Analyzing Problems in Schools and School Systems

A Theoretical Approach

TOPICS IN EDUCATIONAL LEADERSHIP

Larry W. Hughes, Series Editor

Gaynor • *Analyzing Problems in Schools and School Systems:*
A Theoretical Approach

Analyzing Problems in Schools and School Systems

A Theoretical Approach

Alan Kibbe Gaynor

Boston University

LEA LAWRENCE ERLBAUM ASSOCIATES, PUBLISHERS

1998   Mahwah, New Jersey   London

Lawrence Erlbaum Associates, Inc., Publishers
10 Industrial Avenue
Mahwah, New Jersey 07430

Cover Design by Kathryn Houghtaling Lacey

Library of Congress Cataloging-in-Publication Data
Gaynor, Alan K.
Analyzing problems in schools and school systems : a theoretical
approach / by Alan Kibbe Gaynor.
p.   cm. — (Topics in educational leadership series)
Includes bibliographical references (p.) and index.
ISBN 0-8058-2643-2 (cloth : alk. paper)
1. School managment and organization—United States—Case
studies. 2. Organizational sociology—United States—Methodology—Case studies. 3. Education—United States—Methodology—Case studies. I. Title. II. Series.
LB2805.G338   1998
371.2'00973—dc21   97-37752
                                                          CIP

Books published by Lawrence Erlbaum Associates are printed on
acid-free paper, and their bindings are chosen for strength and dura-
bility.

Printed in the United States of America
10 9 8 7 6 5 4 3 2

*To Lucy Warres Finkston
and Mary Doris Rice*

Contents

Preface   ix

PART I: METHODOLOGY

Chapter 1   Conceptual Framework and Overview   3

Chapter 2   Describing and Documenting Problems,   12
             Stakeholders, and Decision Makers

Chapter 3   Analyzing the Causes of a Problem   24

Chapter 4   Developing a Solution Strategy and   30
             Recommendations to Stakeholders

PART II: THEORY SKETCHES

Chapter 5   Bureaucratic Theory   39

Chapter 6   Social Systems Theory   53

Chapter 7   Political Systems Theory   69

Chapter 8   Leadership Theory   87

Chapter 9   Burrell and Morgan's Meta-Framework   95

Chapter 10   Systems Thinking: Modeling   108
               Problem Systems

Chapter 11   Conclusion: Problem Analysis   131
               as a Hermeneutic Process

               PART III: CASE EXAMPLES

Chapter 12   School to Work: An Analysis   137
               of Vocational Education as Provided
               by Greater Stanton Technical School
               Allen Scheier

Chapter 13   The Implementation of the   171
               Massachusetts Education Reform
               Act of 1993 at the New England School
               for Special Students
               Joseph Robert Dolan

Chapter 14   Analysis of an Organizational   223
               Decision: The Placement Process
               for The Honors Track at Brandywine
               Regional High School
               Alan Bernstein

Chapter 15   Analysis of an Organizational   236
               Decision: The Placement Process
               of the Latin American Scholarship
               Program of American Universities
               Josephine Jane Pavese

               References   266

               Suggested Readings   274

               Author Index   291

               Subject Index   295

Preface

We live in a world which is an impressive and irresistible mixture of sufficiencies, tight completenesses, order, recurrences which make possible prediction and control, and singularities, ambiguities, uncertain possibilities, processes going on to consequences as yet indeterminate. They are mixed not mechanically but vitally.... We may recognize them separately but we cannot divide them, for unlike wheat and tares they grow from the same root.

—John Dewey

This book is directed toward an audience of students in organizational theory and problem analysis classes, and their professors, as well as to school administrators seeking to examine their problems and policies from perspectives that go beyond their own personal experience. Hopefully, the book will provide readers with a logical structure for describing, documenting, and analyzing organizational problems and methodological insights that go beyond those currently available in the literature.

Most importantly, the book explains and illustrates a methodology for describing, documenting, and analyzing organizational problems. The methodology is put forward in Part I, comprising the first four chapters. Chapter 1 previews the major elements of the methodology and includes a flow chart showing a 13-step process from identifying a high priority problem to targeting action recommendations to particular stakeholders. Chapter 2 discusses problem indicators, standards of comparison, and the importance of identifying and profiling stakeholders and decision makers. Chapter 3 moves from problem description to causal analysis. It provides a perspective on causal analysis, supplies guidelines for selecting appropriate conceptual frameworks to use, and employ selected conceptual frameworks to analyze the causes of organizational problems. Chapter 4 is the final chapter in the methodology section. It deals with the very practical task of developing an action strategy based on the causal analyses explained in chapter 3. Specific issues addressed include (a) drawing conclusions from particular theoretical analyses, (b) drawing conclusions across diverse theoretical analyses, (c) formulating and evaluating potential solution strategies, and (d) targeting action recommendations to particular stakeholders.

Because the methodology of this book is theory-based, it is important that readers, in order to understand and practice the methodology, have available to them, within the covers of this book, substantive descriptions of selected organizational theories. Included in Part II are particular examples of bureaucratic (chapter 5), role (chapter 6), political (chapter 7), and leadership (chapter 8) theories.

Also included in Part II are descriptions of two broader theoretical frameworks. Chapter 9 delineates the major elements of Burrell and Morgan's conceptual matrix. The four quadrants of the matrix represent substantially different perspectives on organizational problems and decisions. These perspectives reflect differences in epistemological assumptions about objectivity and subjectivity as well as differences between radical and conservative points of view about the purposes and guiding assumptions of organizations. Chapter 10 discusses systems thinking and offers a methodological approach to viewing the causes of organizational problems developmentally and ecologically from a systems perspective. Such a perspective views reality in terms of circular causality, causal feedback loops, and the importance of time delays and nonlinear effects in the development of organizational problems over time. Problem solutions represent interventions in such developmental systems.

Each of the chapters presents an overview of the theory depicted and a description of its focus, major assumptions, and analytic elements. Examples of the analytic elements are given, questions are suggested for analyzing problems from the perspective of the theory portrayed in the chapter, and an outline is delineated for organizing a typical analytic report. The selected theories exemplify some of the 14 categories of theoretical thought represented in the extensive bibliography at the end of the book.

In Part III the reader finds two pairs of case examples prepared by students in the my organizational analysis classes and advanced policy seminars. The first pair of examples illustrates the problem-analyzing methodology using theoretical frameworks found in the social science literature. The second pair illustrates an approach to critiquing organizational decision making through the lenses of the four paradigms of Burrell and Morgan: functionalist, interpretivist, radical humanist, and radical structuralist.

ACKNOWLEDGMENTS

I am grateful to Karl Clauset, Mark Shibles, and Mary Rice for their reviews of various manuscript renderings and to Clauset for his ideas related to systems thinking and system dynamics. I appreciate, too, the counsel of Judith Berg at the University of Northern Colorado, whose review of the manuscript for Lawrence

Erlbaum Associates brought to my attention flaws in earlier versions of the work and whose advice guided me in shaping the final version. My thanks go also to Naomi Silverman, Senior Editor, Lawrence Erlbaum Associates, and to Larry Hughes, Series Editor, for their help and encouragement with this project. Finally, I am indebted to my students, Alan Bernstein, Joseph R. Dolan, Josephine Jane Pavese, and Allen Scheier, for allowing their work to be included in this book, and to all of my students who have taught me through 25 years how to present organizational theory as a matter of intellectual interest and as a useful tool for organizational leaders.

—*Alan Kibbe Gaynor*

PART I

METHODOLOGY

1

Conceptual Framework
and Overview

Knowledge of a science of organization and administration can never be a substitute for specific experience in a specific organization. The usefulness of the more general knowledge to the administrators of organization comes from the rational understanding it gives of behavior that is largely based on trial and error or repetitive experience. Its immediate practical use is limited. Its ultimate practical value is great, sharpening observation, preventing the neglect of important factors, giving the advantages of a more general language, and reducing the inconsistencies between behavior and its verbal description.

—Chester Barnard (1947, p. xi)

Managers and administrators have a special responsibility for knowing about organizational problems and seeing that something gets done about them.[1] Decisions have to be made and resources mobilized to gain support for needed changes. Even for experienced administrators, thinking through problems, formulating sensible policy ideas, and galvanizing interest and support are not easy tasks.

Typically, administrators are under constant pressure; yet moving an organization is not something you do easily off the top of your head. Regardless of the problems to be addressed, you will achieve better results by following a clear and systematic line of reasoning, pursuing an established set of steps, and availing yourself extensively of other people's thinking. This means drawing fully on your own experience, not just tapping the surface of it. It means taking optimal advantage of the interests others have in the problems that concern you, of the commitment they bring to solving them, and of their special skills and resources. It also means

---

[1]The terms *manager* and *administrator* are used interchangeably in this book. The reason for this is that although functional distinctions have been drawn between them, often suggesting that managers have a broader vision and scope of responsibility than administrators, it is also true that *manager* is typically used in the private sector synonymously with the common use of *administrator* in the public sector, particularly in the public schools. Thus, both managers in the corporate context and public school administrators have responsibility for dealing with organizational problems and a commensurate need for organizational analysis skills.

drawing on the minds of great organizational thinkers, not for answers, but for ways of thinking about the problem so that you do not miss anything important. An effective process for solving organizational problems includes (a) describing and documenting the problem; (b) identifying and describing important stakeholders, positive and negative, and decision makers; (c) using theory to guide you in analyzing the causes of the problem; (d) formulating general strategies to address the causes you have identified; and (e) making recommendations specifically tailored to the interests, powers, skills, and resources of individual stakeholders and stakeholder groups.

It is important to recognize that, although clearly rational, this approach is also fundamentally political. It identifies leadership in policymaking as rational in employing systematic processes to formulate and analyze organizational problems as well as political in its recognition of important stakeholders and its involvement of these stakeholders in defining the problem and debating its relationship to value-laden standards. At root, then, the method outlined in this book lies usefully between the technical–rational (analogous to operations research)[2] and the incremental (Lindblom, 1959, 1965, 1968; Lindblom & Cohen, 1979). Although this methodology separates the problem from the solution in ways that contrast with the views of the pure incrementalists,[3] it accepts practical limits on the amount of information that can be gathered for making decisions (Lindblom, 1959) and the information processing limitations of human decision makers (Simon, 1957a, 1957b).

In this chapter, an overview of the five phases of problem analysis is presented. Then each phase is developed in detail in chapters 2 through 4. Chapters 1 through 4 comprise Part I of the book. Part II incorporates seven additional chapters: chapters 5 through 11. Chapters 5 through 10 sketch a set of selected theoretical frameworks that serve as a backdrop to the practical problem analysis approaches

---

[2]I believe that the method presented in this book avoids the serious flaws associated with what has (often interchangeably) been called "operations research" and "management science." One criticism frequently leveled at operations research is that it is limited to small, well-framed, technical problems. A second criticism holds that operations researchers have a limited set of tools that they apply to problems and that, they therefore shape the problems to the tools. A third criticism is that operations researchers unreflectively serve managerial values.

[3]According to Lindblom (1959) in *The Science of Muddling Through*, the following procedure exemplifies the best approach to policy formulation:

[An administrator given responsibility for formulating policy with respect to inflation] would outline those relatively few policy alternatives that occurred to him. He would then compare them. In comparing his limited number of alternatives, most of them familiar from past controversies, he would not ordinarily find a body of theory precise enough to carry him through a comparison of their respective consequences. Instead he would rely heavily on the record of past experience with small policy steps to predict the consequences of similar steps extended into the future. (p. 79)

The weakness of Lindblom's argument is its assumption of an available population of good solution alternatives. Typically, the critical aspects of effective problem solving lie precisely in imagining policies that address the fundamental causes of the problem over time and comparing them to alternative policies that have been proposed and to those that have been previously tried.

detailed in the first four chapters. Chapter 11 suggests ways in which organizational problem analysis can usefully be understood as a hermeneutic process. The theory sketches include illustrations and guidelines for analyzing organizational decision making and the causes of organizational problems from different conceptual perspectives. Part III (chapters 12–15) presents two case examples of the analysis process described in the book and two examples of critiquing decisions and decisional processes theoretically. These chapters were written by students in my doctoral classes and seminars. An extensive bibliography is included.

PROBLEM DESCRIPTION AND DOCUMENTATION

There are four major tasks involved in describing and documenting organizational problems: identifying specific problem indicators, documenting each of them, examining these indicators in the light of appropriate and persuasive standards of comparison, and presenting to potential stakeholders and decision makers your case that an important problem exists.

Identification

Be clear about why you think you have a problem on your hands. Talk with people, check any records available to you, and identify the specific indicators of the problem. This is important because problems often are cast in vague terms. For example, you may say, "We've got a morale problem!" But what makes you think you've got a morale problem? Absenteeism? Turnover? Error rates? Formal grievances? Informal complaints over coffee and in the cafeteria? Sour faces? When people think they've got a problem, and it's a real problem, there are always concrete trails of evidence, some statistical, others qualitative in nature.

Documentation

After you've made a list of the salient indicators of the problem, try to track down as much documentation for each problem indicator as you can. Do this from records, from memory, and from talking with others. You may find the problem isn't as big as you thought it was. If the problem is serious, perhaps because it is contributing to other important problems, your examination of specific indicators will help you to be clearer about its scope, about how long it's been going on, and whether it's getting worse.

Examination

After you've clarified why you think a serious problem exists, you need to do a little soul searching. Given the concrete evidence, why do you think there is something you would really call a problem? Obviously, you think things should be better in some ways. Why do you think that? Against what *standards* are you evaluating the evidence you have? Why are these standards important? Are there other standards that you could reasonably and persuasively use instead of or in addition to the standards that first came to mind? What values do these standards represent for you? Are these important values? Are they values shared by major stakeholders and decision makers? Values may include, for example, those of effectiveness, efficiency, equity, and justice.

Presentation

When you have clarified to your satisfaction as many reasonable standards as possible—standards you believe will persuade other key audiences about the importance of the problem—prepare a presentation of documentation. Charts, graphs, and tables, both quantitative and qualitative, are helpful in showing how performance fails to meet the expectations embodied in persuasive standards. By illustrating the problem, you validate your belief that a serious problem exists while you also build a compelling case for mobilizing support from others to do something about the problem.

STAKEHOLDERS AND DECISION MAKERS

Now that you have built a solid case in defining and documenting the problem against compelling standards, you need to build a political foundation for effective action that will bring about the changes necessary to reduce or eliminate the problem.[4] Begin by identifying others who have a stake in resolving the problem and those who will most likely be involved in making the decisions and taking the actions required to bring about needed changes. Stakeholders often include groups and individuals who are concerned about the problem as it relates to their own values and political and organizational agendas. Because of their prior words and actions, some stakeholders can be expected to favor needed changes and to work to resolve the focal problem; others can be expected to oppose recommendations for change. These are positive and negative stakeholders respectively. Even stakeholders who are concerned about a problem and would like to do something about it may favor certain solution strategies and oppose others out of self-interest or for theoretical reasons. Moreover, decision makers may or may not be current stakeholders, positive or negative.

---

[4]Changing organizational policies and behaviors always requires support, generally from a coalition of actors within, and sometimes around, the organization. Thus, effective action to deal with organizational problems always has a political dimension, and building a political foundation for taking effective action is crucial.

Make a list of significant stakeholders and decision makers and describe the interests, powers, skills, and resources each would bring to any campaign for the changes needed to remove the major causes of the problem. Be clear about evidence you have of their concerns about the problem. It is not uncommon for people to think others should care about a particular problem, yet have no evidence that these others do care. This is important because, in the last analysis, your major strategic recommendations will focus on involving the positive stakeholders—consistent with their individual interests, powers, skills, resources, and levels of commitment—in doing something about the problem, in dealing with potential negative stakeholders, and in influencing key decision makers, who may or may not presently be stakeholders.[5]

CAUSAL ANALYSIS

The Value of Theoretical Analysis

In complex organizations it is difficult to unravel specific causes of important problems from the welter of factors impinging on a problem situation. Precisely for this reason, you must use to maximum advantage your own experience, the knowledge of others around you, and the insights, written and oral, of experienced managers, consultants, and researchers. Yet arguments persist about the worth of social science theory.

It is broadly understood that the social science disciplines differ in fundamental ways from the natural sciences. Furthermore, it has been strongly argued that management science has not successfully validated significant general laws that reliably predict human behavior or organizational phenomena. MacIntyre (1984) said, for example:

> According to...conventional account—from the Enlightenment through Comte and Mill to Hempel—the aim of the social sciences is to explain specifically social phenomena by supplying law-like generalizations to which the managerial expert would have to appeal. This account however seems to entail—what is certainly not the case—that the social sciences are almost or perhaps completely devoid of achievement. For the salient fact about those sciences is the absence of the discovery of any law-like generalizations whatsoever. (p. 88)

But, even if true, this is not to deny, as MacIntyre himself suggested, the value of the thinking of those who have worked in and with organizations and those who have engaged for long periods in systematic research on various aspects of organ-

---

[5]Decision makers may already hold positions about the problem, for or against doing something about it. Often, however, decision makers, at least initially, may have little knowledge of the situation or hold neutral positions about taking action related to it.

izational life. In fact, as Donaldson proposed (1985, p. xi), their concepts and theories constitute an important source of ideas for experienced administrators seeking help in thinking about their problems.

> If evidence were required that organizational studies contains [*sic*] theoretical and empirical work of both volume and breadth, then this has been amply furnished by the many reviews of the literature (Child, 1977; Etzioni, 1975; Hage, 1980; Hage & Azumi, 1972; Hall, 1977; Khandwalla, 1977; Kotter, Schlesinger, & Sathe, 1979; Mintzberg, 1979).

Most administrators would be glad for help in locating and interpreting various management theories, which represent what have been variously called frames, lenses, and perspectives for thinking about organizational life. Their value lies not in telling experienced administrators what to do, but rather in helping them systematically to focus their experience in different ways as they think about what might be causing their problems and how to solve them. As Bolman and Deal counseled (1984), "Understanding organizations is nearly impossible when the manager is unconsciously wed to a single, narrow perspective." They discussed the concept of organizational frames in the following terms:

> We have consolidated the major schools of organizational thought into four relatively coherent perspectives [the rational systems frame, the human resource frame, the political frame, and the symbolic frame]. We have chosen the label "frames" to characterize these different vantage points. Frames are windows on the world. Frames filter out some things while allowing others to pass through easily. Frames help us to order the world and decide what action to take. Every manager uses a personal frame, or image, of organizations to gather information, make judgments, and get things done. (p. 4)

Once you are clear about the nature of the problem in focus and the way it manifests itself concretely in your organization—presently, historically, and, perhaps, projected into the future—you are ready to think systematically about the causes of the problem. This involves drawing on your experience and talking to others (informally or in focus groups), but also reviewing social science and management theories to highlight important causal dimensions of the problem situation.

It should be clear, of course, that these activities should be done not in linear sequence, one before the other, but cyclically and iteratively, over and over again, so they inform each other. You talk to others out of your own experience; what they say informs your experience. How you use the theoretical literature depends on your experience and what others think about the problem. Finally, applying theoretical frameworks informs your experience and your conversations with others, which leads you to approach the theories anew and from different perspectives, and so on (see also chapter 11).

The Nature of Theoretical Analysis

Among other reasons, many hesitate to delve into the theoretical literature because it is sometimes hard to read and hard to find, requiring translations between theory and practice that demand training. The following steps may guide you in approaching and using the theoretical literature:

1. Drawing on your own experience, your knowledge of the problem, and the advice of others you respect, list the factors that you believe may be contributing to the problem. Then consult reviews of management, administrative, and organizational theory; recognized textbooks in these fields; or the references in this book to identify theoretical frameworks that relate to these factors. Reading various theories of organization may remind you of factors you have missed.

2. Review the textbook descriptions of your chosen theories, locate concise original source materials that describe the theories in greater detail, summarize the research using and testing the theories, and examine important critiques of them.

3. Collect and organize information about the problem and the organizational situation within which it is embedded. Be guided by and remain consistent with the analytic categories and variables in the theoretical frameworks. Interpret the information you have collected according to the ideas and relationships the theories suggest.

4. Generate ideas about possible causes of the problem and likely solutions from the perspectives of the different analytic models. Work with positive stakeholders and focus groups to reassess your assumptions about the problem, its causes, and possible solution strategies. At this point you may find it useful, collectively, to formulate your own model, focusing specifically on this problem and its causes. This is sometimes referred to as modeling the problem system. The systems framework (see chapter 10) is particularly useful for configuring in a single model understandings gained from experience and from applying multiple analytic frameworks to a problem situation.[6]

Think about what would happen if certain types of changes were made. These are called solution strategies. Make a list of solution strategies from different theoretical perspectives. Imagine making the theoretical changes in the real organization. What would be involved? How would they work in reality? Discuss your ideas about causes and solutions with other people who know the problem and the

---

[6]A useful technology for sketching policy models is called causal-loop diagramming. It focuses you on describing how the system should work to correct the problem of concern, encouraging you and your colleagues to think about why corrective action hasn't been taken, or hasn't been effective. Typical discontinuities in correcting problems include displaced goals, important information delays, inappropriate responses (e.g., those that make things worse instead of better), and responses to changing conditions that are either too slow or too rapid. Causal-loop diagramming emphasizes understanding how different factors interact over time and how some factors may increase in importance during different periods of the development of the problem. Systems thinking and causal-loop diagramming are discussed in chapter 10.

organization. Compare solution ideas to those tried previously in your organization or elsewhere. Reassess your proposed solutions in the light of these earlier trials.

5. ~~Develop and rank order a list of reasonable solution strategies. Evaluate these according to the following criteria, sep~~arating satisfactory from unsatisfactory solutions:

   a. How well do these strategies address the causes of the problem you have identified?
   b. How well do they avoid the pitfalls of similar strategies tried earlier here or elsewhere?
   c. How feasible are they in terms of cost and the likelihood that they will be effectively implemented in relation to potential hindering and facilitating factors?

6. Formulate a mobilization strategy. That is, work out tasks and strategies for each of the stakeholders you have identified. Be sure that what you ask them to do is consistent with their individual interests, levels of commitment, powers, skills, and resources. Get commitments from them to accomplish the tasks and to pursue the strategies they can best help to implement.

7. Follow up with support and assistance.

SUMMARY FLOW CHART

For a concise visual overview of the previous text, Fig. 1.1 summarizes the steps typically followed in analyzing organizational problems. Part one of this book discusses these steps in detail. Chapter 2 deals with describing and documenting problems, stakeholders, and decision makers. Chapter 3 explains how you analyze the causes of a problem, and chapter 4 examines the steps to develop a solution strategy and to tailor action recommendations to specific stakeholders.

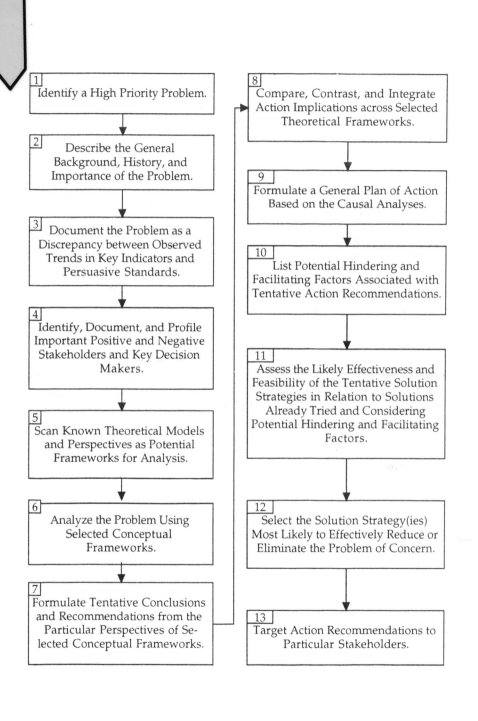

1. Identify a High Priority Problem.

2. Describe the General Background, History, and Importance of the Problem.

3. Document the Problem as a Discrepancy between Observed Trends in Key Indicators and Persuasive Standards.

4. Identify, Document, and Profile Important Positive and Negative Stakeholders and Key Decision Makers.

5. Scan Known Theoretical Models and Perspectives as Potential Frameworks for Analysis.

6. Analyze the Problem Using Selected Conceptual Frameworks.

7. Formulate Tentative Conclusions and Recommendations from the Particular Perspectives of Selected Conceptual Frameworks.

8. Compare, Contrast, and Integrate Action Implications across Selected Theoretical Frameworks.

9. Formulate a General Plan of Action Based on the Causal Analyses.

10. List Potential Hindering and Facilitating Factors Associated with Tentative Action Recommendations.

11. Assess the Likely Effectiveness and Feasibility of the Tentative Solution Strategies in Relation to Solutions Already Tried and Considering Potential Hindering and Facilitating Factors.

12. Select the Solution Strategy(ies) Most Likely to Effectively Reduce or Eliminate the Problem of Concern.

13. Target Action Recommendations to Particular Stakeholders.

FIG. 1.1. The typical seqence of steps in analyzing organizational problems.

2

Describing and Documenting Problems, Stakeholders, and Decision Makers

Whether we wish it or not we are involved in the world's problems, and all the winds of heaven blow through our land.

—Walter Lippmann (1914/1962, p. 83)

Before tackling a problem it is important to be very clear about what exactly concerns you. The clearer you are in documenting the problem, the more effective you will be in clarifying the extent of its damage to the organization and people in it, the degree of interest among important constituencies, and the factors that must be addressed in seeking a solution.

IDENTIFYING A HIGH-PRIORITY PROBLEM

Typically, organizations keep track of important bottom-line indicators. Schools keep records of student grades, attendance, and enrollment. Universities track applications, admissions, and the Scholastic Aptitude Test (SAT) scores of incoming students. Businesses maintain data about sales, profits, productivity, and return on investments. Hospital administrators track patient care; efficiency in the use of personnel, facilities, and equipment; staff performance; payment and reimbursement; cost accounting; and the like. Institutions maintain records about these and other key performance indicators, and problems can be identified by examining such formal records systematically.

Problems also surface in organizations in general and impressionistic ways. In schools there are feelings about staff morale, student motivation and discipline, homework, vandalism, and so forth. In colleges and universities apprehensions may focus on issues such as recruitment, retention, quality of teaching, crime on campus, grant-and-contract activity, or fund raising. In business firms concerns surface about questions related to employee motivation and commitment to work, job performance, product quality, and next-customer satisfaction.

HISTORY AND IMPORTANCE OF THE PROBLEM

It is helpful at the outset, once a problem has been identified, to sketch an overview of its history. In this section of your work, you suggest what information you have about the problem and its development over time. It is important to clarify why the problem is consequential to the organization and to explain how it may, in a kind of domino effect, influence other important problems as well. The task here is to extrapolate the consequences of the problem. Later, you will seek to determine its causes.

PROBLEM INDICATORS

Initial Steps

After you identify general problem areas, a crucial next step is to describe the specific indicators of each problem. Some useful problem indicators are quantitative, such as financial records and data on absenteeism. Others, as discussed below and also as illustrated by Scheier (chapter 12) and Dolan (chapter 13), are basically qualitative.

Where quantitative data are available, a useful step in analyzing an organizational problem is to support general verbal descriptions of the problem with graphs and tables showing the trends in observed indicators of it over time. For example, if you were concerned about low or decreasing *worker commitment*, then absenteeism, job performance measures (e.g., error rates and other behavioral measures of job performance), and the number of grievances filed might be thought of as reasonable indicators.

By way of illustration, a nursing administrator was concerned about downward trends in the job performance of a staff member, a nurse in her hospital (Davis, 1992). In the following series of graphs, the nurse whose performance is of particular concern is referred to as Nurse F.

Figure 2.1 depicts Nurse F's annual performance ratings (1987–1991).[7] It shows how a problem can be documented graphically. In this or other situations, more than one problem indicator could be graphed. It is important to graph problem indicators over reasonable periods of time, not simply for a single point in time, in order to put the problem in historical perspective. Once this is done, your analysis must account not only for a problem that exists presently, but for whatever changes have occurred over the time you establish as reasonable. This stimulates you to think carefully about how factors have changed over time.

---

[7]Problem indicators can be graphed by using different types of measurement scales. Sometimes the scale depicts real units such as dollars, number of days absent, or number of grievances. In this case, the rating scale is "standardized" or "unitized." All the nurses are rated on a scale of 0 to 10. The highest rating a nurse can receive is 10; the lowest rating is 0. Figure 2.2 shows Nurse F's ratings from 1987 to 1991 in relationship to the department standard of 6.0. Figure 2.3 shows Nurse F's ratings during the same time period in comparison to other nurses in the department, all on the same scale.

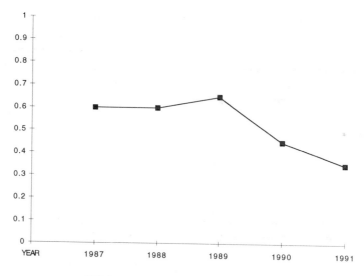

FIG. 2.1. Annual performance ratings of Nurse F.

In this situation, for example, it is important to observe that Nurse F's performance ratings have deteriorated in the last 2 years. Thus, the very manner in which
the problem is documented highlights the change that has occurred. Accordingly,
by documenting the problem longitudinally, the analyst comes to realize the
necessity of the causal analysis to explain the transformations in the situation that
can account for this downward shift in Nurse F's performance ratings.

You will want to identify and collect information about concrete problem
indicators. Frequently, when actual data are examined, it becomes obvious that
there really is no cause for concern and no problem to analyze further. However,
first-stage data collection and analysis often do provide what appears to be sufficient evidence for further documentation and analysis.

Examining the Meaning of the Problem Indicators

Up to this point in the problem analysis, you have assumed that your initial
indicators are good ones. You have collected some trend data. You are temporarily
satisfied that there is evidence of a real problem. Before proceeding further,
however, check with people in the organization as well as with people outside it
who know something about the problem you are addressing.

For example, with respect to worker commitment, maybe others know of reasons
why absenteeism, job performance, and grievances are not really good indicators
of this problem. Perhaps there are other reasons why, in your situation, absenteeism
is high, productivity is low, or grievances are up. Perhaps you should be looking at
other indicators of this problem, collecting data on these, and reexamining the

problem you thought you had. Not only is such an approach to problem analysis logical, it is also consistent with more recent research on organizations suggesting that "facts" cannot be taken at face value without understanding what they mean in particular situations, historically and culturally.

STANDARDS

Let's say you have identified a set of problem indicators that, given the best information you have from knowledgeable people inside and outside your organization, seem to provide reasonable and compelling evidence of a serious problem facing your organization. You have documented the case for the existence of the problem in words and appropriate graphs and tables. Are you ready to go to key people in the organization and say with assurance, "We've got a problem!"? No, not yet.

Although you have moved in the right direction, there is an important dimension of problem documentation that you have not yet addressed. You have data on reasonable and acceptable indicators of the problem, but it is still unclear why, exactly, you think these data are problematic. It is important to establish credible and persuasive standards of comparison. But what are standards? How are they used in dealing with organizational problems, and what makes them persuasive?

What Standards Are

Standards are representations of what you, and perhaps others, in the organization consider ideal, or at least acceptable levels of performance for the variables you have identified as your problem indicators. Any problem is thus defined in terms of discrepancies between the indicators and the standards. These discrepancies describe what is sometimes called a policy gap because changes in organizational or social policy are generally needed to address such problem discrepancies.

Standards related to SAT scores might show, for example, the national (or regional) averages for comparable schools or school districts over the past 10 or 20 years. Implied in a standard is the idea that it is represented in the same quantitative units of measure as its corresponding problem indicator (the SAT scores of your school or school district over the same period). Because this standard is statistical in nature, the local and national (or regional) scores could be compared and contrasted graphically on the same scale. The problem can thus be seen in quantitative terms as the gap between the trend lines associated with the national or regional standards and those associated with the local school SAT scores, which are the problem indicators in this case.

A qualitative approach to describing a policy gap might be to contrast, along the same dimensions, an existing situation with a qualitative ideal-type. For example, in depicting a university program as problematic for corporate training and development professionals, Harrington (1996) contrasted the program's courses with a list of skill and knowledge competencies developed by the American Society for Training and Development (ASTD) and with courses offered by a competitive university. He proposed the ASTD skill inventory, based on extensive research, as the ideal-type. He offered the program of the competing university as a practical alternative standard of comparison.

Thus, instead of portraying the policy gap in terms of differences in statistical trend lines, as with the SAT scores or Nurse F's performance ratings, Harrington constructed a three-column table. The complete set of ASTD competencies was listed in rows in the left column; the elements of the other programs were compared against this qualitative ideal-type in the corresponding rows of the second and third columns of this *qualitative comparison table* (Table 2.1). The policy gap was then portrayed in terms of the programmatic differences between the focal university (University B) and the standards of comparison represented by the ASTD ideal-type, on the one hand, and the competing university (University A), on the other.

TABLE 2.1

A Qualitative Comparison Table: Comparing Programs for Corporate Training
and Development Professionals to the ASTD Ideal-Type

Technical		
ASTD Required Competencies	*University A*	*University B*
Adult learning understanding	How adults learn, Program development in adult and continuing education, Facilitating adult learning, Adult education for social action	Adult learning and training
Career development understanding	Assessing and facilitating career development, Vocational appraisal, Career development of women	None
Competency-identification skills	None	None
Theories of adult development	Developmental psychology: Adulthood and the life span, Psychology of adjustment, Personality development and socialization, Psychological factors in later life, Sociology of the life course	None
Employee counseling skills	Counseling in business and industry, Life-skills counseling, Cross-cultural counseling	None
Training and development theories	Staff development and training, Design and evaluation of training programs, Advanced staff development and training, New technologies for learning	None

Business		
ASTD Required Competencies	*University A*	*University B*
Business understanding	Functions of organizations	None (see School of Management)
Management and leadership understanding	Introduction to management systems, Management science, Executive selection and development, Leadership and supervision	None (see School of Management)
Organization-behavior understanding	Organizational psychology, Psychological aspects of organizations, Organizations and interpersonal behaviors	Organizational analysis

Note. Adapted from Harrington (1996).

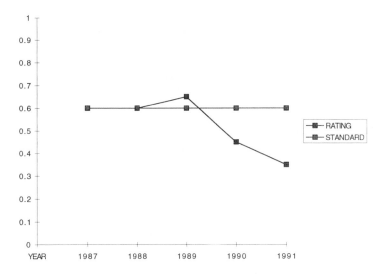

FIG. 2.2. The emerging discrepancy between Nurse F's performance ratings and the standard for the department, 1987–1991.

Note, however, that in contrast to the statistical examples of Nurse F's performance ratings and school or school district SAT scores, the indicators and standards of comparison are cross-sectional, not longitudinal, in nature.

Continuing with the example of Nurse F, whose performance ratings have declined over time (Davis, 1992), Fig. 2.2 shows the performance ratings of the nurse in relation to the department standard, which has been established at a minimum of 6.0 on a scale of 0 to 10. Notice that nurse F's performance ratings declined and were below the department standard in 1990 and 1991, but not before. Notice, too, that in this case, the department standard, constant at 6.0 for the entire time period (1987–1991), is shown as a straight line across the graph.

It is not unusual to display problem indicators against more than a single standard. In the illustrative case, Davis displayed Nurse F's performance not only against her own past history (see Fig. 2.1) and the department standard (see Fig. 2.2), but also against the performance of the other nurses in the department (Fig. 2.3). The graph shows that in 1990 and 1991 Nurse F's performance ratings were below those of the other nurses in the department, all of whom met or exceeded the department standard during this period.

How Standards Are Used

Standards thus become points of reference against which problems are defined and illustrated and solutions are measured. The areas of discrepancy between problem indicators and standards define problems and guide you later in seeking to understand the causes of the problem. Thus, your exploration of problem causes always

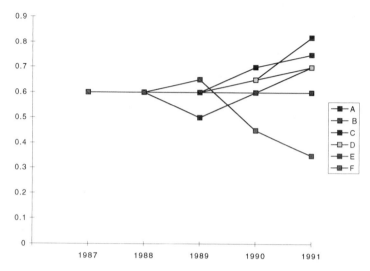

FIG. 2.3. Nurse F's performance versus that of other nurses, 1987–1991.

seeks to understand what factors have contributed to creating the discrepancy between the problem indicator and its corresponding standard(s).

What Makes Standards Persuasive

Although "source" is never a substitute for intellectual defensibility, standards are often persuasive, at least in part, because their sources are respected. Understanding this leads us to recognize the importance of having sources for standards. It also leads us to inquire why some sources are more respected than others and why people differ in the respect they hold for different sources. What, then, are examples of different types of sources?

1. *Past performance.* In setting standards for appropriate levels of absenteeism, reference might be made to past levels of absenteeism that were lower than they are today.

2. *The performance of reputationally comparable organizations.* Implied here are schools, colleges, corporations, or hospitals "like us," a meaning that generally is culturally determined. Often, in these situations, institutions exist to whom we traditionally compare ourselves. We might, for example, compare ourselves to other schools with similar demographic characteristics, other Ivy League universities, other Fortune 500 companies, or other major area teaching hospitals.

3. *National, state, or regional institutional standards.* In this case, we would be prepared to compare ourselves to the average performance (or some other standard, such as the average of the top 10%) of similar organizations in the nation, state, or region.

4. *Standards established by an appropriate professional association.* These would include, for example, associations of teachers, administrators, or curriculum specialists.

5. *Federal, state, and local regulations.* There are many examples of regulatory requirements having to do with such issues as racial and ethnic balance in schools, allocations of resources by gender, services provided to students with disabilities, plant safety, environmental control, cost containment, personnel qualifications, and the like that represent legal standards that must be met.

6. *Ethical standards.* Although ethical standards may seem more abstract than the other types of standards described, and their sources more vaguely defined, they are fundamental in defining organizational problems. Whereas your initial recourse in describing ethical standards may appeal to religious, philosophical, literary, or historical principles and situations, it is helpful to translate such references into working standards, quantitative or qualitative, that can be compared against your problem indicators. In general, you want to determine what statistical performance trends or qualitative characteristics would be logically consistent with the ethical principles from which you are drawing. Having done this, and having made the logical case for so doing, you can display such ethical standards in the same graphical formats[8] or qualitative comparison tables that you have used to display standards from more prosaic sources.

Although this list does not exhaust the possible sources of standards for displaying and analyzing organizational problems, it does illustrate the concepts of standards and sources of standards.

However, listing and illustrating various types of sources of standards does not explain what makes them persuasive. They are persuasive to the extent that they signify for particular audiences important values implicit (for them) in those sources. When we compare ourselves to standards derived from different sources, we do so because we value what those sources represent. Thus we compare ourselves to performance standards set by other schools, colleges and universities, corporations, hospitals, and professional associations because we feel that we ought to live up to such standards. Similarly, we know that we ought to obey the law. Moreover, we may argue that we must live up to higher ethical standards that come down to us through our spiritual and intellectual heritage.

When we make the standards and sources of our standards explicit, we expose our values and our definition of the problem to rational discussion among reasonable people. This exposure of the problem (i.e., of the data and the standards that define the problem) provides the essential foundation for widespread ownership of

---

[8]On the basis of ethical values, such a statistical standard would typically be constant rather than variable, and would be represented in a graphic display as a straight line (see the department standard in Fig. 2.2).

the problem and for broad participation in finding its causes and implementing solutions that work as effectively as possible.

Challenges to the Open Discussion of Standards and Values

It is crucial, if real problems are to be squarely faced, that assumptions about the status quo not be treated as given and that value debates be open, deep, and authentic. The identification and examination of alternative standards is important in exposing alternative value positions and in encouraging discussion of value differences, not in the abstract, but in relation to the problem under discussion. However, research suggests that people are commonly inhibited in making their views known and in openly challenging "the design, goals, and activities of their organizations" (Argyris, 1976, p. 367).

Argyris (1976) has long studied how "single-loop" organizational learning processes, as he calls them, undermine effective decision making and problem solving. His review of the literature confirms the dominance in firms and agencies of the single-loop learning model, a mode of organizational behavior that undermines interpersonal trust and inhibits the free flow of valid information, especially to those at the highest levels of authority.

> [T]he literature suggests that the factors that inhibit valid feedback tend to become increasingly more operative as the decisions become more important and as they become more threatening to participants in the decision-making processes; that is, valid information appears to be more easily generated for less important and less threatening decisions. This is a basic organizational problem for it is found not only in governmental organizations, but also in business organizations, schools, religious groups, trade unions, hospitals, and so on. (pp. 366–367)

STAKEHOLDERS AND DECISION MAKERS

Stakeholders in the Problem and in the Solution

There are important side benefits to be derived from a thorough and participative problem documentation and analysis project such as described (e.g., identifying and building support for doing something about the problem). However, the main product of such an endeavor is the formulation of a plan of action that builds on the understandings developed about the historical and immediate causes of the problem and includes recommendations for resolving the problem.

Unfortunately, too many plans of action developed to address important problems direct their recommendations willy-nilly without strategic focus. It is crucial that recommendations be derived systematically from your causal analysis and targeted scrupulously toward potential supporters consistent with their interests, levels of commitment to resolving the problem, and sources of power, skills, and resources. Although it is too early in our discussion to address the relationship between the analysis of causes and the logical structuring of action strategies, it is important at this point to talk about the pivotal role played by those who are called stakeholders.

The most important stakeholders are those who can be described as positive and those who can be described as negative. The questions is, "Positive or negative toward what?", which, unfortunately, has two answers, although one would be complicated enough. There are those who are positive or negative toward the problem, how it is described and documented, and there are those who are positive or negative toward the solution strategy, to the recommendations proposed for resolving the problem. Thus, in describing your stakeholders, their interests, and their characteristics, it is important for you to consider their positions with respect to both the problem and to the solutions that seem to follow from your analysis of the problem causes.

Positive Stakeholders

Positive stakeholders in a problem are those who are concerned about it, committed to its resolution, and likely to support a reasonable solution strategy. It is important to know who these people are and what powers, skills, and resources they can bring to the problem-resolution project. In general, it is self-deluding to make recommendations about what powerful people should do to resolve a problem when there is no evidence that these people care about the problem and want to do something about it. From a political-organizational perspective, it is essential to know those people at all levels of the organization, and sometimes outside of the organization, who are committed to the changes that must be made, and who will work to address the root causes of the problem.

Specifically, you want to build a list of positive stakeholders and use them in the problem analysis project as sources of information about problem indicators, appropriate standards, and causes, then finally as agents of change. Using stakeholders as agents of change implies recommending to them roles they can effectively play in implementing a feasible plan of action and supporting them in these roles.

Stakeholder roles in the plan of action should be based on and consistent with the stakeholders' positions, powers, skills, resources, and levels of commitment in relation to the problem-solving project. Incorporating a table of stakeholders (Table 2.2)[9] at the outset of the problem analysis project, complete with annotations about relevant characteristics, completes your foundation for being certain that you:

---

[9]The data are shown in Table 2.2 in chart form, but you may find it more convenient in your own reports to display the same information in outline form. For example, each stakeholder can be identified by Roman or Arabic numeral (I, II, III, etc., or 1, 2, 3, etc.) or simply underlined in heading format (e.g., The School Principal), and the five types of information can be reported in subheadings marked by capital or lowercase letters (A, B, C, etc., or a, b, c, etc.). Whereas tables can facilitate easy comparisons among stakeholders, reporting this kind of information in outline form eliminates the rigorous space limitations and graphics problems associated with tables.

TABLE 2.2

Illustrative Layout for a Table of Stakeholder Characteristics

Stakeholders	Basis of Interest in the Problem	Position of Authority	Extent of Power to Act on the Problem	Key Skills and Resources	Level of Commitment to Solving the Problem
Number 1					
Number 2					
...					
...					
Number n					

1. Understand the nature of the problem and have identified appropriate problem indicators.
2. Have sufficient organizational support for the project or have shaped the project to match the organizational support you have.
3. Have identified appropriate and persuasive standards against which to define and illustrate the problem.
4. Have involved in the process the people who have the greatest concern for the problem, those whom you will engage appropriately in analyzing the causes of the problem and in taking action to address the problem in effective ways.

Negative Stakeholders

Whereas positive stakeholders constitute potentially valuable resources in the effort to bring about the changes required to close the policy gap, you can generally anticipate and identify those who are likely to oppose these changes. It is important to know as much about these negative stakeholders as you know about the positive stakeholders. Thus, you should profile negative stakeholders in the same way that you profile their positive counterparts. Whereas action recommendations will be made to positive stakeholders, you will want to formulate and implement actions in your strategic plan to deal with the potential opposition of negative. A table similar to that shown in Table 2.2 is as helpful for negative as for positive stakeholders.

Decision Makers

Your action plan must focus effectively on the causes of the problem, direct the actions of positive stakeholders in support of your solution strategy, and learn from or deal with the potential actions of negative stakeholders. It must also zero in effectively on those who will be most influential in making the key decisions related to implementing changes in policy required to solve the problem of concern. You must know these decision makers, their interests, and their values. You also must know the gatekeepers who control access to them.[10] Thus, in the final analysis, your solution strategy must deal effectively with the causes of the central problem, using positive stakeholders to influence negative stakeholders and decision makers.

---

[10]For further explication of these issues, see also chapter 7, "Political Systems Theory."

3

Analyzing the Causes
of a Problem

*The human condition forces us to sail into the future with our gaze fixed on the past,
plotting our course not on charts that detail the shoals and ledges of the seas ahead,
but on the only charts mankind possesses—and they depict only the seas astern.
Theory teaches us both how to map the waters already under the counter, and how to
plot a course through those uncharted waters before the bows.*
— Robert B. Seidman (1992, pp. 76–77)

A PERSPECTIVE ON CAUSAL ANALYSIS

Think for a minute about how you go about analyzing a problem, even if you make
no attempt to use theory in a formal way. Likely, a part of the process you go through
is to think about what common threads or themes run through the events, sometimes
over years, that have characterized the problem situation that concerns you. You try
to make sense out of what has been happening in terms of the patterns familiar to
you from your own experience. You may involve others in this reflection as well.
Making sense of the problem situation thus becomes a kind of matching procedure
in which you characterize both the events in the problem situation you are trying
to analyze and those you have experienced at other times and places, relating one
set of events to the other.

Such relatively informal thinking is essentially similar to more formal procedures of using theories to analyze problem situations. It is important to recognize
these similarities for two reasons: (a) to realize that using formal theories is an
extension of what you have been doing most of your life and, therefore, is not
strange to you, and (b) to build on this existing experiential platform in learning
and using systematic approaches to analysis.

Emphasizing the act of *characterizing* makes us realize that even in everyday
reflection, which we may not think of as theoretical activity, we select some "facts"
to attend to rather than others and we generalize (i.e., recontextualize) these facts

24

to give them meaning (Hanson, 1958). That is, we transform the infinite detail of everyday life and history into patterned generalizations.

We do this partly because we have access to only part of the full universe of data in any situation, and partly because we filter the data we can observe on the basis of the generalizations we carry forward from prior experience, some of it emotionally charged. These generalizations take the form, consciously or not, of values, attitudes, and beliefs about how people are likely to act and how the world works. Some of the generalizations are more open to awareness and reason than others (Rokeach, 1968). We engage in selective patterning also because the human brain appears capable of remembering and processing only a finite quantity of information (Simon, 1957). Finally, after transforming observed (partial) data into generalized patterns that have meaning for us, we draw conclusions about what is likely to happen if we do this or that, then formulate plans of action for dealing with our various aims and difficulties.

In describing these cognitive processes we do not imply that all problem solvers are as thoughtful as others. Clearly, some of the general procedures may sometimes be abridged, distorted, or omitted. Also, diverse actors and groups may simultaneously engage, collaboratively or competitively, in analogous processes that may or may not lead to the same conclusions. Diverse actors and groups may, as a result, compete among themselves in what, for example, have been variously referred to as "garbage cans" (Cohen & March, 1974; Cohen, March, & Olsen, 1972; March & Olsen, 1976; Padgett, 1980), "organized anarchies" (Cuban, 1975; March & Olsen, 1976), "loosely-coupled hierarchies" (Weick, 1982), and conflictual political systems (Dahrendorf, 1959; Easton, 1965; Lindblom, 1965). These distinctions argue for more not less persistent attempts at clear thinking.

Clear thinking benefits significantly from explicit logic and from systematically using a wide range of conceptual frameworks independent of one's own experience and the biases that idiosyncratic experience engenders. It is not that any of the theoretical frameworks in the management and social science literature are unbiased or value neutral. Rather, it is better for administrators to have their personal conceptions challenged by a range of alternatives than to be left alone with their own often unreflected, even unconscious biases. This is important with respect both to microtheories[11] that focus our attention on particular dimensions of organizational life and to macrotheories that focus us on broader organizational (Bolman & Deal, 1984; Forrester, 1968) and social perspectives (Burrell & Morgan, 1979; Foster, 1986; Morgan, 1986).[12]

---

[11]For example, Allison (1971); Arnold (1981); Bacharach, Bamberger, Conley, and Bauer (1990); Blake and Mouton (1964); Calder (1977); Fiedler, Chemers, and Maher (1976); Getzels and Guba (1957); Graen (1969); House and Mitchell (1974); Lawrence and Lorsch (1967); Ouchi (1981); Salancik and Pfeffer (1977); Schoonhoven (1981); Vroom and Yetton (1973).

[12]Interestingly, both must be examined in terms of the central values on which they rest (e.g., instrumental concerns of effectiveness and efficiency vs. moral concerns about justice and equity and their underlying assumptions about agency, society, human nature, and the human condition).

Ultimately, it is helpful to recognize that whether your theorizing is informal or formal, based solely on your own experience or systematically inclusive of others', largely intuitive or consciously mindful, the processes are generically similar. The generic process includes several stages, regardless of the degree to which they are made explicit in practice:

1. You select facts based on your access to information and preexisting values, beliefs, knowledge, and attitudes.
2. You give meaning to these facts on the basis of assumptions, understandings, and conceptual frameworks that you make more or less explicit on the basis of values, beliefs, and attitudes (that you also make more or less explicit).
3. You imagine various scenarios and judge what is likely to happen given different courses of action. You simulate first theoretically (i.e., abstractly); then you translate the theoretical possibilities into action scenarios including real people in a concrete situation.
4. You finalize action plans on the basis of what you think will happen in the tangible situation.
5. You continue this process in the light of newly discovered information and theories.

Next we discuss how you and your fellow stakeholders can use existing theories to understand what is causing important problems in your organization. Just as the emphasis in chapter 2 is on being explicit and systematic in describing and documenting problems and stakeholders, so the emphasis in this chapter is on using conceptual frameworks from the social science and management literature.

SELECTING APPROPRIATE CONCEPTUAL FRAMEWORKS TO USE

Definition and Perspective

The term conceptual framework includes a broad diversity of structured ideas about organizations as well as their elements and workings. These ideas are structured in the sense that conceptual frameworks include sets of related elements and suggest the nature of the relationships among these elements. Other terms commonly used include theory, model, and theoretical framework. I believe that the term conceptual framework is more inclusive than the others although all are frequently used interchangeably. Conceptual frameworks typically vary from highly specific microframeworks to broad macroframeworks, from verbal descriptions to schematic representations and mathematical models.

The elements of any particular conceptual framework define its boundaries and characterize its particular focus. Each suggests a certain way of looking at problems and calls attention to a certain set of elements and relationships as the possible causes of a particular problem. For example, the bureaucratic framework (chapter 5) focuses on structural elements such as hierarchy of authority (centralization), division of labor (specialization), and written rules and policies (formalization); the social systems model (chapter 6) emphasizes role, role stress, psychological needs and dispositions, and cultural values; and the political framework (chapter 7) calls attention to decision makers, gatekeepers, and political constituencies.

Each theoretical framework requires the collection of data related to its constitutive elements and the dynamic relationships among them. While accenting certain variables and relationships, it ignores others that are central to alternative frameworks. The boundaries of a framework are established by the factors that it incorporates, excluding others that remain outside its boundaries. Thus, each analytic framework constitutes a lens for examining the causes of a problem from a particular perspective.

Matching Conceptual Frameworks for Analysis With the Problem Situation

Every conceptual framework, narrow or broad, is useful precisely because it focuses your thinking on particular elements in the situation that might be contributing to the problem. Your first task (after describing and documenting the problem and the principal stakeholders and decision makers) is to select the conceptual frameworks you want to use in your analysis. This is essentially a scanning and matching job. Because you already know a lot about the problem situation, the next step is to scan the list of conceptual frameworks in your knowledge and choose those that seem relevant to your situation and problem. But how do you do this?

Often this is difficult for the practicing administrator who, not being a professional researcher, has relatively limited knowledge of the theoretical literature. Consult various textbooks that describe different theoretical frameworks, including those referenced in this book, as well as works by real leaders (Barnard, 1938; Bennis & Nanus, 1985). Scan the elements included in each of the conceptual frameworks. Make a list of conceptual frameworks with elements that seem pertinent to your problem situation.

Although you probably have some initial ideas about what is causing the problem, you may be stimulated by examining these summary descriptions of major frameworks to think of additional elements that had not occurred to you previously (see, also, chapter 4 and the bibliography at the end of this book).[13] In fact, some people think it helpful to examine the problem from the perspective of theoretical

---

[13]You should consult original sources related to theories of particular interest. Textbooks typically reference such sources.

frameworks that don't seem to match the causes of the problem you have in mind. A colleague has a poem in her office with a line that says, "Plug us into the wrong socket and see what blows—or what lights up!"

USING SELECTED CONCEPTUAL FRAMEWORKS
TO ANALYZE THE CAUSES OF YOUR PROBLEM:
AN OVERVIEW

Notice, that by following the method to this point, you will have chosen your analytic frameworks by comparing the elements in a large population of conceptual frameworks with what you perceive to be important elements in your problem situation. Although reading the summary material and perhaps some of the additional reference material on these conceptual frameworks will enhance your ideas about what elements in your situation might be relevant as possible causes of the problem, you will have focused first on your problem situation and then matched the elements in each conceptual framework to that situation. In other words, you will have started with the situation and then evaluated each conceptual framework in relation to the situation. The next step in the analysis process is to reverse this perspective.

After selecting your set of analytic frameworks, you should use each in turn to examine your problem. Whereas in selecting the analytic frameworks to use, you examine each of a large number of conceptual frameworks from the perspective of the elements operating in the situation, in the actual analysis, you should examine the problem situation from the perspective of each of the conceptual frameworks you have selected for analysis.

Making this switch in perspective is crucial and sometimes difficult for inexperienced analysts. However, you must initially let each conceptual framework drive its own analysis. Then great effort and careful judgment should go into comparing and contrasting insights gained from different theoretical investigations in order to recognize major themes and patterns among them, then to integrate discrete theoretical insights into a systemic understanding of the problem causes.

Guidelines are presented in each of the theory chapters (chapters 5 through 10). These are intended to illustrate how each analytic framework leads you to collect certain kinds of data and to ask questions directed at the potential causal factors highlighted by it. Compared and contrasted, the guidelines also make you aware of how different theories lead you to ask different questions and collect information about alternative causes of the problem.

Discussed in chapter 9, the work of Burrell and Morgan (1979) provides a unique basis for examining not only organizational problems, but also organizational decisions from two important perspectives. One perspective concerns the extent to which information used to define and contextualize organizational problems and decisions can be viewed from putatively subjective rather than objective view-points. The other perspective focuses the analyst's attention on the extent to which problems, decisions, and analyses emphasize description and instrumental issues of effectiveness and efficiency rather than agentry and moral issues of justice and equity.

In chapter 10, systems theory is presented as a potential framework for portraying, in developmental terms, broad understandings of problem causes over time frames of interest. These broad understandings may well derive from qualitative field research substantially informed by multiple theoretical frameworks such as those delineated in this book. They are cast in terms of the interactive effects of major causal factors over time. Systems thinking emphasizes the importance not only of interaction (typically referred to as "circular causality") but also of delays and nonlinearities.

Before deciding on a final solution strategy, you should evaluate the results of analyses using different conceptual frameworks, including those not included in this book (see, too, the case examples in Part III). You should also interpret these theoretical understandings in relation to the history, culture, politics, and environment of your organization. It is only then that you can formulate an action plan, with specific recommendations for particular stakeholders. Developing a solution strategy and keying action recommendations to stakeholders are the subjects of the next chapter.

4

Developing a Solution Strategy
and Recommendations
to Stakeholders

Leadership over human beings is exercised when persons with certain motives and purposes mobilize, in competition or conflict with others, institutional, political, psychological, and other resources so as to arouse, engage, and satisfy the motives of followers.

—James MacGregor Burns (1978, p. 18)

OVERVIEW

The emphasis in chapter 3 is on selecting theories from the literature on organizations to use as analytic frameworks in analyzing the causes of organizational problems and on the importance of being faithful in your analyses to the particular elements and relationships characterizing separate frameworks. Some general guidelines are provided.

This chapter focuses on drawing conclusions about the causes of the problem, formulating and evaluating potential solution strategies, and making action recommendations to specific stakeholders (see Steps 7 through 13 in Fig. 1.1).

DRAWING CONCLUSIONS
FROM A SINGLE THEORETICAL ANALYSIS

As previously discussed, the central principle governing theoretical analysis is to let the theories drive the analyses. The analytic method explained in this chapter has straightforward procedures:

1. Scan the literature for theories that fit the problem situation.
2. Analyze the causes of the problem in terms of the particular elements and relationships described in each of these analytic frameworks.

3. Formulate a general solution strategy that addresses the causes you identify.
4. Evaluate the likely effectiveness and feasibility of this solution strategy in relation to solutions that have already been tried elsewhere and in light of potential hindering and facilitating factors.
5. Finally, target specific action recommendations to individual stakeholders and stakeholder groups.

Thus, the first step in the analytic process is to examine the situation, at present and historically, from the perspective of one model after another, with each analysis performed independently of the others. Examining the situation from the perspective of a theory implies several discrete steps:

1. *You collect information in the situation relevant to each element in the theory.* For example, with respect to "division of labor," an element of bureaucratic theory (see chapter 5), you would collect information about job descriptions, work flows, and their effectiveness. With respect to "political constituencies," an element of political systems theory (see chapter 7), you would seek to identify the major groups in the political community who have been, or might in the future be, active in making demands on key decision makers for particular policies, goods and services, rules and regulations, and so on. With respect to leadership theory (see chapter 8), you would, among other things, seek out information about how effectively a "vision of the future" has emerged and been articulated among members of the organization.

2. *You collect information about relationships described or implied in the theory.* For example, from a political systems perspective, you might examine relationships between different constituencies and gatekeepers in order to understand why some constituencies are more effective than others in channeling their political demands to those who make decisions related to them. In contrast, from a social systems perspective (see chapter 6), you would investigate the relationships between the psychological, physiological, and cultural characteristics of individuals and the culture, environmental pressures, and work demands of the organization in order to understand the individual's workplace behavior and to envision changes in these relationships that might reduce or eliminate the problem of concern. Alternatively, from an ontological–epistemological perspective (see chapter 9), you would analyze the nature of organizational decisions and decision making (i.e., types of issues identified as decisional questions, decision making procedures, information sources used in making decisions, etc.) by comparing and contrasting them across the functionalist, interpretive, radical humanist, and radical structuralist paradigms.

3. *You draw conclusions from these kinds of information about what might be contributing to the problem and what steps might be taken to resolve the problem.*

The method requires you to reiterate these steps, first using one analytic framework, then another, until you have dealt with most of the potential sources of the problem.

DRAWING CONCLUSIONS ACROSS THEORETICAL ANALYSES

The next stage in the methodology involves synthesizing the results of these discrete theoretical analyses. Essentially this is an exercise in qualitative or hermeneutic analysis. Having deliberately collected information related to the problem from a variety of theoretical, perhaps even epistemological and ontological, perspectives (Astley & Ven, 1983; Benson, 1977; Burrell & Morgan, 1979; Clegg & Dunkerley, 1980; Ferguson, 1984; Foster, 1986; Mills & Tancred, 1992), you must examine these data for logical patterns of causation.

To what extent are the causes you perceive discretely embedded within particular theories such as those already mentioned or others, for example, those of motivation (Miskel & Ogawa, 1988; Ouchi, 1981; Pfeffer & Lawler, 1980; Salancik & Pfeffer, 1977; Vroom, 1964), investment (Ghemawat, 1991), work processes (Deming, 1986; Rummler & Brache, 1991), or leadership (Barnard, 1938; Bass, 1981; Bennis & Nanus, 1985; Fiedler, Chemers, & Maher, 1976; Foster, 1988; Greenfield, 1984; Hodgkinson, 1991; Immegart, 1988; Jago, 1982; Peters & Austin, 1985; Pfeffer, 1977; Schein, 1985; Sergiovanni & Corbally, 1984; Trice & Beyer, 1991; Vroom, 1976; also, see chapter 8). Alternatively, to what extent do these causes represent themselves in the form of themes and patterns across theoretical perspectives? In the end, you must identify both the causes that can be seen exclusively from a single theoretical perspective and those that interact across elements from different conceptual frameworks.[14]

FORMULATING A TENTATIVE SOLUTION STRATEGY

A solution strategy is a general statement describing how you believe you can best address the causes of the problem. Although theoretically derived, such a strategy is not effectively cast in theoretical terms. The theoretical understandings must be transformed from the abstraction of theory to the concreteness of everyday life and action. The theoretical understanding may be, for example, that there are significant "disconnects" in coordinating work flow across "vertically managed organizational functions" (Rummler & Brache, 1991). The solutions required can be expected to mandate significant changes for people in the organization, likely discomfiting

---

[14]Systems thinking is particularly devoted to understanding the causes of a problem across different theoretical frameworks and across diverse organizational boundaries. It is discussed in chapter 10.

many of them. The theory has to be recast into plain language, and the solutions must be specified in the concrete terms of organization charts, work groups, and job descriptions. In fact, for the solution to be effective, many people must participate both in framing the problem and in shaping the final solution strategy. Thus, theory can usefully inform actions, but it cannot determine precisely what actions will work effectively.

EVALUATING THE TENTATIVE SOLUTION STRATEGY

Considering the Likely Effects
of Potential Hindering and Facilitating Factors

Lytle (1993) wrote of "the change formula" in the following terms:

- *Dissatisfaction with the status quo (need for change).* People must be sufficiently dissatisfied with present conditions. They must feel the need for change, which at times must be real pain.
- *Desirability of the change (vision).* People collectively must be attracted to the proposed vision of the new organization.
- *Practicality of the change (process of change).* A change effort must be seen as practical and feasible. People must understand how to start the change effort and proceed toward the end goal.
- *Cost of change: Economic and social.* People will resist the change if the cost of changing (both economic and social) is felt to be too high. (p. xiii)

For every solution strategy, implying certain changes in policy, structure, and behavior, there will be individuals and groups in favor and against, and there will be constraining and supporting conditions. Constraining conditions can be financial, political, cultural, and structural (including the historical dimensions of these elements). Supporting conditions include not only political, cultural, and financial support, but also the availability of human, information, and technical resources, as well as favorable structural and environmental circumstances (Gaynor & Evanson, 1992, pp. 47–49). The extent to which particular solution strategies are satisfactory or unsatisfactory must be judged against these potential hindering and facilitating factors.

Considering the Results of Remedies Already Tried

Not only must you evaluate the feasibility and likely effectiveness of alternative solution strategies in relation to relevant existing and historical conditions both positive and negative, but you also must assess them in the light of related solutions already tried in your organization and elsewhere. You should seek out information on these trials and weigh the satisfactoriness of your tentative solution strategy(ies) against the prior experience of others. If similar solutions failed previously, for what reasons are they likely to succeed or fail in the present situation? If they were successful elsewhere, how likely is it that they will be successful again under the existing conditions in your organization and its environment?

Deciding on a Satisfactory Solution Strategy

It is only after considering all of these factors and issues that you can reasonably and convincingly advocate a particular solution strategy. Thus, you must show that your proposed solution strategy meets the following conditions:

1. It addresses the major causes of the problem in persuasive ways.
2. It builds on potential facilitating factors and deals with potential hindering factors in ways that make it likely to be implemented.
3. It builds on previously successful solution strategies and avoids the pitfalls of previously failed solution strategies so as to give confidence in the probability of its effectiveness.

TARGETING ACTION RECOMMENDATIONS
TO SPECIFIC STAKEHOLDERS

Former Speaker of the U.S. House of Representatives Thomas P. ("Tip") O'Neill is reputed to have said that "all politics is local." In the same sense, all organizational change is implemented by the actions of the people in and around organizations. In the end, your solution strategy is only as good as the people who will support it and take action on its behalf. It is crucial that you translate your solution strategy into distinctive action recommendations tailored to the interests, skills, power, and resources that characterize each and every positive stakeholder you identified and profiled earlier. Your action plan is not complete until you have reexamined these profiles (see Table 2.2) and laid out detailed action recommendations for those who are interested and able to help in the campaign to address the focal problem.

SUMMARY AND PREVIEW

Part I of this book describes and illustrates a problem analysis methodology, which includes several major stages of description and analysis. This methodology emphasizes the importance of describing the problem for analysis clearly, and of documenting its existence in as much detail as possible, using quantitative and qualitative data. It stresses the significance of using appropriate and persuasive standards of comparison to compare and contrast trends over time associated with problem indicators. Such standards place the problem in a value context without which it has little meaning. In fact, raising the issue of standards to explicit consciousness, and purposely seeking to consider the problem from the different perspectives of alternative standards provides a depth of understanding that otherwise is hard to achieve and communicate to others.

The methodology described in Part I also accents the essentiality of stakeholders, positive and negative, and decision makers (as well as gatekeepers). It clearly shows that a central element of the method is the deliberate introduction of theory into the process of causal analysis. Importance is laid on seeking out as wide a range as possible of alternative conceptual frameworks that bear on the problem and its causes, including those representing significant paradigmatic dissimilarity. Summary descriptions of a range of organizational theories are provided. Altough procedural steps are suggested in relation to different parts of the analytic process, the final analysis of causes from multiple theoretical perspectives is portrayed as essentially qualitative in nature, a search through "chunks" of data (Tesch, 1989), collected through disparate conceptual lenses, for themes and patterns of causality that make situational sense.

The point is made that theoretical understandings, no matter how interesting and valid, must ultimately be translated back into the language and action of everyday organizational life. In the end, action recommendations shaped to the interests, skills, power, and resources of particular stakeholders are crucial. Consideration of diverse hindering and facilitating factors is equally imperative. Final solution strategies must clearly address the major perceived causes of the problem, be consistent with solutions previously tried, and be feasible in relation to potential hindering and facilitating factors.

Part II of the book is comprised of seven chapters, six dealing with particular theoretical frameworks. The first four chapters describe fairly well-bounded theories focusing on clearly defined substantive areas. Chapter 5 describes bureaucratic theory, chapter 6 role theory, chapter 7 political systems theory, and chapter 8 leadership theory.

Chapters 9 and 10 are more general and open in nature. They can be thought of as macrotheories. Chapter 9 summarizes the epistemological matrix of Burrell and Morgan (1979) and chapter 10 describes and illustrates systems thinking and the use of causal-loop diagrams as an approach to modeling organizational problem systems. Chapter 11 portrays organizational problem analysis as an hermeneutic process.

Part III presents four examples that apply the analytic methodology described and illustrated in the book. They were done originally for policy courses and seminars at the Boston University School of Education. The chapter by Scheier deals with a policy problem in a vocational school; that by Dolan analyzes issues in a special education school related to educational reform in Massachusetts; the decisional analysis chapters by Bernstein and Pavese deal, respectively, with the placement of students in the honor track of a regional high school and the selection of Latin American scholars to study in universities of the United States.

PART II

THEORY SKETCHES

5

Bureaucratic Theory

Experience tends universally to show that the purely bureaucratic type of adminis-
trative organization—that is, the monocratic variety of bureaucracy—is, from a
purely technical point of view, capable of attaining the highest degree of efficiency
and is in this sense formally the most rational known means of carrying out imperative
control over human beings. It is superior to any other form in precision, in stability,
in the stringency of its discipline, and in its reliability. It thus makes possible a
particularly high degree of calculability of results for the heads of the organization
and for those acting in relation to it. It is finally superior both in intensive efficiency
and in the scope of its operations, and is formally capable of application to all kinds
of administrative tasks.

—Max Weber (1947, p. 337)

More has been written about organizations from a bureaucratic perspective than
from any other. The organizational literature is replete not only with research and
analyses based on bureaucratic theory itself, but with adaptations and extensions
of bureaucratic theory and research, analyses, and critiques of the theory and of
variations on the bureaucratic theme. These include theories, studies, instruments,
and critiques of various aspects of organizations as bureaucratic structures, tensions
involving people in bureaucratic organizations, as well as related concepts such as
decision making, leadership, motivation, organizational politics, and systems theory. Even cultural, critical theory, and poststructural perspectives on organizations
represent reactions to traditional views of bureaucracy.

AN OVERVIEW OF MAX WEBER'S WORK
ON BUREAUCRACY

It is interesting that so much has been written about bureaucracy in the corporate
context when, in contrast, Max Weber's work focused on bureaucracy in governmental administration. In fact, he expressed concern about the danger of bureaucratic officials usurping the legitimate authority of political leaders (Bendix, 1960):

By definition…[bureaucratic] officials are more knowledgeable and so more power-ful than their superiors, unless special provision is made for effective supervision. A bureaucracy that uses its knowledge and capacity for concealment to escape inspec-tion and control jeopardizes legal domination by usurping the rule-making or deci-sion-making powers that ideally should result from the political and legislative process. (p. 445)

Weber was interested essentially in understanding bureaucracy as a form of what he called "legal domination" and in perceiving legal domination in historical contrast to other forms of authority—traditional authority and char-ismatic authority—that had prevailed on the Continent in earlier times (Bendix, 1960):

Like the other types of authority, legal domination rests upon the belief in its legitimacy, and every such belief is in a sense question-begging. For example charismatic authority depends upon a belief in the sanctity or exemplary character of an individual person, but this person loses his authority as soon as those subject to it no longer believe in his extraordinary powers. Charismatic authority exists only as long as it "proves" itself, and such "proof" is either believed by the followers or rejected. The belief in the legitimacy of a legal order has similarly circular quality. "Legal domination [exists] by virtue of statute….The basic conception is: that any legal norm can be created or changed by a procedurally correct enactment" (Kotter, 1982). In other words, laws are legitimate if they have been enacted; and the enactment is legitimate if it has occurred in conformity with the laws prescribing the procedures to be followed. This circularity is intentional. (pp. 413–414)

Nonetheless, the vast majority of bureaucratic analyses have been of business organizations and, as noted, have been based on innumerable variations and extensions of Weber's original descriptions of the essential characteristics of bureaucratic organizations (Weber, 1947, pp. 330–334). Translating from Weber's original writings, Bendix (1960) indicates that "Where the rule of law prevails, a bureaucratic organization is governed by the following principles":

1. Official business is conducted on a continuous basis.
2. It is conducted in accordance with stipulated rules in an administrative agency characterized by three interrelated attributes:

    a. The duty of each official to do certain types of work is delimited in terms of impersonal criteria.
    b. The official is given the authority necessary to carry out his assigned functions.
    c. The means of compulsion at his disposal are strictly limited, and the conditions under which their employment is legitimate are clearly de-fined.

3. Every official's responsibilities and authority are part of a hierarchy of authority. Higher offices are assigned the duty of supervision, lower offices, the right of appeal.
4. Officials and other administrative employees do not own the resources necessary for the performance of their assigned functions, but they are accountable for their use of these resources. Official business and private affairs, official revenue and private income are strictly separated.
5. Offices cannot be appropriated by their incumbents in the sense of private property that can be sold and inherited. (This does not preclude various rights such as pension claims, regulated conditions of discipline and dismissal, etc., but such rights serve, in principle at least, as incentives for the better performance of duties. They are not property rights.)
6. Official business is conducted on the basis of written documents. (p. 418)

He adds that under legal domination, therefore, the bureaucratic official's position is characterized by the following attributes:

1. He is personally free and appointed to his position on the basis of contract.
2. He exercises the authority delegated to him in accordance with impersonal rules, and his loyalty is enlisted on behalf of the faithful execution of his official duties.
3. His appointment and job placement are dependent upon his technical qualifications.
4. His administrative work is his full-time occupation.
5. His work is rewarded by a regular salary and by prospects of regular advancement in a lifetime career. (pp. 420–421)

Thus we see the list of bureaucratic characteristics commonly reproduced in textbooks:

1. A Continuous Organization of Official Functions Bound by Rules
2. Division of Labor and Functional Specialization
3. Functional Authority
4. Functional Specificity of Authority
5. Hierarchy of Authority
6. Technical Competence to Conform to Technical Rules or Norms
7. Separation of Administration from Ownership
8. Written Rules, Orders, Policies, and Decisions and the Universal Application of Them
9. Contractual Relationships

Weber was convinced that bureaucracy would become the dominant form of organization in the modern world. Some of Weber's observations in this regard seem prescient (Bendix, 1960):

1. In Weber's view a system of bureaucratic rule is inescapable. There is no known example of a bureaucracy being destroyed except in the course of a general cultural decline. (p. 450)

2. To those who expect a socialist society of the future to create a major social transformation, Weber pointed out that in a centrally planned society bureaucratic tendencies would mount still higher. The division of labor and the use of special skills in administration would increase, and a "dictatorship of the bureaucrats" rather than a "dictatorship of the proletariat" would result. (pp. 450–451)

3. Universal bureaucratization was for Weber the symbol of a cultural transformation that would affect all phases of modern society. (p. 451)

4. At the end of this road Weber envisaged a society in which social status depends on educational qualifications and governmental office, much like the classic Chinese model except that the education would be technical rather than humanistic. (p. 453)

Keeping in mind Weber's transcendent concern with government and with the rule of law in society, it is not surprising to witness the consideration he gave to bureaucracy in a democratic society. It is interesting the extent to which he foreshadows the concerns of poststructuralist thought (Bendix, 1960, pp. 430–431). Also, concerned about the relationship between bureaucratic administration and the political powers to be served by it, Weber was disquieted by the possibility that legitimate political authority would find itself dominated by the technical expertise and inherent secretiveness of bureaucratic functionaries (Bendix, p. 444).

It is apparent that while, as a sociologist, Weber was a careful observer of the nature and power of bureaucratic organization, he brought to his understanding of the potentialities of this type of administrative organization a sweeping view of history and a thoughtful knowledge of political philosophy. This is not always the portrait of Weber depicted in textbooks of organizational theory.

BUREAUCRATIC THEORY AS A FRAMEWORK FOR ANALYSIS

To use any conceptual framework for analyzing a problem situation, you need to understand the elements of the framework and then organize your analysis around these elements. We have identified nine elements of Weber's bureaucratic theory. A bureaucratic analysis requires that we examine our real-life situation in terms of these nine structural elements.

A Continuous Organization of Official Functions
Bound by Rules

Weber saw bureaucratic organizations as having life spans that transcended those of their employees. He perceived their relative permanence as one aspect of their technical superiority. The theory suggests implicitly that significant discontinuities or instabilities in such broad characteristics of the organization as its identity, goals, sources of support, and leadership might create or contribute to important problems. In your bureaucratic analysis, you should seek out information about such discontinuities or instabilities. Should you discover evidence of them in the past, in the present, or over time, you should consider and investigate whether these have created or contributed to the problem of concern. The following example illustrates an investigation of the impact of organizational discontinuities (Scheidler, 1992). The writer was analyzing the causes of teacher stress in a new public high school program:[15]

> An institution outside the School Department bureaucracy, Ocean City University, proposed the creation of the New Standards Program in 1985, and the School Department accepted the idea and the plan to create the program at Ryan High School. This created discontinuity in the school environment....For example, the program's classes are untracked and meet for double periods on alternate days, and the grading system drops the grade of "D" and allows for multiple chances to complete assignments, institutionalizing a grade of "Incomplete." These changes create a new kind of organizational environment involving regular teacher meetings, a double-period teaching schedule, and fundamental changes in the grading system which affects how teachers and students work. In doing this, the university goals supplanted the School Department's goals, which established tracked classes, teacher isolation and a conventional grading system....
>
> Major funding was obtained by the university to initiate the new program. This funding went only to this new program, and the first four teachers and Program Coordinator were funded to be released from their classes to plan for a semester....The funding for some teachers and not others added to discontinuity. Currently the program costs twenty percent more because New Standards Program teachers have one less class than regular teachers have, under the university principle of reduced teaching load and a common planning period....

Division of Labor and Functional Specialization

A key characteristic of bureaucratic organization is the extent to which roles and functions are specialized. This is related, of course, to maintaining technical competence as a crucial characteristic of job performance. The emphasis in bureaucratic organizations is on hiring people with specialized skills and defining their job functions in terms of these skills. In considering potential problems related to division of labor and work specialization, you may find it useful to consider issues such as these:

---

[15]Pseudonyms are used for school, city, and university names.

1. To what extent is there work that is necessary in the organization for which no one has clear performance responsibility?
2. To what extent is there overlapping or conflicting responsibility for the same job functions?
3. To what extent does division of labor produce undesirable effects on job performance or product quality (e.g., separating responsibility for quality control from production responsibility)?
4. To what extent are there disconnections in the flow of work or information between individuals or units of the organization? (see also Rummler & Brache, 1991)

The following excerpt (Yang, 1992) illustrates an analysis of problems associated with division of labor and functional specialization. The paper deals with a development agency in China. Yang described the problem as follows "Currently, one of the major manifested problems is that funds are not raised in time to implement the projects, which causes a pattern of consistent delay of project implementation." She went on to explain:

> Presently, there are five divisions: Administrative; Education; Medical and Health; Social Welfare and Relief; and Rural Development. Each has a special function as indicated by the name of the division.
>
> The Administrative Division is responsible for the overall administrative work of the foundation, such as general correspondence, public relations and accounting. The other four divisions are organized according to the nature of the projects for which they are responsible leading to an overlap in functions and confusion as to who should be responsible for certain tasks.
>
> Also at times it is difficult to determine to which division a project belongs....Many projects are delayed because they do not technically fit the definition of projects belonging to a certain division.
>
> Commonly, there is a lack of communication between divisions, and staff tend not to know what is going on in the foundation as a whole. Sometimes, one division is overloaded with work while others do not have much to do. Even if requests for help are made by a particular division, staff of other divisions are unable to grant much help because of their lack of knowledge of projects other than their own. Functional specialization hinders the sharing of human resources between divisions and undermines the ability to shift human resources from one division to another in responding to emergency situations.

Functional Authority

According to Weber, bureaucratic functionaries charged with performance responsibilities must be given sufficient authority to discharge their responsibilities. Attending to this issue, you should seek to identify situations in which people are not given enough authority to do their work effectively. Yang (1992) addressed this question in relation to her problem of concern:

Generally, the staff at AD Foundation are not given enough authority in decision making. First of all, projects are not approved within the division responsible for them. Not getting involved in the process of project approval, project coordinators who are responsible for proposal writing and coordinating do not have much of a say in the decision-making process of projects to be approved. Approved projects are usually assigned to them no matter whether they like them or not, and very often, they have to develop a proposal the way they are told to instead of giving the opportunity to express their own opinions concerning the project. As a result, the project coordinators are not very enthusiastic about their projects. Because they are not penalized for not doing their job on time, some of them even deliberately put aside projects they do not feel like doing. Neither do they feel in the position to propose any change toward the present practice of proposal writing or professionalize the fund-raising process. This certainly contributes to the persistence of project delay since the establishment of the foundation.

Functional Specificity of Authority

Do not confuse the question of functional specificity of authority with that of functional authority. Functional authority reminds us to look for problems related to people not having enough authority to do their jobs well. While asserting that people require adequate authority to carry out their assigned functions, Weber reminds us that in bureaucratic organizations, which are legal–rational organizations governed by contractual relationships, people are not expected to wield more authority than is necessary to meet their responsibilities. Cultural expectations in bureaucratic organizations are that the authority of superior officials will be reasonably limited, in contrast to the unlimited authority of kings, feudal lords, and tribal chiefs. The theory asserts that problems can arise when people in bureaucratic organizations are perceived to be overstepping the accepted bounds of their authority. In thinking about your organizations from a bureaucratic perspective, you should look for situations like this that may be contributing to your problem of concern.

Scheidler (1992) described the situation in her school as problematic in this regard:

In the New Standards Program, the authority of the Assistant Principal and the Program Coordinator often impinge upon each other. The Assistant Principal has stated that he feels the Program Coordinator intrudes upon his authority. He has stated that the students are very confused about what authority he has. In contrast, the Program Coordinator has asserted that his authority has been undermined by the Assistant Principal and by the teachers, as well. Some teachers question the Program Coordinator's authority, and feel their authority is impinged upon, for example in the scheduling of new courses. On the one hand, the Program Coordinator is defined by the Union contract as a teacher and, therefore, some teachers feel that he is going beyond his legitimate authority and impinging on their rights. On the other hand, the Program Coordinator believes he has been given responsibility and authority by the university's governing principles to comment on other teachers' classes, how teachers use their time, and to create new courses.

Hierarchy of Authority

Hierarchical authority is central to bureaucratic theory. Bureaucratic organizations are complex. Different units of complex organizations are assigned responsibility for diverse functions. Such units operate in subenvironments with sometimes dramatically different degrees of certainty and stability. To maintain their effectiveness, such units must be structurally differentiated in terms of such things as standard operating procedures and reward systems. At the same time, the structural and functional integrity of the organization as a whole must be maintained. Units must be aligned toward common goals (Lawrence & Lorsch, 1967; see also Senge, 1990).

Although some highly differentiated organizations, operating in rapidly changing technological and market environments, use a variety of devices (e.g., special coordinators, ad hoc teams, even matrix organizations) to help maintain organizational alignment, the primary bureaucratic mechanism of what is called *integration* is the bureaucratic hierarchy. In examining the organization from the perspective of its hierarchy of authority, you should think about questions such as the following:

1. To what extent are goals and functions in the organization clear, coherent, widely accepted, and consistent with changing realities?
2. To what extent are authoritative directives known, clearly understood, and generally followed?
3. To what extent are the activities of different units of the organization consistent with one another and with the broad goals of the organization?
4. To what extent do different units of the organization have sufficient discretion to adapt to unique and changing realities that affect them at the unit level, and to do so in adequate time?

Yang (1992) offered two examples of problems related to hierarchy of authority. The first suggests dysfunctions from overcentralization of authority; the second intimates problems related to a lack of hierarchical control when it is required.

1. At the present stage, overcentralization of authority at the Executive Staff level directly contributes to the lack of planning in fundraising operations. Since decisions concerning the number and type of projects to be implemented are made at the Executive Staff level, each division has very limited choices in projecting and making plans for fundraising. Staff members are expected to be responsive to their project assignments. The staff of each division has to follow the plan for fundraising of projects set by the executive staff even if they think the plan is not feasible. This often causes fundraising activities to be disorganized and leads to persistent delays in implementing projects.

2. As mentioned earlier, there is an overlap of functions between divisions, which causes confusion as to who should be responsible for particular projects. Although divisions on the same level of the hierarchy can negotiate with each other, there are

occasions when consensus does not occur. This then requires someone at the higher level of the hierarchy to help resolve the problem; however, the General Secretary often has difficulty doing so because division heads also constitute the Executive Staff. In reality, they have more power in technical matters, which includes specifying projects and deciding to which division each belongs.

Technical Competence to Conform to Technical Rules or Norms

According to Weber, one source of the relative effectiveness of bureaucratic organizations is their emphasis on the technical competence of people to carry out their specialized functions. This emphasis can be seen in systems of recruitment, selection, training, and performance evaluation. The theory asserts that lack of technical competence erodes the performance effectiveness of the organization. You should ask, then, to what extent problems are caused because recruitment and hiring practices, training, and supervision fail to guarantee that members of the organization will have the necessary knowledge, skills, and motivation to perform well the functions they are expected to perform.

Scheidler (1992) found problems of this type in the New Standards Program:

> No training is provided Program Coordinators for the type of program leadership, organizational management, and budget and scheduling duties they are given....Without efficient, fair, timely scheduling of classes each semester, efficient meeting facilitation, and smooth facilitation of teachers' work with each other and with students, conflict is created among the entire group of teachers. These responsibilities of scheduling, conducting meetings and managing teachers are technical competencies and can be learned. The Program Coordinator is not competent in these skills, creating stress. Teachers have not been trained in these areas either.

Separation of Administration From Ownership

Typically, problems regarding inadequate separation of administration from ownership relate either to dysfunctional interference by policymakers in the day-to-day administrative operation of the organization or to dysfunctional interference in policymaking by administrators, including problems of providing adequate, timely, and accurate information to policymakers. The general question you should ask is this: To what extent are problems caused by the lack of clear and effective distinctions between those who set broad policy for the organization and the professionals who administer those policies on a daily basis? Most frequently, problems related to separation of administration from ownership derive from the interference of policymakers in everyday administration of the organization. In the following example, Yang (1992) suggested that significant problems are created by too much separation between policymakers and administration.

There has been a tendency on the part of the Board of Directors to set policies too broad to be confined to one interpretation which can be clearly understood by the administrators. Sometimes, conflicting elements are found in policies made. Administrators are often uncertain what the correct interpretation of these policies is and how to actualize them in order to bring about the expected outcomes. Some administrators feel that the board does not have enough knowledge of the work of the Foundation to set up policies meaningful to the administration; therefore, implementation of the board's policies becomes difficult. This has a substantial negative effect on fund-raising operations because decisions about implementing a project often depend on how policy is defined. If the definition is not clear, no decisions can be made about a project. Therefore, a number of projects are delayed because there are doubts about whether implementing them would adhere to board policies.

Written Rules, Orders, Policies, and Decisions and the Universal Application of Them

The general expectation in bureaucratic organizations is for clear performance expectations and the fair application of explicit and coherent policies and regulations. The general question you should address is this: To what extent are problems caused by the lack of clear policies and job expectations applied in uniformly fair ways? Scheidler (1992) illustrated several problems related to implementing the new program in Ocean City that derive from inadequate written policies:

1. The Ocean City Teachers Union contract is a 96-page document which spells out the rules which govern the work of teachers and department heads. In 1985 an appendix was added which included new rules for the operation of the New Standards Program at Ryan High School. This appendix was proposed in a meeting of the Ocean City Teachers Union by the Union president in September, 1985, and unanimously accepted by the membership.

2. In practice, several new provisions have caused stress in the organization:
   a. The nonsupervisory, nonadministrative role of the Program Coordinator is not clear.
   b. The use of the planning period is not spelled out in the Union contract.
   c. Rules governing the selection of the Program Coordinator have further contributed to the problem because in the process of the Program Coordinator selection the Ocean City University representative was in direct opposition to the elected teacher representative on the committee. The faculty representative was overruled, causing dissatisfaction among teachers who sided with their elected teacher selection representative.
   d. The responsibilities of the Program Coordinator are unclear to teachers.
   e. Teachers have been unable to file a Union grievance against the Program Coordinator because of a teaching schedule or perceived harassment because he is considered to be a teacher, though one who has scheduling responsibilities.

f. The lack of other written rules, orders, policies and decisions has created tensions over the seven years of the program. Now different teachers in the program have different ideas of what the policies and rules should be. Teachers behave differently. Again, this has created conflict and stress.

Contractual Relationships

Weber emphasized distinctions among sources of authority: tradition, charisma, and law. He saw authority in bureaucratic organizations as being rooted in laws and contracts. He saw this in contrast to how authority was legitimated in traditional societies, by inherited status. He also saw bureaucratic authority in contrast to charismatic authority (i.e., authority deriving from the perception that an individual possesses special attributes, perhaps embodies a higher cause).

An important question related to this dimension of the bureaucratic model is this: To what extent are problems caused by conflicts deriving, knowingly or otherwise, from competing sources of authority? Yang (1992), describing a situation in The People's Republic of China, presented an interesting perspective on this question:

> The sources of authority in bureaucratic organizations are essentially rooted in laws and contracts. Given the uniqueness of the Foundation being a new nongovernmental organization with a religious orientation in a socialist state, the identified problem is to be examined in the context of a larger historical discussion which concerns conflicts among authority rooted in competing sources of authority: law, contracts, policies, tradition, charisma, technical knowledge and skill, recognized experience, etc....
>
> One cause of the problems lies in the competition between charisma and technical knowledge and skills as sources of authority. Decisions to approve a project proposed by a certain social institution are not always based on purely technological considerations, such as the degree of technical sophistication of the project or the technical competence of the institution or the staff of the Foundation to undertake the project. In some cases approval is granted because the president of the Board of Directors, Mr. G. X. Tang, is in favor of the project. Mr. Tang is the Bishop of the Protestant church[16] in China. He plays an important role in the Three-self Movement[17] of the Chinese Christian Community and the process political democratization in China. The reason that he is able to exert a strong influence over administrative decisions is because many view him as a great leader in the religious and political arena; therefore, they tend not to contradict his opinions.

---

[16]The Chinese Protestant Church is nondenominational. However, its practice has the orientation of the British Anglican Church, which is headed by the Bishop.

[17]Three-self Movement, initiated in the early 1950s, advocates self-government, self-support, and self-propagation of the Chinese Churches, which is viewed as significant in averting foreign dependence of the Chinese Church.

FORMULATING CONCLUSIONS
AND RECOMMENDATIONS

Policy recommendations should be developed that are consistent with the analysis; that are consistent with the interests, commitments, and capacities of important stakeholders; and that hold reasonable promise for successful implementation.

QUESTIONS FOR ANALYZING PROBLEMS
USING BUREAUCRATIC THEORY

The following are questions consistent with bureaucratic theory that can be used as guides to bureaucratic data collection and analysis:

 Continuous Organization

To what extent is the problem of concern caused or exacerbated by significant instabilities or discontinuities in such characteristics as identity, goals, sources of support, and leadership?

 Division of Labor

To what extent are there gaps and overlaps of necessary functions among people in different roles?

To what extent is the configuration of specialized roles contributing to problems?

To what extent are observed problems related to trade-offs between short-term efficiencies in defining roles and job functions and the long-term need for greater flexibility in a changing environment?

 Functional Authority

To what extent are people not given enough authority to make the decisions necessary to perform the functions they are expected to perform?

To what extent is lack of needed authority contributing to the problem of concern?

 Functional Specificity of Authority

To what extent are people exercising more authority than is necessary to perform their functions?

To what extent are such transgressions, or perceived transgressions, contributing to the problem of concern?

To use for structural frame.

 5. *Hierarchy of Authority*

To what extent are ~~goals and functions in the organization unclear~~, incoherent, not widely accepted, and inconsistent with changing realities?

To what extent are ~~authoritative directives not known~~, not clearly understood, and not generally followed?

To what extent are the ~~activities of different units of the organization incon-~~ ~~sistent with each other and~~ with the broad goals of the organization?

To what extent do different units of the organization have ~~insufficient~~ ~~discretion~~ to adapt in a timely fashion to unique and changing realities that affect them at the unit level?

To what extent does the managerial structure fail to address important problems and conflicts between different units of the organization or to what extent is the hierarchy structured so that such problems and conflicts can be resolved only at very high levels of the organization?

To what extent do any of these hierarchical dysfunctions contribute to the problem of concern?

 6. *Technical Competence*

~~To what extent are problems caused because recruitment and hiring practice~~s, training, and supervision fail to produce members of the organization who have the necessary knowledge, skills, and motivation to perform well the functions they are expected to perform?

 7. *Separation of Administration from Ownership*

To what extent do those with the ~~responsibility to set policy fail to do so~~, or fail to do so clearly and competently?

To what extent do ~~those charged with setting policy interfere with~~ the day-to-day administration of the organization?

To what extent do administrators interfere with or overly influence policy formulation?

To what extent do any of these transgressions contribute to the problem of concern?

8. *Written Rules and Their Universal Application*

To what extent is the problem of concern caused by ~~lack of clearly written~~ ~~rules and regulation~~s?

To what extent is the problem of concern caused by failure to apply written rules and regulations in uniform, fair, and effective ways?

 9. *Contractual Relationships*

To what extent is the problem of concern caused by conflicts between legal–rational (bureaucratic) authority and authority based on personal or ideological charisma, tradition, or both?

To what extent is the problem of concern caused by tensions between beliefs in the universal application of rules and the differential application of rules for different people in different situations?

AN ILLUSTRATIVE OUTLINE
FOR A BUREAUCRATIC ANALYSIS

The following outline illustrates a bureaucratic analysis. Note that the outline covers only that section of a report that deals with analyzing the problem system from the perspective of bureaucratic theory in particular. The larger report would also include sections on the problem and important stakeholders, their description and documentation, analyses from alternative theoretical perspectives, and recommendations for taking action to deal with the problem.

I. Problems related to individual structural elements

    A. A continuous organization of official functions bound by rules
    B. Division of labor and functional specialization
    C. Functional authority
    D. Functional specificity of authority
    E. Hierarchy of authority
    F. Technical competence to conform to technical rules or norms
    G. Separation of administration from ownership
    H. Written rules, orders, policies, and decisions and the universal application of them
    I. Contractual relationships

II. Problems related to interactions among elements

III. Summary and discussion of the major structural issues related to the policy problem of concern

IV. Conclusions and recommendations from a bureaucratic perspective

6

Social Systems Theory

Conflict and ambiguity tend to pose for the individual special problems of adjustment.
How each man feels about these problems and how he reacts to them depends upon
two further sets of factors. The first of these is his personality, considered as a set of
predispositions formed throughout his previous life history. The second includes all
his contemporaneous relationships with the members of his role set....Both these sets
of factors will affect the behavior of his role sender toward him. Both will also tend
to condition his reactions to conflict and ambiguity, and both, finally, may themselves
be modified by the particular coping patterns he adopts in response to role conflict
and ambiguity of long standing.
—Kahn, Wolfe, Quinn, and Snoek (1964, p. 35)

AN OVERVIEW OF THE THEORY

Role theory, that is the conceptual framework that examines people in organizations
in terms of the ways in which they meet the expectations other significant people
have for their job performance, is in an important sense a corollary to bureaucratic
theory. Whereas the theory of bureaucracy (Weber, 1946, 1947) highlights structural relationships in organizations, especially structures of control and coordination, role theory emphasizes the factors that influence the work behavior of
individuals in organizations. These factors include those that shape people's perceptions of their jobs, motivate them to fulfill organizational expectations for job
performance, and engender stress for them as they seek to meet the expectations
that define their roles in the organization.

As noted in the discussion about bureaucratic theory in chapter 5, Weber focused
on describing the purely structural characteristics of large, efficient organizations.
Bureaucratic theory describes "functionaries" but makes no mention of people, per
se, except in terms of such characteristics as "technical expertise" and how people
are organized and managed to carry out their functions effectively and efficiently.
What bureaucratic theory lacks is any explicit recognition of what McGregor
(1960) was later to call "the human side of the enterprise." In broad terms, at least,
Weber was aware of the negative possibilities inherent in bureaucracy:

The very measures that ensure a bureaucracy against the abuse of authority and the encroachment of privilege—the certified qualification of appointees, regular promotions, pension provisions, and regulated supervision and appeals procedures—can give rise to new status privileges buttressed by monopolistic practices. (Bendix, 1960, pp. 430–431)

Certainly, Weber (1946) was aware of his structural emphasis and the dehumanizing potential of bureaucratic organizations:

Bureaucratization offers above all the optimum possibility for carrying through the principle of specializing administrative functions according to purely objective considerations. Individual performances are allocated to functionaries who have specialized training and who by constant practice learn more and more. The "objective" discharge of business primarily means a discharge of business according to calculable rules and "without regard for persons" [emphasis in the original]. When fully developed, bureaucracy also stands in a specific sense, under the principle of *sine ira ac studio.* Its specific nature, which is welcomed by capitalism, develops the more perfectly the more the bureaucracy is "dehumanized," the more completely it succeeds in eliminating from official business love, hatred, and all purely personal, irrational, and emotional elements which escape calculation. This is the specific nature of bureaucracy and it is appraised as its special virtue. (pp. 215–216)

Thus the tension in bureaucratic theory between the structural (what has been called the "nomothetic") side of the organization and the human (what has been called the "idiographic") side is inherent in the theoretical nature of bureaucracy. This tension was particularly highlighted by the work of Taylor (1856–1915), which was directed toward maximizing the efficiency of production processes (Taylor, 1911a, 1911b).

A pervasive reaction to purely structural theories of organizational efficiency arose initially from research begun in 1924 at the Hawthorne Plant of the Western Electric Corporation. This work began in a Tayloristic search for efficiency related to the levels of illumination at the plant. Its end result, however, was to make prominent the social–psychological effects of simply attending to workers (Roethlisberger, 1956), a finding credited for initiating the "human relations" movement, especially as promoted by Elton Mayo (Hollway, 1991, pp. 68–71). In the more than six decades since the Hawthorne studies, there have been diverse threads of research and theory dealing with the tension between workers and organizations. Miskel and Ogawa (1988) discussed selected aspects of this work related to work motivation, job satisfaction, and organizational climate. However, the relevant literature extends even beyond the considerable range covered in Miskel and Ogawa's review.

Those areas of knowledge that focus on people in the workplace and that affect practice in work organizations…cannot be subsumed under one title, because they reflect many different approaches which are often theoretically inconsistent and even contradictory. They include scientific management; industrial, occupational and social psychology;

human factors; human relations; and organizational behaviour. At the engineering end, ergonomics overlaps with industrial psychology. At the social end, industrial sociology overlaps with organizational behaviour. (Hollway, 1991, p. 4)

Given the broad range of literature on the diverse factors affecting the workplace behavior of people in organizations, the selection of an illustrative analytic theory for this book was particularly difficult. In the end the decision was to present a theory that is conceptually broad, one that I have found analytically useful, and which has seen considerable application in the field of education (Getzels & Guba, 1957; Getzels, Lipham, & Campbell, 1968; Lipham, 1988). Social systems theory, as it is called, seeks to understand and explain human behavior in work roles according to the interaction of cultural, organizational, psychological, and physiological factors.

SOCIAL SYSTEMS THEORY
AS A FRAMEWORK FOR ANALYSIS

As formulated by Getzels and others, social systems theory proposes an extended set of hypotheses about how the dynamics that characterize the relationship between an individual and a social system help us to understand the behavior of the individual in that social system. Typically the social system is an organization. It could, however, just as well be a family, club, or neighborhood gang.

The precise focus of the theory is on the social behavior of a single individual, presumably someone whose actions are perceived as contributing to the problem of concern that you described and documented in the initial stage of the problem analysis. Sometimes, as we shall see in the example included in this chapter (Spiegelberg, 1989), it is useful to examine the behavior of a representative individual, although this poses some problems because of the switch in the level of aggregation and undoubtedly produces some stereotyping. However, we often are interested in understanding the social behavior of rather homogeneous groups in relation to organizational expectations and pressures; social systems theory focused on representative individuals can be helpful in understanding the problem dynamics.

Every analysis using social systems theory as a conceptual organizer must examine the problem situation systematically in terms of these elements and the relationships among them. Social systems theory defines the behavior of the individual as manifesting a kind of transaction between the organization (identified in the model as the "institution") and the individual. Getzels and his colleagues used the Greek-rooted terms *nomothetic* and *idiographic* to refer, respectively, to these two dimensions of the transaction. Nomothetic derives from a root that refers to order (thus, it refers to the organizational component of the social system); idiographic refers to the individual.

The nomothetic, or organizational, dimension is represented in terms of trans-actions, or cross-pressures, between the organization and the culture within which it exists. Individuals are represented in terms of cross-pressures among their respective personalities, physical constitution, and the complex of subcultures with which they identify. Thus, both individuals and organizations are conceived within larger environments to which, presumably, they must adapt.

The theoretical position is that the behavior of an individual can be understood better in terms of the dynamics of interaction among all these elements. The essential elements of the model (Getzels et al., 1968) are arrayed as follows:

1. The culture of the organization as characterized by its ethos (i.e., its domi-nant, competing, and shifting values over time).
2. The organization as a structure of roles and role expectations.
3. Individuals as reflected in their personalities (i.e., their needs and their dispositions to act in ways that satisfy their needs).
4. Individuals as gifted and constrained by the various dimensions of their physical constitutions, conditions that define their potentialities.
5. Individuals as socialized by and carrying the values of whatever subcultures with which they identify to one degree or another.

As suggested in the next section, each of these primary elements is implicitly complex, with wide-ranging implications for analyzing problem situations.

The Stance of the Analyst in Social Systems Analysis

The task of the analyst using the social systems model is to put him or herself in the existential position of the person whose behavior is seen as problematic in order to understand why he or she is displaying the problematic patterns of behavior. The theory offers a guide for the analyst in identifying crucial elements for analysis.

→ Charles - admin v. prof.
Nomothetic Elements

Organizational Culture and Values

The theorists (Getzels et al., 1968) define organizational culture in terms of its outside environment:

> The expectations for behavior in a given institution not only derive from the require-ments of the social system of which the institution is a part but also are related to the values of the culture which is the context for the particular social system. The expectations in the school, for example, are related to the values of the community. (p. 92)

Thus, the theory hypothesizes that values external to the organization exert pressure on it in ways that help to shape its configuration of roles and role expectations. However, recent scholarship emphasizes the further importance of the internal culture(s) of the organization (Deal & Kennedy, 1982; Gregory, 1983; Kozuch, 1979; Sarason, 1971; Schein, 1985; Sergiovanni & Corbally, 1984; Smircich, 1983; Turner, 1972). These combined perspectives imply that a full range of cultural values, within and beyond the boundaries of the organization (often interacting), help determine how roles and role expectations are defined within the organization.

Examples of Descriptions of Organizational Culture and Values. In describing the culture and values of an organization, the analyst attends particularly to those dimensions that affect the focal individual and those aspects of the individual's behavior that the analyst perceives as problematic. In a situation that one of my students examined (Spiegelberg, 1989), the problem was a rising student dropout rate in a high school, and the analysis focused on one student, Ira, who was seen as representative of students dropping out of school. In discussing the culture and values of the school, Spiegelberg addressed the following issues: state certification requirements for teachers, graduation requirements for students, and funding formulas for school districts; the value placed on education in the school district; the backgrounds and special educational interests of members of the school board, the superintendent, and the high school principal; the discipline policy of the school; policies with respect to smoking and chemical abuse; school counselors and counseling programs; the curriculum and scheduling; testing policies; regional school evaluation procedures; the educational backgrounds of the faculty; and student organizations and extracurricular activities in the school. The following discussion of counseling programs in the school illustrates the analyst's method:

> Out of four counselors, three of them are new to the school within the last four years. One of the counselors is responsible for chemical abuse problems and setting up "groups." The other three counselors see themselves as crisis counselors in contrast to providing guidance to students about classes/registration, universities, and vocations. If a student fails a class or classes, the counselors meet with the parents and student each quarter to discuss the problem.

> A strong program in the school is group counseling which was begun in 1980–1981. The School District has now provided training for approximately half of the faculty so they are prepared to work with "groups." Group sessions are eight weeks in length, and each group meets once a week. A student may sign up for a group, or a counselor may suggest a group to him or her. For the next session, the student may continue to sign up for the same group, a different group, or can stay in home room.

> The various groups include career exploration, eating disorders, family relationships/changes (death, divorce, blended families), relaxation (teaching techniques to relax), stress management (focuses on talking about problems), self-esteem, insight (looking at their own chemical usage), concerned persons (people concerned about other people's chemical usage), academic concerns (over- or underachieving), new

students, helping each other (girls that are or have been pregnant), peer pressure, after care support (kids coming back from chemical treatment), and depression. If a different type of group is needed, this decision is made in a special committee created for this purpose. This program has kept many students from dropping out and has helped them to perform better in school.

Roles and Role Expectations

Getzels et al. (1968) defined role and role expectations succinctly in the following terms:

> Roles represent positions, offices, or statuses within an institution....Roles are defined in terms of role expectations....The expectations define what the actor, whoever he may be, should or should not do under various circumstances while occupying the particular role in the social system. (p. 61)

These writers added that, depending on the situation, there is more or less flexibility for people to shape their roles consistent with their personalities:

> The proportion of role and personality factors at least potentially determining behavior will...vary with the specific system, the specific role, and the specific personality involved. (p. 81)

They also quoted from Parsons and Shils (1951, p. 23):

> An important feature of a large proportion of social roles is that the actions which make them up are not minutely prescribed and that a certain range of variability is regarded as legitimate....This range of freedom makes it possible for actors with different personalities to fulfill within considerable limits the expectations associated with roughly the same roles without undue strain. (p. 62)

They described degrees of flexibility that can exist across a range of situations. Roles can vary from those dominated by organizational expectations to those in which there is a great deal of room for people to express their personalities. The full range of possibilities is displayed as a continuum.

It turns out in real life that role expectations are richer for analysis than they might appear on first consideration. First, there usually is not a single set of role expectations; instead, people have different ideas about what any particular individual is supposed to do and how he or she is supposed to do it. In the terminology that sociologists use, each individual is embedded in a role set, which is made up of all the people who have an interest in how the individual does his or her job and who are in a position to pressure the individual to do it their way. Some are more powerful than others. Getzels et al. (1968) described the role set this way:

list of expectations.

> Role set refers to the pattern of role relationships and concomitant complementary expectations which an individual has by virtue of occupying a single position—the position of teacher necessarily entails role relationships with pupils, colleagues, administrators, and so on. (p. 84)

This explication of the construct is consistent with its general exposition in the social–psychological literature. For example, Kahn et al. (1964) portrayed the concept in quite similar terms:

> Organizations consist ultimately of the patterned and concerted activities of their members. Thus considered, each individual's role in the organization consists of his part in the total pattern of activity. The study of the impact of an organization upon an individual, therefore, may be approached through the observation of the role behavior of its members as they affect the individual. For any particular person it is useful to restrict our observations to the role behavior of those members of the organization who have direct contact with him in the course of their work, the roles thus selected being labeled a role set. It is a key assumption of this approach that the behavior of any organizational performer is the product of motivational forces that derive in large part from the behavior of members of his role set, because they constantly bring influence to bear upon him which serves to regulate his behavior in accordance with the role expectations they hold for him. (pp. 34–35)

Some members of the role set are clearer than others about what they want. Also, people are more or less consistent about what they expect from the individual. Thus, the individual has to deal with the cross-pressures from diverse role expectations for his or her role within the organization and other roles outside the organization. Furthermore, the individual has to deal with his or her own ideas about what the job should be about.

Social systems theory highlights the importance of examining the performance pressures on the individual that emanate from significant members of the role set. This implies listing what Getzels and his colleagues called the major *role senders* (Kahn et al., 1964), identifying for the individual their major expectations—for what he or she should do (substance) and how he or she should do it (style). It also implies identifying how role senders make clear what they expect, how clearly they do so, and what sanctions they wield when the individual fails to meet their expectations. Spiegelberg (1989) described the network of role expectations surrounding Ira, her representative potential high school dropout.

The following from Spiegelberg (1989 [computer file]) is a partial [list of expectations school personnel have for students:]

Administrators, counselors and teachers expect students to:

- Be familiar with the information in the handbook and to abide by the school rules (i.e. no smoking, fighting, drugs, or alcohol)

- Attend classes and be on time
- Do their assignments and participate in class
- Be courteous and responsible.

Counselors expect students to:

- Follow the attendance procedures for absences
- Sign up for appropriate classes during registration which are needed to meet graduation or competency requirements (i.e., required or remediation courses)
- Know that counselors can help them with other problems such as mediating a problem between a parent and teacher or signing them up in an appropriate group session.

Teachers expect students to:

- Be aware of each teacher's tardy policy
- Follow the attendance procedures for absences
- Make up work in advance for prearranged absences and field trips
- Request extra help if they fall behind in class or do not understand the assignment.

Spiegelberg also included a list of the key expectations students hold for each other. These also constitute a dimension of the organizational culture.

Students expect other students to:

- Attend classes and be on time
- Do their assignments
- Abide by school rules
- Do not cause disruptions in classes
- Participate in activities (i.e., clubs or athletics and/or attend school functions)
- Be considerate of other students and faculty.

Multiple Role Conflict. Individuals are also subject to cross-pressures from role expectations across multiple roles. Getzels et al. (1968) described multiple roles as follows:

> The term "multiple roles" refers to the complex of roles and concomitant *independent* expectations associated with the various positions in which an individual finds himself—the same individual as teacher, father, deacon, and so on. (p. 84)

Thus, these writers distinguished the independent expectations associated with multiple roles from the complementary expectations that characterize role sets. They further suggested the complexity of pressures from both types of expectations:

Individuals are subject to pressures arising both from the conflictual expectations of their multiple roles and from their role-set in the given organization. (p. 84)

Idiographic Elements

There are three elements that comprise the idiographic section of the model: subcultural values, constitutional potentialities, and personality needs and dispositions.

Subcultural Values

Getzels et al. (1968) explained this concept in the following terms:

Not only is personality related to its biological substratum…but it is also *fundamentally and integrally related to the values of the culture in which the organism grows up.* The human organism is not born with a ready-made set of culturally adaptive attitudes and reactions any more than it is born with a culturally adaptive language or set of religious beliefs.…The child must learn…to acquire certain culturally adaptive attitudes, values, and beliefs. The process of *socialization* is designed to help the child to do just this. (pp. 103–104)

In addition they stated:

At first the parents are the objects of identification. Later he may add older siblings, favorite neighbors, community heroes, school personnel, and other important figures in the various social systems in which he comes to play a part. In making these identifications, he not only assumes the outward manners and expressive behavior of his "significant others" but also attempts to incorporate their values and attitudes. (p. 104)

Spiegelberg (1989) described the principal components of Ira's subculture:

Ira's cultural background is different from the majority of students in the school. One source of difference is the high value placed on education; Ira's family does not. In fact, Ira is subject to many of the same circumstances that research lists as indicators for potential dropouts, i.e., broken home, older than classmates because of retention, parents who did not graduate from high school, and siblings who dropped out of school.

Ira comes from a broken home and has three brothers and three sisters. His mother did not graduate from high school and the family is in the lower socioeconomic class. His brother dropped out of school last year. Ira's mother is overburdened with her own problems so his education is a low priority to her. She would like Ira to quit school and get a job which would help the family financially. Her aid for dependent children decreases if she works, but if the children work, it does not. She does not call the attendance office to excuse his absences. In fact, she often does not wake him up in the morning for classes and he does not have an alarm clock. She is also unable to help him with his homework and she does not encourage him to do it. He also does not have a quiet place to do it.

His friends do not encourage him to attend school since they have many of the same problems and some of them who have already dropped out of school encourage Ira to quit. They are a subgroup whose main purpose is to disregard authority. Ira's fighting and chemical dependency is condoned by his subgroup although it is not acceptable to others.

Spiegelberg summarized these subcultural expectations as follows:

Ira's mother expects Ira to:

• Drop out of school since she doesn't feel it is necessary for him to continue
• Help family financially by getting a job
• Stay out of trouble.

Ira's friends expect Ira to:

• Drop out of school, disregard authority
• Use chemicals with them
• Have time to associate with them.

Constitution and Potentialities

Getzels et al. (1968) cited Bakke and Argyris (1954, pp. 13–14) in providing a sense of what they mean by the constitution and potentialities of an organism as they affect the individual's personality. Bakke and Argyris identified four aspects of an individual's biological constitution:

(1) "Biological equipment with its inherent capacities"; (2) "Impulses to activity" that lead to experience and the acquisition of abilities; (3) Physiological, psychological, and social abilities; and (4) Predispositions such as "reflexes, habits, attitudes, prejudices, convictions, sentiments, [and] intentions." (pp. 90–91)

Spiegelberg (1989) described Ira in terms of his potentialities:

Although Ira feels overwhelmed by school because of his lack of education skills, he sees a diploma as the one pathway that could ultimately help him to be successful. He is aware that he is not prepared to hold down a very rewarding job even though his mother keeps encouraging him to quit school and go to work. When he dropped out of school a year ago, he checked back into school at the beginning of the next semester. His success in auto mechanics two years ago is probably the "life line" that he continues to remember. Physiologically, his chemical dependency also affects his performance. He requested to be placed in a "group" for chemical dependency. The counselor found that Ira was unable to work within the "group" structure so she arranged individual therapy for him. Since Ira is aware that he has a problem, he may be able to eliminate the chemical dependency through the individual therapy sessions.

Need-Dispositions

Getzels et al. (1968), described five aspects of need-dispositions. The first of these refers to "forces within the individual":

Every human being has a characteristic style of life. Not only is he a creature of his biological drives or animal necessities, but he strives to fulfill wants having no apparent relationship to the maintenance of merely physiological well-being. (p. 70)

A second need-disposition relates to goal-orientation:

Need-dispositions refer to tendencies to achieve some end state. As Kluckhohn and Murray (1953, p. 15) say, "Conforming with Lewin and many others, we may use the term 'need' or "need-disposition" to refer to the roughly measurable 'force' in the personality which is coordinating activities in the direction of a roughly definable goal. (pp. 72–73)

A third aspect relates to cognitive, perceptual, and other forms of behavior:

Need-dispositions influence not only the goals an individual will try to attain in a particular environment but also the way he will perceive and cognize the environment itself. A person with a high need for dominance tends to structure the environment in terms of its opportunities for ascendance; a person with a high need for affiliation, in terms of its opportunities for sociability; and a person with a high need for cognizance, in terms of its opportunities for understanding. (p. 73)

Fourth, Getzels et al. (1968) suggested that need-dispositions vary in specificity:

Insofar as a need-disposition is general, it can find expression in a variety of situations, and the same person can move with ease into numerous roles. (p. 75)

Finally, Getzels et al. suggested that need-dispositions are "patterned or interrelated" (p. 75). Referring to Maslow, they make the point that "the relation among needs is not that they exist randomly like a great many sticks lying around side by side, but that they lie like a nest of boxes, one box containing three others, each of these containing ten others, each of these ten containing fifty others, and so on" (p. 76).

In part, Spiegelberg (1989) discussed Ira's need-dispositions in the following terms:

If one were to use Maslow's scale, his most salient present needs are belonging, self-esteem, and self-actualization. He has a need to associate with other students. However, the friends he chooses have similar problems so they have not provided a positive influence. His auto mechanics teacher took a personal interest in him two years ago. This was the first teacher whom Ira felt had really cared about him succeeding. This teacher has been supportive, understanding, and caring. The class Ira took from him was the first one in which Ira actually felt real success and achievement. As Ira meets his needs for belonging and self-esteem, he will probably stop fighting. Fighting has been his primary way of venting his aggression, frustration, and hostility. It has given him the self-esteem he needed (since he has always won).

Sources of Role Stress

Role Discrepancies, Conflicts, and Cross-Pressures

Discrepancies, conflicts, and cross-pressures between role expectations, on the one hand, and the individual's own values, constitutional characteristics, needs, and dispositions on the other constitute, according to the model, important sources of tension and stress. Stress commonly derives from the following sources and affects organizational performance, which Getzels et al. (1968) referred to as ["social behavior"]:

1. *Discrepancies* that may exist between the individual's own needs (and dispositions to behave in certain ways to meet those needs) and the expectations others hold.
2. *Competing demands* for time and energy to meet expectations related to different roles in which the individual serves (e.g., spouse, parent, multiple job holder), what is called "multiple role conflict."
3. *Conflicting demands* among role-senders (members of the "role set") in the organization, what is called "intrarole conflict."
4. *Lack of ability* to meet the role expectations of self and others.
5. *Lack of time* to meet the role expectations of self and others, what is called "role overload."
6. *Lack of clarity* about the role expectations of others or lack of insight into one's self-expectations, what is called "role ambiguity."
7. *Value differences* between the values implicit in the role expectations of others, one's own values, and the values of important personal reference groups, what is called "value conflict."

Spiegelberg (1989) discussed, in her analysis, some of the sources of stress for Ira:

Stress caused by the organization. He is extremely frustrated because of his low level of success in the academic areas. The academic classes cause him stress since he has never been successful in these courses. He feels hopelessly behind before he even starts a new course. His inability to pass the competency tests creates a great deal of stress for him since failing to pass these competencies will eventually keep him from graduating. It is stressful to Ira that he cannot take elective courses like auto mechanics or welding. Since he was successful in auto mechanics, he would like to take one of these elective courses. It bothers him that the administrators seem inconsistent with discipline in regards to his fighting and disruptive behavior compared to some other students.

Stress caused by conflicting demands of the organization and the mother and friends. There is conflicting stress caused by his mother in regards to the attendance policy.

She does not follow the procedures for calling in to excuse his absences. Consequently, he is unexcused and cannot make up the work for a grade. He feels that there should be other ways for him to be excused when he misses classes, since his mother will not call. For example, students who do not live with a parent/guardian can call the attendance office to excuse themselves. Many of his absences are caused because his mother insists that he stay home to help her.

Stress caused by mother and friends. Ira wants to attend school but his mother and friends try to discourage him from going to school. However, they have different reasons. His mother wants him to go to work and his friends want him to "run around" with them. Ira would like to help his family but he realizes that he is not qualified to find a satisfying job without a high school education. His mother wants him to stay out of trouble and she is unaware that he has a problem with chemical abuse. His friends encourage his fighting and chemical abuse.

Class pressures. In his classes he feels pressure from the students and the teachers because he is late for class. The first period teacher does not want to hear any excuses as to why he is late; she just deducts points from his grade for each tardy. Since his mother does not care if he goes to school, she will not help him to get there on time. When he is tardy for other classes, it is because he is outside smoking with his friends. The stress is caused by trying to be with his friends who are disregarding school rules and knowing that he will also be tardy for class. Stress is also caused because of the variety of tardy policies. Also, cross-pressures are caused by homework assignments. It is difficult for him to do his homework since no one at home can help him with it, and he does not have a quiet place to study. However, the teachers expect the homework to be completed for each class. When he does fail classes, his mother will not go to school to meet with a counselor. Consequently, the counselors and teachers feel that both Ira and his mother are not interested.

Misperception as a Potential Source of Distortion and Misunderstanding

Another dimension of behavior and stress is related to the distinction between real and perceived role expectations. You may misperceive what others expect you to do; you may act on erroneous perceptions; or you may suffer stress because of misunderstandings about what you are expected to do. Such distortions are important in some situations. In using the social systems model as a lens for analysis, you should consider whether misperceptions of role expectations play an important part in sustaining problem behavior. You should also examine whether the important members of the role set (i.e., the role senders) may be misperceiving the role performance of the individual. This is a complementary form of misperception that can contribute to performance problems in the social system. Spiegelberg did not discuss these issues in her analysis of the dropout situation in Laramie High School.

Dynamic Analysis

The social systems framework can be used to analyze a situation at a particular point in time. This is illustrated in Spiegelberg's work. It can also be used to examine the consequences of changing conditions over longer periods of time. In doing the former, what we might call static analysis, the analyst seeks to describe the various elements of the model and to explain the problematic behavior of the individual in terms of cross-pressures among the elements. However, sources of role stress in organizations, and what may be viewed as problem behaviors, can result from dynamic changes in aspects of the organization and individuals in the organization over time. The following examples illustrate the idea:

1. Environmental pressures produce changes in the culture of organizations (e.g., changes in the financial and information industries of the United States deriving from deregulation) that, in turn, lead to sometimes dramatic changes in roles and role expectations.
2. Environmental pressures lead to significant shifts in personnel (e.g., affirmative action legislation) that, in turn, alter the configuration of subcultures in organizations; the dynamics between individuals in an organization who have different needs, dispositions, potentialities, and values; and the role expectations of the organization as represented in its traditional members.
3. Changes in the values or lifestyle of an individual alter how he or she responds to traditional role expectations.
4. Changes in the personality or physical constitution of an individual (e.g., as the result of personal development, aging, or trauma) alter how he or she responds to traditional role expectations.

One of the most interesting applications of the social systems model takes the form of dynamic analysis.

FORMULATING CONCLUSIONS
AND RECOMMENDATIONS

Policy recommendations should be developed that are consistent with the analysis; that are in keeping with the interests, commitments, and capacities of important stakeholders; and that hold reasonable promise for successful implementation.

QUESTIONS FOR ANALYZING PROBLEMS
USING THE SOCIAL SYSTEMS MODEL

The following questions consistent with the social systems theory can be used as guides to social systems data collection and analysis:

1. What individual behaviors are contributing to the problem defined for analysis?
2. What members of the role set are most concerned about these behavioral discrepancies from expectations? Are there other members of the person's role set who find his or her performance consistent with their expectations?

3. To what extent is the individual's role behavior contributing to the problem defined for analysis because of:

   a. Discrepancies from widely shared role expectations?
   b. Differences in role expectations for the individual among important members of the role set?

4. To what extent do the role expectations that members of the role set hold for the individual seem rational or irrational with respect to the goals of the organization

   a. To the individual him- or herself?
   b. To important others in the role set?

5. To what extent are the problem behaviors the result of the lack of clarity of role expectations

   a. To the individual, him or herself;
   b. To important others in the role set?

6. To what extent are the problematic aspects of the individual's behavior attributable to describable and documentable:

   a. Needs and dispositions of the individual?
   b. Constitutional aspects of the individual, including dimensions of giftedness and handicap?
   c. Particular values of the individual?

7. To what extent have there been significant changes in the organization or its environment, or in the individual or his or her environment, that may be contributing to the problematic behaviors:

   a. Changes in the environments of the organization, the individual, or both?
   b. Changes in the roles and role expectations of the organization?
   c. Changes in the needs and dispositions of the individual?
   d. Changes in the constitutional aspects of the individual (capacities and potentialities)?
   e. Changes in the values of the organization, the individual, or both?

AN ILLUSTRATIVE OUTLINE
FOR A SOCIAL SYSTEMS ANALYSIS

The following outline can be used for a social systems analysis. The outline covers only that section of an analytic report that deals with analyzing the problem system from the perspective of social systems theory in particular. The larger report would also include sections on the problem and important stakeholders, their description and documentation, analyses from alternative theoretical perspectives, and recommendations for taking action to deal with the problem.

I. The role set

    A. Members

    B. Sources and types of pressure

II. The configuration of role expectations among different members of the role set

    A. Expectations for what the individual should do (substance)

    B. Expectations for how the individuals should do what they do (style)

    C. The clarity of various role expectations

    D. The accuracy with which the individual perceives various role expectations

    E. The changes in different role expectations over time

III. The consistency of different and changing role expectations with various dimensions of the individual's needs, dispositions, potentialities, and cultural values

IV. Sources of role stress for the individual

    A. From the discrepancies that may exist between the individual's own needs (and dispositions to behave in certain ways to meet those needs) and the expectations others hold

    B. From competing demands for time and energy to meet expectations related to various roles in which the individual serves (multiple role conflict)

    C. From the conflicting demands among members of the role set in the organization (intrarole conflict)

    D. From lack of ability to meet the role expectations of self and others

    E. From lack of time to meet the role expectations of self and others, what is called role overload

    F. From lack of clarity about the role expectations of others or lack of insight into one's self-expectations, what is called role ambiguity

    G. From value differences between the values implicit in the role expectations of others, one's own values, and the values of important personal reference groups, what is called value conflict.

    H. From changes in role expectations, individual or organizational values, or the individual's needs, dispositions, or constitutional capacities

V. Summary and discussion of the major social system dynamics related to the problem of concern

VI. Conclusions and recommendations from a social systems perspective

7

Political Systems Theory

[I]t is highly useful to depict a political system as a set of interactions through which valued things are authoritatively allocated for a society.
—David Easton (1965, p. 153)

AN OVERVIEW OF THE THEORY

Political activity characterizes not only decision making at the national, state, and local levels within the larger society; it shapes decision making in organizations as well.

The *political frame* views organizations as arenas of scarce resources where power and influence are constantly affecting the allocation of resources among individuals or groups. Conflict is expected because of differences in needs, perspectives, and life-styles among different individuals and groups. Bargaining, coercion, and compromise are all part of everyday organizational life. Coalitions form around specific interests and may change as issues come and go. Problems arise because power is unevenly distributed or is so broadly dispersed that it is difficult to get anything done. (Bolman & Deal, 1984, p. 5)

Political science can be viewed as the study, in societies, communities, and even organizations, of the processes by which "valued things are authoritatively allocated" (Easton, 1965, p. 153). The discipline of political science, with its historical roots in the moral philosophy of the ancient Greeks (Easton, 1991; Scribner & Englert, 1977), is a changed and divided field of study. Waldo (1975) characterized political science in the 19th century in the following terms:

In a view of the entire period from the establishment of the first colleges to 1880, several evolutionary trends are evident. One is simply an increase in the stock of materials on which to draw for instruction, as well as increasing diversity in those materials. The works of Montesquieu, Guizot, Adam Smith, and de Tocqueville, for example, were drawn on to some extent when they became available. Another trend was toward differentiation and secularization. "Philosophy" was becoming differentiated and divided into separate pursuits. Not only was "natural" philosophy separating from "moral" philosophy, but "political philosophy" was becoming distinct from "ethics." History and economics were beginning to develop self-awareness; and the study of law was moving rapidly toward professionalization. (p. 25)

By the late 19th century, those who were doing "political science" were describing existing legal systems; they "assumed that there was a reasonably close fit between what constitutions and laws said about the rights and privileges people held in various political offices and the way in which they acted in those offices" (Easton, 1991, p. 38). Later in the 19th and 20th centuries political scientists entered into the description of the "informal activities out of which public policy was formed," without, however, drawing clear distinctions between facts and values and with little debate over methodology (Easton, 1991, p. 41). These "formal–legal" and "traditional" periods were displaced by "behavioralism" (not to be confused with Skinnerian "behaviorism") (Easton, 1991, pp. 42-43).

Once political theory took on a behavioral cast, the field of study became differentiated in a number of significant ways. First, political scientists divided themselves between those whose research focused on understanding the political behavior of groups and individuals (Kessel, Cole, & Seddig, 1970) and those whose work focused on political systems, for example, in terms of theories of political economy, operations research, game theory, and systems theory (Eulau, 1969; Greenstein & Polsby, 1975).

Second, especially since the 1960s, there has been an increasing separation between political science and policy studies.

[I]t is quite clear that the discipline can now be disaggregated into an infinite number of policy specialists—all organized and constrained by the practical problems of the moment. So, apart from defense policy, and security policy, and foreign policy, and arms control policy, we have our specialists in housing, welfare, transportation, education, technology, and energy. The list is endless. By their nature, and by their thrust, they constitute a centrifugal force—literally fleeing from the center of the discipline. (Landau, 1988, p. vii)

Policy studies tend, in fact, to be closer to economics than to political science, although it may not always be clear that this attraction is judiciously derived.

That is, such fields as policy analysis, policy evaluation, and policy implementation are seen increasingly as separate fields, quite distinct from political science....If, however, they presume to draw little from political science, they frequently, and quite thoughtlessly, attach to economics. (Landau, 1988, p. vii)

In a very important sense, whereas modern political science tends more to the theoretical and the value-neutral, the policy sciences emphasize the practical and the value-expressive.

At the most general or inclusive level of meaning, theory and policy refer to two distinct ends of knowledge. Science has always been animated by these two general aims. On the one hand, it has promised unified knowledge and the discovery of a theoretical order able to make sense of the apparent multiplicity of individual occurrences. On the other hand, it has promised increased control over the environment. The tension between these two ends is not particularly strong in modern natural science because theoretical achievement has become an important ingredient of engineering success. No such reconciliation has occurred in the social sciences, for the role and even the nature of theory in an empirical field of study that increasingly justifies itself in terms of its potential contribution to rational public policy are far from obvious. Consequently, a conclusive or consensual answer to the question of the optimal relationship between such a science and political theory is not likely to emerge in the foreseeable future. (Portis & Levy, 1988, p. xv)

A third form of division within political science is that between the post-structural, commonly neo-Marxist schools of political thought and the traditional main stream of political science. Marxist thought tends to be macro-political and is closer in important respects to political economy and policy analysis than to traditional political science. A rich moral philosophy, systematically developmental and historically dynamic, neo-Marxism can be seen, in these senses, to be conceptually related to systems thinking. For example, such a phrase as "institutionally sedimented," often seen in the critical theory literature, seems directly akin to the systems theoretical concept of "accumulation" (Forrester, 1968). However, in contrast to systems analysis, neo-Marxist thought is deeply values-oriented, rooted in an action philosophy, and, especially in its radical humanist dimensions, strongly voluntarist in its ontology.

Despite their obvious differences, the connections between these two schools of thought can be seen in the following brief observation by J. Kenneth Benson (1982), a noted critical theorist:

One of the objectives of policy sector analysis is to explain the emergence, the maintenance, and the transformation of interorganizational patterns....[I]nterorganizational patterns would be explained at the level of the total social formation, i.e., the whole society conceived as a multileveled structure of social relations containing contradictions and undergoing periodic crises of development. (p. 147)

Benson's focus, while critical, is deeply developmental and dynamic and, in these ways, akin to traditional systems thinking. It is my view that in important ways critical theory is characteristically systemic. In fact, it may appropriately and usefully be characterized as radical systems analysis (Habermas, 1973). I point out the common threads between these two systems of thought, often characterized in dichotomous terms, in order to suggest that systems theory, despite its historically conservative cast, may be usefully employed more broadly than previously realized.

POLITICAL SYSTEMS THEORY
AS A FRAMEWORK FOR ANALYSIS

In this chapter, as in the previous ones, it was necessary to decide on the presentation of a particular theoretical framework for analysis. The decision was made to present David Easton's political systems theory for several reasons. First, it is historically at the heart of political science, per se. Second, as Bolman and Deal (1984) have pointed out, contingency theory and systems theory are the two main strands of traditional organizational theory. Third, systems theories, as does the social systems model presented in the previous chapter, provide a good balance between breadth and specificity for analysis. Finally, as suggested earlier, political systems theory is as compatible with radical as it is with conservative analysis. In short, my belief is that the political systems model provides an unusually useful framework for looking at organizational problems in terms of the conflicts and cross-pressures on decision makers emanating from powerful individuals and groups with different, frequently conflicting, interests and goals.

Although political science concerns itself mainly with the processes of decision making in the purely political world of municipal, state, and national government (e.g., Easton, 1965, diagram, p. 374), it is, as suggested in the opening paragraphs of this chapter, often useful to explore the dynamics of organizational problems from a political perspective. There are at least two reasons for doing this. First, because decision making is at the heart of the administrative enterprise, there is no reason to assume that decision making processes are all neatly subsumed hierarchically, even in largely bureaucratic structures. Political perspectives on bureaucratic decision making tap a significant reality (Bacharach & Lawler, 1980; Bacharach & Mitchell, 1981; Hills & Mahoney, 1978; Pfeffer, 1981; Pfeffer & Salancik, 1983; Rowan, 1982; Tucker, 1981; Zald, 1970). Easton (1971) himself alluded to this:

> A policy, in other words, whether for a society, for a narrow association, or for any other group, consists of a web of decisions and actions that allocate values. (p. 130)

Easton's work is the classic example of political systems theory. Whereas bureaucratic theory describes the structural elements and relationships that organizations manifest in the name of order and efficiency, and whereas social systems theory seeks to open for analysis the tensions and stresses that derive from the persistent struggle to conform diverse individuals to universal bureaucratic norms, political scientists such as Easton see the world of conflict as the normal world and understand the dynamics of problem situations in terms of what Lindblom (1965) called "partisan mutual adjustment." Thus, Easton's model of the political system provides an important lens for examining the politics of decision making in the microworld of organizations as well as in the macroworld of party politics.

Like all formal conceptual frameworks, Easton's theoretical framework comprises a number of elements and relationships among them. The configuration of these elements and relationships constitutes an extended hypothesis about the nature of an observed reality. It focuses our analysis of the causes of our problem precisely on these elements and relationships. The basic model includes six elements: (a) political constituencies, (b) demands, (c) supports, (d) decision makers, (e) decisions and actions, and (f) feedback to political constituencies. These are conceived as a circular feedback loop characterized by the following essential dynamics of the political system:

1. Political constituencies make demands[18] on decision makers and seek to influence them through providing and withholding supports[19] (and threatening to do so).
2. Decision makers forge decisions[20] and take actions that are observed by diverse constituencies through various formal and informal channels of public and private communication.
3. Constituencies adjust their demands and supports, in subsequent rounds of political activity, in response to the feedback they receive about the decisions and actions of decision makers.

Thus, Easton's theory is truly systemic in the sense that it models causal influences developmentally over time (see also, in this regard, the discussion of systems thinking in chapter 10 of this book).

As always in formal analysis, data must be collected from the problem situation that describe, as well as possible, each element and relationship in terms of people, structures, artifacts, events, and interpretations in the real world. The political systems model encourages us to organize our thinking in terms of these analytic categories and to use them in seeking to understand the situation from its particular perspective. This implies again, as always, that we perceive the elements of the model as overlapping with elements in the real problem situation that appear to be important in understanding the problem dynamics. This perception is exactly what informs our decision to call first of all on the political systems model.

Conceptual Overview

In the parlance of systems theory, the political model is truly dynamic (see also chapter 10 in this book on systems thinking). That is, it includes a feedback cycle that, at least conceptually, implies the ongoing operation of the system over time.

---

[18]Easton defined demands for (a) allocations of goods and services, (b) regulations of behavior, (c) participation in the political system, and (d) value symbols.

[19]Easton described supports in terms of (a) goods and services, (b) respect for regulations, (c) voting and political activity, and (d) respect for public authorities.

[20]Paralleling the four categories of demands, Easton discussed decisions about (a) allocations of goods and services, (b) regulations of behavior, (c) participation in the political system, and (d) value symbols.

Easton (1965) commented on this view:

> Outputs not only help to influence events in the broader society of which the system
> is a part, but also, in doing so, they help to determine each succeeding round of inputs
> that finds its way into the political system. (p. 152)

Because the system is cyclical, you can begin at any point in the flow and continue
iteratively. As Easton (1965) said, "It does not matter where we break into the
systemic feedback loop to begin our analysis of it" (p. 382). For example, one could
begin with the decision makers.

1. Information about the decision makers' decisions and actions finds its
   way through available channels back to diverse political constituencies,
   perhaps with differential rates of speed and levels of completeness and
   accuracy.
2. These constituencies interpret the information they receive and evaluate its
   meanings and implications.
3. The constituencies respond to the information by forwarding, through available channels, corresponding demands to the decision makers, along with
   increases or diminutions in levels of support for what Easton (1965) called
   "the regime" (pp. 191–198).
4. The decision makers make decisions and take action.

Because the cycle is circular, you can, from an analytic perspective, begin it
anywhere. Thus, for example, the following version of the cycle is as valid as that
just described. In fact, this second version may, from a practical perspective, be
more useful because most analyses begin with an examination of the authorities'
past decisions and actions as they are seen to contribute to the particular problem
being addressed. Easton (1965) suggested that this is the case in reminding us that
"[t]he production of outputs that act as stimuli for the members is…the first phase
of the feedback process" (p. 401):

1. The decision makers make decisions and take action.
2. Information about these decisions and actions finds its way through available
   channels back to diverse political constituencies, perhaps with differential
   rates of speed and levels of completeness and accuracy.
3. These constituencies interpret the information they receive and evaluate its
   meanings and implications.
4. Through available channels, diverse constituencies communicate demands
   to the decision makers, along with evidence of support and indications of
   likely future levels of support conditional upon decisions made and actions
   taken by the decision makers.

An iterative feedback view is both incremental and developmental in nature. It suggests a longitudinal perspective in which one attends mainly to processes. An important implication of this description is that we can discern the importance of stress as a driving force in the political system—stress as a consequence of events that have transpired as well as those that may possibly occur under imaginable conditions. Sources of stress on decision makers are discussed in several of the following sections.

Elements

Political Constituencies

Easton (1965) described in broad terms those who input demands:

> Persons acting in and stimulated by their roles in any environmental system may thereby be led to demand binding decisions of some sort. (p. 54)

In doing a political analysis of your problem situation it is important that you describe the important sources of demands to the political system. These descriptions constitute a major part of your analysis. In the course of describing these political constituencies, be sure to include descriptions not only of constituencies that are politically active at the moment, but also those who, under certain conditions, may become active in the future. This latter task is the more difficult one. Such potential constituencies, not currently active, are called *latent constituencies*. Your analysis should include reference to both active and latent constituencies, especially if you perceive latent constituencies as potentially active players in feasible action strategies.

One of my students used the Easton model to analyze a problem related to the criteria used in selecting students for a special program for gifted students. The program is referred to as Project EXCEL (PE). The student identified the problem in terms of several problem indicators (Tarver, 1989, pp. 4–9):

1. The identification process equated achievement test performance with intelligence in a way that gave an advantage of as many as 15 points to those students whose achievement test scores were particularly high.
2. Up to 15% of the school population was identified as gifted, three times the 5% limit authorized by the state.
3. Many of the identified students were ultimately not successful in PE, with a "failure" rate of about 30%.
4. In a fewer, but significant, number of cases the PE identification system failed to reidentify for continuation in the program students whose progress in the program had been exceptional, which angered some parents.
5. The population of PE was disproportionately located in schools attended by children from middle- and upper-income homes.

6. Many classroom teachers had attempted to sabotage the program either by ceasing to refer any students or by referring all their students.

This student's term paper illustrates several different components of a political systems analysis. The first of these focuses on the political constituencies with an interest in Project EXCEL and the history of their respective demands, supports, and levels of influence related to the program for gifted students. A summary table (Table 7.1) is included here (Tarver, 1989, p. 16).

Decision Makers

In general, Easton (1965) described what he called "authorities" (i.e., decision makers) in the following terms:

They must engage in the daily affairs of a political system; they must be recognized by most members of the system as having the responsibility for these matters; and their actions must be accepted as binding most of the time by most of the members as long as they act within the limits of their roles. (p. 212)

TABLE 7.1

Tarver's Summary of Demand History, Support, and Influence

Demand Constituencies	Demand History	Influence
Classroom teachers	Inconsistent	*Manifest Support:* Most direct responsibility to support to students
	Activity depends largely on demands of other constituencies	*Latent Support:* Building principals; parents of nonidentified students
		Influence: Large numbers of members
Program teachers	Steady success in demands and growth of staff and budget in K–8	*Manifest Support:* Legal mandate to provide services; generous state funding formula
	No success expanding into 9–12	*Latent Support:* Parents of identified students
		Influence: Ownership of the problem provides incentive for resolution
Parents of identified students	Few demands but great success with those	*Manifest Support:* Level of involvement in schools
		Latent Support: Contact with school board members
		Influence: Includes many leading members of Jacksport
Parents of nonidentified students	Few demands with little success	*Manifest Support:* Large number of voters and taxpayers
		Latent Support: Classroom teachers (in certain circumstances)

Easton went on to indicate such "occupants of authority roles as elders, paramount chiefs, executives, legislators, judges, administrators, councilors, monarchs, and the like" (p. 212) as commonly recognized decision makers in political systems. It is important in doing your political analysis to identify as decision makers those in your situation who make binding decisions on matters related to your problem of concern and actions taken toward its resolution. This is not always obvious. Sometimes, for example, under pressure, final decisions are displaced to higher level decision makers. As a case in point, we have seen labor negotiations over financial issues displaced from municipal to state levels when the political stakes are high enough.

Whom you choose to define as the decision makers has important ramifications for your political analysis. This choice will tend to set boundaries for data collection and analysis, determining to a great extent the size of the arena within which the drama is perceived to be played out, who the constituencies are, and the nature of the political communication channels. In a certain sense, defining the decision makers also defines the level of aggregation of the political system. It is important to define the level of aggregation accurately with respect to the scope of the decision being made and the constituencies involved.

In the following excerpt, Tarver (1989) described a single key decision maker relevant to policies concerning Project EXCEL:

> At its inception, the superintendent assigned Project EXCEL to the authority of the Assistant Superintendent of Elementary Education, who is now Mr. John Leroux. In that role, Mr. Leroux makes all final recommendations for program action to the superintendent. (Although the Superintendent must always be considered the district's official key decision maker, he has never taken any action related to PE other than that recommended by the assistant superintendent. To consider Mr. Leroux the primary gatekeeper instead of the key decision maker might be technically correct in terms of the levels in Easton's model, but it would be "spiritually" incorrect in terms of practice in Jacksport.)
>
> Mr. Leroux cannot accurately be said to favor substantially either gatekeeper. In making decisions, he does tend to support the principals over Ms. McGeever. This may be due to the fact that his ascension to the position of assistant superintendent followed a 20-year career as a building principal in Jacksport; the current principals have been colleagues rather than subordinates for most of Mr. Leroux's time in Jacksport. In addition, during his years as principal, Project EXCEL was not a program of particular interest to him. The program was the "brainchild" of the previous assistant superintendent, a career-bound (rather than place-bound) administrator.
>
> Mr. Leroux cannot be said to treat PE unfairly when assessing the needs of all the programs for which he is responsible. Most often, though, he attempts to avoid making decisions in situations of conflict, not wishing to alienate any of the gatekeepers and their constituencies. As a result, PE has remained status quo for the last four years. (Although this problem might be analyzed in terms of leadership weaknesses, the

problem of Jacksport's ID procedure is really due more to struggles among constituencies than to Mr. Leroux's action or nonaction.) (pp. 22–23)

Demands

Although in my opinion Easton (1965) does not do so definitively, he actually does distinguish demands from other less public, less organized, and less insistent points of view:

> Members also put in expectations, opinions, expressions of motivations, ideologies, interests and statements of preferences. At times these may be identical with demands; at others they may be just partial determinants of these demands. (p. 47)

It is my sense, given Easton's subsequent discussions of the importance of stress on decision makers as a driver of the political system, that to be considered political demands, inputs from constituencies must be channeled in ways that give them political force. Demands must create pressure for action on the decision makers, whether or not the decision makers respond to that pressure. Given the reality of multiple constituencies, political systems are frequently characterized by conflicting and competing demands. In a sense, the object of political analysis typically is precisely on conflicting and competing demands and on understanding why at certain times and in relationship to certain issues the demands of particular constituencies are more fully met than those of other constituencies.

By way of illustration, I had a student some years ago who wrote a proposal for a doctoral dissertation. His intent was to identify all of the significant political constituencies, active and latent, in two communities to determine the demands of each constituency and to assess the extent to which the demands of the various constituencies found their way into the agenda of the School Committee, were acted upon, and resulted in favorable or unfavorable action. This type of research exemplifies the importance of competing and conflicting demands as a component of political analysis. See Tarver's (1989) table of constituencies (Table 7.1) for descriptions of the demands made on the political system by different constituencies in regard to Project EXCEL.

Demand Flow

Demands flow in a political system through what Easton (1965) called communication channels. He contrasted the complex communication channels in modern society with "the absolute dominance of face-to-face relationships" in simple societies:

> But in modern societies, the communication channels for demands are highly diversified and structurally very differentiated [including]…interest groups, parties, opinion leaders, mass media, political leaders, legislatures, and relevant unorganized publics….Each subsystem may modify the demands coming to it, both as to their numbers and content, or it may stop them entirely under appropriate circum-

stances....[I]t is thereby capable of performing an intrasystem gatekeeping function. (pp. 118–119)

Describing the relevant communication channels leading to decision makers and understanding how their use and the effectiveness of their use differs among constituencies is an important dimension of political systems analysis.

Tarver (1989) described the political channels and gatekeepers who shaped and controlled the flow of political demands related to the program for gifted students:

There are just two channels to the key decision maker: the building principals and the program coordinator. The building principals are the primary gatekeepers in this situation. As full members of the district's administrative team, the principals have the most direct line of communication and the strongest influence with the decision maker, the assistant superintendent, John Leroux. Building principals meet with Mr. Leroux weekly to discuss current issues in the district. Mr. Leroux is heavily overburdened in terms of the number of programs and staff groups for which he is directly responsible. As a result, he often relies on his primary staff, the principals, in handling a variety of situations in the schools. (p. 19)

Supports

Easton (1965) discussed the importance of both overt and covert support of political communities (pp. 171–189), regimes (pp. 190–211), and authorities (pp. 212–219). Overt support, by its nature, is the more evident. Discussing national political systems, Easton illustrated the concept of overt support, positive and negative, with the following examples:

[W]e may defend a decision by the courts of the land, vote for a political candidate, pay taxes willingly, or voluntarily join the armed forces. We may engage in riots against the government, refuse to pay taxes, resist authority at every turn, join forces with a separatist movement, migrate to another country, or participate in a revolution against the existing regime. (p. 159)

Analogous examples can be given at other political levels. For example, school district political systems depend on support from students in attending school, participating actively in classes, and following school regulations. Similarly, they depend on teachers to come to work, prepare their classes, and engage in a variety of curricular and extracurricular activities. Further examples can be given of overt support in school districts, and comparable examples can be given in other types of political systems. Easton (1965) argued, though, that in the long term covert support provides a reservoir of stability for political systems. He said, "Supportive behavior may involve more than externally observable actions alone" (p. 161).

As we shall see, consistent with his emphasis on the importance of stress as the force driving the dynamic behavior of political systems, Easton posited erosion of support and its perception by decision makers as a source of stress to which leaders typically respond. Thus, identifying the sources of support for the authorities, for the regime,[21] and for the political community,[22] takes its place as a primary component of political systems analysis.

In thinking about support and erosions of support, it may be crucial to distinguish between objective levels of support and those perceived by the decision makers. It is often important, both in understanding the historical dynamics of a political system and in formulating strategies for change, to understand what constituencies the decision makers believe to be important sources of support. Frequently, decision makers underestimate the importance of significant sectors of support that are simply taken for granted.

It should be noted that, from a political systems perspective, an essential strategy of passive resistance movements is to call the attention of decision makers to formerly taken-for-granted constituencies and types of support. Historical examples include work-to-rule tactics in labor negotiations as well as mass movements such as those led by Mahatma Ghandi and Martin Luther King. Thus, changing the perceptions of decision makers about the relative contributions of various constituencies to total levels of political support may be as important as changing the levels of support, themselves. Tarver (1989) described the supports, manifest and latent, associated with each of the relevant constituencies she identified in the last column in Table 7.1.

Decisions and Actions

Easton (1965) discussed political decisions and actions as "outputs." He described two types of outputs: authoritative and associated (p. 353). Authoritative outputs include statements such as "binding decisions, laws, decrees, regulations, orders, and judicial decisions" as well as performances that he referred to as "binding actions." Associated outputs include statements in the form of "policies, rationales, and commitments" and performances such as "benefits and favors." Four types of outputs include decisions about (a) allocations of goods and services, (b) regulations, (c) opportunities for participation, and (d) symbolic statements and actions. Most political analyses focus on decisions and actions perceived as problematic and try to understand them at least partly in terms of disproportionate power among diverse constituencies. Power in this sense is generally thought of in terms of the ability to influence political decisions and actions.

In Table 7.2, Tarver (1989) displayed along with a list of constituencies and their demands, a corresponding list of desired outputs. Each of what she referred to as "sample outputs" describes a policy output that would be consistent with that

---

[21]Easton defined the regime as the "basic procedures and rules" for resolving controversy and reaching binding decisions.

[22]Easton quoted Firth (1951) in this regard: "A human community is a body of people sharing in common activities and bound by multiple relationships in such a way that the aims of any individual can be achieved only by participation in actions with others" (p. 41).

TABLE 7.2

Key Demand Constituencies, Demands, and Sample Outputs

Demand Constituencies	Demands	Sample Outputs
Classroom teachers	Exclusive control over student-by-student ID decisions	Program policy statements establishing individual classroom teachers' final say in all ID decisions
Ideology: strong control	Wider participation in program	
Program teachers	Greater participation in ID decisions	Changed ID procedures and administrative hierarchy
Ideology: effective system; increased control	Accurate referrals from classroom teachers	Funds to support training aimed at greater system accuracy
	Better match between definition and ID practices	
Parents of identified students	ID of certain talents initiating services for those talents	Expanded programming; changed program policy regarding annual ID decisions
Ideology: service expansion; status quo for ID	Stable program population	Maintenance of city-wide ID
Parents of nonidentified students	No identification for giftedness	Abolishment of Project EXCEL
Ideology: all kids are gifted	Enrichment services provided for all students	Redistribution of funds to provide enrichment for all students

constituency's demands. As you study the history of the actual decisions made and actions taken in a political situation, you should compare the desired outputs of constituencies with those they are able to elicit from the decision makers.

Feedback to Political Constituencies

Easton (1965) expressed appreciation for the substantial complexity of the interacting feedback loops in a political system. He identified six general types of feedback, at the same time recognizing that there are interactions among them that render the feedback infinitely complex (pp. 373–376):

1. Feedback between and among "producers of inputs of support and demands" (i.e., among political constituencies)
2. Feedback between constituencies and interest groups
3. Feedback between interest groups and political parties
4. Feedback between political parties and administrative agencies
5. Feedback among the producers of output, including administrative agencies, legislature, and executive (i.e., the decision makers)
6. Feedback from the producers of output to the producers of input (i.e., from the decision makers to the constituencies).

You should examine the differential involvement of a range of constituencies exchanging information about various issues in feedback systems. In doing so, you should attend to issues of the accuracy, distortion, timeliness, and completeness of receiving and giving information. For example, what is commonly referred to as "public relations" deals significantly with controlling the timing and content of information—and disinformation—destined for different constituencies.

According to Easton (1965), the political system is fueled by information about demands, supports, decisions, and actions and driven by stress. Information is processed through the feedback systems described earlier that comprise Easton's "channels of communication." Tarver (1989) described the information feedback system surrounding Project EXCEL in the following terms:

> Ms. McGeever regularly provides information regarding Mr. Leroux's decisions related to Project EXCEL to the program teachers who, in turn, relate to the parents of their identified students. The principals have opportunities to relay the same information to classroom teachers through daily school bulletins and monthly staff meetings. However, they rarely pass on information related to PE. As a result, classroom teachers and the general parent community gain their information through the program teachers. This gives an extra degree of influence to the program teachers inasmuch as they have at least informal control over the information that is circulated and, thus, the demands generated by the information. (p. 24)

Sources of Stress

Political systems theory describes two types of stress: demand stress and stress from erosion of support, perceived and anticipated.

Demand Stress.   Stress due directly to demands derives from the volume, complexity, and contentiousness of demands (Easton, 1965):

> Stress from a large number of demands will occur if they require greater channel space than is available or that can be readily produced by the system. For example, if the channel is a newspaper or a legislative representative, the paper can carry only so much printed material and the representative can handle only a certain amount of mail or listen to only a limited number of persons in his office or, in developing nations, at the bazaar. (p. 65)

It seems useful to understand the role that patterns of demand stress have played historically in relation to the problem of concern. Also, in formulating your action strategies you should consider the potential utility of tactics designed to play upon patterns of demand stress in the political system you are examining with reference to your problem of concern. Political strategies commonly include elements designed to increase levels of demand stress on decision makers and the keepers of their gates.

Stress on Support. The concept of support is central to Easton's (1965) political systems theory. Easton takes the position that some minimal levels of support are essential to the persistence and effectiveness of a political system, suggesting that systems may experience variations in support in three different ways. To function at minimal levels, political systems must have a stable set of authorities, a stable set of rules and structures, what Easton refers to as a stable regime, and some "minimal cohesion" within the polity, what he calls political community (p. 157).

Responses to Stress on Support

In defining how supports operate to drive the dynamics of a political system, Easton (1965) discussed how "authorities" (i.e., decision makers) respond to perceived or anticipated erosion in support. He identified and discussed several types of response:

1. *Homogenization*: The reduction of "religious, linguistic, or other cultural differences among groups" (p. 249).
2. *Expressive structures*: Providing for each group comprising the polity "institutional recognition in the political sphere and self-expression as a unit" (pp. 250–251).
3. *Representative structures*: Involving either the extension of suffrage or the recruitment of "elites from the groups to occupy some of the authority" (p. 252).
4. *Depoliticizing political issues:* Easton suggested two approaches to this strategy: withdrawing "from the arena of political importance any disputed matter" (a) after significant discord or (b) in anticipation of such discord (pp. 262–263). Examples he gave include prohibitions against governments intruding on religion or freedom of speech or establishing official languages.
5. *Generation of specific support:* Providing outputs in the form of symbols, favorable regulations, allocations of resources, or opportunities for participation in the political system to groups to attract or maintain their specific support for the authorities or the regime (p. 267).
6. *Generation of diffuse support*: Authorities may generate diffuse support, in contrast to specific support, not by providing particular outputs favorable to the interests of particular groups, but rather by calling attention to the general loyalties people have to cultural symbols associated with the authorities or the regime, such as flag, country, and the political community itself. Easton suggested that such general good will "helps members to accept or tolerate outputs to which they are opposed or the effect of which they see as damaging to their wants" (p. 273).
7. *Coercion*: Members may offer minimal levels of support out of fear and the threat of force, at least for some period of time (p. 276).

It seems important to understand from a historical perspective how policies have been enacted and maintained (i.e., "sedimented" in the language of the critical theorists) that represent one or another of these strategies to bolster political support. It is equally important, in considering alternative plans of action to resolve your problem of concern, to appraise how you might seek the enactment of policies related to alternatives among Easton's seven categories of response to erosion of support.

These are the major elements of the political systems model. As you proceed with your political systems analysis, you will want to collect information about all of the dimensions of the political process represented in the model and discussed earlier. Your report should discuss each as it is relevant to the problem situation. Ultimately, your recommendations for action should be based on a careful consideration of the political system dynamics that have contributed to the problem of concern and the changes required to ameliorate the problem.

FORMULATING CONCLUSIONS

Policy recommendations should be developed that are consistent with the analysis; that are consistent with the interests, commitments, and capacities of important stakeholders; and that hold reasonable promise for successful implementation.

QUESTIONS FOR ANALYZING PROBLEMS
USING EASTON'S POLITICAL SYSTEMS MODEL

1. Who are the key demand constituencies relative to the problem under examination?
2. What are, have been, or are likely to be the principal demands of each of these constituencies? What would be important examples of political outputs (decisions and actions by key decision makers) consistent with these demands?
3. To what extent, historically, have the demands of the various constituencies been met by the decision makers (a) in absolute terms, or (b) relative to the demands of other constituencies?
4. What factors might explain apparent discrepancies in the political success of these constituencies: support base; elements of power (time, resources, skill)?
5. Who are the key decision makers relative to the issues that you believe are significantly related to the problem you are analyzing? What are their respective and collective relationships to the several constituencies?
6. What are the major channels through which demands normally reach the decision makers? What groups and individuals are the important gate-keepers?

7. In what ways and to what extent have "demand stress" and "erosion of support" been important factors relative to the issues you are examining?

8. To what extent are constituencies aware of political processes, activities, and decisions that affect them? To what extent and by what means is political information manipulated? To what extent do constituencies receive information that differs significantly in timeliness, completeness, and accuracy?

AN ILLUSTRATIVE OUTLINE
FOR A POLITICAL SYSTEMS ANALYSIS

The following outline illustrates a political systems analysis. The outline covers only that section of an analytic report that deals with analyzing the problem system from the perspective of political systems theory in particular. The larger report would also include sections on the problem and important stakeholders, their description and documentation, analyses from alternative theoretical perspectives, and recommendations for taking action to deal with the problem.

I. The decision makers   *summary table p. 76*

   A. Information about their values

   B. Information about their agendas

II. Decisions made and actions taken by the decision makers significantly related to the problem of concern

III. The identity of the significant constituencies related to the problem and to the political issues surrounding it

   A. Active

   B. Latent   *p. 75*

IV. Demands associated with different constituencies

   A. Manifest

   B. Latent

V. The differential support bases of the various constituencies[23]

VI. Gatekeepers

---

[23]This involves looking into the perceptions of the decision makers. How do they view the ways in which the various constituencies have traditionally provided support to them, have been dangerous to them, or could help or hurt them in the future? How have these perceptions helped to provide political influence unequally to different constituencies?

   A. Information channels to the decision makers

   B. Information processing mechanisms associated with the different gate-keepers

VII. Information feedback to the various constituencies

   A. Differential timing

   B. Differential accuracy

   C. Differential completeness

VIII. Historical patterns of stress on gatekeepers and decision makers

   A. Demand stress

   B. Stress from erosion of support

      1. Real

      2. Perceived or anticipated

   C. Significant types of response by decision makers to stress

IX. Summary and discussion of the major political dynamics related to the problem of concern

X. Conclusions and recommendations from a political systems perspective

8

Leadership Theory

It must be considered that there is nothing more difficult to carry out, nor more doubtful of success, nor more dangerous to handle, than to initiate a new order of things.

—Machiavelli (1513/1942, p. 24)

AN OVERVIEW OF THE THEORY

As much has been written about leadership in one aspect or another as about any other dimension of organizational and administrative theory, with the possible exception of bureaucracy. Comprehensive reviews of the literature include the original classic by Stogdill (1974), updated by Bass (1981). More concise, but highly informative reviews have also been done by House and Baetz (1979), and Jago (1982). Other significant reviews include those by Cartwright and Zander (1968), Fiedler and Chemers (1974), Filley, House, and Kerr (1976), Immegart (1988), McCall (1976), and Schriesheim, House, and Kerr (1976). At the date of this writing, the latest and most comprehensive compendium of leadership theory and research is the third edition of what is now called *Bass & Stogdill's Handbook of Leadership* (Bass, 1990). As Bass stated in the preface to this work, significant changes have occurred since 1981 in the substance and methods of research on leadership:

> The treatment of leadership as a phenomenon in organizational and social psychology has broken out of its normal confinement to the study of the behaviors seen previously mainly in leader–group interactions in the field and laboratory. Cognitive science has provided the freedom to explore leader–follower thoughts and feelings. Organizational science has increased the sophistication of examinations of leadership that are contingent on the context in which leadership occurs. Political science has provided new objective insights into the contrasts of leadership, politics, and administration. Throughout this third edition, the contributions from cognitive social psychology and the social, political, communications, and administrative sciences have been expanded. Methodology has become more sophisticated. More field and longitudinal studies have appeared, along with many helpful meta-analyses. Culture and environment, both inside and outside the organization have taken on a renewed prominence. (p. xi)

In this same introduction, Bass took issue with those who argue that leadership is not real, is not important, is harmful, or that we know little about it. He suggested, to the contrary, that the work reviewed in his compendium of almost 1,200 pages makes clear just how much is known about the subject:

> Worse still are the "know-nothings" who simply know little about the subject and do not take the time to find out. Yet, they declare that we know nothing about leadership. Or, what we know does not matter. Or, leadership does not exist. Or, if it does, it is antidemocratic and interferes with good team efforts. This book should demonstrate the absurdity of such know-nothingism. (pp. xi–xii)

The research on leadership can be categorized for the most part within a four-fold typology classifying studies according to whether they treat leadership as universal or contingent and whether they focus on traits of leaders or leadership behaviors (Jago, 1982).

> Certain perspectives make the implicit assumption that what constitutes successful or effective leadership does not depend on the characteristics of the situation in which the leader operates. Leadership is proposed to be a general as opposed to specific phenomenon....On the other hand, alternative approaches propose that effective leadership depends on specific features of the leader's situation (e.g., characteristics of the task, characteristics of followers)....Secondly, perspectives differ in the way the leadership construct is conceptualized....Leadership can be viewed as a *trait* (or set of traits) distributed in some way among the population....Alternatively, it is possible to focus on observable leader *behaviors* rather than on inherent traits. (p. 316)

Jago's typology seems confirmed 8 years later in an examination of Bass's (1990) table of contents. The major categories around which Bass's review of the literature on leadership is organized in the most recent edition of the *Handbook* are consistent with the earlier classification schema. Major topics dealing with the "personal attributes of leaders," "the transactional exchange," "situational modera-tors," and "the work of leaders and managers," along with discussions of various types of leadership styles (e.g., "autocratic and authoritarian vs. democratic and egalitarian," "directive vs. participative," and "task vs. relations-oriented" leader-ship) cover much of the same range of literature as that classified by Jago.

Not surprisingly, the very definition of leadership has been the subject of much discussion. Bass summarized the modern history of this discussion in the following terms:

> Either by explicit statement or by implication, various investigators have developed definitions to serve the following different purposes: (1) to identify the object to be observed, (2) to identify a form of practice, (3) to satisfy a particular value orientation, (4) to avoid a particular orientation or implication for a practice, and (5) to provide a basis for the development of theory....The definitions indicate a progression of thought, although historically, many trends overlapped. The earlier definitions iden-

tified leadership as a focus of group process and movement, personality in action. The next type considered it as the art of inducing compliance. The more recent definitions conceive of leadership in terms of influence relationships, power differentials, persuasion, influence on goal achievement, role differentiation, reinforcement, initiation of structure, and perceived attributions of behavior that are consistent with what the perceivers believe leadership to be. Leadership may involve all these things. (p. 19)

LEADERSHIP THEORY
AS A FRAMEWORK FOR ANALYSIS

As suggested in the preceding overview, the literature on leadership theory is extensive and highly variable. Many theories could have been chosen as perspectives for examining leadership issues as possible causal factors related to organizational problems. But because the theory sketches in this book can do no more than illustrate a very broad range of organizational theories, it seemed important to choose as an example for analysis a leadership theory that represents the increasing interest in recent years in leadership at the highest levels of organizations at a time when "the proportionate number of studies on college students and younger participants has continued to decrease" (Bass, 1990, p. xi). It is for this reason that the focus in this chapter is on the work of Bennis and Nanus (1985) and their broad theory of institutional leadership.

Bennis and Nanus derived their theory from an interpretation of interviews with 90 top leaders, including company executives, senators, governors, labor leaders, orchestra conductors, film producers, college presidents, and athletic coaches, among others. Perhaps as a result of the qualitative nature of their research, the theory is presented in an arrangement of major and minor themes. The result is a theoretical presentation somewhat less precisely articulated than the presentations of the bureaucratic, social systems, and political systems theories summarized in the preceding chapters of this book, but one that is broadly useful for examining the nature and dynamics of leadership pertaining to organizational problems. In relation to Jago's (1982) typology, this theory focuses on leader behaviors and recognizes the situational nature of leadership in fulfilling what appear to be universally conceived expectations and functions.

MAJOR ELEMENTS OF BENNIS
AND NANUS' THEORY OF LEADERSHIP

Bennis and Nanus identified four crucial functions that leaders must perform effectively: attention through vision, meaning through communication, trust through positioning, and the deployment of self. Leaders must perform these functions if their organizations are, in Parson's (1961) terms, to successfully achieve "pattern-maintenance,"[24] integration,[25] goal-attainment,[26] and adaptation."[27]

Attention Through Vision

In a provocative and thoughtful discussion of the future of the world economy, Lester Thurow (1996) emphasized the importance of maintaining an essential correspondence in a society, or by analogy in an organization, between technology and ideology. It is my sense that Thurow used the term "ideology" synonymously with the idea of an essential and driving vision: "Successful societies have to unite around a powerful story with a sustaining ideology" (p. 257). Bennis and Nanus suggested that effective leaders "set…new direction[s], and they concentrated the attention of everyone in the organization on [them]" (p. 88). Thus, the central focus of their theory of leadership is on the critical significance of "a shared vision of the future" (p. 91) which aligns members of the organization at all levels and "unite[s] the people in the organization into a 'responsible community,' a group of interdependent individuals who take responsibility for the success of the organization and its long-term survival" (p. 211). It is important to note, however, that Bennis and Nanus make no claim that leaders, themselves, invent the visions they proclaim; they make clear that leaders typically draw their ideas for new directions from others in the organization. Furthermore, with an eye toward the other central functions of leadership, they remind us that, although necessary, attention to vision is not enough.

Meaning Through Communication

Having a vision is not sufficient. Leaders must be skillful and persistent in communicating new directions and the changes they imply to all members of the organization. As Bennis and Nanus put it, "[A]n *essential* factor in leadership is the

---

[24] According to Parsons (1961), "the focus of pattern-maintenance lies in the…maintenance, at the cultural level, of the stability of institutionalized values through the processes which articulate with the belief system…." (p. 38) and "the motivational commitment of the individual" (p. 39).

[25] Parsons describes integration in the following terms:

Our recognition of the significance of integration implies that all systems…are differentiated and segmented into relatively independent units….The functional problem of integration concerns the mutual adjustments of these "units" or subsystems from the point of view of their "contributions" to the effective functioning of the system as a whole. (p. 40)

[26] A goal, according to Parsons (1961), is "a directional change that tends to reduce the discrepancy between the needs of the system, with respect to input–output interchange, and the conditions in the environing systems that bear upon the "fulfilment" [*sic*] of such needs" (p. 39).

[27] Parsons (1961) stated that "the primary criterion [of adaptation] is the provision of flexibility, so far as this is compatible with effectiveness; for the system, this means a maximum of generalized disposability in the processes of allocation between alternative uses" (p. 40).

capacity to influence and *organize meaning* for the members of the organization" (p. 39). According to them, the relationship between vision and communication is inextricable: "Changes in the management processes, the organizational structure, and management style all must support the changes in the pattern of values and behavior that a new vision implies" (p. 144). They also stress that, based on their interviews, successful leaders do not entrust to anyone else in the organization basic responsibility for "shaping social architecture" (p. 150).

Trust Through Positioning and the Deployment of Self

Of the four central functions of leadership described by Bennis and Nanus the last two are closely coupled. Both are essential to creating and maintaining the trust without which commitment to change cannot be realized.

Bennis and Nanus defined *positioning* as "the process by which an organization designs, establishes, and sustains a viable niche in its external environments" (p. 156). They suggested that leaders, wittingly or not, choose mainly among four general strategies for positioning the organization. Whereas leaders can, ordinarily ineffectively, simply react to changing circumstances, proactive options include efforts to change the internal structure of the organization, acting to alter key aspects of the external environment of the organization, and working to create structures linking the internal and external environments of the organization.

Changes in the internal environment can be short- or long-term. Typical short-term changes take the form of reallocating financial, physical, and human resources to those units of the organization whose work is central to the new organizational directions implied in the vision. Longer term changes reshape the culture of the organization, for example, through reeducation and through targeted recruitment and hiring policies to reflect "certain values at the expense of others" (Bennis & Nanus, 1985, p. 164). Strategies for influencing the external environment include marketing activities, lobbying, advertising, and structuring linkages with other organizations (p. 165). Bennis and Nanus suggested several approaches to linking the internal and external environments. These include bargaining and negotiation in the short term and "vertical integration, mergers and acquisitions, or innovative systems design" in the longer term (pp. 165–166).

Although effective positioning can engender confidence in leadership based on a sense that members of the organization develop about the knowledgeability and general competence of leadership, it is equally important for the leader to build in others a sense of personal trust. Bennis and Nanus took the position that such trust derives basically from the leader's "deployment of self." Following Donald Michael (Kotter, 1982), they argued that, to gain trust, leaders must seen as exhibiting the following personal characteristics: acknowledging and sharing uncertainty; embracing error; responding to the future; demonstrating such interpersonal skills as listening, nurturing, and coping with value conflicts; and gaining self-knowledge

(Bennis & Nanus, 1985, pp. 188–189; cf. Jentz & Wofford, 1979). They also emphasized the special responsibility of leadership, in contrast to management, for "innovative learning" (p. 194). According to Bennis and Nanus, effective leaders "pull" rather than "push" people on, highlighting for them the significance of their work, the satisfactions of competence, "enhanced performance," and "alignment behind the organization's goals" (pp. 82–83). Effective leaders draw people into a sense of "community" as a component of empowerment and of "enjoyment" in being "immersed in their game of work" (p. 83).

Throughout their discussion of good leadership, Bennis and Nanus reasoned that leadership is not a rare skill, that good leaders are made not born, that they are not necessarily inherently charismatic, and that effective leadership does not essentially involve controlling, prodding, and manipulating others (pp. 221–226). Also, fundamental to their position is the idea that leadership exists throughout effective organizations, not only at the top.

The major themes of Bennis and Nanus's theory of leadership center around attention to vision, meaning through communication, trust through positioning, and the deployment of self. Minor themes for leaders include "doing the right thing"; "managing yourself"; using metaphors and analogies to enliven your thoughts and speech; focusing on the present rather than the past; thinking about solving problems, not assigning blame, in dealing with others; treating everyone with courtesy and attention; and trusting others even when the risk seems high.

FORMULATING CONCLUSIONS

Policy recommendations should be developed that are consistent with the analysis; that are consistent with the interests, commitments, and capacities of important stakeholders; and that hold reasonable promise for successful implementation.

QUESTIONS FOR ANALYZING PROBLEMS USING BENNIS AND NANUS' (1985) LEADERSHIP THEORY

Bennis and Nanus' leadership theory focuses your analysis on issues of leadership in the organization and how failures of leadership may be contributing to the documented problem. In using this framework for analysis, it is important to examine the problematic situation systematically in terms of the major and minor themes that comprise the analytic framework.

Attention Through Vision

1. How and to what extent is the leader's vision or lack of vision for the organization problematic?

Meaning Through Communication

2. How and to what extent do problems exist in communicating a coherent and compelling vision for the organization?
3. How and to what extent has the leadership failed to take into account "the strong undertow of cultural forces" (Bennis & Nanus, 1985, p. 114) in the organization in its attempt to effectively communicate a coherent and persuasive vision for the organization?
4. How and to what extent has the leadership failed to articulate a coherent and persuasive vision clearly and frequently in a variety of ways to diverse audiences throughout the organization and the important parts of its environment?
5. How and to what extent has leadership failed to make the "changes in the management processes, the organizational structure, and management style [that] must support the changes in the pattern of values and behavior that a new vision implies?" (p. 144)

Trust Through Positioning

6. How and to what extent has leadership failed to make its important positions clear to diverse audiences throughout the organization and its relevant environment?
7. How and to what extent is there lack of trust in leaders in various parts of the organization and its environment?
8. How and to what extent has leadership failed to change the internal environment of the organization in ways that are consistent with and supportive of a coherent and persuasive vision for the organization?
9. How and to what extent has leadership failed to change the external environment of the organization in ways that are consistent with and supportive of a coherent and persuasive vision for the organization?
10. How and to what extent has leadership failed to change the linkages between the internal and external environments of the organization in ways that are consistent with and supportive of a coherent and persuasive vision for the organization?
11. How and to what extent has leadership failed to be sufficiently sensitive "to the needs of many stakeholders and failed to establish a clear sense of the organization's position?" (p. 186)
12. How and to what extent has leadership failed "to set [an effective] moral tone by choosing carefully the people with whom they surround themselves, by communicating a sense of purpose for the organization, by reinforcing appropriate behaviors, and by articulating these moral positions to external and internal constituencies?" (p. 186)

The Deployment of Self

13. How and to what extent has leadership failed in "acknowledging and sharing uncertainty; embracing error; responding to the future; becoming interpersonally competent (i.e., listening, nurturing, coping with value conflicts, etc.); and gaining self-knowledge?" (pp. 188–189)
14. How and to what extent are the organizational reward systems out of alignment with a coherent and persuasive vision put forward by leadership?

Minor Themes

15. How and to what extent are there leadership problems related to any of Bennis and Nanus' 'minor themes'?

AN ILLUSTRATIVE OUTLINE
FOR A LEADERSHIP ANALYSIS

The following outline illustrates a leadership analysis. Note that the outline covers only that section of an analytic report that deals with analyzing the problem system from the perspective of leadership theory in particular. The larger report would include, in addition, sections on the problem and important stakeholders, their description and documentation, analyses from alternative theoretical perspectives, and recommendations for taking action to deal with the problem.

    I. Problems of attention through vision

    II. Problems of meaning through communication

    III. Problems of trust through positioning

    IV. Problems of the leader's deployment of self

    V. Problems related to other leadership themes

    VI. Summary and discussion of the major leadership dynamics related to the problem of concern

    VII. Conclusions and recommendations from a leadership perspective

9

Burrell and Morgan's
Meta-Framework

The time is ripe for the practice of an unprecedented kind of administrative science sensitive to the diverse issues of human life and able to deal with them in a variety of settings where they appropriately belong, and of which the formal economizing organization is a case limit.

—A. G. Ramos (1981, p. 74)

In chapters 5 through 8 you encountered a number of analytic frameworks that you have seen explained and illustrated. They may appear to represent a very broad range of theoretical models—and in a sense they do, portraying a variety of social science disciplines—but in another, broader sense, they depict only a narrow band of conceptual possibilities. It seems fair to say that they all fall within what Burrell and Morgan (1979) referred to as the "functionalist" paradigm, perhaps stretched in some instances to include aspects of the interpretive paradigm. In the course of their discussion of the functionalist paradigm, Burrell and Morgan (1979) suggested that "the orthodox approach to the study of organisations 'tends to adopt theories and models of organisational functioning...that are highly oriented towards managerial conceptions of organisations, managerial priorities and problems, and managerial concerns for practical outcomes'" (p. 118).

Burrell and Morgan might have argued that, employing only these conceptual frameworks as lenses through which to view our organizations, we would be very much in the position of the blind men and the elephant. They might have argued that this would be true even if we used all of these various conceptual frameworks—bureaucratic systems, social systems, political systems, leadership systems, and other analytic frames—because, from larger philosophical and ideological perspectives, they all represent basically orthodox perspectives for viewing organizations.

INTELLECTUAL BACKGROUND OF THE FRAMEWORK

Over at least 2,500 years, the philosophy of the Western world has concerned itself with what Ramos (1981) termed the diverse issues of human life. Through the ages philosophers have debated such ontological issues as monism, dualism, and plural-ism and such epistemological issues as the nature of faith and the limits of reason. They have contrasted an ethics of principle versus an ethics of virtue (or character), the particular and the universal, the temporal and the eternal, the objective and the subjective. Although philosophers (e.g., Hegel) tend to believe that such long-standing debates are finally resolved only in the course of their own personal analyses, the continued vitality of these questions suggests that no final answers to them have yet been determined.

> Truth, then, reasoned truth, harmonious experience, absolute system, is the theme of philosophy. Or, in Hegelian language, its theme is the Truth, and that Truth, God. Not a sum, an aggregate, or even what is ordinarily styled a system of truths: but the one and yet diverse pulse of truth, which beats through all: the supreme point of view in which all the parts and differences, occasionally standing out as if independent, sink into their due relation and are seen in their right proportion. (Wallace, 1894/1968, pp. 132–133)

The debates to which Burrell and Morgan (1979) addressed themselves are mainly about issues deriving from the scientific project. Science began to take on a systematically positive form in the course of the 17th century. Early philosophical expositions of the general principles of the scientific project are to be found in Bacon's *Novum Organum* (1620), Newton's *Philosophiae Naturalis Principia Mathematica* (1687), and Locke's *An Essay Concerning Human Understanding* (1690).

Philosophically, the scientific revolution shifted attention from revealed and rationally deduced knowledge, the knowledge of the ancients and the medieval philosophers, to knowledge that is empirically derived and inductively accumulated over time. Bacon suggested, for example, that true knowledge is that which increases human power over the thing.

> For the end which this science of mine proposes is the invention not of arguments but of arts; not of things in accordance with principles, but of principles themselves; not of probable reasons, but of designations and directions for works. And as the intention is different, so, accordingly, is the effect; the effect of the one being to overcome an opponent in argument, of the other to command nature in action. (Bacon, 1620/1960, p. 19)

Scientific knowledge has proven enormously successful in Baconian terms, but by increasing the reach of human power over nature, this shift has had the concomitant effect of narrowing the scope of knowledge defined by scientific canons to the domain of experience that is observable and testable. Thus science systematically excludes from scientific knowledge both metaphysics and creative and expressive thought in the arts and philosophy. The reaction to what in the 20th century has been called the *privileging* of scientific knowledge has been intense among philosophers and other humane scholars. Although their attacks have often been directed against *logical positivism* and the confrères of the Vienna Circle, the implications of these attacks have been broader than logical positivism itself. Actually, the attacks have been against positive science much more extensively construed, against what frequently has been called *scientism*. The first target of the assault by the enemies of scientism is the fundamental flaw at the logical underpinnings of science: The epistemological premises upon which science is founded are, themselves, as Lord Hailsham noted, outside of the purview of knowledge as science defines it.

> While...it may be true that [within] the field of science, its terms of reference...are circumscribed by the proposition that only that exists which can be measured or observed, the proposition itself is one which cannot itself be observed, and is therefore one which cannot be true of all being and if it is asserted as such becomes immediately self-contradictory. (Aeschliman, 1983, p. 20)

Questionable, too, from the narrowly scientific perspective, is the legitimacy of knowledge about many of the most important questions addressed not only in philosophy and the arts, but in the social sciences, as well. The battle over what constitutes the legitimate grounds of knowledge—faith or reason, imagination or a narrowly conceived empirical reality, although bitterly contested in recent decades, has its intellectual roots in the scientistic thrust at the turn of the 17th century.

> [It is] a debate that has raged for centuries between those who assert the primacy of metaphysical knowledge and those who argue for the priority of physical reality. This is an old and important conflict, one fought with asperity in the seventeenth century between men such as Donne, Milton, and the Cambridge Platonists on one side, and Bacon and the Royal Society on the other—the conflict between the Ancients and the Moderns, with philosophers, poets, and theologians ranged against some scientists and many more enthusiasts of science. (Aeschliman, 1983, p. 18)

To the extent that the social sciences have cloaked themselves in the mantle of the natural sciences, fashioning themselves epistemologically in positive terms, they have come under a powerful attack, especially for defining values outside the realm of social scientific knowledge and for limiting legitimate knowledge to what can be explicitly claimed and verifiably observed. Eisner's (1988) is a representative critical voice:

> As Nelson Goodman has said in *Ways of World-Making* (1978), "There may be one world, but there are many versions of it." And, as he says elsewhere, there are as many versions as there are languages to describe them. The research language that has dominated educational inquiry has been one that has attempted to bifurcate the knower

and the known. We use a language that implies that it is possible for the organism to grasp the environment as it *really* is.…We talk about our *findings*, implying somehow that we discover the world rather than construe it.…We write and talk in a voice void of any hint that there is a personal self behind the words we utter: "the author," "the subject," "the researcher," or, miraculously, we somehow multiply our individuality and write about what "we" found.…The motive for such locutions, ultimately, is found in our search for objectivity.…We distance ourselves from the phenomena we wish to understand so that we can see them from the knee of God—or at least close by. (p. 18)

Burrell and Morgan provided a framework that focuses organizational analysis precisely on competing assumptions of objectivity, subjectivity, and intersubjectivity, as well as on goals of productivity and maintaining the *status quo* of power relationships versus those of justice and equity. Such goals and assumptions are crucial in determining the kinds of questions organizations frame in the course of their decisional processes, the procedures they constitute for making decisions, the sources of information they consider important in making decisions, and the people they involve in decision making.

THE BURRELL AND MORGAN FRAMEWORK

Burrell and Morgan suggested that it is useful to view the social science literature in terms of four paradigms. They conceive these paradigms by crossing two bi-polar dimensions: the ideological dimension with the ontological–epistemological dimension. They cast the ideological dimension in terms of radicalism and conservatism, the ontological–epistemological dimension in terms of subjectivism and objectivism. This two-by-two breakout produces four quadrants: objective–conservative, subjective–conservative, subjective–radical, and objective–radical. Burrell and Morgan labeled these quadrants, respectively, the functionalist, interpretive, radical humanist, and radical structuralist paradigms.

The Two Principal Dimensions of the Matrix

The Ideological Dimension. Each of these paradigms is characterized by combining the characteristics of its ideological ideal type with those of its corresponding ontological–epistemological ideal type. Burrell and Morgan (1979) indicated that the conservative ideal-type, what they refer to as "the sociology of regulation," is concerned with the *status quo*, social order, consensus, social integration and cohesion, solidarity, need satisfaction, and actuality. They described the radical ideal-type, what they refer to as "the sociology of radical change," in terms of radical change, structural conflict, modes of domination, contradiction, emancipation, deprivation, and potentiality (p. 18).

The Ontological–Epistemological Dimension. Burrell and Morgan (1979) described the "subjectivist approach to social science" in terms of a nominalist ontology, an antipositivist epistemology, a voluntarist human nature, and an ideographic methodology. They described the "objectivist approach to social science" in terms of a realist ontology, a positivist epistemology, a deterministic view of human nature, and a nomothetic methodology (p. 3).

The Four Paradigms

The Functionalist Paradigm. Burrell and Morgan characterized the functionalist paradigm as combining the attributes of conservatism with those of objectivism. They included in this paradigm such schools of thought within sociology as structural functionalism, systems theory, interactionism, symbolic interactionism, social action theory, Blau's exchange and power model, Mertonian theory of social and cultural structure, conflict functionalism, morphogenic systems theory, behaviorism, and abstracted empiricism. They also included such branches of organization theory as social systems theory, classical management theory, job satisfaction and human relations theories, sociotechnical systems theory, equilibrium theories of organization, contingency theory, quality of work life, theories of bureaucratic dysfunction, the action frame of reference, and pluralist theory, all with a strong focus on empirical research.

The Interpretive Paradigm. Burrell and Morgan described the interpretive paradigm as combining a conservative ideological perspective with a subjectivist epistemological perspective. They included in the interpretive paradigm such philosophic perspectives as hermeneutics, and phenomenology, and such methodological approaches to the study of organizations as ethnomethodology and phenomenological symbolic interactionism.

Radical Humanism. Burrell and Morgan (1979) cast radical humanism at the intersection of radicalism and subjectivism. According to them, the paradigm encompasses critical theory, anarchistic individualism, and French existentialism. They distinguished within critical theory Lukácsian sociology, Gramsci's sociology, and the Frankfurt School. They argued that "if the implications of the radical humanist paradigm are developed in relation to the study of organisations, the result will be an *anti-organisation theory*" (p. 310), a concept that they developed further in terms of several interesting contrasts between antiorganization and organization theory including the following (pp. 322–323):

- The humanities versus science as an "intellectual source of problems"
- Harmony versus competition as the essential human relationship to nature
- Technology as a negative rather than a positive or neutral force.

Burrell and Morgan suggested an interesting list of factors treated as problematic within the radical humanist paradigm (pp. 323–324):

- "Purposive rationality"
- "Rules and control systems"
- "Roles which constrain and confine human activities"
- The "language of organisational life"
- "Ideological mechanisms" of control
- The "worship of technology"
- The "reification" of mystifying concepts.

Radical Structuralism.   Burrell and Morgan portrayed radical structuralism as combining the characteristics of radicalism and objectivism. They included in this paradigm such schools of thought as Bukharin's historical materialism, anarchistic communism, Althusserian sociology, Colletti's sociology, and a number of examples of conflict theory. They suggested that four ideas reside at the center of the radical structuralist paradigm: totality, structure, contradiction, and crisis. Burrell and Morgan put forward a number of fairly concrete ideas for a radical organization theory. Among other factors, they suggested that such a theory would do the following (pp. 366–367):

- Focus on studying "the structure of social oppression."
- Highlight action research that emphasizes revolutionary change.
- Build theoretically on the mature Marx.
- Put the concept of social class at its center.
- Reassess, reinterpret, and build on the work of Max Weber.
- Articulate and extend a theory of the state.
- Be historically rooted.
- Clarify the dynamics of contradiction.
- Found itself on critical theory, not on empirical methodology.
- Define itself as mutually exclusive of traditional organizational theory.

Such a theory would rest on an understanding of the "mutual opposition of interests in terms of broad socioeconomic divisions," would recognize conflict as "an ubiquitous and disruptive motor force propelling changes in society," sometimes a "suppressed feature of a social system, not always evident at the level of empirical reality," and would regard "power as an integral, unequally distributed, zero-sum phenomenon, associated with a general process of social control" (p. 388).

APPLICATION

I developed Table 9.1 which many of my students have found helpful in moving from the seemingly abstract notions of Burrell and Morgan to applying their ideas

TABLE 9.1

Questions about Decisions and Decision Information from the Burrell and Morgan Matrix

	Conceptual Dimensions	
Focus for Analysis	Objective–Subjective	Radical–Conservative
The problem and the decisional content	1. To what extent and in what ways are the definitions of the problem and the decision based on "facts" that are perceived as hard and objective? 2. How could one think of defining the problem and the question from a different, more subjective, inter-subjective, or cultural perspective? 3. What implications might this have for the situation at hand?	1. To what extent are the problem and the decision themselves defined in terms of the status quo? 2. In whose interests are the problem and the decision defined? 3. How could the problem and the decision be defined differently? 4. What difference might it make if the problem and decision were defined differently?
The information base informing the decision	1. How might the sources of information being used to make the decision be broadened to include more interpretive, psychological, cultural, and philosophical perceptions and understandings, with more weight given to diversity in norms and values? 2. How might such a broadening affect the decisional situation?	1. How might the sources of information being used to make the decision be broadened to include people, documents, observations, and statistics that might change the perspective of the decision makers and alter the nature of the decision? 2. What difference might it make if the sources of information used in decision making were broadened?

to practical situations.[28] I focused my students, in using the Burrell and Morgan framework, on decision-making situations, in particular (see chapters 14–15 in this book). Essential in organizational life are the kinds of decisions we make, the kinds of information we use to make these decisions, the procedures we adopt for gathering decision information, and the sources of information we draw on for information in making decisions. Typically, the assumptions that inform decision making in each of these dimensions are not discussed. Often, within the cultures of real organizations, they are essentially not discussible (Argyris & Schön, 1978). Table 9.1 suggests some broad questions for decision making from the two principal dimensions of Burrell and Morgan's matrix: the radical–conservative and the objective–subjective.

---

[28]In their book, Burrell and Morgan addressed an audience of researchers and theoreticians and spoke to issues of theory and research in the social sciences. However, as a teacher I have found that their ideas provide a unique platform for stimulating students to think in a challenging way about their organizations from different philosophical and ideological perspectives. Thus, the examples of application in this book are addressed not to researchers and theoreticians, but primarily to administrators of schools and school systems.

The outline at the end of this chapter suggests an approach for using the Burrell and Morgan framework think about organizational decisions from different paradigmatic perspectives. For each of the four paradigms—functionalist, interpretive, radical humanist, and radical structuralist—the outline describes the assumptions that characterize the paradigm according to Burrell and Morgan and suggests a number questions for mounting a critique of the decision and the decision-making process.

Descriptive Questions

1. What is the nature of the decision being examined?
2. What kinds of information are currently being used to make the decision?
3. Who is currently involved in providing the information being used and in making the decision?
4. What is the current set of procedures for analyzing the information and making the decision?

Critical Questions

1. Is this the type of decision the organization ought to make?
2. Are these the right types and sources of information?
3. Are these the right procedures for collecting and analyzing the information and making the decision?

On the basis of such a critique, recommendations for change can be made from each of the four paradigmatic perspectives. Then these recommendations can be compared and contrasted in thinking about what changes, if any, can and should be made in the particular situation.

ILLUSTRATIVE OUTLINE FOR ANALYZING A DECISIONAL SITUATION FROM BURRELL AND MORGAN'S FOUR PARADIGMATIC PERSPECTIVES

Part 1: The Decision

I. Background statement: Description of the organizational context within which this type of decision is made

II. Description of the type of decision the analysis addresses

III. Description of the decision makers

IV. Description of the present process for making the decision

   A. Information used

      1. Types

      2. Sources

   B. Procedures

      1. For collecting and handling information used
      2. For making the decision

Part 2: Critiquing the Decision Process
From Four Perspectives

  I. The functionalist perspective

   A. Defining assumptions

      1. Focus on objectivity

         a. Reality is objective and can be known by objective methods.
         b. Knowledge is founded on information derived by reproducible scientific methods.
         c. Scientific knowledge is descriptive, describing what is, not what ought to be.
         d. Logical, systematic methods and measures are essential to replicating and assessing the validity of scientific findings.
         e. Knowledge is potentially universal.
         f. Situational knowledge is potentially reducible to universal laws.

      2. Conservative orientation

         a. It is important to understand existing systems.
         b. Conflict is problematic and should be reduced or eliminated.

   B. Critique

      1. *Of the type of decision, itself:* From the functionalist perspective, is this the type of decision the organization ought to make?
      2. *Of the types and sources of information used to make the decision:* From the functionalist perspective, are these the right types and sources of information?
      3. *Of the procedures used for collecting and handling the information used to make the decision:* From the functionalist perspective, are these the right procedures for collecting and handling the decisional information?

4. *Of the procedures used for making the decision*: From the functionalist perspective, are these the right procedures for making the decision?

C. Recommendations for change from the functionalist perspective

II. The interpretive perspective

A. Defining assumptions

1. Focus on subjectivity and intersubjectivity

a. Reality is importantly socially (culturally) constructed and essentially situational.
b. Knowledge of socially constructed reality is of subjective and intersubjective understandings and interpretations.
c. Knowledge is subjectively defined by people.
d. Interpretations are the essential element of knowledge, not objective facts.
e. Whatever objective elements may exist in the universe, knowledge of them is never objective.
f. The knower is inseparable from the known.
g. Knowledge is inherently situational, not universal.

2. Descriptive orientation

a. It is important to understand and describe existing socially constructed realities.

B. Critique

1. *Of the type of decision itself*: From the interpretive perspective, is this the type of decision the organization ought to make?
2. *Of the types and sources of information used to make the decision*: From the interpretive perspective, are these the right types and sources of information?
3. *Of the procedures used for collecting and handling the information used to make the decision*: From the interpretive perspective, are these the right procedures for collecting and handling the decisional information?
4. *Of the procedures used for making the decision*: From the interpretive perspective, are these the right procedures for making the decision?

C. Recommendations for change from the interpretive perspective

III. The radical humanist perspective

  A. Defining assumptions

    1. Focus on subjectivity and intersubjectivity

      a. Reality is importantly socially (culturally) constructed and essentially situational.

      b. Knowledge of socially constructed reality is of subjective and intersubjective understandings and interpretations.

      c. Knowledge is subjectively defined by people.

      d. Interpretations are the essential element of knowledge, not objective facts.

      e. Whatever objective elements may exist in the universe, knowledge of them is never objective.

      f. The knower is inseparable from the known.

      g. Knowledge is inherently situational, not universal.

    2. Radical orientation

      a. Problems relate to moral issues of equity and justice. (Typical cases of injustice involve social class, race, ethnicity, and gender.)

      b. It is important to change existing conditions to achieve equity and justice.

      c. Conflict is normal and necessary.

      d. Individuals are socialized in unjust societies to participate in their own oppression.

      e. It is important to change the consciousness of individuals in unjust societies, especially the consciousness of the oppressed.

      f. Oppressed individuals can transcend their socialized, oppressed consciousness and attain true consciousness in which they understand the nature of their oppression and are thereby empowered to act against it.

      g. Individuals who have achieved true consciousness have the power to act in concert to throw off oppression.

  B. Critique

    1. *Of the type of decision, itself:* From the radical humanist perspective, is this the type of decision the organization ought to make?

    2. *Of the types and sources of information used to make the decision:* From the radical humanist perspective, are these the right types and sources of information?

      3. *Of the procedures used for collecting and handling the information used to make the decision*: From the radical humanist perspective, are these the right procedures for collecting and handling the decisional information?

      4. *Of the procedures used for making the decision*: From the radical humanist perspective, are these the right procedures for making the decision?

  C. Recommendations for change from the radical humanist perspective

IV. The radical structuralist perspective

  A. Defining assumptions

    1. Focus on objectivity

      a. Reality is objective and can be known by objective methods.

      b. Knowledge is founded on information derived by reproducible scientific methods.

      c. Scientific knowledge is descriptive, describing what is, not what ought to be.

      d. Logical, systematic methods and measures are essential to replicating and assessing the validity of scientific findings.

      e. Knowledge is potentially universal.

      f. Situational knowledge is potentially reducible to universal laws.

    2. Radical orientation

      a. Problems relate to moral issues of equity and justice. (Typical cases of injustice involve social class, race, ethnicity, and gender.)

      b. Change is necessary to achieve equity and justice.

      c. The institutions of society, especially government, act to enhance the interests of the empowered against the oppressed.

      d. The relationship between government and economic institutions is of special importance in maintaining oppression.

      e. Educational institutions, including schools and all of the media, have powerful roles in defining the structure of oppression, including language and social relationships.

      f. Changing institutions is necessary for equity and justice.

      g. Conflict is normal and necessary.

B. Critique

1. *Of the type of decision, itself:* From the radical structuralist perspective, is this the type of decision the organization ought to make?
2. *Of the types and sources of information used to make the decision:* From the radical structuralist perspective, are these the right types and sources of information?
3. *Of the procedures used for collecting and handling the information used to make the decision:* From the radical structuralist perspective, are these the right procedures for collecting and handling the decisional information?
4. *Of the procedures used for making the decision:* From the radical structuralist perspective, are these the right procedures for making the decision?

C. Recommendations for change from the radical structuralist perspective

Part 3: Reflections on the Four Critiques

Reflect on your four critiques and the recommendations deriving from them. On the basis of this review, discuss and explain any changes that should be made in the type of decision being made, the information used to make that type of decision, or the process for making it. Take into consideration the nature of the organization as you know it, including its culture and environment. Consider major potential hindering and facilitating factors relevant to any changes you might consider.

10

Systems Thinking: Modeling Problem Systems

Business and other human endeavors are also systems. They, too, are bound by invisible fabrics of interrelated actions, which often take years to fully play out their effects on each other.

—Peter Senge (1990, p. 7)

In this chapter systems thinking is presented as a meta-framework for configuring in a consistent manner insights about the causes of problems, insights derived from different sources and rooted in diverse theoretical foundations. We interest ourselves here in how different factors work together to cause and exacerbate organizational problems over short and long periods of time. Because of its emphasis on essential factors and relationships, systems thinking helps us to distinguish the fundamental elements of a problem from the confusion of absorbing but nonessential details. In the following pages a number of elements fundamental to this way of thinking are explained and illustrated.

The term *meta-framework* is used in discussing systems thinking because, in contrast to the theoretical frameworks discussed earlier in this book, systems thinking is content free. It can be applied to any field of study and any situation. Its focus is on how people and their organizations respond to physical realities and to the actions of other people and organizations in ways that affect the development of opportunities and problems. People and organizations help create and become parts of feedback systems out of which problems develop and opportunities arise.

THE NATURE OF SYSTEMS THINKING

Put in its simplest terms, problem solving is about figuring out the causes of problems and then doing something to temper those causes. When a problematic effect occurs immediately after its cause, such as a bloody nose following a punch to the face, the analysis is straightforward and obvious. However, as effects occur more distantly in time from their causes, identifying the causes becomes more difficult and increasingly less certain. As causes are multiple and contingent in nature, as well as removed in time, identifying them unambiguously is unlikely. By contingent is meant that the effects of one variable on another depend on the presence, intensity, and timing of still other variables. Finally, recognizing that causes are reciprocal, as well as multiple, distant, and contingent, makes causal analysis ever more complex, as much a form of art as science. The term *reciprocal* refers to the spiral nature of cause and effect over time, in which changes in one variable contribute to changes in another, which in turn are implicated in subsequent changes in the first variable. Indeed, this is precisely what Richardson (1991) alluded to in his comprehensive exegesis of "feedback thought" (Richardson, 1991).

Systems thinking takes into consideration all these aspects of causation. Systems thinkers have traditionally formulated models that describe, according to the best knowledge available, precisely the interactive feedback dynamics examined by Richardson in his historical analysis. Such models are typically based on a mixture of quantitative and qualitative information from available documents, observations, and interviews with knowledgeable participants about causal interactions among key variables. The models are longitudinal, situational, and developmental in nature, explaining microtheoretically the historical development of problem systems.

Accordingly, systems models, with rare exception, stand in contrast to the universal theorizing characteristic of the social sciences such as sociology and psychology. In contrast to universal theories, systems models have been formulated most commonly as theories of problems. In this sense, at their best they represent in highly coherent form a combination of qualitative and quantitative understandings about how crucial variables interact over time to engender and modulate significant social and organizational problems. A great advantage of systems models, at least to the extent that they are put into mathematical form and computerized, is that their outputs can be tested for consistency against relevant historical trend data. Additionally, their internal relationships can be examined systematically for coherence and construct credibility. Thus, systems modeling is a particularly powerful method of problem analysis, of gaining insight into the complex causes of problems, thereby laying a foundation for apprehending potential solutions, and for simulating how proposed solutions might actually evolve over time in the problem system.

THE HISTORY OF FEEDBACK THOUGHT

George Richardson (1991) provided a thorough intellectual history of feedback thinking. Citing Mayr (1970), Richardson (p. 18) explained that feedback thought has a venerable history, with written records going back to Ktesibios in Greece in the third century. Again referring to Mayr, Richardson (1991) summarized the early history of feedback thought in the following terms:

> Although feedback devices were used with increasing frequency from the time of Ktesibios, and although formal analysis of their structure and behavior began as early as 1868 with Maxwell's paper "On Governors," the loop concept underlying them remained completely unrecognized until the twentieth century....Before Maxwell, regulators were constructed with little theorizing and much experimenting. (p. 23)

"Maxwell's work," says Richardson, "led directly to extensive use of differential equations in the design and analysis of feedback control devices" (p. 26). Richardson emphasizesd that it was the "control engineer's concept of feedback" that was transferred to human systems analysts' views of the organizational world:

> What emanated most strongly to the social sciences from engineering control theory was that control, or management, requires the feeding back of information. In particular, the necessary information is the "error signal"—the extent to which the actual state of the system differs from the desired state. (p. 31)

Although not explicitly shown, feedback loops were implicit in an early population model of Verlhust (1838), in the predator–prey model of Alfred Lotka (1925), and in L. F. Richardson's arms race model (1919–1939) (Richardson, 1991, pp. 32–41). In Richardson's view (pp. 59–71), loop dynamics were central to Malthus's thinking about population growth (Malthus, 1798), Hume's (1752) theory of trade, Smith's (1776) theory of supply and demand, and in Hegel (1805–1806/1983) and Marx's (1818–1883/1975) theories of the historical dialectic. Richardson saw important examples of feedback thought in John Dewey's work as well:

> In a remarkable ten-page essay published in 1896, John Dewey displayed a conception of the feedback loop in psychological processes that was far ahead of its time. (Dewey, 1896, in Richardson, 1991, p. 75)

Finally, Richardson (1991) cited feedback thinking in Myrdal's (1939) "principle of cumulation," in the old idea that Merton (1948) labeled the "self-fulfilling prophecy," and in Bateson's (1935) concept of "schismogenesis" (pp. 59–90). Circular causality, according to Richardson, was also present in much of the early writing in econometrics, although no connection was made to the "emerging feedback literature in the social sciences." He said:

> We may conclude that although the early econometric authors recognized, in fact clearly intended, the mutual dependencies in their models, they did not picture their systems in loops nor associate patterns of model behavior with loop structure and polarities. Before 1940 the feedback concept had not yet emerged from engineering, and the other loop notions in the social sciences...were not associated with this quantitative, statistical line of thinking. (p. 46)

In summary, Richardson concluded:

The concept of the feedback loop in twentieth-century social science is a blend of intuitions and ideas from at least six intellectual traditions: engineering, economics, biology, mathematical models of biological and social systems, formal logic, and classical social science literature itself. (p. 17)

SYSTEM DYNAMICS MODEL BUILDING

System dynamics is a well-developed methodology joining a wide array of systems tools and procedures (Morecroft & Sterman, 1994) to a basic systems ontology (Forrester, 1968) that emphasizes the fundamental reality of feedback (i.e., of circular causality) in real-world systems. This ontology also holds that systems can be understood best in terms of key variables that define the state of the system at any point in time. These variables have traditionally been called *state variables*. Also essential to this basic systems ontology is the principle that state variables change only incrementally over time and that their rates of change are essential elements of systems. Thus, although state variables affect each other, they do so only through their rates, not directly. Thus, systems are seen to change only incrementally over time. For example, from a system dynamics perspective, although supply and demand affect each other, changing levels of demand influence only changes in supply from one time period to the next. Similarly, supply influences only changes in demand from one time interval to another.

Also important in system dynamics thinking are the effects of time delays on system behavior. For example, in thinking about the impact of demand on supply, it makes a difference, when demand rises, whether current production is running close to capacity. If so, then supply cannot be increased without increasing capacity itself, which will require considerable time to accomplish because capacity can be increased only by building new plants and ordering new machinery. Thus, the time delays involved under these conditions contrast sharply with the relatively quick upward adjustment in production (supply) that is possible when current production is well below capacity. Similarly, improvements in teacher recruitment, selection, training, and supervision, as well as in instructional methods and materials, can be expected to have an impact on changes in student motivation and performance only developmentally over time.

Finally, as a guiding principle, system dynamics thinking encourages its practitioners in their modeling efforts to highlight those variables most under the control of stakeholders, and, in analyzing the causes of problems, to minimize preoccupation with variables outside their control, even when these external variables have important effects on the problems under consideration. The stress in system dynamics analysis is consistently on those variables under stakeholders' control and on their responses to external variables not under their control.

The effect of this emphasis is, on the one hand, to empower stakeholders by focusing their attention on what they can actually do something about and, on the other, to inspirit stakeholders to take responsibility for the effects their own actions and policies have had in generating and sustaining problems historically and will have in influencing the course of these problems in the future. In essence, this perspective makes crucial persistent questions about whether schools can (or should) affect such factors as student motivation, family and peer culture, and student health and nutrition, and whether any or all of these and other factors lie within or outside the influence of schools and school systems. Such system boundary questions lie at the heart of contentious educational policy debates.

The remainder of this chapter is devoted to describing and illustrating a series of steps that comprise the system dynamics methodology. The steps include these:

- Defining a problem
- Listing as comprehensively as possible one's understandings concerning the principal variables and relationships influencing the course of the problem
- Deciding on the focal elements for analysis
- Framing the hypothesis that most clearly describes the central dynamics affecting the problem
- Diagramming the key elements of this causal model
- Specifying the model mathematically
- Using the computer as a tool for examining the logical coherence of the model and probing its policy implications.

Two examples from my own experience are threaded through the chapter for purposes of illustration and clarification. One of these concerns itself with clarifying the essential dynamics that distinguish effective from ineffective schools. The other, on which I am still working at the time of this writing, strives to illuminate the central dynamics of organizational change in an elementary school seeking to integrate computer technology into the teaching of school subjects such as reading, writing, mathematics, science, art, and music.

Defining the Problem for Analysis

Because system dynamics is a problem-focused methodology, preparing the problem for analysis is a crucial first step. The classic approach to this task is to draw on available trend data available to illustrate the development of the problem over a suitable period of time. Thus data are used to describe the evolution of one or more indicator variables over a period long enough to put problematic changes in ample historic or developmental perspective. Two examples follow.

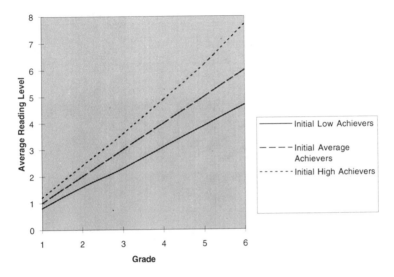

FIG. 10.1. Ineffective schools' reference behavior.

The Effective Schooling Project.   A problem Clauset and I approached in the early 1980s (Clauset, 1982; Clauset & Gaynor, 1982) took a broadly theoretical view of a contrast that was quite an issue at the time, the nature of effective versus ineffective schooling. On the basis of our own extensive experience in schools and many conversations with teachers, administrators, and educational consultants, we posited the problem of ineffective schooling in terms of the following reference behavior, widely regarded as common in elementary schools.

The essence of the problem we posed, without reference to such issues as family background and IQ, was that in ineffective schools initial differences in children's readiness to learn in school were systematically magnified over the course of schooling (Fig. 10.1). Such a dynamic was considered clearly unsatisfactory; it is desirable that, over time, schools should bring the academic performance of initially low-achieving children close to that of initially average- and high-achieving children. Thus, the problem was the discrepancy between historical and desired performance.

The Computer Technology Project.   The problem we are currently addressing[29] centers on the relatively slow historic growth in one particular public elementary school in integrating computer technology into the curriculum. The school is located in an affluent suburban community populated significantly by high-income professional and managerial parents. There is considerable pressure in the community for the evolution of technology in the schools to approximate

---

[29]The work now underway is being done with Nancy Vescuso, a management consultant who is currently pursuing a doctoral program in Human Resources Education at Boston University.

that of the community and the businesses in which parents work. The following graph depicts the problem discrepancy (Fig. 10.2). The trend lines show (community) the average number of hours per week parents spend using computers and (school) the average number of hours students spend per week using computers for academic work.

Generalizations About Establishing the Problem for Analysis. In establishing the problem for analysis, it is important to identify the key indicator variables, each of whose behavior or performance has been observed as problematic over time. Keep in mind, then, that the purpose of the model is to explain this set of behaviors. If the model can explain why the reference variables have been performing problematically over time, then it should provide a basis for examining

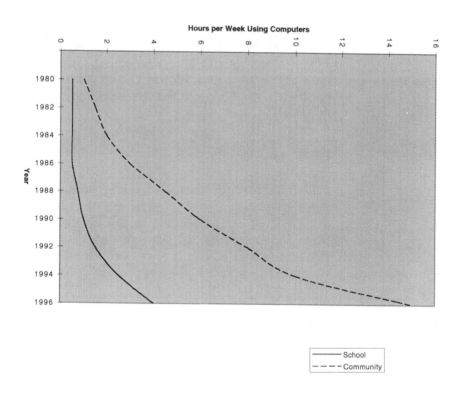

FIG. 10.2. School technology reference behavior.

policies to address these problem behaviors. It also should provide a framework for understanding why past policies have not worked and for evaluating new policies to improve system performance. Sometimes you may identify only a single reference behavior as problematic; that is, you may specify only a single indicator variable. More frequently, you will distinguish multiple reference behaviors. Obviously, a model capable of explaining simultaneously the problematic behaviors of multiple indicator variables engenders more confidence than a model that explains only a single reference behavior.

Listing Initial Understandings About Variables and Relationships

This stage of model development is a brainstorming phase in which one registers every idea that comes to mind about what factors are involved in the problem and how they are related. Examples follow from the school effectiveness and computer technology policy studies mentioned earlier.

The Effective Schooling Project

In the effective schooling project we thought of relationships among such variables as academic performance, which was the central variable of the study, and other factors such as student learning, student motivation, teacher expectations for student achievement, and the appropriateness and intensity of instruction. Although our original notes are no longer available, the following list exemplifies the kinds of thoughts we brought to the project.

1. Academic performance represents the accumulation of learning over time.
2. The rate at which students learn is affected by their levels of motivation to learn.
3. Student motivation to learn is affected by the appropriateness and intensity of instruction.
4. Student motivation to learn is affected by the student's academic performance.
5. The appropriateness and intensity of instruction is affected by the teacher's expectations for any particular student's achievement.
6. In ineffective schools, the teacher's expectations for any particular student's achievement is affected by the teacher's observations of the student's academic performance.
7. Teachers in general are good observers of academic performance.
8. In effective schools, teachers' expectations for student achievement are fixed by professional standards and are relatively unaffected by the observed performance of students.

The Computer Technology Project

Because the computer technology project is currently ongoing, we have extensive notes hypothesizing the variables and relationships that influence the integration of computer technology into the curriculum. These are organized into subsections. You will notice, because this is a brainstorming process, that there is some redundancy in the listing. This is normal because what is most important in brainstorming is to maximize idea generation; redundancies can be cleaned up later.

Administrative Support.   Administrative support for teacher integration of computers into their instruction will be influenced by the following:

1. Expectations of the parents.
2. Extent to which administrators inherently value computers as an object of instruction in schools.
3. Administrators' beliefs about the value of computers in enhancing basic student learnings.
4. Administrators' knowledge about computers in general, as well as their computer skills.

Budget Constraints.   The following will be constrainted by the budget:

1. Investments in computers and training.
2. Purchases of computer facilities, equipment, and software.

Community Expectations.   Community expectations for computer use in the school will be influenced by the following:

1. Community awareness of computer use in other schools and school districts.
2. Degree of computer use in the community.
3. Community's sensitivity to costs.

Computers in Students' Homes.   The availability of computers in students' homes will be influenced by the following:

1. Integration of computers into instruction in the school.
2. Availability of computers in the school (availability may cut both ways).

Investment in Computers.   Investment in computer resources is influenced by the school system's support for the integration of computers into instruction.

Rewards and Incentives. Rewards and incentives for integrating computers into instruction are influenced by the school system's support for it.

School System Support. The school system's support for the integration of computers into instruction is influenced by the following:

1. State standards, if there are any.
2. The community.
3. Budget considerations.
4. School committee politics.
5. The teachers.

Teacher Attitudes. Teacher attitudes regarding the use of computers in the school will:

1. Affect the degree to which they integrate computers into their instruction.
2. Be influenced by their knowledge and skills related to computers and computer software.

Teacher Integration of Computers Into Instruction. Teacher integration of computers into their instruction will be influenced by the following:

1. External rewards and incentives.
2. Student computer skills.
3. The availability of computers for instruction.
4. The availability of computers in students' homes.
5. The availability of necessary materials and equipment.
6. The availability of software in their fields of instruction.
7. The belief that computer literacy is an important basic skill.
8. The degree to which other teachers in the school use computers in their teaching.
9. The degree to which other teachers in their subject fields use computers in their teaching.
10. The degree to which their students use computers.
11. The ease of computers and software use.
12. The expectations of other teachers.
13. The expectations of the administration.
14. The expectations of the parents of their students.
15. The expectations of the students.
16. The extent to which teachers inherently value computers as an object of instruction in schools.
17. The software in their fields of instruction that is available in the school.

18. The technical support they get to do it.
19. The training they get to do it.
20. Teachers' beliefs about the value of computers in enhancing basic student learnings.
21. What teachers know about computers in general, including their computer skills.
22. What they know about using computers in their fields of instruction.

Technology Environment.   The technology enviromnent will be influenced as follows:

1. Changes in the global computer environment will affect the community's expectations for the school.
2. The availability in the school of software in different fields of instruction is influenced by knowledge of the nature and quality of "what's out there."
3. Knowing what's out there is influenced by time and effort expended to examine and evaluate software in the different subject areas.

Training.   Training for integrating computers into instruction will be influenced by the school system's support for it.

Generalizations About Listing Initial Understandings About Variables and Relationships

Having tentatively established the problem with reference to the observed and desired performance of key indicators over time, the analysts then interview knowledgeable people in the organization (e.g., work with focus groups), examine relevant documents, and observe pertinent situations. On the basis of such information they brainstorm and list an emerging set of understandings about the variables and relationships that account developmentally for the behavior of the problem indicators.[30] Dynamic hypotheses are formulated that guide decisions about setting the boundaries of the model, that is decisions about what factors to include and exclude and which to treat as variables rather than constants in the model.

Setting the Boundaries of the Model

The boundaries of a model are established when decisions are made (a) to include certain factors and exclude others from the model and (b) to treat certain factors as

---

[30]It should be noted that hypotheses emerge gradually, and always tentatively, but with greater certainty as the process unfolds. Also, the list of ideas typically contains some redundancies. This, however, is acceptable because the purpose of the brainstorming process is to generate as comprehensive a list of hypotheses as possible about the circular feedback dynamics that drive system performance. Duplication can always be resolved later.

variables and others as constants in the model. The more factors you include in a model, the larger and more complex it is. When you treat a possible variable as a constant, you reduce the size and complexity of the model. How large and complex a model is best?

Although there is no fixed answer to this question, certain observations can be made. Obviously, to be useful a model must include the essential variables and relationships required to explain the historic development of a problem and to facilitate the testing of policy alternatives. Yet, the model must be simple enough to be understandable, and to expose the essence the problem, avoiding confusing details. Models are constructed because the complexity of reality is often too great, so there is always a balance to be achieved, a tension to be resolved between the seeming verisimilitude of complexity and the clarity of simplicity.

In my experience, the essential model, the one that gets at the heart of the problem, is usually smaller and simpler than most clients will tolerate. Clients often insist on the inclusion of variables that, although not always essential, provide a sense of reality that is important for communicating their understanding of the problem causes to important audiences. Again, two examples are offered. Each example includes a description of the essential *dynamic hypothesis* and a *causal-loop diagram* showing the essential elements of the problem theory. However, it is important first to explain the concepts of positive and negative feedback.

Positive and Negative Feedback

The two examples require that you understand the nature of and the distinction between positive and negative feedback. All feedback is either positive or negative. In positive feedback, variables are mutually reinforcing in a pattern of circular causality. For example, in one of the illustrations given later high levels of student motivation to learn spur student learning, which, in turn, stimulates even higher levels of motivation to learn. Similarly, although in the opposite direction, low levels of student motivation to learn tend to diminish learning which, in turn, stimulates a further decline in motivation to learn. Thus, in either case, the feedback is positive in the sense of positive acceleration upward or downward as the feedback cycle continues. The word "positive" as used to describe feedback has no sense of valuing, of good or bad. Rather, it is used in the sense of progressive amplification.

Analogously, negative feedback describes a balancing dynamic that counters tendencies toward acceleration. The quintessential example is the thermostat system, maintaining a dynamic equilibrium around a desired temperature setting. In a thermostat system, when the temperature rises above the desired setting, the thermostat turns the heat off and may trigger air conditioning to bring the temperature back down toward the desired temperature. When the temperature drops too low, the air conditioning (if any) goes off, and the heat goes on to bring the temperature back up to the desired temperature. Thus, whereas positive feedback is self-reinforcing, negative feedback is balancing or stabilizing. Biological organisms are characterized by numerous negative feedback systems to maintain the stability required for survival. Common examples in human beings include systems to maintain blood pressure, heart rate, body temperature, and blood sugar levels.

Population Explosion as an Example of a Positive Feedback Loop. Although traditionally controlled by high death rates due to such factors as starvation and disease, there is a basic positive feedback relationship between the size of a population and the birth rate by which it is increased. For example, freed from high death rates by advances in sanitation and medicine, in the 20th century, populations exploded. The following diagram shows that whereas birth rate drives population growth, the birth rate rises as the size of the population increases (Fig. 10.3). Taking into consideration appropriate time delays (for children born to reach adulthood) there are simply more people to have children. Such a positive feedback loop, uncontrolled by other factors, is clearly self-accelerating.

Blood Sugar Control as an Example of a Negative Feedback System. As indicated earlier, biological organisms require a wide array of negative feedback systems to survive. The stability associated with the normal regulation of blood sugar illustrates such a negative feedback system. The dynamics of this control system are such that as the level of blood sugar rises above the normal blood sugar level, insulin is secreted to increase the metabolism of blood sugar, which has the effect of bringing the level of blood sugar down. As blood sugar drops below normal levels, hunger sets in, and the organism is motivated to eat; ingestion of carbohydrates increases blood sugar (Fig. 10.4). Thus, whereas positive feedback loops are self-reinforcing, negative feedback loops have stabilizing effects.

The Effective Schooling Project

The dynamic hypothesis in the effective schooling project explains the essential difference between ineffective and effective schools very simply. In system dynamics terms, the essential difference between the two kinds of schools lies in the contrast between a system driven at root by a positive feedback loop and one guided by a negative feedback loop. The simplicity of the explanation of what is otherwise a quite complex phenomenon recalls the famous tale of Rabbi Akeba, who, it is told, was asked to explain the *Talmud* while standing on one leg. The great Rabbi

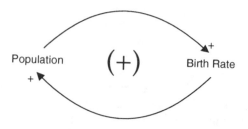

FIG. 10.3. The positive feedback of population growth.

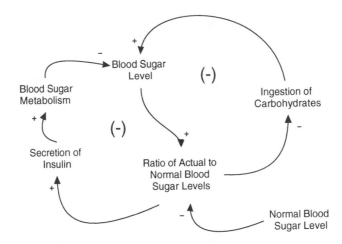

FIG. 10.4. The negative feedback associated with maintaining the stability of blood sugar.

did so by proclaiming, while perched in this uncomfortable position, "Do unto others as you would have them do unto you; all the rest is commentary." Analogously, we explain the essential distinction between ineffective and effective schools in the following manner.

An ineffective school is characterized most importantly by its multiplier effects on children's learning. The learning rate of initially high achievers tends to be exponentially reinforced upward in comparison with other children. The learning rate of initially low achievers tends, also, to be exponentially reinforced, but downward in comparison with other children. Whereas multiplier effects are helpful and desirable for high-achieving children, they are undesirable for low-achieving children. Such self-reinforcing dynamics are typical of positive feedback loops such as those depicted in the Fig. 10.5.

The self-reinforcing effects of motivation and learning are natural, presumably unchangeable. By contrast, however, those linking academic performance and teacher expectations for student learning through the intensity and appropriateness of instruction are socially constructed, or essentially matters of reason and policy. The main point is that in ineffective schools teacher expectations for student learning are driven by the students' academic learning. Because there is evidence in schools that students perceived by teachers as more academically able tend to receive more intense and appropriate instruction (Rist, 1973; Rosenthal, 1991; Rosenthal & Jacobson, 1968), the effect of this set of structural relationships is to reinforce the academic performance of both the initially high- and low- achieving students. High-achieving students are reinforced upward; low-achieving students tend to be reinforced downward. Clearly, such schools are ineffective *in a structural, dynamic sense* for those children who, at any point in time, are low-achieving students.

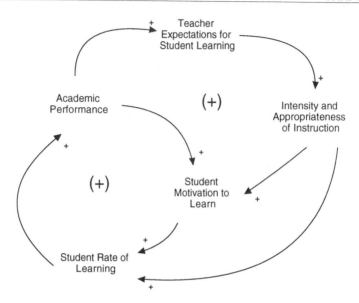

FIG. 10.5. The multipler dynamics of schooling that is ineffective for low-acheving children.

This situation is quite different in effective schools. The dynamics of effective schooling are portrayed in Fig. 10.6. The diagram looks very similar to the one for the ineffective school, but the key difference is that teacher expectations are keyed to stable professional standards for student academic performance, not to student academic performance itself.

As illustrated in Fig. 10.6, teacher expectations for student academic performance are not permitted to fall below professional grade level minimal expectations, and the intensity and appropriateness of instruction is augmented whenever student academic performance is below grade level standards.[31] Thus there is a stabilizing thermostat system put in place for low-achieving children, a negative feedback dynamic that, instead of reinforcing low achievement, seeks to counteract it. It is this distinction that constitutes the dynamic hypothesis about the essential difference between ineffective and effective schooling. As Rabbi Akeba suggested, "All the rest is commentary."

The Computer Technology Project

At the time of writing, the computer technology project was at a point where a tentative dynamic hypothesis had been formulated. Although we were still involved in interviews with school personnel, through which we hoped to gain a more lucid

---

[31]Note the negative sign at the arrowhead between "The Ratio of Performance to Expectations" and "Intensity and Appropriateness of Instruction." Negative signs on arrowheads signify inverse causal effects; conversely, positive signs on arrowheads denote direct causal effects.

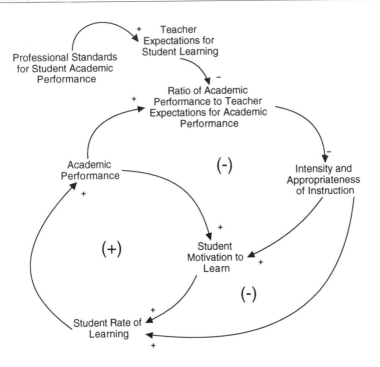

FIG. 10.6. The negative feedback maintaining effective schooling for low-achieving children.

understanding of the basic dynamics of the problem system, we had sufficient information from the interviews up to that point and the documents we had examined to suggest a theory regarding the elements and dynamics of technology change in the school. This hypothesis, as illustrated in Fig. 10.7, crystallizes the initial understandings listed earlier. The causal-loop analysis represents diagramatically the following six basic hypotheses:

1. Computer use tends to be self-reinforcing through increasing teacher and student skills, amount and complexity of software suited to different subject matters and to supporting enriched and individualized instruction, numbers of computers and amount of software, class time spent using computers, and community support for using computers for instruction.
2. Computer use tends to be limited by costs of hardware, software, training, and facilities and by demands on teacher preparation time related to changes in the degree of enrichment and individualization of instruction.
3. Community support for using computers for instruction is influenced positively by the importance of computers in the wider world.

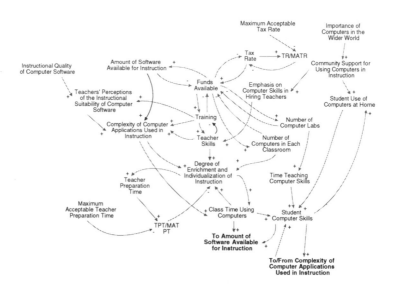

FIG. 10.7. Causal loop diagram of the computer technology model.

4. School finances are constrained asymptotically by the tax rate as a fraction of the maximum tax rate acceptable to the community.[32]

5. Use of computer software for instruction is positively influenced by teacher perceptions of its effectiveness in achieving their instructional objectives.

6. In summary, although there are many potential self-reinforcing loops that could be harnessed to generate growth in the use of computers for instruction in the elementary school under analysis, growth is ultimately bounded by financial constraints related to the willingness of the community to bear the tax burden and by the willingness of teachers to put in the preparation time required to take advantage of the potential of computer instruction to enrich and individualize instruction.

Our central hypotheses highlight the importance of skills and teacher attitude and of student learning as powerful factors in the success or failure of the computer integration effort. Seemingly obvious, such understandings are frequently overlooked in curriculum reform efforts. This is not surprising because attending to the analytic and policy significance of these fundamental causal relationships is made

---

[32]That is, the closer the tax rate gets to the theoretical limit of the maximum acceptable tax rate, the harder it becomes politically to raise taxes any further.

difficult by the extent to which their effects are characterized by time delays of months, or even years (e.g., in the effects of curricular innovations on observable indicators of student learning).

Although causal-loop diagrams easily become complex, they are particularly useful in highlighting mutually reinforcing (+) and balancing relationships (-) among factors. Looking at Fig. 10.7 you can see a number of mutually reinforcing relationships (consistent with the hypotheses described earlier). For example, as students develop their computer skills, they are more likely to use computers at home but as they use computers more at home they tend to improve their skills. Similarly, in a loop that is more difficult to follow in the diagram, the following circular set of relationships tends be self-reinforcing:

1. The greater the amount of software available for instruction (upper-left), the greater the complexity of computer applications used in instruction.
2. The greater the complexity of computer applications used in instruction, the greater the degree of enrichment and individualization of instruction.
3. The greater the complexity of computer applications and the greater the degree of enrichment and individualization, the more class time is devoted to using computers.
4. The more class time spent using computers, the greater student computer skills.
5. The greater student computer skills and the more class time devoted to computer use, the more software teachers will order and the more willing administrators will be to make software available for instruction—and the circle continues.

In evaluating the implications of self-reinforcing (positive) feedback loops, however, you should keep firmly in mind that often they can spiral downward as well as upward. Thus, little available software, little class time spent using computers, and little complexity of software applications tend to block growth in the integration of computers into instruction and keep levels of integration low.

There also are important balancing (negative) feedback loops identified in Fig. 10.7. Balancing relationships tend to define limits to growth. They operate in ways similar to the dynamics of thermostat systems, maintaining (depending on their relative strength) stability and control in the system. Thus Fig. 10.7 highlights the constraining effects of funding, the tax rate, teacher training, and teacher preparation time (to support the enrichment and individualization of instruction associated at its best with integrating computers into instruction). Such loops suggest the leverage points embodying the not necessarily publicized (or even fully recognized) goals of the system.

In this model, as cases in point, the Maximum Acceptable Tax Rate and the Maximum Acceptable Teacher Preparation Time are hypothesized as empirically real goals that constitute powerful curbs on the growth of computer use in the school. Tax constraints, for example, influence such intermediate factors as the amount of training given to teachers to support their effective use of computers in classrooms, the amount of software available, the number and quality of computers available, the number of computer labs, and so forth. Although to some extent the implicit system "goals" around taxes and work loads are cultural givens in particular situations, the community's willingness to provide financial support depends on the value it places on using computers in instruction, and the teachers' willingness to take on more demanding work loads depends, at any particular point in time, on their perceptions of the instructional suitability of computers and computer software and their impact on what and how well children learn.

Implicit in this view is the belief, supported by a reasonable reading of case studies of innovation in schools (Berman, 1981; Berman & McLaughlin, 1975a, 1975b, 1977, 1978, 1979; Huberman & Miles, 1984; Rosenblum & Louis, 1981), that change efforts are fundamentally unstable until they have been fully institutionalized. Thus, lacking adequate levels of support in the form of training, technical assistance, and physical resources, innovation is more likely to spiral downward than upward toward effective institutionalization. According to this diagnosis, organizational change efforts for a long time remain sensitive to administrative error and the lack of political will to sustain the collateral effort required to persevere in innovative ventures. This seems especially true of the integration of computer technology into the curriculum because, by its nature, such integration can never be fully institutionalized. Computer technology is likely to remain too evolutionary to be fully institutionalized, both in general and in terms of educational applications.

Generalizations About Boundary Setting

The basic guides to determining the variables for inclusion in a system dynamics policy model are the reference behaviors and the dynamic hypothesis. The reference behaviors show the historic trends associated with key indicators of the problem being addressed in the policy analysis. Because the model is intended to explain the essential causes of these historic trends in terms of circular feedback loops, the variables in the model must include all the indicator variables as well as the other variables implicated in the analysts' hypotheses about the major feedback dynamics. External variables, out of stakeholders' control and not included in the positive and negative feedback loops comprising the system model, should be kept to an absolute minimum. Under no circumstances should the primary explanation of the problematic behavior of the indicator variables reside in such external variables. External variables (i.e., those outside feedback loops) should be included in the model only for purposes of examining how the system responds to them. Understanding such responses and their effects over time may be important in understanding the sources of policy problems.

Specifying the Model Mathematically

It is not the purpose of this chapter to detail to any significant degree the methods and procedures for constructing mathematical computer models. Suffice it to say that mathematical model building is the most sophisticated form of system dynamics analysis. No other form of system dynamics analysis includes the degree of specification of mathematical models and, for this reason, no other form of modeling approaches the precision and clarity of mathematical modeling. There are several popular software applications that permit the mathematical specification of system dynamics levels and rates, different types of delays, and the auxiliary variables used to show rate structures more clearly.[33]

Specifying a model mathematically is a very detailed piece of work. It is also, unfortunately, very technical in nature. The following example is part of the effective schools model (Clauset, 1982), examples of which have been shown in the preceding pages of this chapter.[34] You will recall that the dynamic hypothesis (see Figs. 10.5 and 10.6) suggested that student motivation to learn is affected by teacher expectations for student learning, the appropriateness and intensity of instruction, and student academic performance. The following section explains how equations have been formulated to represent these ideas.[35, 36]

Student Reading Motivation Coflow

Motivation to learn to read is carried from grade to grade as a changing characteristic of students in different cohort groups. The level [state] equation which structures this flow is identical *in form* to that which structures other coflows:

(1) L2RM.K=L2RM.J+DT*(L2RMIN.JK+L2RMC.JK-L2RMX.JK), where:

L2RM.K = the new level of total motivation to learn to read;

L2RM.J = the old level of total motivation to learn to read;

DT = the time period of computation;

L2RMIN.JK = the inflow rate during the last period of computation;

---

[33]These include, among others, *Dynamo,* developed by Pugh-Roberts Associates, Cambridge, MA, *Stella,* developed by High Performance Systems, Hanover, NH, and *DYSMAP,* developed by the University of Bradford and the University of Salford in England. Several generations of each have been made available.

[34]The model was written in the 1982 version of *Dynamo.*

[35]Because dynamic models show changes in state variables from one time period (DT) to the next, technical notations in the equations include the use of subscripts to designate the values of state variables in different time periods. These time periods are called the "old" and the "new" time periods and are designated respectively by the subscripts ".J" and ".K" and combinations thereof. Because rates effecting changes in state variables operate in time intervals, they are shown as operating in "the last period of computation" (.JK) and in "the next period of computation" (.KL).

[36]Motivation in this set of equations is shown to be affected also by the behavior of other students. For purposes of simplicity, this was not shown in Figs. 10.5 and 10.6.

L2RMC.JK = the rate of change during the last period of computation; and

L2RMX.JK = the outflow rate during the last period of computation.

Again, the key theoretical component is the change rate (L2RMC). Change in motivation (CL2MR.K) is described as closing a discrepancy between the current level of motivation (L2MR.K) and the indicated level of motivation (IL2MR.K). This occurs over an adjustment time (MAT):

(2) CL2MR.K = (IL2MR.K-L2MR.K)/MAT.

The indicated level of motivation (IL2MR.K) is determined by an equal weighting of motivation from four sources:

(3) IL2MR.K = (IL2MRA.K+IL2RTX.K+IL2MRI.K+IL2MSB.K)/4, where:

IL2MRA.K = the indicated level of motivation from reading achievement;

IL2RTX.K = the indicated level of motivation from teacher expectations;

IL2MRI.K = the indicated level of motivation from appropriateness and intensity of instruction in reading; and

IL2MSB.K = the indicated level of motivation from grade level student behavior.

The effect of reading achievement on motivation is based on the discrepancy between current reading achievement and grade level standards. The indicated level of motivation from teacher expectations is the product of the current level of motivation (L2MR.K) and the multiplier for the effect of teacher expectations (ML2MTX.K). This multiplier is based on the discrepancy between teacher expectations and current reading achievement. The indicated motivation from appropriateness and intensity of instruction in reading and the indicated motivation from grade level student behavior vary with the ratio of current conditions to the normal condition. Precise effects are described in a series of table functions (not shown here).[37, 38]

Testing for Logical Coherence

Two of the advantages of specifying a policy model in such detail are that its behavior can be examined in terms of both internal and external validity. In terms of its external validity, the statistical and graphic outputs of the model can be compared with and contrasted against relevant historic trend data. From the perspective of internal validity, the impact of variables on each other can be scrutinized time period by time period and evaluated for construct validity and logical coherence.

---

[37]Table functions represent values in a graph showing the effect of one variable on another at different values of the influencer variable. Thus it is possible to represent nonlinear effects in the model.

[38]The quoted material is taken from Appendix A, Documentation for the School Effectiveness Model, pp. 179–181 of a version of Clauset's dissertation prepared for publication but ultimately never published. This version, entitled *Closing the Learning Gap: Effective Schooling for Initially Low Achievers*, was written in 1982 by Karl H. Clauset, Jr., and Alan K. Gaynor.

Examining Policy Implications

When models behave in ways consistent with the known historic performance of the real system, they give interested observers confidence in their utility for policy analysis. The ability of computer models to reproduce known historic system behaviors constitutes a kind of *concurrent validity*. To the extent that they are able to predict system behaviors into the future, they would show *predictive validity*. However, because it is important to believe that a model generates the right behavior for the right reasons, there is always strong interest in assessing the internal structure of the model. Other analysts want to be assured that the internal structure, the mathematics of the model, makes sense. They want to have confidence in its *construct validity*.

When various interested parties are satisfied that a computer model constitutes a credible representation of reality, it can be modified to represent alternative policy choices and their implications can be assessed in terms of the behavior of the model. This is an important value of computer modeling, although most system dynamicists I know believe that engaging the organization in the modeling process yields the most important organizational outcomes.

QUESTIONS FOR ANALYZING PROBLEMS USING SYSTEM DYNAMICS THEORY

The following questions are typically addressed in the course of analyzing a problem system from a system dynamics perspective:

1. What are the key indicators of the problem?
2. What have been the historic trend behaviors of these indicator variables (over a period of time long enough to characterize the problem developmentally)?
3. Against what desired trends over the same period of time are the indicators perceived as problematic?
4. On the basis of relevant information from interviews, observations, and document analyses, what variables and relationships seem important in understanding the trend behaviors of the indicator variables?
5. What basic positive and negative feedback loops seem most essential in explaining system behavior over time (dynamic hypothesis)?
6. Given these essential dynamics, why have past policies to correct the problem failed? What proposed policies are likely to be more successful?

AN ILLUSTRATIVE OUTLINE
FOR A SYSTEM DYNAMICS ANALYSIS

I. The problem

    A. General description and time frame of the problem
    B. Indicator variables
    C. Performance trends and discrepancies with desired performance trends

II. Research on key variables and relationships

    A. Interviews
    B. Observations
    C. Document analyses
    D. Understandings about key variables and relationships

III. Key causal feedback loops

    A. Positive feedback loops
    B. Negative feedback loops
    C. Dynamic hypothesis explaining the causes of the problem developmentally in terms of the interactions among feedback loops over time

IV. Mathematical Modeling (Optional)

    A. System dynamics flow diagrams and equations
    B. Comparison of system outputs with historical indicator trends
    C. Examining the model in dynamic equilibrium
    D. Testing the model for sensitivity to changes in parameters
    E. Examining the microdynamics of model behavior
    F. Testing policy alternatives

V. Conclusions and policy recommendations

11

Conclusion: Problem Analysis as a Hermeneutic Process

Theoretical Bildung *goes beyond what man knows and experiences immediately. It consists in learning to allow what is different from oneself and to find universal viewpoints from which one can grasp the thing, "the objective thing in its freedom," without selfish interest.*

—Hans-Georg Gadamer (1975, p. 14)

Although it presents a conceptual framework for problem analysis and a theoretical approach to analyzing the causes of organizational problems, all of which may be thought of as decidedly abstract, this book is essentially pragmatic in nature. Systematic problem description and theoretical analysis are valid precisely to the extent that they are seen as useful in raising good questions and in guiding data collection and analysis toward wise decision making. As Stephen Toulmin said in a televised interview in the course of a program titled "A Glorious Accident" (National Public Television, 1996), "Theory has to be justified as a form of practice. It isn't that practice has to answer before the high court of theory."

From the very beginning of the problem analysis process, problems are defined in relation to values. Within the system of analysis presented in this book, you embody your values in the standards of comparison against which you define the problem. Inescapably, you specify the indicators of the problem in relation to the values you hold dear and which you perceive to be violated in ways that you characterize as problematic. Later, you hypothesize the causes of the problem, intuitively at first, then systematically in relation to theories that seem relevant to the problem situation.

Interesting is the extent to which problem analysis turns out to be a hermeneutic process. Treating the organizational situation as a kind of text, you examine it progressively in circular fashion. Initially, you sense that something is wrong in the situation, and you list examples, both anecdotal and statistical, of the intuitively perceived problem. Having identified the major qualitative and quantitative dimensions of the problem, you then examine more systematically what standards of comparison you might use to illustrate how the situation might reasonably appear if the problem were resolved.

Would important qualitative dimensions of the situation be different? You can, for example, contrast the major qualitative characteristics of the present and desired situations in the left- and right-hand columns of a table. Moreover, you could ask if the year-to-year trends of key statistical indicators should be different? Graphical comparisons are generally effective in highlighting such contrasts.

A critical part of the problem analysis process involves comparing and contrasting alternative standards of comparison among themselves in order to evaluate not only which seem more valid but also because in drawing such comparisons you inevitably analyze more deeply the values at stake in relation to the perceived problem. Then, in typically hermeneutic fashion, having clarified the value domain, you reevaluate the indicator domain; salient values may have emerged that suggest new or better indicators. Thus, there is an analytic reciprocity between the specification and examination of values and indicators that extends your understanding of the problem and enriches the power of the analysis.

Once you have closed the circle of analysis between problem indicators and standards of comparison, you are engaged in a second stage of hermeneutic study. The search for appropriate theoretical perspectives for causal analysis is also an iterative process. Typically, you sense spontaneously some likely causes of the problem and are able to list them. Such an opening list provides a first entry into the search for potentially useful theoretical frameworks. Having this initial list, you can explore the sorts of theories that characterize the literature on organizations as well as the literatures of the social science disciplines, checking for a fit between their content and orientation and the causes that first came to mind. Needless to say, it is more than likely that in the course of such an exploration additional possible causes of the problem will emerge. Thus, you tend progressively to realize a correspondence between hypothesized causes and theoretical perspectives from which further causal hypotheses can be drawn.

Thus, in such a way, as you scan your initial list of potential causes, you are drawn to theories of bureaucracy, leadership, motivation, decision making, role, politics, intergroup dynamics, politics, games, systems thinking, and so forth, within the organizational literature, or to other theories in disciplines such as economics, psychology, sociology, and social-psychology. As you examine such theories you expand your list of possible causal factors and relationships. This circular process continues in a manner that refines your understanding of the causal nexus until you achieve a sense of resolution.

The fruit of problem analysis is a solution strategy. Solutions must be consistent with the problem as you have described and documented it, with the theory of causation that emerges from the causal analysis, with an assessment of the effectiveness of solutions that have been tried in the past, and with the cultural, political, economic, and sociotechnical characteristics of the school and school district in which the reform effort is being addressed. Finally, the strategy must be consistent with the interests, commitments, skills, and resources of the stakeholders who are concerned about the problem and want to resolve it.

The relationship between the stakeholders and the solution strategy constitutes a third stage of hermeneutics. A key to this third stage is an understanding that although there may be stakeholders interested in resolving the problem, their final commitment to its resolution is contingent on the particular nature of the solution strategies under consideration. This is because particular approaches require financial, social, and professional obligations and touch upon values that go beyond those inherent in the problem, itself. Thus, you must in the end negotiate, in recommending and implementing solution strategies, what politicians know as the "art of the possible." You always transact, in a process analogous to the iterations between text and interpretation of the hermeneutic circle, the values that define the problem, your understanding of what solutions can be expected to work, and the effects of alternative solution strategies on various stakeholders.

PART III

CASE EXAMPLES

In the following sections are two pairs of examples of the analysis types described and illustrated in this book. In one pair you find first an organizational problem in a school environment detailed and documented. Then each author identifies a set of stakeholders who are aware of the problem and want to do something about it. Finally, the author proposes recommendations tailored to these stakeholders that address the causes uncovered analytically.

In the other pair of examples each author presents a significant organizational decision for analysis, describing the nature of the decision, the kinds of information used to make it, the sources of this information, the people involved in making the decision, and the decisional process. The author then critiques the decision (Is this the kind of decision the organization should be making at all?) and the various aspects of the decisional process (Is this how the decision should be made?) using criteria represented in the normative assumptions of each of Burrell and Morgan's four paradigms: functionalist, interpretivist, radical humanist, and radical structuralist. Finally, the author analyzes the feasibility for the organization of action recommendations corresponding to the these diverse critiques.

The problem analysis chapters were prepared in an advanced policy seminar and were then revised and submitted as doctoral comprehensive examination papers. The decisional critiques were written as papers in a course in organizational analysis. Although the chapters have been reformatted to match the editorial style of the book, they are substantially unchanged from when they were submitted as class papers.

Students have consistently found sample papers very helpful in understanding the processes of problem description and causal analysis. I hope you find these chapters useful in the same way.

12

School to Work: An Analysis of Vocational Education as Provided by Greater Stanton Technical School*

Allen Scheier

EXECUTIVE SUMMARY

Vocational education in an organized form has existed in this country since the early part of the 20th century. The theory behind vocational education is that public schools can and should prepare students to enter the work force. It recognizes the fact that not all students are capable of or interested in pursuing a college education. Since the Industrial Revolution, a demand has always existed for skilled and semiskilled workers. For many years, vocational education has played an integral role in meeting this demand.

Greater Stanton Technical School has been providing students from the Greater Stanton area with a vocational and academic education since 1965. In recent years, however, very few of Greater Stanton's graduates are found working in jobs that relate to their vocational training. This represents a problem.

There are a number of possible reasons why graduates of Greater Stanton are choosing not to enter the trade they have studied. This analysis points to two primary reasons why this is happening. The first reason is that students enrolled in vocational education programs must choose a trade before they are prepared to do so. The second reason revolves around the role of human capital theory in the changing global economy. On the basis of these two causes, recommendations may be formulated to address this problem. These recommendations apply not only to

---

*This chapter was originally submitted as a term paper for the Advanced Policy Seminar, Department of Administration, Training and Policy Studies, School of Education, Boston University, Fall 1996. Names have been altered to protect the identities of the school and key participants.

Greater Stanton, but also are applicable to vocational education as a whole.

As we approach the 21st century, the economic structure of this country and the world is changing. Despite these changes, there have been very few changes in the methods our public education system uses in preparing students to enter the work force. For vocational education to maintain its role, it must be willing to adapt to the demands of this new global economy.

PROBLEM BACKGROUND

The existence of vocational education in the United States dates back to the manual education movement of the late 19th century. In its early form, manual education was less concerned with education than it was with morality. Such education was targeted primarily at juvenile delinquents and the disadvantaged, with the belief that social evils could be corrected by moral uplift, and manual labor was seen as the best method of inculcating morality (Lazerson & Grubb, 1974). With the growth of industrialism came a shift away from the need for unskilled manual laborers to a need for laborers who possessed specific skills. All parties concerned with industry and education began to recognize the connection between the two. The future of industry depended on the educational system providing skilled workers.

Initially, vocational education aimed to provide students with a strong academic background coupled with the skills for applying that knowledge to a trade. At its inception, vocational education did not focus on specific trades. In "A Place Called School," John Goodlad (1984) observed:

> Initially, instruction in the manual arts was introduced into the curriculum largely to provide for the simultaneous development of hand and head. The medium for the activity—paper, wood, metal, or soil—called for skill in the use of hands while presenting a problem for the mind. The purpose was not to prepare carpenter, tinsmith, and gardener, although one might become some of all three, but to provide alternative avenues for intellectual development and the honing of some useful skills. (pp. 238–239)

Under this system, a graduate of a vocational education program would acquire knowledge and thinking skills from the academic curriculum coupled with the ability to apply that knowledge and these skills as a skilled laborer.

The basic framework for the creation of federally financed vocational education came about as a result of the Smith-Hughes Act of 1917. This act created the system of vocational education that was largely separate from the existing educational system. This system of vocational education has gone substantially unchanged until the recent passage of the Perkins Act of 1990, which was simply a series of amendments to the Perkins Act of 1984. These amendments included some very powerful new requirements for vocational education: Vocational and academic education should be broadly integrated; vocational education should move from narrow, occupationally specified skill-based training to broad-based vocational instruction; vocational education should forge strong links with economic development efforts in the community (Wirth, 1992).

The general goal of vocational education as it exists today is to provide students with a regular academic education combined with trade-specific knowledge and skills so that they may become productive members of the workforce. A graduate of a vocational school should have

- Opportunities for full-time employment in a trade
- The ability to be trained for employment in a different trade
- The academic skills required to pursue further education
- General work skills that are useful in a variety of occupational settings
- Work experience and the foundation of a work ethic.

In its ideal form, vocational education has the ability to offer education in a variety of areas including basic academic education, career development, vocational knowledge, living skills, and occupationally specific skills (Pautler, 1990). An effective vocational education program should increase the range of choices available to its graduates.

Since it was established in 1965, Greater Stanton Technical School has offered students the opportunity to earn an academic education along with the skills and knowledge associated with a specific trade. On graduating, students receive a high school diploma and a certificate denoting their proficiency in their chosen trades. Currently, graduates of Greater Stanton receive a certificate in one of the following trades: allied health, autobody, automotive, cad/machine/drafting, carpentry, construction/painting, cosmetology, culinary arts, distributive education, data management, electrical, electronics, food technology, graphic communications, industrial electronics, metal fabrication, and plumbing. With their diplomas and certificates, graduates have the options of entering the work force in their trade or continuing their education.

THE PROBLEM

Problem Statement

Very few graduates of Greater Stanton Technical School are members of the work force in the specific trade for which they have been trained. These students who are not utilizing the knowledge and training associated with their trade are choosing to continue their education at the college level, working outside their trade, finding themselves unemployed, or serving in the armed services. This fact represents a significant waste of time, money, and effort on the part of the students and the educational system that serves them.

Importance of the Problem

In our society, it is very difficult to dispute the value of an education. Education is universally viewed as an investment in one's future. Parents and teachers constantly remind children of the significance that studying and learning will have in their future. Obviously, not everything learned in school is useful in life. Rather, education is considered to be a steppingstone to bigger and better things. By exposing children to a wide variety of knowledge and skills, we help them make decisions about their future vocations.

Students enrolled in vocational education programs have supposedly already decided on their vocations. These students spend a great deal of time learning skills and knowledge associated with specific trades. If these students never utilize these skills and knowledge, then time was wasted that could have been put to better use.

Who is Disadvantaged by the Problem?

The population most disadvantaged by this problem at Greater Stanton is the population the school is designed to help the most: the students. Students attending Greater Stanton Technical School split their time in school between their chosen "shop" and academic classes. For 4 years students alternate between "academic week" and "shop week." Students spend an entire week in their shop working in and learning about their trade. The following week is spent in academic classes such as algebra, English composition, and American history. Also during this week, students spend part of their time in "related," a class that is held in the shop area that deals with academic knowledge related to that specific trade. Although students spend half their time in shop week and half in academic week, the existence of "related" during the academic week means that less than 40% of a student's time in school is spent in academic classes. This structure is similar to that used in other vocational schools.

A significant part of the vocational education experience is the co-op program. At the end of their junior year, students who have exhibited proficiency in their shop and are in satisfactory academic standing are eligible to work outside of the school during their shop week. Instead of coming to school for that week, they work at local businesses related to their trades. This provides the students with paying jobs as well as real-world work experience in which they are able to apply much of what they have learned in school. This arrangement is then carried over into their senior year. In an average year, 75% of the senior class "goes out on co-op." The experience given to these students in these jobs is an important component of their vocational education experience.

The essence of the problem is that students are spending over 60% of their time in high school learning specific trade-oriented knowledge that most of them do not use. This represents a waste of time and resources on the part of students, teachers, and the school. Students who graduate receive a high school diploma, but those students have likely not learned as much academic and general knowledge as graduates of a comprehensive high school. This is evidenced by the low Scholastic Aptitude Test (SAT) scores of the school's graduating seniors. On average, the school's highest academically ranked students score below the 25th percentile on the SAT. Such students going on to college are likely to be at a serious disadvantage. If they opt to enter the work force in different trades, they will likely need to be retrained in the skills and knowledge related to those trades.

Certainly not everything learned in any high school is of great value later in life. There is, however, a difference between learning general academic knowledge, some of which may be of value at some point in life, and learning a specific trade. The former provides a person with knowledge that could be used in a variety of professions, whereas the latter is knowledge mainly of value for only one profession. Acquiring academic knowledge opens avenues for further knowledge in a wide range of subjects. Learning knowledge associated with a specific trade does just the opposite.

High school is a very important time in the life of an adolescent. Decisions made at this point in a student's life can have far-reaching effects. For a student to decide on a career at 14 years of age, then spend the better part of the next 4 years studying that trade, only to decide to do something else, is problematic.

How the Problem Affects Other Important Problems.   A majority of those graduates who do not enter a specific trade either enroll in college or enter the work force in another trade. Those who enroll in college find themselves at a serious disadvantage due to their lack of substantial academic preparation. These students are often placed in noncredit remedial courses to make up their deficiencies. Already frustrated by their academic deficiencies, these students must now cope with the additional work, time, and expense associated with remediation.

Those students who choose to enter the work force in a different trade often lack the general thinking skills employers seek. Many are forced to enter unskilled or semi-skilled positions. Those fortunate enough to find skilled work often must be retrained with new skills at their or their employer's expense.

Another important factor to be taken into account is the socioeconomic status of the population served by Greater Stanton. Students enrolled at Greater Stanton Technical School are faced with a number of hurdles. To begin with, most of them reside in a depressed, inner city community. This community has some of the highest rates of crime, unemployment, teen pregnancy, drug use, and welfare dependency in the state of Massachusetts. Many students see the world of work as a way out. The promise of a good education and a good job is very appealing, perhaps their only hope for escaping their environment. When the promise of vocational education becomes an empty promise, many of these students find themselves trapped in their environment. Instead of working their way out or contributing to the improvement of their community, they become a part of the problem.

TABLE 12.1

Current Status of Recent Graduates

	Number of Students	Percentage
Working in trade	23	17%
Working outside of trade	44	32%
Attending college	51	37%
Military service	17	12%
Unemployed	3	2%
Total	138	100%

Problem Indicators

In an informal survey of graduates from Greater Stanton Technical School within the past 5 years, students were asked what they were currently doing or had been doing since graduation. Table 12.1 illustrates their responses.

With only 17% of its graduates entering their fields of study, this school is clearly not meeting the basic goals of vocational education. It would be unrealistic to expect 100% of the graduates of any vocational school to be working in their chosen trades, but one would certainly expect more than 17% to be doing so. This is especially true when one considers that, at the time of graduation, roughly 75% of the students are working in their trades at their co-op job.

On the basis of the statistics reported in Table 12.1, it is possible to argue that the goals of vocational education are still being met. One goal is to prepare students to enter the work force, which almost 50% of those surveyed have done. Unfortunately, as shown in Table 12.2, many of the graduates employed outside of their trade hold unskilled, menial positions. Some do hold semiskilled positions, but the requirements for those positions are unrelated to the trade the students studied while in school.

There is no evidence to suggest that the specific vocational training of these students contributes to their current job requirements. Many of these positions could be held by comprehensive high school graduates, college graduates, and even high school dropouts.

Another goal of vocational education is to provide students with an adequate academic education so they may continue their education. The implied intent, however, is that they will continue their education in a field related to their trade. In some cases this is true, but often students' majors in college are totally unrelated to the trades they studied in high school. Table 12.3 gives examples of students' trades and their collegiate majors.

For these students the trade-specific knowledge and skills they learned for over three years in high school have little to no value for them. These students also tend to be at a disadvantage when compared with their collegiate peers who graduated from comprehensive high schools in which the emphasis is placed on academic knowledge and college preparation. Each of these students has had difficulty dealing with the academic rigors of college.

TABLE 12.2

Sample Jobs Held by Vocational School Graduates
Who Are Not Working in Their Trade

Student	Trade	Current Job
SM	Allied health	Cashier
MF	Allied health	Secretary
SD	Carpentry	Nutrition store manager
JD	Carpentry	Pizza restaurant/delivery
JH	Carpentry	Bartender
JL	Cosmetology	Nurse's aide
DB	Culinary arts	Mover
MG	Culinary arts	Medical records clerk
DP	Data management	Restaurant supervisor
PS	Data management	Waitress
YP	Data management	Stitcher
KB	Data management	Circuit board assembler
MD	Electrical	Cab driver
DR	Electrical	Grocery store manager
JS	Electronics	Sheriff
KG	Industrial electronics	Bank teller
AV	Machine shop	City hall clerk
VN	Metal fabrication	Hardware store salesman
PA	Plumbing	Receiving director
IT	Plumbing	Police officer

TABLE 12.3

Sample College Majors of Vocational School Graduates

Student	Trade	College Major
AC	Allied health	Paralegal studies
KW	Automotive	Radiology
JS	Data management	Education
PC	Electrical	Broadcasting
IM	Electrical	Physical therapy
MN	Electronics	Computer science
DH	Electronics	Physical therapy
RE	Graphic communications	Business
SM	Graphic communications	English
DT	Metal fabrication	Business
JC	Painting & decorating	Criminal justice
JB	Plumbing	Engineering

STANDARDS

Since its inception in the early 20th century, the definition of vocational education has changed considerably. The most recent, comprehensive definition taken from the American Vocational Association Fact Sheet defines vocational education as

> The segment of education charged with preparing people for work. It is the backbone of the nation's employment-related education and training programs. It responds to this charge through a variety of programs that offer instruction in related basic education, career development, general vocational knowledge, improved family living skills, and occupationally specific preparation. (Pautler, 1990, p. 267)

Although this definition applies to vocational education at all levels it would not be unreasonable to examine only secondary vocational education through the lens of this definition. Given that perspective, secondary vocational education may be defined as education designed to provide students with the skills and knowledge they will need to enter the work force in a specific trade after graduation. Because education is considered to be more of a state and local function than a federal one, an analysis may be done only on a state by state basis.

In the state of Massachusetts the rules and regulations governing vocational education are outlined in the Chapter 74 regulations (Commonwealth of Massachusetts, 1977, p. 5), which define "vocational education" as, "education of which the primary purpose is to fit students for profitable employment."

The regulations further state:

> The major goal of vocational education is to prepare students to seek, acquire and succeed in a specific trade, technical, or occupational field requiring specialized or technical skills for entry into that field.

In 1990, in response to legislation designed to improve vocational education, the Chapter 74 regulations were revised. In the revised regulations (Massachusetts Department of Education, 1980, p. 3) vocational education was called "vocational technical education" and redefined as

> the approved type of education, purposefully designed to educate and prepare students of all ages for employment and continuing academic and occupational preparation through a balance of classroom instruction, supportive services, and occupational experience to develop life-long skills so that upon completion of vocational technical programs, students are qualified to pursue directly or indirectly, opportunities emanating from such vocational technical programs.

Furthermore, the regulations (p. 4) redefined the goals of vocational technical education with a stated purpose:

> to provide equal access to high demand quality programs for all students and to prepare students to seek, acquire, and succeed in a specific technical or occupational field requiring specialized or technical competencies for entry into that field for employment, entrepreneurship, or further education.

This revised definition of vocational education did broaden its goals, but the fact remained that the primary goal of vocational education in the state of Massachusetts is to prepare students to enter the work force in a specific trade. This is the standard against which I have chosen to measure the success of the vocational education provided by Greater Stanton Technical School.

Alternative Standards

There are various ways of approaching these issues. The question is whether this is a problem only at Greater Stanton or throughout the entire vocational education system. One possible answer is a comparison of the figures from Table 12.1, which examined the status of recent graduates of Greater Stanton with the statistics for vocational schools throughout Massachusetts. A summary of these data is given in Table 12.4. When the percentage of Greater Stanton's graduates who work in their trade is compared with the state average, there is a clear disparity.

A second alternative way of examining this situation is to remember one of the general purposes of public schools: to engage children in their own learning. Proponents of vocational education argue that its curriculum addresses the learning styles of students who are "turned off" by the traditional secondary school curriculum. They further argue that the option of vocational education prevents many of these students from dropping out of school altogether. These arguments do have some validity, but the question arises as to whether one of the goals of our educational system should be to keep students in school even if they are not getting anything out of it. By accepting this as a goal of schools, we reduce the schools' role for many students to that of baby-sitter.

In the case of Greater Stanton, approximately 40% of the students who enter the school never graduate. Some transfer to other schools where they do complete their studies, but many also simply drop out. If one accepts the argument that a goal of high schools is to keep students in school, then Greater Stanton is not effectively meeting this goal.

TABLE 12.4
Current Status of Recent Massachusetts Vocational School Graduates

	Greater Stanton Graduates	Massachusetts 1992 Graduates	Massachusetts 1991 Graduates
Working in trade	17%	36%	36%
Working outside of trade	32%	20%	20%
Attending college	37%	29%	27%
Military service	12%	6%	7%
Unemployed: Not in labor force	2%	9%	10%

Rationale for Standards

The theories on which vocational education is based have a great deal of merit. Our society expects all able-bodied citizens to work for a living. The idea of public education providing students with a high school diploma and marketable job skills so that they may successfully enter the work force is very appealing.

Since America's Industrial Revolution there has always been a demand for skilled and semiskilled workers. Although this sector of the economy has undergone a number of transformations over the past 100 years, a consistent demand for skilled workers has always existed. This is true not only in large corporations, but also at the small business level. Large businesses will always need skilled laborers as well as occupations such as auto mechanic, plumber and carpenter that are an integral part of every type of community throughout this country. Vocational education provides these occupations with their skilled workers.

Important Values Reflected in the Proposed Standards

Vocational education provides an avenue into the work force for many students who, for a number of reasons, are rebuffed by the regular high school curriculum. Students with technical and manual skills that are not fostered by traditional education will benefit greatly from a vocational curriculum. Those who are rebuffed by or drop out of a traditional academic high school can be engaged in learning skills and knowledge through vocational training. Vocational education effectively addresses students whose learning styles are not met by the traditional high school curriculum.

Vocational education can also provide a significant service to students from poor socioeconomic backgrounds—the lower class. Furnishing these students with marketable job skills that enable them to enter the work force provides the opportunity for them to work their way out of poverty into the working class.

Why the Proposed Standards Are Persuasive

Vocational education is an elective form of education. Students opt to enroll in a vocational school instead of a comprehensive high school. Once enrolled in the school, they choose what trade they want to study. For these students, the promise of learning concrete work skills that will enable them to find gainful employment is very appealing. Students enrolled in vocational education have the expectation that they will be employable or employed in their trade when they graduate. On the basis of the definition and goals of vocational education, a majority of graduates of a vocational program would be expected, in some way to make use of the vocational skills they have learned.

Discrepancy Between Documented Indicators
and Proposed Standards

Vocational education is designed to educate students in the skills and knowledge of a certain trade so they may enter the work force in that trade. Within a few years of graduation, a majority of Greater Stanton's graduates are not utilizing the vocational skills and knowledge they learned while in school. If the basic goal of vocational education is to prepare students to enter the work force in a specific trade, then clearly a problem exists. The low percentage of graduates who are actually working in their trade represents an enormous waste of time, effort, and resources on the part of both the students and the school system.

If graduates of the school were not choosing to enter their trade, but were still successful, then it could be said that the school is still meeting its goals. Unfortunately, this is not the case. Most graduates working outside of their trades are not utilizing the skills they learned in school. The majority of those who enroll in college not only are not using the vocational knowledge they learned in school, but also are at a serious disadvantage from an academic standpoint.

It would seem that graduating from a vocational school has not been advantageous for a vast majority of the graduates. In fact, for many, the vocational school experience becomes a handicap.

Summary

It is not unusual in our society for people to change careers a number of times over the course of their lifetime. It is also not unusual for high school students in the midst of adolescence to be constantly changing their career goals and aspirations. Therefore, it would be unrealistic to expect every graduate of a vocational school to be working in the trade for which they have been trained. Still, it seems that there must be other methods for teaching vocational skills and knowledge that prepare students for work, while providing them with academic skills in a way accounts for the dynamic nature of adolescence.

STAKEHOLDERS

Stakeholder 1: Superintendent-Director

Basis/Evidence of Interest.   The present Superintendent Director (SD) has held the position since 1991. Having taught and administered three other secondary vocational programs in Massachusetts, she clearly understands and endorses the basic tenets of vocational education, but she also recognizes the need for an adequate academic education. In her tenure as SD she has expanded the academic component at the expense of the vocational component. She has proposed plans for "block scheduling" academic subjects and for the "clustering" or consolidating shops that provide similar skills. Her primary concern at the moment is the low performance of Greater Stanton in the Massachusetts Educational Assessment Program (MEAP) in which the school has consistently placed at or near the bottom.

Power to Act on the Problem. The SD has the support of a majority of the school committee and therefore possesses a significant amount of power over this problem. In the past she has combined shops that taught similar skills and closed shops teaching skills that were no longer of value in the workplace. She also possesses the power to alter the scheduling scheme of the school to increase or decrease the time spent on academic subjects.

Level of Commitment to the Problem. Although the SD is aware of the problems that exist at Greater Stanton, her commitment to the solving of these problems is questionable. She is often away from the building and, therefore, unaware of the day-to-day activities. She rarely has any dealings with individual students and she does not have a great deal of support among the faculty. The general belief is that her career is more important than the education of the students. Still, what is good for the school will also be good for her career, so she does possess an interest in the problem.

Stakeholder 2: Principal

Basis/Evidence of Interest The school's principal has worked at the school for over 20 years. He is in his second year as principal. Before serving as principal, he held the title of academic coordinator. Before that, he spent many years as an English teacher. The principal is a well-educated man who clearly recognizes the value of an academic education, but who also acknowledges the positive characteristics of vocational education. He maintains ties with many of the school's graduates, so he is aware of the problems they face in the workplace and in furthering their education. He has often expressed frustration over the lack of "success" experienced by many of these graduates.

Power to Act on the Problem. The principal is a highly respected man amongst the students, faculty, and administration of the school. He also receives a great deal of support from the school committee and from the community. By the nature of his position, he does not have a great deal of power over administrative and policy decisions. His concerns have more to do with the day-to-day activities of the school and the health and welfare of the students. He primarily draws his power from his broad range of support. Being a very popular and charismatic man, he is able to effectively utilize the "bully pulpit" to influence the decision making process.

Level of Commitment to Problem. The principal is very much committed to the school and its students. He is very involved in the day-to-day operations of the school, maintaining a very visible presence. He consistently has put the education and well-being of the students first. Given his level of commitment to the students, he is also very committed to the solution to any problem that disadvantages them.

Stakeholder 3: Co-Op Coordinator

Basis/Evidence of Interest The role of the co-op coordinator is to find co-op jobs for eligible students. Needing to provide local businesses with qualified students who are willing to work, he maintains close ties with hundreds of local employers. These businesses often employ students each year, so it is important that the students be well qualified. The fact that so few of the students that he places in co-op positions end up working in that field is of great concern to him. The co-op coordinator also is responsible for tracking graduates of the school to determine the percentage of graduates who are employed in their trade. It is in his best interest to have a high percentage of graduates working in their field of study. He recognizes that the percentage of graduates doing so is too low. It is important to note that he spent many years as a shop teacher before becoming the co-op coordinator. He is committed to the theories of vocational education, but he recognizes that changes need to be made.

Power to Act on the Problem. The co-op coordinator possesses the power to place students in jobs in their trade. He not only finds employment for current students, but he is often contacted by businesses seeking graduates who are looking for full-time employment. The co-op coordinator serves as the primary liaison between the school and the business community served by the school. He has very little power in school-based policy decisions.

Level of Commitment to the Problem. The co-op coordinator expresses a great deal of concern about the low percentage of graduates employed in their trade. He recognizes this as a problem for himself, the school, and for vocational education as it exists at the school. He would like to see more students entering the work force in the trade for which they have been trained.

Stakeholder 4: Teachers

Basis/Evidence of Interest. Greater Stanton employs approximately 200 classroom, shop and related teachers. Shop and related teachers, those directly concerned with the vocational curriculum, constitute approximately 65% of the teaching staff. The existence of each shop is based on a demand in the community for the particular skills it teaches. In the past, specific shops have been closed or combined with other shops when there was no longer a demand for that particular trade. Vocational teachers are concerned not only with the preservation of their jobs, but they are also concerned about providing the local business community with qualified workers. These teachers, many of them graduates of vocational education programs themselves, believe in the value of a vocational education. Academic teachers recognize that the primary focus of the school is on the vocational curriculum, but they are also aware of the significant percentage of graduates who go on to further their education. Just as vocational teachers want to make sure that graduates possess the necessary skills to enter the work force, the academic teachers want to provide students with adequate academic preparation for further education.

Power to Act on the Problem.   Individually, teachers possess very little power to affect policy decisions, but collectively they are very powerful. Greater Stanton has a very active teachers' union that in the past has played a significant role in policy decisions.

Level of Commitment to Problem.   As expected with any large group of people, within the teaching staff there are varying degrees of commitment to this problem. It is tempting to believe in an ideal world where all teachers are committed to the well-being of their students. A cynic, however, would argue that the teachers are very committed to this problem simply as a matter of self-preservation. The reality is actually a combination of both beliefs.

HYPOTHESIZED CAUSES OF THE PROBLEM

Review of Possible Causes

There are several possible explanations for why this problem exists. These possible causes may be placed in two different categories: psychosocial issues and economic issues. The following discussion is a brief overview of the possible causes of the problem broken down categorically.

Psychosocial Issues

Are Students Developmentally Prepared?   In their first year at Greater Stanton Technical School students are placed in an "exploratory program" in which they are able to sample briefly six different shops. Students spend each of their first 6 shop weeks in a different shop. At the end of this exploratory period students are asked to choose their preferred shop. Those who have performed well usually will be placed in their first or second choice.

This entire process raises two significant questions. First, have the students adequately explored their career options by examining only six shops for 1 week each? In a span of 5 days is a student fully exposed to the knowledge and skills they will be taught and need for the next 3 years. Do they fully grasp the ramifications of the career path they are choosing? Are they made fully aware of the options that will be available to them when they graduate? Have they received adequate career education and guidance? In most cases, the answer to these questions would be no.

The second, overriding, question is this: are 14- or 15-year-old adolescents developmentally able to make career decisions? It is true that the concept of work plays a very important role during this period. Developing skills that are useful in the workplace can help adolescents make the difficult transition into adulthood by introducing them to the adult world associated with work (Mussen, Conger, Kagan, & Huston, 1979). There is a difference, however, between providing general work skills coupled with career education and providing vocational education in which students are taught trade-specific skills and knowledge. The former prepares students to work in a variety of trades, the latter to work in only one trade.

In preindustrial America this was not a concern. Most children grew up working with their families in the family business or trade. It was natural for them to continue in that line of work as an adult. The Industrial Revolution and the ensuing birth of big business changed this. Children today tend to be more detached from their parents' work and, therefore, less sure of their occupational identity.

According to developmental psychologist Erik Erikson, this struggle over occupational identity is the main problem for contemporary adolescents (Stern & Eichorn, 1989). Vocational education addresses this need for an occupational identity. Adolescents, especially those growing up in an inner city environment, have many important decisions to make about their lives. The opportunity to resolve their vocational concerns is very powerful. However the question remains as to whether 14- or 15-year-olds have developed enough occupational identity to choose their own occupations, or whether this decision is better put off until later in their development.

Why Do Students Enroll at Greater Stanton Technical School?

Another possible cause of the problem revolves around the reasons why students enroll in vocational programs. If the difficulties associated with developing an occupational identity are universal to adolescents, then why are some drawn to vocational training whereas others opt for academic training. In The Shopping Mall High School the authors observe:

> Even in the most selective programs, many voc/tech students are different from top-track students in one important respect: for them, school has not been a winning experience. They are students who have not really learned to cope. As a result, "social skills" or "survival skills" have to be emphasized—thus the rules of work and community life that top track students already know and largely respect. (Powell, Farrar, & Cohen, 1985, pp. 131–132)

Many of these students do not enroll in vocational education because they want to learn a specific trade. Rather, they lack the confidence in their ability and desire to succeed in an academic setting. Enrolling in a vocational school becomes "the easy way out."

Students who enroll at Greater Stanton Technical School tend to fall into this category, but there is another factor that influences their decision. Over 70% of Greater Stanton's student body reside in the city of Stanton. Students in the Stanton public schools have three options for high school: Greater Stanton Technical School, Stanton High School, or one of the local parochial or private schools. For most of these students, the cost of the latter is prohibitive. Many students who could go to Stanton High School choose not to because of safety concerns. The school is located in a densely populated area at the city's center. Crime and violence are commonplace in this neighborhood. The school and neighborhood are easily accessible to gangs and drug dealers. Greater Stanton Technical School, on the other hand, is located on the boundary between Stanton and a neighboring community. It is approximately one mile away from the nearest residential area. When asked why they chose to attend Greater Stanton Technical School instead of Stanton High School, most students will say that their parents would not send them to Stanton High or that they were afraid to go to Stanton High. The bottom line is that many students who choose to enroll at Greater Stanton Technical School are not doing so because of the vocational curriculum and the opportunity to learn a trade. They are doing so because it is the lesser of two evils.

How is Vocational Education Perceived?   Another possible cause of this problem is the negative perception many people hold of vocational education, which has a reputation of attracting students who are not able or willing to handle the academic work of a comprehensive high school. In general, potential employers do not see vocational high school programs as a prime source of skilled or even trainable workers. In fact, participation in a vocational education program often stigmatizes a worker in the eyes of a potential employer (Aring, 1993). Not only does this perception of vocational education exist in the community, but it also exists within the school itself. Teachers know that their students tend to be less motivated and weaker academically, so they tend to lower their expectations for them. Students, aware of the stigma associated with vocational education, suffer a self-fulfilling prophecy. They lower their own expectations for themselves based on the generally held belief that they are not as smart as their peers enrolled in an academic-oriented program. They also tend to lower their own vocational aspirations. Often they chose to learn the skills of a trade because they do not believe they can do any better.

Economic Issues

Are Good Jobs Available?   When it is seen that only 17% of Greater Stanton's graduates are employed in their trade of study, the first question that comes to mind concerns whether there is a demand in the community for these trades. Considering the number of students employed through the co-op program, it would appear that jobs are available to those who want them. Many students working in their trade still work for the business that employed them as a co-op student. Still, most students in the co-op program choose to leave their co-op job and their trade altogether. What then are the economic factors that influence a graduate's decision to leave his or her trade?

The most simplistic answer to this question is wages. The jobs may be available, but they do not pay enough for graduates to make a satisfactory living. In a survey conducted of 1996 graduates of Greater Stanton 3 months after graduation, the average salary for those still employed in their chosen trade was $6.75/hr. In comparison, a 1991 and 1992 survey of graduates of Massachusetts secondary vocational schools working in their trade reported an average wage also of $6.75/hr. In the same survey, graduates of postsecondary vocational education programs reported average wages in excess of $10/hr. Granted, these wages are primarily for entry level positions and would be expected to grow as time passes. Yet one could not classify a job paying $6.75/hr as a "good" job. Students who have spent 4 years learning the knowledge and skills associated with a specific trade expect that their investment will yield a good job. Given the low wages associated with working in their trade, it should not be surprising that many graduates opt to leave it for further education or for a different, more lucrative, occupation.

This discussion of wages raises deeper questions related to the changing economic structure and policies of this country and the role that education plays. Vocational education is predicated on the theory that skilled labor will always be in demand. This has not changed, nor, in all probability, will it ever change. The problem is centered around the theoretical relationship between economics and education in the context of a changing global economy.

THEORETICAL CAUSAL ANALYSIS

Human Capital Theory

One most effective method of analyzing the relationship between economics and education is through the use of human capital theory. The basic tenet of this theory is that people are a form of capital in which we invest. Decisions about how much and what kind of education to acquire, expenditures on health care, and occupational decisions are all placed in a maximizing framework. The essence of the theory is that the costs and benefits of these decisions are carefully weighed in a rational manner before decisions are made (Osterman, 1989). As is true with any investment, success is measured by the rate of return or the profit realized on the investment.

Education is considered to be an investment in people that will yield a return for the individual and for society. Because education provides individuals with skills and knowledge useful in the marketplace, it then follows that an increase in education results in an increase in personal income as well as in the productivity of people (Squires, 1979). Possessing a good education does not guarantee success, but it certainly helps. Besides the fact that possessing a wide range of knowledge and skills increases the range of occupational choices available to an individual, there is a direct correlation between education and income and an inverse relationship between education and unemployment (Becker, 1964). Not only does empirical evidence exist that education is related to future success, but education also has become one of society's basic values. From the earliest stages of their cognitive development, children are constantly reminded of the value of a good education by their parents, teachers, and society as a whole.

Human capital theory also serves as an economic theory for the analysis of occupational choice. In discussing Richard Freeman's (1971) work, *Market for College Trained Manpower,* Paul Osterman (1989) observed:

> The individual surveys the range of occupations and forms expectations about the future income streams of these occupations. From these expectations, he or she applies a discount rate and determines the present discounted value of each income stream. The individual also calculates the costs of acquiring the human capital necessary to enter the occupation and arrives at the net present value of each occupation. The individual then maximizes a utility function whose arguments are net present value, unearned income, and the nonpecuniary characteristics of each job. The occupation that maximizes the utility function becomes the occupational choice. (p. 253)

This analysis presupposes that an individual possesses the knowledge and skills needed to adequately analyze the job market and the range of options available. Obviously, the better the education a person has, the more options are available, and the clearer are the decisional costs and benefits.

Human capital theory is especially applicable to the problems faced by low-income workers. According to the theory, increasing the education level of this population has a number of benefits. Most importantly, additional education raises workers' skill levels, and thus, their incomes. Then, too, as low-income workers become more skilled, the supply of low-skilled workers declines, resulting, according to the laws of supply and demand, in an increase in the demand for low-skilled workers. Because they are now more in demand, low-skilled workers are able to command higher wages. Finally, as the supply of skilled workers increases, the demand for such workers declines resulting in a decline in their wages. The end result is that productivity increases and the distribution of income becomes more equal (Squires, 1979). Human capital theory gives credence to the belief that lower-class children will be able to work their way into the middle class through education. Given the population served by Greater Stanton Technical School, this aspect of human capital theory is especially relevant.

Human capital theory can also be applied to the choices faced by prospective employers. These employers must apply some form of measurement to evaluate job applicants. Obviously, experience and level of education would be two of the primary characteristics employers would examine. In evaluating the credentials of any applicant, an employer will not only determine whether the applicant is qualified for the job, but also the costs associated with training such an employee. In reference to this issue, Lester Thurow (1975) defined the concept of a "labor queue." This theory is based on the belief that a majority of the skills any worker will need are most likely learned on the job. Therefore, employers tend to rank potential employees in a labor queue and place the most educated and skilled at the top of the list. Those with few skills or low levels of education, and therefore the most expensive to train, are relegated to the bottom of the list. Applicants at the front of the queue are most likely to obtain the most desirable and best paying jobs. To ensure a spot near the front of the queue, workers must not only possess work experience and skills, but also an education that has provided them with the cognitive skills necessary to learn new skills.

Human Capital Theory and Vocational Education

Because vocational education has the dual goal of educating students and providing them with specific occupational skills, human capital theory can also be applied to many of its problems. Ideally, vocational education should help create human capital by providing students with the skills and knowledge necessary to evaluate their options. To fully understand the relationship between human capital theory and vocational education, this relationship must be examined in the context of the changing world economy.

Since the time that vocational education was created, there have been important changes in this country's and the world's economic structures. Perhaps the greatest influence on these changes has been the advent of computer technology, which has been a revolutionary development in the workplace. Computers have completely altered the way business is conducted.

On the production level, many production jobs are being taken over by computer-driven robotics. Workers not replaced by this technology find that their work increasingly relies on high-tech machinery requiring complicated skills to operate. At higher levels, the existence of computers has completely changed the areas of research, design, management, and communications. One result of this increasing reliance on computers in the workplace is the development of an "electronic text" in which the fundamental nature of work is shifted from action-oriented skills to intellectual skills (Zuboff, 1988). To be successful, businesses must not only be able to use this computer technology, but they also must be able to access and understand the wealth of information that is now available.

Related to the growth in computer technology is the continuing development of a global economy. In the past, the United States was the undisputed world economic leader when it came to industry, but times have changed. In *Education and Work: The Choices We Face*, Arthur Wirth (1993, p. 363) stated:

> American corporations that can no longer generate large earnings from the high-volume production of standard commodities are gradually turning toward serving the diverse special needs of customers dispersed around the globe....National corporations are being transformed into international corporations with offices and personnel located all over the world.

The development of this global economy is partially attributed to the continuing development of third world countries, but it also may be attributed to the development of computer technology. This technology, in the form of facsimile machines, telecommunication networks, and computer modems has enabled designers and engineers to exchange information at the push of a button.

These changes in the economic structure of the world have a profound effect on America's economic and educational systems. In the past, a well-skilled worker could earn a decent wage working in a factory, but those days are past. This is due in part to the shifting of many industries to third world countries where labor is cheaper, but it is also because of a shift in the economic structure of this country. The U.S. economy is shifting from a production-based economy to one that is service based. In fact, it is estimated that by the year 2,000 approximately 88% of the work force will be employed in the service sector (Wirth, 1992, p. 159). Although many of these jobs will be unskilled or semiskilled positions, many of the new jobs will be related to the continued growth of computers and technology. These jobs will require a variety of higher level thinking skills that a good education can provide. Not only will workers need knowledge and skills associated with new technologies, but they also will need to be capable of adapting to a fast-changing marketplace.

In *The Work of Nations: Preparing Ourselves for 21st Century Capitalism*, Robert Reich outlined the skills that he believed would be the vital skills for employment in the 21st century. Reich (1991) defined the following four skills as those of a "symbolic analyst":

- *Abstraction*: The ability to discover patterns and meanings and to examine reality from a variety of angles
- *System thinking*: The ability to see different parts and how they relate to each other and to the whole
- *Experimentation*: The ability to use observation and experimental techniques to analyze and solve problems
- *Collaboration:* The ability to work and communicate with a variety of people possessing different values and perspectives.

Although Reich prescribed the skills of a symbolic analyst for the 21st century, these skills are certainly valued now in the workplace today, yet it would be difficult to find a school whose curriculum includes these skills in its goals and objectives.

Reich's recommendations are similar those put forth by Richard J. Murnane, a professor of education, and Frank Levy, a professor of urban economics (Murnane & Levy, 1996). Murnane and Levy focused primarily on the skills that students will need as high school graduates if they are successfully to enter the work force at a decent wage. They define three basic sets of necessary abilities:

- Hard skills, such as basic mathematics and problem-solving skills
- Soft skills, such as the ability to communicate effectively, present topics, and collaborate with others
- Computer literacy.

Murnane and Levy argued that people must see themselves as economic free agents in a global marketplace (Warsh, 1996). In accord with the theories of human capital it must be recognized that a work force educated with these skills is an economic necessity.

Whether one subscribes to Reich's theories or to those of Murnane and Levy, it seems clear that the skills necessary to succeed in the changing marketplace must be taught in the public schools. These observations concerning the relationship between changes in the global economy and education have been the target of various contemporary reports related to education reform. For example, a recent publication of the Carnegie Forum on Education and the Economy entitled, *A Nation Prepared: Teachers for the 21st Century*, supported the restructuring of public education from a human capital theory perspective:

> In the future, high-wage level societies will be those whose economies are based on the use of a wide scale of very highly skilled workers, backed up by the most advanced technologies available....When [workers] are well educated, they more than pay for their high salaries by adding more to the value of the products they create and the services they offer than less skilled workers can possibly match. (DeYoung, 1989, p. 108)

The findings of this report provide further support for the growing relationship between human capital theory and education.

If the primary goal of vocational schools is to provide students with work skills, then it seems that they are the perfect forum for the inculcation of these skills. According to some sociologists, however, specific vocational and occupational training programs in secondary schools have proven inefficient in the formation of human capital (DeYoung, 1989, p. 142). The problem remains that vocational schools tend to teach narrow, job-specific skills when what is really needed is broad-based skills. This problem exists not only at Greater Stanton Technical School, but it may also be endemic to vocational education as it exists today. The problem at Greater Stanton Technical School is further complicated by the socioeconomic status of the students. The vocational education they are receiving is not adequately developing them as human capital, so many of them are unable to move out of poverty.

Summary of Causes

Four aspects of human capital theory relate to this problem as it exists at Greater Stanton Technical School. First is the notion that education is considered to be an investment in human capital. Most important, Greater Stanton's responsibility is to provide an adequate vocational and academic education to its students, who are not receiving the skills they need. Second is the use of human capital theory to explain how and why individuals make occupational decisions. Graduates of Greater Stanton Technical School are clearly weighing their options and choosing not to enter their trade. Third is the important relevance of human capital theory to the lower class and low-income workers. Most of Greater Stanton's students reside in a poor, depressed inner city environment. Finally, prospective employers use the labor queue to assess job applicants. Graduates of Greater Stanton Technical School lack the necessary skills to be in a good labor queue position.

It would be impossible to point to any one factor as the cause of this particular problem. Two, however, seem worth addressing. The first is the developmental issue surrounding the choice of a trade that students are forced to make. Having these students choose an occupational pathway at the age of 14 or 15 is too soon. Adolescents at this age do not possess enough knowledge or experience to make such a decision. The second concerns the development of human capital. Greater Stanton, and for that matter, most vocational schools, are not teaching the skills and knowledge students will need successfully to enter and maintain their places in the work force. At Greater Stanton, this is the case presently, but it is also a major concern for the entire system of secondary vocational education. Any proposals aimed at this problem should, at the very least, address the issues brought forth by these two causes.

POLICY RECOMMENDATIONS

In the past 20 years education reform has been a very hot topic on both the federal and state levels. Interestingly enough, most of the reports on what is wrong with our public schools and the ensuing proposals designed to fix them give only minimal attention to vocational education. The problem at Greater Stanton Technical School is a problem shared by many vocational schools. Certain characteristics in the nature of vocational education as it exists today contribute to this problem. Some attempts have been made to address these issues at different levels.

Problem Solutions Already Tried/Currently Being Tried

Perkins Act.   On the federal level the greatest effort aimed at solving many of the problems associated with vocational education culminated in September of 1990 with the passage of the Carl D. Perkins Vocational and Applied Technology Education Act of 1990. The new Perkins Act's main goal was to shift away from the traditional job-skills orientation of vocational education and toward the broader purpose of using vocational education as a vehicle for learning academic and other types of thinking skills (Wirt, 1991). This was to be accomplished by the following four changes:

1. *The integration of academic and vocational education:* The goal was to restructure the vocational education curriculum so that it helps students develop thinking skills associated with an academic education. One method for accomplishing this was to bring more academic content into the shop area either by a change in curriculum or the addition of academic teachers to shop areas.
2. *The federal government directing financial resources to those vocational schools where the needs for improvement was greatest:* Basically, vocational schools that served high proportions of poor families would be targeted to receive extra federal funds.
3. *A shift in power over the control of vocational education with power taken away from the state and given to the local districts.* This not only meant that the local district had more control over expenditure decisions, but also that these local districts had the power to initiate and implement their own individual reform measures aimed at their particular school population.
4. *A clear distinction made between secondary and postsecondary vocational education programs:* The goal was to recognize the value and popularity of postsecondary vocational education.

Whether the Perkins Act will be successful depends primarily on the implementation of its recommendations at the local level. The policies discussed here and the ensuing analysis of these policies are made possible because of the Perkins Act.

Integration.   One key piece of the Perkins Act designed specifically to address the problems associated with secondary vocational education was the call for the integration of vocational and academic curricula.

Currently, there is a very little cohesion between what is taught in the academic classroom and what is taught in shop. Integration of the two areas would provide students with a stronger academic background coupled with a better understanding of the skills and knowledge required in the workplace. Under an effective integration plan, vocational education would be used as an alternate method for teaching the academic concepts and skills that students in an academic program learn. This could prove beneficial to all students in three primary ways (Wirt, 1991):

- It would supply more context and motivation for the learning of higher order thinking skills than currently exists in schools.
- It would provide students with more opportunities to apply what they are learning to real-world settings.
- It would offer students a wider range of intellectual and work-related skills than they are currently receiving.

The movement toward integration is suited for meeting the long-term interests of both students and the labor market (Grubb, et al, 1991, p. 22). It directly addresses the issues associated with human capital theory elucidated by Reich and Levy and Murnane by teaching broad, academic-based skills and knowledge instead of job-specific skills.

To implement such a plan, vocational and academic teachers would work together creating and organizing courses and curricula designed to address the concerns of both. Ideally, students deciding to pursue further education would receive a stronger academic education, whereas those opting to enter the work force would be equipped with the cognitive and work skills they will need to acquire a good job.

Greater Stanton implemented a pilot integration project 3 years ago. One shop and four academic teachers, one each from the special education, mathematics, English and social studies departments, were selected to participate. The academic and shop teachers collaborated to develop an integrated curriculum that would meet the needs of both. The students spent their regular time in shop, but during their academic week they were placed in their own academic classes where the academic curriculum was directly related to the skills and knowledge the students were utilizing in shop.

Exploratory Program.   Approximately 4 years ago, Greater Stanton Technical School began an exploratory program for the school's freshmen. This program was born out of the recognition that students were not prepared to choose a shop when they first enrolled at the school. Often during the first few months of school students would be dissatisfied with the shop they had chosen. These students would either transfer to a different shop or to a different school. Frequently, students who switched shops also had to change their academic schedules to allow for their related classes. This constant movement in and out of shops and classes created a great deal of strain on teachers, the guidance department, and the schedulers.

The exploratory program allows students to sample different shops before making a final choice. At the beginning of the school year, freshmen go on a "mini-exploratory" tour of all the shops they can select. Once they have been introduced to all of the shops, they select six shops they want to explore further. For the first two terms of their freshman year they spend each of their shop weeks in a different shop. As students pass from shop to shop, each shop teacher keeps a record of the students' performance in the shop. At the end of the 6-week cycle students are asked to rank, in order of preference, their choice for a shop. On the basis of students' preferences, their performance in a given shop, and teacher recommendations, the guidance department then places students in appropriate shops.

Clustering.   A second vocational education reform that has been discussed is that of "clustering." The general idea behind clustering is that different shops tend to have a common curriculum of general skills and knowledge that can be applied in a variety of work settings. By clustering these shops together, focus can be placed on general skills and knowledge rather than the very specific trade knowledge. Clustering also incorporates some of the theories and practices associated with integration. Academic teachers are assigned to a particular cluster of shops in which they teach the academic knowledge associated with that particular cluster of shops.

In the past, Greater Stanton Technical School has applied some principles associated with clustering by combining shops that teach similar skills.

Table 12.5 illustrates the number of shops that existed in 1976 compared with 1996. The difference between 1976 and 1996 is that there has been some clustering of similar shops. Two examples are Data Management, created as a combination of the Business Records & Machines with clerical shops and Food Technology & Hospitality, a combination of Child Study, Clothing & Modeling, and Home Management. These combinations were not created as a result of a particular mandate or policy aimed at improving vocational education. They were created over a period of time due a combination of changes in the job market and a recognition of the overlap of certain shops.

Recently, there has been some discussion at Greater Stanton Technical School concerning the further clustering of shops. Although there is not a concrete plan in existence yet a sample clustering is illustrated in Table 12.6.

This is just a rough outline of how a cluster plan at Greater Stanton might appear. The idea behind these categories is the grouping of shops that teach the same or similar skills. Focus would then be placed on general skills and knowledge associated with that particular cluster. Once students master those, they would move on to more specialized skills.

New Problem Solutions

The following three new problem solutions programs build on many of the theories behind the solutions that have already been tried. These new solutions have two unifying factors that seem to be missing from previous attempts:

TABLE 12.5

A Comparison of Shops at Greater Stanton Technical School
1976–1996

Shops in 1976	Shops in 1996
Air conditioning/refrigeration	Allied health
Autobody	Autobody
Automotive	Automotive
Business records & machines	CAD/machine/drafting
Carpentry	Carpentry
Child study	Construction & painting
Clothing & modeling	Cosmetology
Commercial art	Culinary arts
Cosmetology	Distributive education
Culinary arts	Data management
Clerical	Electrical
Distributive education	Electronics
Drafting	Food technology & hospitality
Electrical	Graphic communications
Electronics	Industrial electronics
Heavy equipment	Metal fabrication
Home health	Plumbing
Home management	
Machine	
Metal fabrication	
Multimedia	
Painting & decorating	
Plant maintenance	
Plumbing & pipefitting	
Radio & TV	
Upholstery	

TABLE 12.6

Greater Stanton Technical School:
Possible Shop Clusters

Cluster	Shops
Building trades	Carpentry, construction & painting, electrical, metal fabrication, plumbing
Communications & technology	CAD/machine/drafting, data management, electronics, graphic communications, industrial electronics
Interpersonal trades	Allied health, cosmetology, food technology & hospitality
Service/business trades	Autobody, automotive, culinary arts, distributive education

162

1. They recognize the growing need for academic skills on the part of graduates and the growing desire for academic skills on the part of employers. Providing students with these skills increases their value as human capital.
2. They postpone the vocational career decision students now face too early until they have been more thoroughly educated about all of their options.

Freshman Exploratory/Career Education Program.   One problem of Greater Stanton's existing exploratory program is that students are able to explore only six shops for a brief period of time. If students opt to enroll in a vocational school with a shop in mind, the time permitted to sample each shop seems too short. Such students have not had the opportunity to understand all of their options.

An alternate method for accomplishing the goals of the exploratory program is to eliminate the concept of shop week for freshmen. Instead of alternating between shop week and academic week, freshmen would be enrolled solely in academic classes. One of these classes would be a course in career education. At the end of their freshman year, students would choose their shop. Such a program would have a number of positive effects:

- It increases awareness of careers and career paths. Students would receive broad education about the various shops in the school and an opportunity to sample the shops that interest them most.
- It addresses the developmental issues associated with vocational identity. By waiting until the end of their freshman year students will have a better understanding about the world of work and their place in it.
- Increased time is spent in academic classes allowing the school to emphasize need for both academic knowledge and problem-solving skills. This not only addresses the growing need for these skills in the workplace, but it also closes the existing gap between time spent in academics and that spent in shop.

2+2/3 Program.   This program would carry the theories behind the Freshman Exploratory/Career Education Program one step further. Students would spend their first 2 years entirely in academic classes. At the same time, they would continue to receive career education and an opportunity to sample different shops. At the end of the 2 years students would enroll in the shop they have chosen. For these 2 years the alternating week structure would remain intact, but because students have already completed much of their academic course work, a greater emphasis could be placed on the related class by having it meet three or four times per day instead of the current twice per day. Again, this program recognizes the increasing need for academic skills and the problems associated with vocational development.

At the end of their 4 years students would receive both a high school diploma and a certificate denoting proficiency in their trade. If they so desire, students would have the opportunity to spend one more year at the school solely for further shop training and education. This part of the program would be akin to a postsecondary vocational education program. It recognizes the growing need for skills and knowledge associated with a specific trade beyond what is taught in high school.

Academic Track. This plan could be adopted as an additional feature to either of the two plans that have already been offered. This proposal is aimed at students who have changed their minds and decided that they want to go on to further education. These students would have the option of entering an academic track in which they would be enrolled in only academic, college preparatory courses. Given that a high percentage of Greater Stanton's graduates go on to further education, the addition of an academic track would better prepare these students to do so.

ANALYSIS AND EVALUATION
OF PROPOSED POLICIES

A number of issues must be examined when analyzing and evaluating any policy recommendations. Primarily, any recommendations must satisfactorily address the two primary causes of the problem. First, the new policy must deal with the developmental issue. Students either must be better educated about their career options or the decision on which career path to take must be postponed. Second, any new policy must recognize the contribution that vocational education can make to the development of human capital. This means that vocational education programs must forgo much of the traditional trade-specific knowledge in favor of computer, thinking, problem-solving, and communication skills.

Any proposal that calls for an added emphasis on academic education at the expense of vocational education will create a further problem. Although there is a great deal of cooperation between shop and academic teachers, each group clearly has its own agenda. Academic teachers are products primarily of academic programs. In most cases, they believe that a strong academic education is more important than vocational training. Shop teachers, many of whom are products of vocational education programs, tend to be staunch supporters of vocational education. Although the teaching staff as a group is a stakeholder in this problem, its members will not always agree on the same solution. Academic teachers, in general, would favor an increase in the time students spend in academic courses. Shop teachers, of course, would oppose any such measure, but would support an increase in the time students spend in shop or related. Any solution must be acceptable to both groups.

Integration

Although it is too soon to fully evaluate the integration program at Greater Stanton Technical School, a number of problems have already arisen. The main problem is that integration does not address the developmental concern of forcing adolescents to decide on a career path before they are ready. Proponents will counter with the argument that the students in the integration program will be better prepared academically, so they will be better prepared to change careers. The evidence, however, does not support this assertion. Students who have transferred out of a shop involved in the integration project into another shop are also taken out of the academic classes associated with their former shop. Experience has shown that these students are behind their peers who have not participated in the integration project. These students spent so much time learning academic knowledge associated with their shop that they were unable to keep up with the standard academic curriculum.

On such a small scale, it does not appear that integration will be successful. For success, everybody in a particular school must be committed to its implementation. Teachers with varying backgrounds must be willing and able to work cooperatively at developing a fully integrated curriculum. True integration requires nothing less than a full restructuring of high schools (Rosenstock, 1991).

Exploratory Program

Many problems associated with the exploratory program have already been indicated. Although it is a small step in the right direction, the exploratory program does not address the two primary causes of the problem. Students are still forced to make a decision on what trade they want to learn well before they are developmentally prepared to do so. This program also does nothing to address the need for more academic skills. If it does not address the causes of the problem, it is an unsatisfactory solution.

Clustering

The theories behind clustering have a great deal of merit. The basic premise for teaching general skills and knowledge rather than trade-specific skills and knowledge does address the two primary causes of the problem. By enrolling in a cluster of shops instead of a specific shop, students have more time to evaluate different vocational paths before making a decision on which to follow. By learning more general knowledge and skills, the value of graduates in the work place increases.

The problem associated with clustering is that it calls for a major restructuring of the vocational school's component. Currently, each of the 17 shops operates as a separate entity with a department chair and a number of shop teachers. One or more members of this group also serve as the related teacher for the shop. Each shop, with the approval of the administration, has power over decisions concerning curriculum and expenditures for that particular shop. Each shop maintains a variety of ties with the business community. These networks often provide equipment and supplies for the shop, and they provide avenues for graduates or students seeking employment as co-op students. Many of the ties that make up these networks have had a long-standing relationship with the school. Some are graduates of the school who have established their own businesses in the community.

To cluster a number of these shops together would require a drastic shift in the power structure. Instead of individual shops having control, the power would need to rest in the form of a cluster chairperson. This would mean that many department chairs and shop teachers would be forced to relinquish much of the power that they now possess. This would not be an easy task. Thus there likely would be a great deal of resistance to a proposal such as this from those who would stand to lose power. As with integration, an effective clustering program would require a full restructuring of the school.

Freshman Exploratory/Career Education Program

Implementing this policy would require the least amount of restructuring while still addressing the causes of the problem. With its extra career education, this option provides students a better understanding of their career options and the ramifications that their shop decision will have. An argument can be made that these students still are not adequately developed to make such a decision, but it is an improvement over the current system. As an additional benefit of this program, students would spend more of their freshman year in academic classes in which their academic deficiencies can be addressed.

Unfortunately, this extra time in academic content areas is not significant when the entire secondary high school experience is considered. Alone, this policy will not solve the problem, but it would help, and it would be simple to implement.

2+2/3 Program

A 2 + 2/3 policy clearly addresses the causes of the problem. In their first 2 years students will receive ample career education and counseling to enable them to make an informed choice of careers. There is still no guarantee that students will stay in the career they choose, but at least they will be making an informed choice when the time comes to choose a shop. The additional time spent in academic classes will provide students with the additional academic preparation necessary either to continue their education or to be competitive in the job market.

The problem with this solution is that it again calls for a significant restructuring of the school. Eliminating the vocational component portion of the first 2 years creates a number of potential problems. First, there will be a greater need for classroom space and teachers. Currently, there is a shortage of classroom space at Greater Stanton Technical School, but there are plans to enlarge the school building. If this construction does occur, it will provide the necessary classroom space. The need for additional classroom teachers is more problematic. Hiring more classroom teachers depends on finding the funds to pay their salaries.

Academic Track

The establishment of an academic track would enable students to forgo all vocational training in favor of academic courses. The academic track would aim to prepare students for college. Students in the academic track would go to classes every day just as they would in a comprehensive high school. The concept of an academic track would work best in conjunction with some form of exploratory program. Students would still have the opportunity to try different shops and receive career education. After doing so, they would make the choice between enrolling in a specific shop to learn a trade or entering the academic track.

This proposal adequately addresses the possible causes of this problem. Students would not be forced to choose a career path before they are ready. They would have an opportunity to explore different shops without being forced to make a choice. If students opted to enroll in the academic track, they would receive a stronger academic background. If they decided to go on to college they would be adequately prepared. If they chose to enter the work force they would possess the academic skills that increasingly are of value. Students in the academic track would have the opportunity to take electives in different shops enabling them to gain valuable work skills and experience. This plan also addresses the dilemma of school choice that faces many of Greater Stanton's students. Those students who wanted an academic education, but did not want to go to the local high school, could enroll in the academic track at Greater Stanton Technical School.

The problem with the institution of an academic track revolves around the basic mission of the school. Purists and vocational educators would argue that students enroll in a vocational school to learn a trade. Students wishing an academic education are free at any time to leave Greater Stanton and enroll in the local comprehensive high school. Many students who change their minds do this, but is it necessary, and is it in the best interest of the student to be forced to transfer to another school?

A possible compromise would be to institute an academic track only for seniors. At this point, most students have decided whether they want to go on to college or work in their trade. Those who planned to go on to college, and whose academic performance was satisfactory, could forgo their senior year of shop and the co-op program in favor of a concentration of academic courses designed to prepare them for college.

RECOMMENDATIONS DIRECTED
TO STAKEHOLDERS

The principal, the vocational coordinator, and the teachers at Greater Stanton do not possess very much power over large-scale policy decisions. They do, however, possess a great deal of power to initiate projects on their own. The following are recommendations directed at these stakeholders.

Teachers

- Academic teachers need to make their curriculum more relevant, providing connections between what they are teaching in class and what students will need in the workplace.
- Shop teachers must integrate more academic skills and knowledge into the shop curriculum.
- Shop teachers must acknowledge the growing value of academic skills over vocational skills and begin to emphasize the importance of the former.
- In the absence of any formal integration project, shop and academic teachers must create curriculum units that use the theories of integration.
- Shops can take it on themselves to cluster shop students together when common skills are being taught.
- All teachers must encourage students to continue their education beyond high school.

Vocational Coordinator

The vocational coordinator should:

- Discuss with local businesses the skills that will be needed, and make recommendations based on his or her findings.
- Bring representatives in from local businesses and industry to discuss the future needs of workers in the workplace. These presentations should be directed at teachers and students.
- Develop a formal clustering plan for shops that teach similar skills.
- Interview graduates to determine what skills and knowledge have proven to be of value to them working in their trade.
- Create partnerships and collaboratives between local businesses and the school.
- Evaluate the vocational curriculum to determine what skills and knowledge are outdated.

Principal

The principal should:

- Create committees to study the advantages and disadvantages of the existing integration and exploratory programs.
- Form committees to evaluate new proposals including the Freshman Exploratory/Career Education Program, the 2+2/3 Program, and the Academic Track.

- Provide in-service education programs for teachers on integration, clustering, and the Perkins Act.
- Allocate planning time for groups of teachers to create integrated curriculum units.
- Provide in-service education on the changes in the economy and its relevance to education.
- Present a new image of the school to the public. Instead of a focus on individual shops, emphasis should be placed on the general skills and knowledge that will be of value in the future workplace.

Although these stakeholders do not have the ability to institute large-scale policy decisions, they do have the power to influence the decisions of the superintendent-director. Most of the power to implement any policy change at Greater Stanton must meet with the approval of the SD. The following recommendations are directed solely at the SD.

Superintendent-Director

The SD should:

- Provide funding for in-service education and training programs for teachers related to integration, clustering, economic changes, and the Perkins Act.
- Allocate extra funds for small scale integration projects.
- Institute the Freshman Exploration/Career Education Program.
- Create an academic track for seniors planning to go on to college.
- Maintain a more visible presence among teachers and students in both the academic classrooms and the shops.

BROAD STRATEGIC POLICY RECOMMENDATIONS

The two aspects of the Perkins act of 1990 that will greatly assist Greater Stanton Technical School are the section that gives individual vocational schools more autonomy concerning policy issues and decisions and the section that provides additional funds for schools serving poor families. At Greater Stanton Technical School, most of the power to dictate policy is held by the SD, who must recognize the complex relationship between the socioeconomic population served by the school, the changing global economy, and the need for higher ordered academic skills in the workplace.

It is clear that a problem exists and that this problem cannot be solved with minor changes. Greater Stanton Technical School must make up its mind that it recognizes the changing needs of the population it serves and that it is willing to do whatever it takes to solve its problems. If this means that the entire school needs to be restructured, then that is what must be done. Although this would not be a popular course of action, it is clearly what is needed.

SUMMARY AND FINAL RECOMMENDATIONS

Vocational education has always played an important role in the educational process. It will continue to do so, but it must begin to adapt to change. Instead of teaching trade-specific skills to prepare graduates to work in a specific vocation, it must begin to give graduates broad-based academic, thinking, and problem-solving skills that will be applicable to a variety of occupational and educational settings. Instead of preparing students for an occupation, it must begin to prepare workers, people who are prepared for a variety of occupations.

Many of the problems associated with vocational education at Greater Stanton Technical School can be identified. Currently, Greater Stanton is not meeting many of the goals of vocational education, but has the potential to become a model for other vocational education programs. To do this, however, those with the power to make or influence policy decisions, must consider the possibility of a complete restructuring of the school. If this does not occur, the problems at the school will continue to go unresolved.

13

The Implementation of the Massachusetts Education Reform Act of 1993 at the New England School for Special Students*

Joseph Robert Dolan

PART I: EXECUTIVE SUMMARY

Problem Statement

The Common Core of Learning and the Curriculum Frameworks outline academic standards and expectations for all students attending public schools in the Commonwealth of Massachusetts. Teachers and administrators are under pressure from the state department of education to redesign their curricula to include the knowledge and skills standards outlined in these documents. In addition, professional development activities should be tied to the elements of the curriculum frameworks, and schools are required to concentrate 990 hr of school time on instruction in the core academic subjects.

The problem facing teachers and administrators of the New England School for Special Students (NESSS) is that there is a gap between the standards of the profession as defined by the Massachusetts Education Reform Act of 1993 and the practices of the NESSS educational program. NESSS students follow a highly individualized educational program because they have severe physical and cognitive limitations. Teachers and administrators of NESSS are attempting to solve this problem and maintain the integrity of their academic program.

---

*This chapter was originally submitted as a term paper for the Advanced Policy Seminar, Department of Administration, Training and Policy Studies, School of Education, Boston University, December, 1996. Names have been altered to protect the identities of the school and key participants.

Causes of the Problem

Using a conceptual framework designed by James Q. Wilson (1989), the researcher has found that NESSS teachers and administrators define their essential tasks on the basis of several factors, and this definition of tasks reinforces the policy gap. The unpredictable behavior of the student population, the prior experiences of NESSS teachers, the professional norms of special education teachers, the mandates outlined in the Chapter 766 special education regulations, the undefined and broad goals of NESSS, and an organizational culture that places the physical health and mental well-being of students ahead of academic standards reinforce the policy gap described in Table 13.4.

Policy Recommendations

This policy gap could be remedied if NESSS medical staff and faculty worked together to create an NESSS common core of learning and a set of curriculum frameworks for each academic program. A curriculum framework for the medical program also could be established. The professional standards defined by the Massachusetts Education Reform Act would guide NESSS in the creation of these documents, allowing NESSS to meet the individual needs of its students.

PART II: THE PROBLEM

General Description and Historical Background

The Massachusetts Common Core of Learning and the Massachusetts Curriculum Frameworks outline academic standards and expectations for all students attending public schools in the Commonwealth. Teachers and administrators are under pressure from the state department of education to redesign their curricula to include the knowledge and skill standards outlined in these documents. Schools are held accountable for student learning on the basis of an evaluation system that is closely tied to the Frameworks' learning goals. According to the Massachusetts Department of Education (1994a), this evaluation system will be "a much more comprehensive approach [to assessment] including portfolio evaluation, performance tasks, and other more authentic assessment techniques" (p. 14). In addition, professional development activities should be tied to the elements of the Common Core of Learning and the Curriculum Frameworks, and schools are required to concentrate 990 hr of school time to instruction in the core academic subjects during a 180-day school year.

The problem facing the NESSS teachers and administrators is that there is a "gap" between the standards of the profession as defined by the Massachusetts Education Reform Act, and the practices of the NESSS educational program. NESSS students follow an academic program different from that of a traditional public school. This program is highly individualized because of the student population's special needs. The description of the problem and its indicators are outlined in a later section. The purposes of this section are to describe the school and to place this problem in a broader historical context.

The New England School for Special Students

The New England School for Special Students (NESSS) offers educational and medical services to students with severe handicapping conditions. The rehabilitative needs of the children under care include cerebral palsy, muscular dystrophy, spina bifida, trauma-based disability, and other congenital or physically debilitating disorders. Children matriculate at the school to receive the medical care and individualized education that public schools cannot provide because, in general, public schools in the Commonwealth do not have the faculty expertise, medical services and expertise, and facility accessibility that NESSS provides its students. NESSS is also attractive to parents and their children because the school's educational environment encourages age-appropriate social experiences and extracurricular activities. In contrast, public school students with severe special needs often spend nonschool hours in unhealthy isolation at home; this behavior is especially common with public high school students who are often shunned by their peers. NESSS students participate in student government activities, athletic events, and yearly musical concerts and recitals in order to build healthy social relationships.

Historical Context of the Problem (1954–1983)

Students with special needs have struggled along with other so-called minority groups to gain greater access to public education in the United States (Martin, 1979). Historically, special-needs children were excluded from public schools because it was believed that they did not have the cognitive abilities to be educated in regular classroom settings. As Martin (1979) wrote:

> Most states allowed the exclusion of handicapped children if they were deemed incapable of benefiting from a program of public instruction. One reason for this was undoubtedly discriminatory—schools did not want to be bothered with children who were different. A ruling of the Wisconsin Supreme court (Beattie v. State Board of Education) revealed this feeling when it allowed the exclusion of a cerebral palsied child because of "his depressing and nauseating effect on teachers and school children...[because] he required an undue portion of the teacher's time." (p. 12)

Over the last 50 years, federal and state laws and various court decisions have provided special-needs students with greater access to public schooling. Specifically, the cases of Brown v. the Board of Education, and the Pennsylvania Association for Retarded Children (PARC) v. Commonwealth of Pennsylvania; and the passage of Education for All Handicapped Children Act of 1975 by Congress provided handicapped children greater access to public schools.

In 1954, the Supreme Court ruled in Brown v. the Board of Education of Topeka that separate public schools for White and African American children were unconstitutional as this practice violated the Fourteenth Amendment's equal protection of the laws mandate (Ducat & Chase, 1988). Chief Justice Earl Warren, in his majority opinion, stated:

> Today, education is perhaps the most important function of state and local governments. Compulsory school attendance laws and the great expenditures for education both demonstrate our recognition of the importance of education to our democratic society. It is required in the performance of our most basic public responsibilities, even service in the armed forces. It is the very foundation of good citizenship. Today it is the principal instrument in awakening the child to cultural values, in preparing him for later professional training, and in helping him to adjust normally to his environment. In these days, it is doubtful that any child may reasonably be expected to succeed in life if he is denied the opportunity of education. Such an opportunity where the state has undertaken to provide it, is a right guaranteed to all on equal terms....(Ducat & Chase, 1988, p. 642)

Advocates for children with special needs saw this constitutional principle as extending to handicapped children. Thus the Fourteenth Amendment could be used to force state and local governments to provide special-needs students with a free and appropriate public education (Martin, 1979). In 1971, PARC brought suit against the Commonwealth of Pennsylvania because mentally retarded children were denied admission to public school programs. The Pennsylvania federal district court ruled that it was unconstitutional for handicapped children to be excluded from public schooling, and schools needed to provide special services to these children so that they could receive a free, appropriate public education. Martin (1979) quoted a passage from the federal district court's ruling:

> Expert testimony in this action indicates that all mentally retarded persons as capable of benefiting from a program of education and training; that the greatest number of retarded persons, given such education and training, are capable of achieving self-sufficiency, and the remaining few, with such education and training, are capable of achieving some degree of self-care; that the earlier such education and training begins, the more thoroughly and the more efficiently a mentally retarded person can benefit at any point in his life and development from a program of education and training. (p. 14)

These events led Congress to pass into law the Education for All Handicapped Children Act (PL 94–142) in 1975. This law defines the processes and procedures by which children with special needs are educated in public school settings. Three important provisions protect the educational rights of special needs students:

The Individual Education Program (IEP).　　Each student who is diagnosed as in need of special education must have an IEP developed by a team of educators and medical specialists (Cushner, McClelland, & Safford, 1992). An IEP documents the nature of the student's special need, the goals for student learning, the teaching methodology appropriate for the student's learning style, the special equipment required for learning, and the evaluation methods that will be used to assess student progress.

Procedural Due Process. Students cannot be labeled as in need of special services unless the school has (a) notified parents of the child's special need as determined by the teachers who work with the child, (b) provided documentation of the student's special need on the basis of a nonbiased assessment mechanism and, (c) received parental permission to place the student in a special education program (Cushner, McClelland, & Safford, 1992).

The Least Restrictive Environment. Students with special needs must be educated in settings that allow for contact, integration, and co-learning with students who are not handicapped (Cushner, McClelland, & Safford, 1992). Special-needs students cannot be isolated from their peers in public school settings because they are in need of the services outlined in the IEP.

Historical Context of the Problem (1983–1996)

Since the late 1970s and early 1980s, educators and elected officials have become increasingly interested in improving the overall "quality" of education that children receive in public schools, rather than expanding the civil and educational rights of low-status groups. This trend is influenced by important changes in the American economy such as the end of cold war era military expenditures, the increasing competitiveness and globalization of the economy, and the pervasiveness of communication technologies in the private sector (Drucker, 1994; Reich, 1992; Toch, 1991).

In response to economic and social changes, educators and elected officials advocate standards-based educational reforms. Educational standards define the knowledge and intellectual skills that all children should have and be able to demonstrate regardless of where they attend school (Furhman, 1993; Gagnon, 1995). Furhman (1993) explained the elements and purposes of standards-based reforms (or systemic reforms) this way:

> The first is the establishment of ambitious outcome expectations for all students, including specification of the knowledge and skills to be expected for every student. Standards would be set at a high level, requiring deep understanding of subject matter and sophisticated reasoning ability. The second is the coordination of key policies in support of ambitious outcome expectations, which would be reflected in curriculum frameworks that lay out important topics and understandings. Student assessment, instructional materials, teacher licensing, and staff development would all be tied to the frameworks. In that manner, key policies would send coherent messages about instruction....Third, the governance system would be restructured to support high achievement by according schools more flexibility in meeting the needs of their students. (p. 2)

Advocates of standards-based, systemic reforms also argue that because American children do not follow as rigorous an academic program as do students in

Germany, Japan, or France, the competitiveness of American industries is threatened in the global marketplace. Gagnon (1995), a French historian and professor of education at Boston University, spoke to this issue:

> In 1991, in two school systems at opposite ends of the earth, about two-thirds of the corresponding Japanese and French age groups completed markedly more-demanding academic programs, which included foreign languages. In both countries about half the students were in programs combining technical and liberal education. Even disregarding foreign languages, relatively few of our young people graduate from academic programs that are as rigorous as those abroad. For fully equivalent programs, a generous estimate of American completion would be 15%—about a quarter of the French and Japanese completion rate....To our shame, a disadvantaged child has a better chance for an equal and rigorous education, and whatever advancement it may bring, in Paris or Copenhagen than in one of our big cities. (p. 67)

Perhaps the standards movement began in 1983 with the publication of *A Nation at Risk* (1983/1995) by the National Commission on Excellence in Education. The authors of this report warned that the quality of American education was "being eroded by a rising tide of mediocrity that threatens our very future as a Nation and a people" (p. 396). Furthermore, "[i]f an unfriendly foreign power had attempted to impose on America the mediocre educational performance that exists today, we might well have viewed it as an act of war" (p. 396). The commission used strong and direct language to bring attention to the perceived failings of public education, and to build political support for reform. Toch (1991) explained:

> The powerful language of *A Nation at Risk*, its brevity, its alarming message, as well as the prestige of a number of its authors and the fact that they wrote with the imprimatur of the federal government, focused national attention on public education like no other single event since the Soviet Union's launching of Sputnik in 1957. The response to the report was so great that within ten months of its release 150,000 copies had been distributed by the U.S. Department of Education, another 70,000 had been purchased through the Government Printing Office, and several million additional copies and extended excerpts were estimated to be in circulation through reprints in the general and professional press. (p. 15)

The National Commission on Excellence in Education (1983/1995) found, among other things, that (a) the academic demands required of students had declined since the 1960s as "[t]he proportion of students taking a general program of study [had] increased from 12% in 1964 to 42% in 1979" (pp. 397–398); (b) students were afforded a high degree of choice in curriculum offerings that resulted in less enrollment in the core academic courses, especially math and science; (c) schools in the U.S. spent approximately 6 hr a day on instruction in a 180-day school year as compared to 8 hr a day on instruction in a 220-day school year in other industrialized countries; (d) school textbooks were "written down" by their publishers to ever lower reading levels in response to perceived market demands (p. 399); and (e) the expectations for the level of knowledge and abilities students needed to demonstrate to graduate from high school were low. In the end, the commission recommended, in part, that (a) all high school students enroll in a program consisting of 4 years of English, 3 years of math, 3 years of science, 3 years of social studies, 2 years of foreign language for the college bound, and ½ year of computer science; (b) the school day and the school year be extended; and (c) colleges and universities "adopt more rigorous and measurable standards, and higher expectations, for academic performance and student conduct" (pp. 401–402).

The Commission based its conclusions on data collected at the state and national levels, but this high degree of aggregation makes it difficult to understand the causes of this problem. Beginning in the early 1980s, Powell (1985/1995), and Sizer (1986), among others, reasoned that the organization of public schooling contributed to the low academic standards for learning and poor student performance.

Powell argued that the organization of the typical high school academic program is analogous to that of a "shopping mall." The shopping mall high school is a place where students select programs that fit their individual tastes and desires. These programs also vary in academic quality and expectations for student learning. Students with so-called "average" abilities can pass through a high school program and graduate without having learned intellectually challenging content. Powell (1985/1995) observed:

> The shopping mall high school defines its responsibilities primarily as offering vast opportunities. Learning is there for the taking and is not undervalued. But learning is just another consumer choice, which may or may not be selected. Students can browse, or even stand back from the products of most educational shops, without penalty. The school will press itself to offer opportunity but will not press students to choose wisely among its offerings or to engage deeply with any of them....Students who do not want to learn, or who do not know what they want, can pass through quietly and graduate. (p. 178)

Further, Powell argued that, in the shopping mall high school, average students are not pushed by teachers to achieve at high levels. Teachers focus on building self-esteem in students instead of setting high standards for achievement.

Sizer (1986) also believed that high school academic programs were seriously flawed, but he believed that raising academic standards would not improve student learning unless programs were fundamentally restructured. He based his conclusion on the following observations: (a) secondary school curricula stressed the acquisition of broad, unconnected content that did not allow for students' mastery of subject matter, (b) students were not challenged to think and reason on a high level, and they did not have to demonstrate real competence in learning tasks to graduate; and (c) instructional pedagogy relied on teacher as deliverer of information, which contributed to dry and boring teaching of content.

In addition, Sizer (1986) argued that the organization of the school day, the length of the school year, and the instructional load of teachers needed to be changed. He illuminated this point by describing the dilemma of Horace Scott, a fictitious high school English teacher:

Most jobs in the real world have a gap between what would be nice and what is possible. One adjusts. The tragedy for many high school teachers is that the gap is a chasm, not crossed by reasonable and judicious adjustments. Even after adroit accommodations and devastating compromises—only *five minutes per week* of attention on the written work of each student and an average of ten minutes of planning for each fifty-odd-minute class—the task is already crushing, in reality a sixty-hour work week. For this, Horace is paid a wage enjoyed by age-mates in semiskilled and low pressure blue-collar jobs and by novices, twenty-five years his junior, in some other white collar professions. Furthermore, none of these sixty plus hours is spent replenishing his own academic capital. That has to be done in addition, perhaps in the summer. However, he needs to earn more money then, and there is no pay for upgrading his teachers' skills. He has to take on tutoring work or increase his involvement at the liquor store. (p. 20)

For Sizer, the solution to this problem would be the creation of the essential school based on the nine common principles outlined at the end of *Horace's Compromise.*

Ten years after the publication of *A Nation at Risk*, the Massachusetts state legislature passed the Massachusetts Educational Reform Act of 1993. According to Robert Antonucci (1995), this act is the most ambitious educational reform initiative in the history of this state. It is seen as fundamental to restructuring this state's educational system to improve the academic performance of all students.

Summary

The purpose of this overview was to show how educational policies have changed from the *Brown* decision to the present. Educators and elected officials have shifted their attention from expanding the civil rights of low-status groups to raising the academic standards for all students. It is within this context, that NESSS teachers and administrators are aware of the problem.

Explanation of the Importance of the Problem

An examination of this problem is important for two reasons. First, the Massachusetts Common Core of Learning and the Curriculum Frameworks represent the most ambitious and comprehensive education reform initiatives in the history of this state. This study is an example of how one school is struggling to change familiar educational practices in order to embrace these new standards. Ultimately, educational reform can be successful only if teachers and administrators change their educational practices at the school level to incorporate the standards and expectations of the Common Core of Learning and the Curriculum Frameworks. If schools do not implement these standards, educational reform will fail to meet its objectives. This will have a detrimental effect on the quality of life for individuals and communities in this state as well as on the health and vitality of this democracy in the long term.

Second, this study is an example of how low status groups are affected by standards-based reforms. As shown in this chapter, raising academic standards places low-status groups in a highly disadvantaged position because they need extra care, resources, and remediation to reach the new standards for learning. This problem raises important questions about how much responsibility elected officials have to mandate opportunity to learn standards for the poor and special-needs students who are severely at a disadvantage. At this time, policy-makers in this state apparently have not considered this issue.

Who Is Disadvantaged by the Developing Situation, and How Does This Problem Affect Other Important Problems?

The gap between the standards of the profession and the design of the NESSS academic program places NESSS students, teachers and administrators, and parents at a disadvantage. The problem under consideration also affects other important educational problems.

Students.   First, NESSS students are the most disadvantaged by the developing situation. The standards in the Common Core of Learning and the Curriculum Frameworks require that students learn a high degree of knowledge and skills at a very fast pace. NESSS students, however, have a variety of physical and cognitive limitations that determine the amount of information that can be learned and the pace at which content can be taught. In general, NESSS students because of their limitations cannot learn content at the same pace or in the same way as other so called "regular" students. These special students need extra time and special adaptations in order to learn well, but even when these accommodations are made, learning, for them, is an extremely slow process.

The slow pace of student learning may affect the performance of these students on the state assessment test. In Massachusetts, all students will be required to pass the state examination to graduate from high school. This test will be administered in 10th and 12th grades, and students who do not pass this test will not be able to graduate from high school. This form of high-stakes testing places NESSS students in a disadvantaged situation. If the students do not learn the knowledge and skills outlined in the Curriculum Frameworks—due to their physical and cognitive limitations—they will fail the state assessment. This means they will not graduate from high school and will need to attend NESSS until they can graduate. This situation is also problematic because students can attend NESSS only until the age of 22 years because state financial support is discontinued at that time. Students who have not passed the exam by age 22 will need to seek help from other social service agencies to receive a high school diploma. In the end, if NESSS students do not receive a high school diploma, they will not attend college nor hold a solid vocational job in the community. As these opportunities become limited, students will depend more on federal and state aid for existence. This behavior will greatly affect their ability to live happy, productive lives.

Because the Curriculum Frameworks are designed so that the knowledge and skills to be learned are acquired over a lifetime in school, NESSS students are at a disadvantage. These students often come from a variety of school districts with education programs that vary in quality. This is especially true for the high school students who enter NESSS as teenagers. Some students simply are better prepared to learn the knowledge and skills outlined in the Curriculum Frameworks than others. The teachers and administrators must fill in the gaps in students' learning created by diverse school experiences so that they can pass the state assessment test.

Teachers and Administrators. Second, NESSS teachers and administrators also are disadvantaged by the developing situation. Systemic reforms are designed to hold teachers and administrators accountable for the extent to which students learn at high levels. This determination is based on how well students perform on the state examination. If NESSS students do poorly on the state test, this will reflect on the teachers' and administrators' level of professionalism, which could have important consequences for this group.

First, William Weld, the present state governor, wishes to privatize NESSS services to reduce the size of the executive branch's administrative structure. He may see low student performance as a justification for privatizing NESSS. However, many of the school's teachers and administrators believe that this public institution can protect the civil and educational rights of the students better than a private institution driven by profit.

Second, poor student performance on the state examination may justify limiting teachers' pay. If teachers are perceived as not doing their job well, the state department of education may not authorize pay raises. This is particularly important because the teachers who work for the state department of education have not had a pay raise in 5 years; this trend could continue if students do poorly on the state test.

Finally, the existence of high standards for student learning and high-stakes testing places pressure on teachers to fill in the knowledge and skills gaps in their own education. Many teachers may have to contribute out-of-pocket funds to increase their own knowledge because the school does not compensate teachers for non-school-sponsored professional development activities.

Parents. Finally, parents, too, are disadvantaged by the developing situation. Many NESSS parents are from modest educational and socioeconomic backgrounds and have selected NESSS because it has a reputation of providing a high standard of care and education at a moderate cost. These parents place a high degree of trust in this institution to educate their children to live happy, productive, and independent lives. If students do poorly on the state assessment test, then parents will lose their faith in the institution. This loss of trust may lead to high degrees of cynicism about the competence of the teachers. Parents may also feel a need to enroll their children in high-cost, private institutions that they cannot afford. This move may facilitate financial instability for these families.

Description and Documentation of the Problem

The Problem

The problem facing NESSS teachers and administrators is that there is a gap between the standards and expectations of the Massachusetts Education Reform Act of 1993 as outlined in the Curriculum Frameworks, the Common Core of Learning, and the accountability procedures built into the law and the design of the NESSS academic program. NESSS teachers and administrators are struggling with ways to comply with the standards outlined in the law while maintaining the integrity of the institution.

Proposed Standard for Comparison

The Massachusetts Education Reform Act of 1993 is the professional standard that all schools in the Commonwealth must follow. The Common Core of Learning outlines the essential knowledge and skills that all students should know and be able to demonstrate. The elements of the Common Core have been translated into curriculum frameworks for the content areas of math, science, English, social studies, technology, health, and the visual and performing arts. The knowledge and skills outlined in the Common Core are categorized into three broad areas: thinking and communication, gaining and applying knowledge, and working and contributing. These three areas are subdivided into essential knowledge and skills domains for each broad area of the common core. Tables 13.1, 13.2, and 13.3 describe the

TABLE 13.1

Elements of the Common Core of Learning

Thinking and Communicating	
Read, write and communicate effectively	*Define, analyze and solve complex problems*
• Read and listen critically for information, understanding and enjoyment.	• Make careful observations and ask pertinent questions.
• Write and speak clearly, factually, persuasively, and creatively in standard English.	• Seek, select, organize, and present information from a variety of sources.
• Distinguish fact from opinion; identify stereotyping and recognize bias.	• Analyze, interpret, and evaluate information.
• Read, write, and converse in at least one language in addition to English.	• Develop, test, and evaluate possible solutions.
Use mathematics, the arts, computers, and other technologies effectively	• Develop and present conclusions through speaking, writing, art, and other means of expression.
• Apply mathematical skills to interpret information and solve problems.	
• Use the arts to explore and express ideas, feelings, and beliefs.	
• Use computers and other technologies to obtain, organize, and communicate information and to solve problems.	

Note. Source: Massachusetts Department of Education (1994b, pp. 3–4).

TABLE 13.2

Elements of the Common Core of Learning

Gaining and Applying Knowledge

Acquire, integrate, and apply knowledge in the core academic areas of
- Literature and language
- Social studies, history, and geography
- Mathematics, science, and technology
- Visual and performing arts; health.

Note. Source: Massachusetts Department of Education (1994b, pp. 3–4).

TABLE 13.3

Elements of the Common Core of Learning

Working and Contributing	
Study and work effectively	*Demonstrate personal, social, and civic responsibility*
• Set goals and achieve them by organizing time, work space, and resources effectively.	• Accept responsibility for one's own behavior and actions.
• Monitor progress and learn from both success and mistakes.	• Know career options and the academic and occupational requirements needed for employment and economic independence.
• Manage money, balancing competing priorities and interests, and allocate time among study, work, and recreation.	• Treat others with respect and understand similarities and differences among people.
• Work both independently and in groups.	• Learn to resolve disagreements, reduce conflict, and prevent violence.
• Work hard, persevere, and act with integrity.	• Participate in meaningful community and/or school activities.
	• Understand the individual's rights, responsibilities and roles in the community, state, and nation.
	• Understand how the principles of democracy, equality, freedom, law, and justice evolve and work in society.
	• Analyze, develop, and act on informed opinions about current economic, environmental, political, and social issues affecting Massachusetts, the United States, and the world.

Note. Source: Massachusetts Department of Education (1994b, pp. 3–4).

elements of the Common Core of Learning. In addition, the Massachusetts Education Reform Act mandates that schools concentrate 990 hr of school time to instruction during a 180 day school year (this is about 5.5 hr of instruction per day) and that professional development activities be closely linked to the elements of the knowledge and skills standards. Table 13.4 juxtaposes the elements of this standard with the practices of the NESSS educational program.

TABLE 13.4

A Comparison Between the Elements of the Massachusetts Education Reform Act
and the Elements of the New England School for Special Students' Academic Program

Massachusetts Education Reform Act	NESSS Academic Program
The Common Core of Learning states that all students should be able to:	NESSS students vary in cognitive abilities and academic skills based on nature of individual special needs.
• *Think and communicate* by reading, writing, and communicating effectively, using mathematics, the arts, computers, and other technologies effectively, and defining and solving complex problems.	Highly individualized educational program (IEP) outlines the knowledge and skills each student should know and be able to demonstrate on the basis of his/her special need.
• *Gain and apply knowledge* by acquiring, integrating, and applying essential knowledge in the core academic areas of literature and language, math, science, technology, visual and performing arts, and health.	
• *Work and contribute* by studying and working effectively, and by demonstrating personal, social and civic responsibility.	
Curriculum Frameworks outline the knowledge and skills all students should know and be able to demonstrate in the core academic areas of math, science, English, social studies, technology, foreign language, and visual and performing arts.	The academic program does not follow a standardized curriculum. No documentation exists that explains the design of the academic program.
State assessment mechanism evaluates the extent to which all students have learned the knowledge and skills outlined in the Curriculum Frameworks.	Highly individualized assessment mechanisms are used by teachers and administrators based on the student's special need.
Student assessment is conducted in 4th, 8th, and 12th grades.	NESSS does not have a traditional grade structure. Age-appropriate school activity is based on individual special need and cognitive skill. Students are sorted into a cluster system based on individual special need.
There are 990 hr of instructional time in a school year. This time is about 5.5 hr of instructional time per day over a 180-day school year.	School time is divided between instructional time in the classroom, and medical attention in the hospital component.
Professional development is based on acquiring the knowledge and skills to teach the knowledge and skills outlined in the Curriculum Frameworks.	Professional development is based on acquiring the knowledge and skills to teach students with severe special needs.

Rationale.   This standard is selected as the basis of comparison for four reasons. First, it represents what many educators believe to be the elements of a high-quality academic program. Good academic programs have clear, explicit standards and expectations for all students, and are intellectually coherent.

Second, this standard represents what many educators believe to be the elements of high-quality professional practice. Educators engaged in good professional practices evaluate the substance, quality, and relevance of their academic programs on a continual basis. They question the premises on which the academic program is based; they reinforce good practice; and they update and change practices that are obsolete. In this way, organizational members are in the process of continuous improvement rather than relying on tradition or unexamined habits to guide professional activities.

Third, this standard is selected because the NESSS academic program will be evaluated on the basis of this standard, so the school's administrators and teachers are faced with the task of implementing it in the school. NESSS is a subordinate unit within the Massachusetts Department of Education's bureaucratic structure. Thus there is more direct pressure on NESSS to adhere to this standard than there is on public schools, which are not directly administered by the state.

Finally, this standard represents what elected officials believe schools must do to improve the quality of the workforce in a technological economy. The Massachusetts Board of Education (1995) made this point:

> Unfortunately, the successes of our public education system have not kept pace with the changes occurring in our society. The simple fact is that the education system Massachusetts pioneered over a hundred years ago is no longer preparing the majority of our citizens for the challenges that they will face in the emerging information age. By the end of the century as many as 85% of the jobs will require higher order thinking skills while fewer than 50% of the population currently exhibits such skills. The 50% who lack these skills will be forced to compete for the 15% of unskilled jobs in a dangerous game of musical chairs in which both employers and employees are guaranteed to lose out.
>
> To make matters worse, over the last twenty years, as the economy increasingly demands high-skilled workers, educators have consistently reported a decline in students' readiness to learn. Inadequate family support, pervasive violence, television induced passivity, and other societal problems contribute challenging new factors to an overwhelmed education system.
>
> The Massachusetts Education Reform Act provides the Commonwealth with the opportunity to move back into the vanguard of educational excellence. Passed in June 1993 after more than two years of vigorous debate by business, education and community leaders, the Act lays the foundation for a fundamental change in the way our public education system operates by establishing clear standards of accountability with expectations for
>
> • All students to achieve high standards;
> • All educators to exhibit professionalism;
> • All schools to continuously improve; and
> • All communities and the state to provide schools with consistent, equitable support. (pp. 1–2)

Important Values Reflected in This Standard.

Three important values are reflected in this standard. First, it reflects the prevailing value that schools play a role in maintaining the health and vitality of the nation's economy through the sorting and training of the workforce (Spring, 1996). As Spring noted: "[T]he most important arguments given for the support of public schooling are that education increases national wealth and advances technological development" (p. 18). In the same way, Reich (1992) argued that, in the technological society, individuals are under increasing pressure to learn the analytical skills necessary for manipulating complex information in the workplace. For Reich, this means that schools must prepare students to think analytically and to solve problems. He justified his position this way:

> We are living through a transformation that will rearrange the politics and economics of the coming century. There will be no national corporations, no national industries. There will no longer be national economies, at least as we have come to understand the concept. All that will remain rooted within national borders are the people who comprise a nation. Each nation's primary assets will be its citizens' skills and insights. Each nation's primary political task will be to cope with the centrifugal forces of the global economy which tear at the ties binding citizens together—bestowing ever greater wealth on the most skilled and insightful, while consigning the less skilled to a declining standard of living. (p. 3)

Second, public schools serve the important social functions of maintaining social order, "improving social conditions, and reducing social tensions caused by economic equalities" (Spring, 1996, p. 12). Glenn (1987), in his study of the history of common school in the United States and Europe, found that Horace Mann wanted to create a public school system in Massachusetts in order to reconcile social differences created by the increasing diversity of American society caused by immigration. As Glenn observed, "The term [the common school] refers...to a program of educational reform, indeed of social reform through education. The heart of this program, which we will call 'the common school agenda,' is the deliberate effort to create in the entire youth of a nation common attitudes, loyalties, and values and to do so under the central direction by the state" (p. 4).

Finally, this standard is a statement of what the state believes individuals need to learn if they are going to pursue individual notions of the good life. For example, the skills of critical thinking, problem solving, hard work, civic and social involvement, and respect for self and others are seen in this standard. In this way, elected officials and educators outline the habits of mind and qualities of character necessary for individual happiness and the maintenance of this democracy. These leaders are not assuming a neutral position as to what constitutes a good and happy life: A notion of the good is outlined in the Common Core of Learning and the Curriculum Frameworks.

Alternative Standard

Public law 94-142 is the alternative standard of comparison in this analysis. This law states that: (a) all students are entitled to an individualized educational program, (b) all students are educated in the least restrictive environment, and (c) all students are guaranteed procedural due process rights.

Rationale.   For more than 20 years this standard has been the cornerstone of educational practice for special education teachers and, by law, NESS must adhere to this standard in its practices. NESSS is in full compliance with this standard. First, each student has an individualized educational program (IEP) as determined by the professional planning team. Second, NESSS offers the least restrictive environment for students: The facility is designed with automatic doors for easy access to the building, wide hallways to allow movement of students in wheelchairs, and classrooms equipped with computers that allow for student learning. Finally, all students are guaranteed procedural due process rights as the Professional Planning Team (PPT) meets with parents at least once a year to discuss student progress in the academic program.

Important Values Reflected in This Standard.   A fundamental principle of U.S. democracy is that all individuals, regardless of their status in society, should have an equal chance to pursue a fulfilling, happy life. This pursuit begins with a high-quality public education and, as Justice Earl Warren stated, it should be afforded to all on equal terms. Spring (1996) noted:

> America's democratic ideology has promised equal opportunity for all citizens. Equality of opportunity means that all members of society are given equal chances to enter any occupation or social class. It does not mean that everyone will have equal incomes or equal status; rather, all have an equal chance to compete for any place in society. Ideally, equality of opportunity should result in a social system in which all members occupy their particular position as a result of merit and not as a result of family wealth, heredity, or special cultural advantages. (p. 81)

Public law 94–142 is intended to guarantee equal access to public schooling so that students learn the skills and knowledge necessary to pursue their own notions of the good life. In this way, equality of educational opportunity is extended to students with severe special needs by requiring that school systems adhere to a strict set of procedural requirements.

There are two problems with this standard. First, following procedural guidelines alone does not ensure that students will learn the habits of mind and qualities of character necessary for them to earn their place in this society. In some cases, as accommodations are made for students on the basis of PL 94–142, expectations for what they can do are diminished. This is especially problematic for students with severe special needs because their physical limitations can lead teachers to place substandard academic demands on them in the name of accommodating for individual differences.

Second, this standard, as a procedural guideline, does not address the larger issue of how to ensure that all students are exposed to high-quality academic programs, regardless of where they attend school. Regular education students and students with severe special needs cannot pursue democratic opportunities if they have not had a high-quality public education. In the end, NESSS must balance two important standards—the Massachusetts Education Reform Act and PL. 94–142—so that the students have procedural guarantees as well as exposure to a rigorous, coherent academic program.

Problem Indicators

A discrepancy exists between the standards established by the Massachusetts Education Reform Act and the design of the NESSS educational program. This problem places students, teachers and administrators, and parents at a disadvantage and contributes to other educational problems. The policy gap is illuminated by comparing the elements of the Massachusetts Education Reform Act of 1993 and the practices of the NESSS educational program.

Comparison Between the Standards Established by the Massachusetts Education Reform Act and the Elements of the New England School for Special Students' Academic Program.   The Massachusetts Common Core of Learning and the Curriculum Frameworks define the knowledge and skills that all students should know and be able to demonstrate. In addition, the Massachusetts Education Reform Law requires that all schools in the Commonwealth devote approximately 5.5 hr per day to instructional time so that students can learn the knowledge and skills mandated in the essential content areas of math, science, English, social studies, technology, and foreign language, and the performing and visual arts. Professional development and student assessment should be closely tied to the Curriculum Frameworks. Teachers and administrators will be held accountable for student achievement based on the results of the assessment mechanism designed by the state. Table 13.4 describes the elements of the Massachusetts Education Reform Act.

Table 13.4 also describes the elements of the NESSS academic program, which is organized in a way that is very different from the program of a traditional public school. Each student has an IEP, which is mandated by PL 94–142. The IEP outlines in a very specific way the nature and severity of the student's special need, the goals for the student's learning, the student's learning style, the appropriate instructional methodology to meet the prescribed learning goals, and the necessary assessment mechanism to evaluate the student's learning.

In addition, NESSS does not follow a traditional grade structure as do public schools. The school is divided into elementary and secondary components, but students follow a sequence of learning based on the IEP rather than a knowledge and skills sequence determined by individual grade levels. This is not to suggest that all students at NESSS do not learn age-appropriate or grade-appropriate content, but that the nature and the complexity of the content learned is determined by the severity of the student's special need.

In the secondary school, students are divided into three distinct clusters. Cluster A is for students whose cognitive abilities function below an elementary school level. These students receive a vocational education and will move to a residential setting after graduation because of their level of cognitive abilities. Cluster B functions as an academic program. Students learn both academic subjects and vocational skills that will allow them to attend institutions of higher education after graduation or enter the world of work. Cluster C students have cognitive abilities that function on an elementary school level. These students receive a vocational education and functional academic skills that will allow them to perform simple work tasks. They may work in the community after graduation.

In general, the NESSS academic program is characterized by a high degree of individualized instruction and knowledge acquisition as well as a high degree of medical care. Students split time between medical care and instruction. This means that the amount of classroom time is limited compared to that of a traditional public school. Professional development is often based on those activities that will improve the faculty's and staff's ability to teach students with severe special needs.

Presentation of Stakeholders

Positive stakeholders are defined as individuals or groups that are aware of the problem and will work to see its resolution. Negative stakeholders are individuals or groups that are also aware of the problem, but may resist efforts to solve the problem. There are four positive stakeholders and one negative stakeholder in this problem.

Positive Stakeholder 1: Allen Cameron, Chief Administrator, Educational Services in Institutional Settings (ESIS)

ESIS, a unit of the Massachusetts Department of Education's administrative structure, provides educational services for students who live in facilities under the control of the Massachusetts Department of Mental Health, Public Health, and Youth Services, and the County Houses of Correction. NESSS is a subunit of the ESIS organizational framework. Allen Cameron has over 20 years of experience working in ESIS. He is well informed on the trends and changes in educational policies in Massachusetts, and is working with Commissioner Antonucci to define how the new educational standards will apply to students educated in ESIS schools. He is also very influential in determining the kinds of resources NESSS will receive in order to implement the standards of the Massachusetts Education Reform Act.

In August 1996, Cameron conducted a summer institute on educational reform. There, he informed NESSS teachers and administrators that the new standards will apply to NESSS students. Cameron encouraged faculty and administrators to support the mandates of education reform and to implement the standards of the profession in their programs He also pledged his efforts to gain resources to help NESSS update its academic program.

Positive Stakeholder 2: Carol Kaplan, Principal of NESSS

Carol Kaplan has been a special educator for the past 20 years. Most of her experience has been working with students in ESIS schools, so she understands the needs and dispositions of students with unusual physical and cognitive limitations. Carol attended the summer institute in August of 1996. She supports education reform, and she has pledged her efforts to update the academic program to meet the new standards. She has a strong working relationship with Allen Cameron, and she understands the processes and procedures that should be followed to gain the resources necessary to implement reforms. In addition, Carol understands the dynamics involved in creating changes to educational programs because she has often worked with other teachers and administrators during her career to improve programs for special needs-students.

Positive Stakeholder 3: Dr. Margaret Reilly, Executive Director, Potentials Inc.

Dr. Reilly is the former principal of NESSS. In 1996 she became the director of a nonprofit organization that works closely with the NESSS Board of Directors to gain grants from private and governmental foundations in order to provide educational programming and services for NESSS students. Dr. Reilly is aware of the problem as she has attended many seminars and professional development activities in which standards-based reforms have been discussed. As former principal, she understands the design of the NESSS educational program, the needs of NESSS students, the professional norms that guide the behavior of NESSS teachers, and the procedures needed to implement reform. She also has a strong working relationship with Cameron and Kaplan. In the end, Reilly's strength is her ability to work with the Board of Directors to gain the support and resources necessary to implement reforms at NESSS.

Positive Stakeholder 4: Claretta di Stefano, NESSS Faculty Member

Claretta di Stefano has been a faculty member at NESSS for 10 years. She attended the summer institute in August of 1996, and she has worked with Carol Kaplan to design a plan to update the NESSS academic program to meet the new standards. Claretta recently finished a Certificate of Advanced Graduate Study at Harvard University in educational administration, so she is well informed about standards of the Massachusetts Education Reform Act. She has a very positive working relationship with Carol Kaplan and Margaret Reilly, and she is highly respected by both the faculty and students. Her positive relationship with members of the faculty makes her very influential in building support for reform with faculty members.

Negative Stakeholder 1: Mr. Raymond Scott, parent

Raymond Scott is a parent of a student at NESSS. He also works for the Massachusetts Department of Education. On various occasions, Mr. Scott has been an outspoken critic of attempts on the part of the state to make the new professional standards apply to students with special needs. His point of view is very persuasive because many parents and teachers are afraid that common standards will place some students in a highly disadvantaged position. Mr. Scott has spoken to Reilly about this issue in the past. As a member of the Department of Education he is well informed on the state and federal regulations that apply to special-needs students. As a parent of an NESSS student, he understands the design and purposes of the school's academic program. He could work to undermine efforts on the part of Cameron, Reilly, Kaplan, and di Stefano to implement the standards of the profession.

PART III: AN EXAMINATION
OF THE PROBLEM CAUSES

Theoretical Perspectives on the Problem Causes

Possible Causes of the Problem and Possible Conceptual Frameworks for Analysis

The purposes of this section are to (a) speculate, in an informal way, on the possible causes of the problem described in Table 13.4 and (b) propose three conceptual frameworks that may be useful for determining the causes of this problem. In this section, the conceptual frameworks and the causes of the problem are considered in a broad and incomplete way. This discussion is a preliminary step to the analysis outlined in a later section of this chapter.

First, a conceptual framework developed by Lawrence and Lorsch (1967) may be helpful in illuminating the causes of this problem. They argued that effective and efficient organizations have units that are highly differentiated yet highly integrated within the organization. *Differentiation* is defined as "the state of segmentation of the organizational system into subsystems, each of which tends to develop particular attributes posed by its relevant external subenvironments" (p. 4). *Integration* is defined as "the process of achieving unity of effort among various subsystems in the accomplishment of the organization's task" (p. 4). Lawrence and Lorsch insisted that subunits must be correctly aligned with demands of their subenvironments, and that subunits must create structures that respond to these demands. Further, they saw it as essential that the organization develop integrative devices to help the subunits work together in accomplishing the goals of the organization.

To make a causal analysis based on Lawrence and Lorsch's model, the researcher would seek out information about how the academic and medical programs at the school perform their functions relative to the demands of their sub-environments. Perhaps he or she would need to know how these functions have changed as a result of shifts, over time, in the school's sociopolitical environment. Also, the researcher would need to know the extent to which the academic and medical components are integrated. It is difficult for the organization to implement the standards of the Common Core of Learning and the Curriculum Frameworks if the organization has not achieved a unity of effort among the various programs.

NESSS has altered its educational practices and organizational designs in response to changes in its larger sociopolitical environment. Founded in 1907 by Dr. Edward H. Bradford, NESSS was the first school in the Commonwealth to provide medical services and educational instruction for students with severe special needs. In early years, the school served students with primarily physical limitations, and its educational program resembled that of a traditional public school.

As medical technology eliminated physical disabilities such as polio and tuberculosis, and federal and state laws were developed to protect the educational rights of special needs students, the NESSS student population changed. The new student population had both physical and cognitive limitations. Therefore, the school's academic program became more individualized and nontraditional in design. The medical program also offered more complex medical and rehabilitative services to students.

Following the ideas of Lawrence and Lorsch (1967), the changes described in the NESSS student body and the associated changes in its educational and medical component have created an organization that is highly differentiated. The individual academic components are responding to very particular and dissimilar demands in their relative subenvironments causing the academic program to be incoherent. Furthermore, the academic and medical components are also responding to very particular and dissimilar demands in their relative subenvironments. This high degree of differentiation makes it difficult for the organization to achieve the integration necessary for implementing the standards of the Massachusetts Education Reform Act.

Second, the conceptual framework developed by Wilensky (1967) would be helpful in illuminating the causes of the problem. Wilensky argued that for an administrative leader to make good decisions that will allow the organization to operate efficiently and effectively, she or he needs high-quality intelligence. Wilensky defined intelligence as "the problem of gathering, processing, interpreting, and communicating technical and political information needed in the decision-making process" (p. 1). He contended that administrative leaders often receive vague, distorted, or incomplete information, which can lead to inappropriate decisions.

Therefore, administrative leaders need to develop good intelligence-gathering mechanisms in order to receive high-quality information.

NESSS teachers and administrators may not be receiving the information needed to implement the standards of the Common Core of Learning and the Curriculum Frameworks. To make this analysis, the researcher would seek out data concerning both the quality and quantity of information that teachers and administrators are receiving from external intelligence sources. Also, he or she would need to know the extent to which this information informs the daily practices of NESSS teachers and administrators.

The Massachusetts Department of Education (1995) offered suggestions to show how schools can change their academic programs to incorporate the standards of the Common Core of Learning, and the Curriculum Frameworks. This information shows how traditional public schools can update their practices. Because NESSS is not a traditional public school, this information, in varying degrees, is not useful to its teachers and administrators.

Moreover, this document is full of vague language, undefined terms, and educational jargon (Delattre, 1996). Vignettes of how teachers are incorporating the knowledge and skill standards in their classrooms are utilized instead of clear, practical suggestions that all teachers in all kinds of schools can utilized to update their programs. NESSS is also receiving conflicting information based on the public statements of Dr. John Silber, Chairman of the Massachusetts Board of Education. Dr. Silber openly criticizes the standards in the Common Core of Learning and the Curriculum Frameworks. In fact, he has ordered that the curriculum frameworks for English and social studies be rewritten to include what he believes are clear, measurable, substantive intellectual standards. In the end, intelligence that is vague, incomplete, contradictory, and not practical does not allow NESSS to update its practices.

Third, a conceptual model developed by Wilson (1989) may be helpful in illuminating the causes of the problem. Wilson (1989) argued that the behavior of individuals in organizations is determined by incentives not directly controlled by the organization's owners. The circumstances in which individuals work, the beliefs they bring to their job, the political interests in an organization's environment, and the culture of the organization determine, in varying degrees, the way that individuals define the essential tasks of their job. Thus, the researcher would seek out information about how NESSS teachers and administrators define their essential tasks (i.e., the procedures that should be followed to fulfill the job requirements of being a teacher).

School teaching is not an activity that can be easily supervised, coordinated, and routinized. In general, teachers often determine the tasks of their job on the basis of powerful professional norms and the needs and behaviors of their students. For example, because all NESSS teachers are special educators, they follow practices and procedures (i.e., the IEP) particular to that profession. Also, their students have severe physical and cognitive handicapping conditions, so the teachers and administrators develop formal practices and individual habits that serve students' needs.

The conceptual models developed by Lawrence and Lorsch (1967) and Wilensky (1969) are useful in illuminating the causes of the problem, but they are not selected for use in this study. It appears that NESSS is characterized by high degrees of differentiation and low degrees of integration. The school is also receiving low-quality information from its primary intelligence source. These types of analyses are useful, but they do not provide insight into why teachers and administrators create these designs or how they respond to the information provided to them. Formal structures arise because individuals design them to meet the needs of their job. In this way, organizations are deliberately created by individuals. Therefore, the conceptual model designed by Wilson (1989) is particularly useful for understanding the causes of the problem because it provides a conceptual framework showing how individuals behave in an organization. The next section provides an additional rationale for selecting Wilson's analytical model.

A Discussion of the Problem Causes

Wilson's Bureaucratic Model Selected for Analysis

The problem facing NESSS teachers and administrators is that there is a gap between the standards and expectations of the Massachusetts Education Reform Act of 1993 as outlined by the Curriculum Frameworks, the Common Core of Learning, and the accountability procedures built into the law and the current practices of the NESSS academic program. The causes of this problem are illuminated using the elements of an analytical model developed by the political scientist, James Q. Wilson (1989).

Rationale. Wilson's model is selected for two reasons. First, it is a theoretical framework of how public (or government) bureaucracies operate and why public policies are implemented (or not) in government agencies. This observation is important because many organizational theories can be applied to either private or public organizations, but Wilson's model is concerned only with how government bureaucracies behave. For Wilson (1989), "a government agency is a monopoly provider of some service and is supported by a legislative appropriation that is paid for by taxes extracted from citizens who may or may not benefit from that agency" (p. 33). Government agencies are not profit driven. They have goals that serve the public interest, and they are governed by political institutions that respond to public demands. In this way, government agencies have organizational characteristics and tendencies different from those of private sector organizations.

Second, Wilson believed that public policies cannot achieve their objectives unless elected officials understand how situational imperatives, individual beliefs, organized political interests, and organizational culture influence the work of individuals in public organizations. Further, as Wilson (1989) observed:

> There are two ways to look at government agencies: from the top down and from the bottom up. Most books, and almost all elected officials, tend to take the first view. The academic perspective, much influenced by Max Weber (and lately by economic theories of the firm), typically centers on the structure, purposes, and resources of the organization. The political perspective draws attention to the identity, beliefs, and decisions of the top officials of the agency. These are important matters, but the emphasis given to them has caused us to lose sight of what government agencies do and how the doing of it is related to attaining goals or satisfying clients. (p. 11)

> By looking at bureaucracies from the bottom up, we can assess the extent to which their management systems and administrative arrangements are well or poorly suited to the tasks the agencies actually perform. (p. 12)

Thus analyzing the causes of the problem with Wilson's model illuminates how the habits and characteristics of individuals in street-level units may contribute to causing the problem under consideration. In addition, this model is appropriate for the following reasons: (a) NESSS is a street-level, public institution; (b) the school is managed by a state agency; (c) the school serves an important public function; and (d) NESSS is governed by a political institution that is very responsive to public demands and organized interests.

Elements of Wilson's Theory

Overview

This section is an overview of Wilson's conceptual model. The next section defines the terms of the model and applies these concepts to NESSS. For Wilson (1989), understanding the way in which operators (i.e., rank and file employees or, in this case, NESSS teachers and administrators) define their essential tasks is important for understanding how public agencies operate. Simply stated, essential tasks are the procedures that operators follow to accomplish the functions of their jobs.

Consider Fig. 13.1. The chart reads from top to bottom with the relationships between the elements shown by arrows. According to Wilson, when the organization's goals are clear and operators can easily derive their essential tasks from these goals, then the circumstances operators encounter in doing their jobs, their personal beliefs, and the external pressures of organized political interests have a low degree of influence in defining the essential tasks of operators. As Wilson saw it, all organizations have a culture, but when the goals are clear and the culture is widely shared, the agency has acquired a sense of mission.

Again, consider Fig 13.1. When the organization's goals are unclear and operators cannot easily derive their essential tasks from these goals, then circumstances,

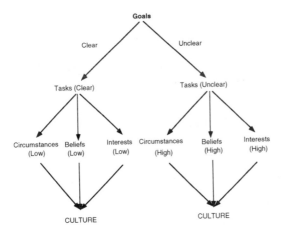

FIG. 13.1. Elements of Wilson's bureaucratic model.

beliefs, and political interests have a high degree of influence in defining the essential tasks of operators. In examining Fig. 13.1, consider the conditions under which the elements of the model have a high degree of influence in defining the essential tasks of operators:

Circumstances.   Situational imperatives can define the essential tasks of operators when goals are unclear and the operator is interacting with a client whose behavior can change in rapid and unpredictable ways. Situational imperatives also define essential tasks when the situation requires the operator to act cautiously or in a different way, or when one task easier to perform than another more difficult task. Peer expectations have an influence when circumstances are hostile and dangerous.

Beliefs.   Prior experiences have an influence when an organization is newly formed, its goals are vague, and its tasks are undefined. Professional norms have influence when (a) the role of the operator is not clearly defined, supervised, coordinated, or routinized and (b) the operator has a high degree of professional training and is associated with a profession group outside the organization. Wilson used the term *bureaucratic personality* to describe the extent to which the organization employs operators who have predispositions that are risk aversive, conformist, and highly procedural in outlook.

Interests.   Organized political interests can also be influential, depending on the type of political environment an agency occupies. This relationship is further defined in the next section.

In Wilson's view, all organizations have a culture created by interaction of the factors described. In the end, an organization's culture is influential in determining which tasks are important and the extent to which new tasks should be resisted by the organization. Some organizations have multiple, competing cultures that can determine which tasks should be performed by operators.

An Application of Wilson's Theory

This section (a) defines the terms in Wilson's model, (b) sets forth illustrative questions derived from the elements of the model, and (c) applies the constituent elements of the model to NESSS to illuminate the causes of the problem.

Circumstances

Wilson (1989) argued that studies of public agencies often focus on how organizational structures, decision-making processes, planning practices, or legislative oversight policies influence the way in which governmental units determine their essential tasks. He believed that this kind of analysis is inadequate because the internal life of an organization and the way in which rank-and-file employees determine their tasks are shaped, in varying ways, by circumstances that are not explained by conventional academic analyses. For Wilson, the essential tasks of operators are determined by (a) the extent to which organizational goals are clearly defined, and measurable; (b) the situational imperatives that operators encounter on a daily basis; and (c) the expectations of peers. Wilson (1989) wrote:

> What operators do will depend on the situations they encounter (what they see as the "critical environment" problem), their prior experiences and personal beliefs, the expectations of their peers, the array of interests in which their agency is embedded, and the impetus given to the organization by its founders. For any distinct bureaucratic unit, these factors combine to produce an organizational culture—a distinct way of viewing and reacting to the bureaucratic world—that shapes whatever discretionary authority the operators may have. When that culture is a source of pride and commitment, the agency has acquired a sense of mission. (p. 27).

The next section describes the circumstances that shape operator behavior and shows how circumstances at NESSS contribute to causing the problem under consideration.

Defining Tasks on the Basis of Organizational Goals

Wilson (1989) made a distinction between two types of organizational goals: operational and general. He defined these terms thus:

> By goal I mean a desired future state of affairs. If that image can be compared unambiguously to an actual state of affairs, it is an operational goal. If it cannot be so compared, and thus we cannot make verifiable statements about whether the goal has

been attained, it is a general goal....Public agencies rarely have single, clear goals. Their ends are often general and multiple. (p. 34)

According to Wilson (1989), the Social Security Administration has well-defined, clear, operational goals. Thus this agency's operators can easily determine the nature of their tasks. In Wilson's view, this agency operates with a high degree of efficiency and precision. He wrote:

The Social Security Administration (SSA) has operational goals, at least with respect to the retirement program it administers, and has the freedom and resources with which to pursue them. It is required by law to send a check each month to every eligible retired person in the nation. The amount of the check is determined by an elaborate but exact formula, the eligibility of the recipient by well-understood laws and regulations. The SSA performs this task with remarkable precision, considering that it pays out claims of one kind or another to 35 million people and collects taxes from 110 million more. (p. 35)

As Wilson (1989) noted, most governmental organizations have general rather than operational goals, which makes defining essential tasks problematic for operators because the tasks of the organization must be derived from goals that use such vague and unclear language that "reasonable people will differ as to the meaning of such words" (p. 33). General, multiple goals also create the problem of determining which goals are most important, but even when individuals "agree on the meaning of one goal, they will disagree as to what other goals should be sacrificed to attain them" (p. 33).

Wilson's discussion of the way an organization's goals determine the essential tasks of operators is useful in illuminating the causes of the problem Consider the following questions:

1. To what extent are the NESSS goals reasonable, clear, measurable, and consistent?
2. To what extent are the NESSS goals multiple, conflicting, or overlapping?
3. To what extent can the NESSS teachers and administrators reasonably derive their essential tasks from the school's goals?

NESSS has general goals, and this reinforces the policy gap described earlier. Consider excerpts from the NESSS program guide (Massachusetts Department of Public Health, 1993):

New England School for Special Students offers multiply challenged children and young adults a unique opportunity to grow as individuals. We begin with the premise that each student can and should be allowed to reach his or her fullest potential. Our goal is simple: to help each student adapt to the least restrictive environment possible at school, at home and in the community. (p. 1)

NESSS provides for an abundance of life. We offer our students a supportive environment that allows them to grow as individuals, to learn about themselves, their abilities and capabilities, and the world around them. Our students learn to reach their fullest potential, working towards goals that may once have seemed impossible. (p. 2)

Direct access to comprehensive medical care ensures we maximize each child's own level of health and overall functioning. The NESSS hospital and outpatient center provide complete, on-campus program of medical and health care services. Our staff remains highly qualified in diagnosing, treating and caring for pediatric and young adolescent patients, particularly those who are physically or cognitively challenged. (p. 3)

A strong education plays a vital role in determining every child's future. Clearly, NESSS students are no exception. Each prepares for the challenges of life at NESSS by developing his or her skill level to its full potential....Our pledge: every NESSS student will learn to adapt to the least restrictive environment possible, both at home and within the community. (p. 4)

As Wilson observed about most public sector organizations, this school has broad, vague, general goals. Terms such as helping students to reach their "fullest potential" or affording each child the "opportunity to grow as individuals" are difficult to operationalize and even more difficult to measure. Because the school's goals remain vague, undefined, and difficult to measure, NESSS teachers and administrators are likely to define their essential tasks on the basis of circumstances they encounter on their job and the beliefs they bring to their daily work. This trend reinforces the policy gap depicted in Table 13.4.

Furthermore, NESSS must balance two competing goals: educational, and medical care goals. The competition between these goals also makes it difficult for NESSS's teachers and administrators to define their essential tasks. The discussion of organizational culture illuminates how competing goals create a culture that favors the goals of medical care over the goals of teaching and learning, a trend that reinforces the policy gap shown in Table 13.4.

Defining Tasks on the Basis of Situational Imperatives

According to Wilson (1989), when organizational goals are vague, situational imperatives become important in determining the essential tasks of rank-and-file employees (i.e., teachers and administrators at NESSS). "When you report for work the behavior of your clients and the technology available will powerfully shape what you do, no matter what the stated goals of the organization may be" (Wilson, 1989, pp. 36–37). To illustrate his point, Wilson described how situational imperatives shape the essential tasks of police officers. Police are often confronted with situations that require them to "impose authority on people who are unpredictable, apprehensive, and often hostile" (p. 37). These situations "lead the street cop to define the job, not in terms of 'enforcing the law', but in terms of 'handling the situation'" (p. 37). Wilson further explained that "[t]he situation defines the outer limits of his or her freedom of action, and thus the outer limits of what will be determined by organizational goals or individual personality" (p. 38). In this way, "situational factors so powerful [make] organizational goals all but meaningless" (p. 39).

Wilson's discussion of how situational imperatives define the essential tasks of operators is helpful in illuminating the causes of this problem. Consider the following questions:

1. To what extent are NESSS teachers and administrators in situations with students who act in unpredictable ways?
2. How does the behavior of students influence the way in which NESSS teachers and administrators decide what they should teach and what students should learn?

As previously discussed, the NESSS goals are broad, vague, and difficult to measure. Therefore, situational imperatives help to define the essential tasks of teachers and administrators at NESSS because, like police officers, they are in situations with clients (i.e., students) who act in fluid, unpredictable ways. Situational imperatives contribute to the policy gap described in Table 13.4 in three important ways.

First, Wilson (1989) maintained that when the decisions of operators are "subject to...political scrutiny after the fact, people making those decisions will have a natural tendency toward caution" (p. 41). The medical conditions of NESSS students can change in rapid, unpredictable ways. When students appear ill or request to see a member of the medical staff, teachers are willing to excuse them from instructional settings. Teachers are willing to err on the side of caution in these situations because their decisions have important legal ramifications for the organization. Situational imperatives based on the medical conditions of students contribute to reducing students' time in instructional settings, thus reinforcing the policy gap depicted in Table 13.4.

Second, in addition to the changing medical conditions of students, NESSS teachers and administrators are faced with students whose self-image and self-perception can change in unpredictable ways. This trend is especially prevalent as students approach adolescence and begin to perceive more clearly their physical and cognitive limitations. When students exhibit signs of self-doubt, or low self-esteem, teachers react by trying to build up their self-image. At times, teachers do not place rigorous academic demands on students for fear that this may reinforce feelings of inadequacy. An unintended result of this practice is that NESSS teachers have a tendency to supplant high-quality academic standards with low-quality standards. This trend makes implementing the knowledge and skills standards in the Curriculum Frameworks and the Common Core of learning problematic for the school's teachers and administrators, again reinforcing the policy gap described in Table 13.4.

Third, Wilson (1989) contended that:

> [e]ven when goals are relatively clear, the situation can define the tasks if one way of doing the job seems easier or more attractive. (p. 42) In this way, operators will attend to tasks which are "technically easier to find, describe, assess and control rather than the latter. (p. 42)

The differing cognitive abilities of students and the slow pace of student learning make holding students to rigorous, demanding academic standards difficult for teachers. Instead, they reduce teaching and learning to simple, routine tasks that are easy to teach, easy to learn, and easy to assess. Also, when students are asked to learn rigorous content and skills, they resist and place pressure on teachers to reduce the demands of the academic workload. Teachers generally comply with this request because they do not want to feel guilty for causing feelings of discomfort in students, or gain a negative reputation among students. Selecting easily performed teaching and learning methods contributes to the policy gap shown in Table 13.4.

Defining Tasks on the Basis of Peer Expectations

Wilson (1989) insisted that the expectations of peers have a significant effect on the way operators define their essential tasks. For example, the actions of combat soldiers are greatly determined by peer expectations. Wilson (1989) wrote:

> Soldiers fight when the men next to them fight. Soldiers fight well when they are members of cohesive small groups and led by officers they trust; they fight poorly when the group lacks cohesion and the officers cannot inspire trust. Their generalized attitudes and political views—how they feel as individuals about soldiering, patriotism, or the war—seem much less important. (p. 46)

Wilson also explained:

> Peer expectations not only affect how hard people work at their jobs; they can affect what they decide the job is. Soldiers will stand and fight rather than cut and run (here peer expectations induce rather than limit performance); miners will dig in dangerous—but not too dangerous—places; narcotics agents will buy and bust rather than watch and wait; police officers will decide when and how to use force and make arrests. (p. 48)

For Wilson, peer expectations are very influential when conditions are dangerous and hostile. In a much less dramatic way, peer expectations at NESSS may be reinforcing the policy gap shown in Table 13.4.

The Extent to Which Peer Expectations Define the Essential Tasks of NESSS Teachers and Administrators.   Perhaps teachers are placing peer pressure on each other not to hold students to the knowledge and skills standards in the Curriculum Frameworks and the Common Core of Learning. Perhaps teachers are placing pressure on each other not to put forth the effort needed

to implement the mandates of the Massachusetts Education Reform Act. Because the researcher is not a member of the faculty, and peer expectations are difficult to determine unless he is part of the group, it is difficult to determine the extent to which negative peer expectations contribute to causing the policy gap. On the basis of his experience as teacher at NESSS, the researcher suspects that peer expectations may have limited influence. However, he has not observed this trend in any significant way while conducting this study.

Beliefs. As Wilson (1989) pointed out, the beliefs of operators can shape, in varying degrees, the way in which essential tasks are defined in public agencies. This trend is especially influential when the role of operators is not clearly defined by the organization. Wilson observed:

> But other tasks, like those of a police officer or schoolteachers are unroutinized. What these people do importantly depends on varying and unpredictable circumstances....Personal beliefs can have a large effect on how tasks are defined when the role to be played is not highly specified by laws, rules, and circumstances and when the operator playing the role receives relatively weak rewards from the organization itself. (p. 54)

Wilson said further:

> To varying degrees, all of these operators [schoolteachers, police, diplomats, scientists, etc.] bring to their work predispositions about how the job ought to be done. These predispositions come from their prior experiences, their sensitivity to professional standards...and perhaps their personality characteristics. When such operators play a role that is weakly defined, they will tend to play it in ways consistent with these predispositions. (p. 55)

As discussed earlier, Wilson surmised that when organizations have undefined goals, situational imperatives and peer expectations will help to define the essential tasks of operators. In the same way, when the roles of operators in a public agency are not clearly defined, prior experiences, professional norms, and bureaucratic personality (i.e., bureaucratic norms) will help to define essential tasks. These "beliefs" are most influential when the work of operators can neither be easily routinized nor easily supervised within the organization.

Defining Tasks on the Basis of Prior Experiences

Wilson (1989) maintained that the prior experiences of operators will define, in varying ways, the essential tasks of an organization. This trend is especially strong when the public agency is newly created and its goals are ambiguous and undefined. Wilson observed:

> When a government agency is created, it is not assembled out of people who are blank slates on which the organization can write at will. Except for young employees getting their first jobs, the operators will have worked for other organizations, often other

government agencies. Indeed, most new agencies are formed out of bits and pieces of old ones...These people had learned certain ways of doing things. If a new agency has ambiguous goals, the employees' prior experiences will influence how its tasks get defined. (p. 57)

In addition, Wilson insisted that, as the new agency grows and matures over time, organizational experiences learned during the development process will determine, in varying degrees, how essential tasks are defined. He wrote:

As time passed and experienced was gained, some definitions of the task prospered and others waned. The key factors that determined the survival of a given task definition was, first, how workable it was (could people in fact get the job done) and how strongly it was supported by external allies (other agencies and groups in Congress). (p. 56)

Wilson's discussion of how prior experiences define the essential tasks of operators is helpful in illuminating the causes of the problem. Consider the following questions:

1. To what extent do the prior experiences of NESSS teachers and administrators contribute to causing the problem under consideration?
2. To what extent do the experiences of NESSS teachers and administrators, gained while working at the school, help to define their essential tasks?

NESSS teachers and administrators typically have been teaching at NESSS for 15 to 20 years. In fact, NESSS has not hired a new teacher in last 5 years due to budget cuts at the Department of Education and the general stability of the faculty. Before teaching at NESSS, most teachers did not have experience working with students who had severe special needs. Therefore, they did not bring any prior experiences to NESSS about how to work with the NESSS student population. Most teachers learned their tasks by working directly with these students on a daily basis over a number of years.

In this way, essential tasks have been learned by trial and error. Tasks that have seemed to help students learn have been repeated; tasks that have not seemed to help students learn have waned. NESSS teachers, like most teachers, keep "mental notes" on what tasks are essential to helping students learn well. This trend reinforces the policy gap as NESSS teachers, like most teachers, continue to follow teaching methodologies developed over years of experience. They often do not consider new methodologies, especially, when, on the surface, these methodologies do not appear applicable to the student population. The knowledge and skill standards in the Curriculum Frameworks and the Common Core of Learning are not considered by NESSS teachers and administrators because, in varying degrees, they do not believe that these methodologies will help students learn well. Their prior experiences often prevent them from considering how the state standards can be implemented at NESSS.

Defining Tasks on the Basis of Professional Norms

As with prior experiences, professional norms are important for defining the essential tasks of operators, who learn these norms through specialized training designed to develop particular habits, characteristics, and dispositions of a particular profession (e.g., physician, lawyer, engineer or teacher). Wilson (1989) defined a professional this way:

> A professional is someone who receives important occupational rewards from a reference group whose membership is limited to people who have undergone specialized formal education and have accepted a group-defined code of proper conduct. The more the individual allows his or her behavior to be influenced by the desire to obtain rewards from this reference group, the more professional is his or her orientation. (p. 60)

The behavior of a professional is not completely shaped by organization-controlled incentives because the standards of the external group often define the way tasks are performed. In contrast, a bureaucrat is "someone whose occupational rewards come entirely from the agency" (p. 60). As Wilson sees it, professional norms are very powerful in shaping essential tasks when the role of the operator is not clearly defined, difficult to routinize, and difficult to supervise.

In the same way, Lortie (1969) contended that teaching is a profession that is not easily routinized, coordinated, and supervised. The activities of teachers are determined in various ways by hierarchical controls, collegial controls, and the amount of autonomy afforded to teachers. These controls shape the way that teaching and learning is defined in a school. Lortie (1969) wrote:

> There are occupations carried on within organizations whose members claim professional status and who declare allegiance to a specialized colleague group which transcends any single organization. In this instance, the several strands of hierarchical control, collegial control and autonomy become tangled and complex. (p. 1)

> Elementary teaching is a case in point. The role of the elementary teacher is defined in diverse and contradictory terms. As an "employee," the teacher is a salaried worker subject to the authority of the public body which employs her. Continual claims to "professional status" presume the existence of a unified occupational group with a system of collegial controls. The rhetoric of "teaching as an art," however, projects autonomy rather than control; to use the artist as prototype is to stress individuality rather then standardization through bureaucratic and collegial controls. Each definition implies alternative sources of control or, antithetically, the absence of external control. (p. 2)

In part, Lortie's point reinforces the thinking of Wilson: Collegial controls and professional norms help to define the tasks of operators and act as sources of control in schools.

Wilson's discussion of how professional norms influence the way in which operators define their essential tasks is helpful in illuminating the causes of this problem. Consider the following questions:

1. To what extent do the professional norms, and training of NESSS teachers and administrators contribute to causing the problem under consideration?

Professional norms reinforce the policy gap in two important ways. First, all the teachers at NESSS have professional training as special educators. In fact, all of them have at least a master's degree in special education. This training socializes them to think of the students in highly individualized ways. They believe that each student is different and should be taught according to his or her particular learning style. Perhaps all teachers, in varying degrees, learn this think this way, but for NESSS teachers, accommodating for individual differences is a fundamental concept. This concept is first learned in their undergraduate education courses, then reinforced in graduate programs and professional development activities. In addition, NESSS teachers are trained as methodological experts. The emphasis on the acquisition and demonstration of high levels of pedagogical content knowledge is considered fundamental to being a high-quality special educator.

These professional norms work against the implementation of the Curriculum Frameworks and the Common Core of Learning. NESSS teachers and administrators believe that the standards established by the Education Reform Act are a form of standardized curricula. A standardized curriculum forces NESSS teachers to act like traditional public school teachers. In other words, the Common Core of Learning and the Curriculum Frameworks cause them to impose a set of knowledge and skills on students without considering the individual needs and learning styles of each student. Moreover, standardized curricula cause NESSS teachers to teach in standardized ways, which violates the professional norm of teacher as pedagogical expert.

2. To what extent do NESSS teachers see state-mandated standards for student learning as an undue encroachment into their professional space?

Teachers believe that state standards force them to "teach to the test," which restricts their professional judgment with respect to content and methodologies that are most relevant to helping students learn well in their classrooms. This kind of behavior by NESSS teachers is not unusual; it is a well-known professional norm. As Lortie (1969) noted, a teacher protects his or her authority in the classroom by not welcoming high degrees of supervision or advice about teaching by outside sources. The classroom is a teacher's sphere of influence, and it should be respected by the state, the principal, and other teachers. Lortie (1969) observed:

In describing how the principal should act, teachers stress his obligation to be accessible and ready to help them when requested. Teachers stress that good colleagues are those who show a willingness to share their knowledge and effective practices with other teachers. In either case, teachers feel that initiation should come from the teacher who desires help and advice; neither the principal nor colleagues should offer unsolicited assistance. Teacher culture, apparently, permits the individual teacher to approach a peer or a subordinate. But most teachers apparently see the exchange of technical assistance as theirs to control; ideas and suggestions may be solicited from various sources, but it is the teacher who tests them in the crucible of classroom experience. The norms maximize teacher freedom to seek assistance without granting authority to those who give it. (p. 39)

In the end, a strong professional ethos leads to reinforcing the policy gap. NESSS teachers and administrators are socialized through their professional training and professional development activities to reject those mandates that appear, on the surface, to be standardized curricula and therefore reduce their ability to individualized the academic program. Furthermore, state-mandated standards unduly infringe on the teacher's authority in the classroom. These professional norms contribute to the policy gap described in Table 13.4.

Defining Tasks Based on Bureaucratic Personality

Wilson (1989) observed that a "bureaucratic personality" is best defined as a disposition on the part of operators that is risk-averse, conformist, and highly procedural in outlook such that "they worry more about following the right rule than about achieving the ultimate goal" (p. 69). He commented:

There are aspects of organizational life that make people risk averse. Indeed, it would be surprising if they did not, since organizations are created in the first place to reduce uncertainty and risk. All organizations by design are enemies of change, at least up to a point; government organizations are especially risk averse because they are caught up in a web of constraints so complex that any change is likely to rouse the ire of some important constituency. But political and organizational pressures for conformity are very different from the presumed tendency of bureaucracies to either recruit or be especially attractive to individuals with risk-averse, conformist personalities. Insofar as we can tell from the few studies that have been done, the presumption is untrue. (p. 69)

Wilson (1989) maintained that sociologists who study public agencies differ over the extent to which individuals who work for public bureaucracies develop a bureaucratic personality. He cited studies that seem to show that under certain conditions, "[b]ureaucrats as a whole revealed a personality disposition that...was idealistic and strongly oriented toward achievement" (p. 69) and "did not turn out to be conformist or cautious" (p. 69). In the end, Wilson seemed to leave this issue unresolved as he did not consider in a rigorous way the conditions under which operators may exhibit a bureaucratic disposition.

Given this limitation in Wilson's work, a strong bureaucratic personality among NESSS teachers may contribute to the policy gap.

Consider this question: To what extent do NESSS teachers and administrators develop conformist, risk-aversive, or inflexible behaviors based on their continual association with NESSS?

As with the discussion of peer expectations, it does not appear that NESSS teachers exhibit a bureaucratic personality such that they are risk aversive or inordinately focused on procedural details. Most NESSS teachers, at least on the surface, appear flexible and care about the well-being of their students. This element of Wilson's model does not reinforce the policy gap described in Table 13.4.

Defining Tasks on the Basis of Pressure From Political Interests

Organized political interest groups can be influential in determining essential operator tasks based on the kind of political environment an agency occupies. Wilson (1989) outlined a typology of possible political environments:

> To oversimplify, a government agency can occupy one of four kinds of political environments: It can confront (1) a dominant interest group favoring its goals [clients politics]; (2) a dominant interest group hostile to its goals [entrepreneurial politics]; (3) two or more rival interests groups in conflict over its goals [interest group politics]; or (4) no important interest group [majoritarian politics]. Which kind of environment they face will shape the forces working on operators as they try to define their tasks. (p. 76)

Public agencies are more likely to be influenced by interest groups when (a) the legislative branch mandates that the agency serve the needs of a particular group, (b) the continued existence of an agency is based on support of a particular interest group, (c) operators are recruited from the social movement that worked to create the agency, and (d) operators need important information from interest groups in order to perform essential tasks. Wilson also insisted that even when an interest is influential, it must compete with other organizational incentives that define essential tasks: the clarity of organizational goals, situational imperatives, peer expectations, prior experiences, professional norms, and the predispositions of operators (bureaucratic personality). In the end, Wilson cautioned that it is difficult for an agency's tasks to be shaped by interests because the political system has developed mechanisms that restrain "capture." The increase in access points to the political system, the limitations on contributions to political campaigns, and the decentralization of political power in the U.S. Congress reduces the ability of a single interest to capture a public agency.

In a similar way, Chubb and Moe (1990) argued that interest groups are influential in shaping the essential tasks of public agencies, especially public schools. For Chubb and Moe, democratic political structures (i.e., school boards, state legislatures, Congress) allow powerful interests to compete for the formulation of legislation that supports their political ends. Because public schools are governed by democratic institutions, they are easily captured by political interests. Chubb and Moe (1990) wrote:

> In this sense, democracy is essentially coercive. The winners get to use public authority to impose their policies on the losers. Teachers' unions, for example, might prevail over the opposition of administrators or parents on some issues. On others, business groups might succeed in imposing reforms fought by unions. What makes this peculiar form of coercion broadly acceptable is that public authority does not belong to any individual or group. It is up for grabs. Anyone who plays by the rules and gains popular support has the same right as anyone else to take control of public authority and to specify the legitimate interests for everyone. (p. 29)

Perhaps the notion that public policy formulation is an "all or nothing" competition between contending groups is debatable, but Chubb and Moe's proposition reinforces the view of Wilson that interests can be influential in shaping the essential tasks of public agencies in general, and public schools in particular.

Wilson's discussion of how political interests influence the way essential tasks are defined is helpful in illuminating the causes of the problem. Consider this question: To what extent do important political interests in the school's political environment influence the way NESSS teachers and administrators define their essential tasks?

As described by Wilson (1989) and applied to NESSS, the special education lobby in Massachusetts is highly influential in defining NESSS core organizational tasks because: it is the dominant group in the NESSS political environment and the school has a direct mandate by the state legislature to educate and provide medical services for students with severe handicapping conditions. As described by Chubb and Moe (1990) and applied to NESSS, this lobby's influence is based on laws and mandates established by the state legislature in response to the demands of the special education lobby.

The Commonwealth of Massachusetts has the most generous special education law of any state in the country, which is based, in varying degrees, on the special education lobby's influence in the state legislature. Because NESSS has a mandate from the state legislature to service students with severe handicapping conditions, the school very carefully adheres to the mandates outlined in the special education law. These mandates are described in the Chapter 766 regulations that define the core tasks of NESSS teachers and administrators (Massachusetts Department of Education, 1994c). Three important regulations in Chapter 766 contribute to the policy gap described in Table 13.4.

First, the Chapter 766 regulations afford the planning and placement team (TEAM) a high degree of discretionary authority over determining the extent to which a student is in need of special educational services and the type of educational program a student will follow. Unlike TEAMs in states such as Connecticut or

Vermont, TEAMs in this state do not have to use a formal evaluation mechanism such as a standardized test to determine a student's need of special services. The TEAM makes a determination of a student's special need primarily on the basis of professional norms, prior experiences, and professional judgment. Second, Massachusetts is a noncategorical state. This reinforces the discretionary authority of the TEAM because a student does not have to fit into some predetermined rubric (i.e., mentally retarded, ADD, or learning disabled) to receive special services.

These two regulations, working together, create the policy gap. Under the Chapter 766 regulations, the TEAM has a high degree of discretionary authority to plan a student's educational program. It should be reemphasized that the TEAM does not have to prove a student's need or the appropriate educational program based on some quantifiable data. If the TEAM believes that a student needs special services, then the student is afforded the services to the extent determine by the TEAM. In this way, the TEAM can decide the kinds of knowledge and skills a student should know and be able to demonstrate. If it decides that the standards outlined in the Common Core of Learning and the Curriculum Frameworks do not apply to a particular student, then the student is not held accountable to these standards.

Third, when students have been categorized as needing medical care as well as educational services, the amount of time a student will spend in an instructional setting is determined by the physician. This regulation creates the obvious problem of reducing instructional time. NESSS students are allowed to miss instructional time with a physician's order, and the teachers and administrators acquiesce to this order. It is difficult for the school to organize the academic program to meet the 990-hr standard of instructional time based on this stipulation in Chapter 766.

In the end, the Chapter 766 regulations are designed to protect the interests of the special education lobby. Massachusetts has the highest proportion of special-needs students of any state in the country because it affords such a high degree of discretion to its special educators. It is difficult for the school to implement the standards outlined in the Common Core of Learning and the Curriculum Frameworks because of the way Chapter 766 regulations define the essential tasks of NESSS teachers and administrators.

It should be noted that the extent to which the Chapter 766 regulations have precedent over the standards outlined in the Massachusetts Education Reform Act is unknown by NESSS teachers and administrators. The Massachusetts Department of Education and the state legislature have not enacted regulations or legislation that attempts to resolve this situation. Therefore, the school continues to follow the mandates outlined in Chapter 766 while trying to implement the standards of the Massachusetts Education Reform Act.

Defining Tasks on the Basis of Organizational Culture

Thus far, Wilson's conceptual model of how public agencies behave has focused on the way operators define their essential tasks in terms of factors that have varying and competing influence within the organization itself. As discussed earlier, when an agency's goals are vague and undefined, essential organizational tasks are defined by the imperatives of the situation and the expectations of peers. Moreover, when the role of an operator is not clearly defined, not easily routinized, and not easily supervised, professional norms, prior experiences and the predisposition of employees may have a role in shaping the core of an agency's tasks. Organized political interests have a role in shaping the agency's core tasks as well.

According to Wilson (1989), these elements, working together, form an organization's culture: "Every organization has a culture, that is, a persistent patterned way of thinking about the central tasks of and human relationships within an organization" (p. 91). In this way, an organization's culture determines the essential tasks of the organization and how they should be performed. Wilson (1989) maintained that a healthy public agency is not merely a coordinated system of rules and procedures. Rather, "a viable organization...is an institution that has been 'infused with value' so that it displays a 'distinctive competence'" (p. 92). Ideally, "[a]n organization acquires a distinctive competence...when it has not only answered the question 'What shall we do?' but also the question 'What shall we be?'" (p. 92). When an organization has clear goals and "a culture that is widely shared and warmly endorsed by operators and managers alike...[it] has a sense of mission" (p. 95). For Wilson (1989), the ideal type of agency has a strong sense of mission:

> A sense of mission confers a feeling of special worth on the members, provides a basis for recruiting and socializing new members and enables administrators to economize on the use of other incentives. (p. 95)

> Able administrators will not want to let their agencies' culture be formed by the chance operation of predispositions, professional norms, interest group pressures or situational imperatives. Such executives will try to shape that culture by plan in order to produce not only a widely shared but warmly endorsed culture—in short, a sense of mission. (p. 95)

Despite his idealism, Wilson (1989) admitted that it is very difficult to create a sense of mission within an organization:

> No administrator finds it easy to create a sense of mission....When goals are vague, it will be hard to convey to operators a simple and vivid understanding of what they are supposed to do. Thus tasks will get defined in ways over which administrators have very little control, with the result that the definition adopted by the operators may be one that the executive does not intend and may not desire. Since government agencies often have more than one goal and thus engage in more than one kind of task, they will have many competing cultures that cannot easily be fused into a shared sense of mission. (pp. 95–96)

Wilson outlined three ways in which organizational culture shapes an agency's core tasks. First, culture determines which tasks have priority. Wilson (1989) called this trend selective attention. "[T]asks that are not part of the culture will not be attended to with the same energy and resource as are devoted to tasks that are part of it" (p. 101). Second, multiple competing cultures define essential tasks. "Organizations in which two or more cultures struggle for supremacy will experience serious conflict as defenders of one seek to dominate representatives of the others" (p. 101). Finally, "organizations will resist taking on new tasks that seem incompatible with its dominant culture" (p. 101).

Wilson's discussion of how organizational culture defines the essential tasks of teachers and administrators is helpful in illuminating the causes of this problem. Consider the following questions:

1. To what extent does the organization's culture influence NESSS teachers and administrators to attend to some tasks more than others?
2. To what extent does the organization's culture influence NESSS teachers and administrator to resist new tasks?
3. To what extent do multiple, conflicting cultures contribute to causing the problem under consideration?

The organizational culture of NESSS is formed by the organization's goals, the situational imperatives facing NESSS teachers and administrators, the professional norms and prior experiences of special education teachers, and the influence of interest groups in defining the school's essential tasks. The interaction of these elements creates an organizational culture that stresses the individual growth and well-being of students, high degrees of individualization in the educational program, and high degrees of individualized medical care and attention. The school's culture is problematic because it resists new organizational tasks, selectively attends to some organizational tasks more than others, and creates multiple conflicting cultures. These factors make the implementation of the Curriculum Frameworks and the Common Core of Learning difficult for the organization, and reinforces the policy gap in Table 13.4.

Resisting New Tasks. The school's culture is characterized by practices of faculty and administrators designed to provide for individual growth and feelings of well-being in students. Teachers and administrators actively promote this culture by creating a learning environment that is nurturing, comfortable, caring, and gentle in its treatment of students. Faculty members, staff, and administrators are careful not to speak harshly to students, nor to diminish students with unkind words, and they are constantly praising students for work completed.

In many ways, this organizational culture represents the highest ideals for the ethical treatment of students and the highest ideals for a positive learning environment, so it is difficult to argue that this culture is problematic. However, it becomes problematic in relation to the Massachusetts Educational Reform Act when teachers resist pushing students to reach rigorous content and skills standards because they do not want to cause high levels of student discomfort and anxiety, which they believe are detrimental to individual growth.

In the researcher's view, this practice is prevalent at NESSS. Teachers often unconsciously resist implementing the Curriculum Frameworks and the Common Core of Learning because this standard is not compatible with the school's culture. In this way, the school's culture contributes to the policy gap when NESSS teachers and administrators resist new tasks (i.e., the Curriculum Frameworks and the Common Core of Learning) because they are not seen as compatible with a culture that stresses individual growth and well-being based on self-esteem development.

Selective Attention.   The school's culture is also characterized by high degrees of individualization in the academic program. In this way, the school's faculty and administrators focus on tasks that are by fiat, by situational imperative, and by professional training compatible with a school culture that emphasizes the individual needs of students. Again, it is difficult to argue that this organizational culture is problematic. Most educators would agree that all students should be treated as individuals and perhaps have IEPs to enhance student learning. A culture that attends to highly individualized tasks becomes problematic when it creates incoherence in the school's academic program. Earley, Magno, and Amico-Porcaro (1995) conducted a study of the NESSS academic program at the request of the NESSS Board of Directors and found the following:

> Given the nature of the needs of the students, it is to be expected the IEP is the focus of curriculum content. However, it was unclear whether staff have clearly articulated the rationale for decision making regarding the movement of students within instructional settings. Currently, grouping strategies includ[ing] standardized and informal assessments form the basis of team decision making. It appears that there is a need to clearly define and clarify entrance and exit criteria for grouping for instruction, specifically in the high school academic areas and vocational areas. (p. 8)

> Communication among teachers within and across the various instructional levels appeared limited. Opportunities for collaborative planning and decision making need expanding. Increased communication among staff members provides opportunities for planning interdisciplinary thematic instruction. (p. 8)

> The program is so highly individualized it would be difficult to know where students would be if educated in a regular education program. (p. 8)

> The academic program will be enhanced by providing more challenging content for those students with higher ability. The emphasis for instruction for students appears to focus on lower order thinking skills. (p. 9)

> The expected emphasis on meeting individual needs has diminished the use of interdisciplinary teaching and "instructional" themes to connect various disciplines. Teachers need more opportunities to develop, observe and study a variety of instructional groupings, practices and ways of collaborative planning and problem-solving. (p. 8)

This kind of incoherence makes it difficult for the school to implement the Curriculum Frameworks and the Common Core of Learning. The organizational culture selects practices that stress individualization without considering how the academic program holds together in a logical manner.

Multiple Conflicting Cultures.   As described in the section on defining tasks based on the goals of an organization, NESSS has two competing goals which creates two competing cultures: the teaching and learning culture (i.e., teachers and administrators), and the medical care culture (i.e. physicians, therapists, nurses). The medical care culture seems to be the dominant group at the school because of the students' complex medical conditions. The goals of medical care have priority over the goals of teaching and learning in all situations. Students miss time in instructional settings on a continual basis, making it difficult for teachers and administrators to teach at high levels and hold students to high standards of learning. This trend makes it difficult for the school to implement the Common Core of Learning and the Curriculum Frameworks.

In the end, it appears that the school has not defined a continuum of essential medical conditions requiring immediate attention by a physician and prolonged absence from classes by students, as well as those simple, routine medical treat- ments or therapies (e.g., a dentist appointment or a meeting with the speech pathologist) that could be scheduled around or integrated with instructional time. Earley, Magno, and Amico-Porcaro (1995) observed:

> More [t]herapeutic services need to be implemented within the student's instructional program. In order to [be] more effective and efficient [s]peech and language, occu- pational and physical therapists need to be more fully integrated into the student's instructional program. Methodologies for integrating the student's therapies within classroom content must be explored and piloted to reduce the continual pull-out of students from the classroom to the therapy room. (p. 9)

The NESSS culture does not support the academic development of students. In fact, educational goals appear to fall behind the goals of individual growth, well-being, and medical care. It is difficult for NESSS teachers and administrators to implement the Curriculum Frameworks and the Common Core of Learning when academic goals are not attended to in the same manner as the other goals.

PART IV: POLICY RECOMMENDATIONS

Presentation of Recommendations

Recapitulation

As Part II demonstrates, the problem facing NESSS teachers and administrators is the policy gap between the standards and expectations of the Massachusetts Education Reform Act of 1993, as outlined in the Common Core of Learning and the Curriculum Frameworks and the accountability procedures built into law, and the current practices of the academic program at the NESSS. As Part III demonstrates, the way that NESSS teachers and administrators define their essential tasks contributes to the policy gap described in Table 13.4. Using Wilson's (1989) bureaucratic model as the framework for analysis, the researcher has shown how vague and undefined goals, situational imperatives, prior experiences, professional norms, pressure from organized political interests, and the school's culture contribute to the cause of this problem. This section is primarily concerned with ameliorating this problem by considering (a) problem solutions already tried, (b) problem solutions proposed during the course of the current debates, (c) new solution recommendations, and (d) solutions which are unsatisfactory for solving this problem.

Problem Solutions Already Tried

The Massachusetts Educational Reform Act of 1993 represents the first formal attempt to outline common standards for schools in the state. This is therefore a new issue for the school's faculty and administrators, and they have not attempted to solve this problem in any meaningful way to date. However, there has been an attempt to create common standards within the ESIS system. ESIS provides educational services for students who live in facilities under the control of the Massachusetts Department of Mental Health, Public Health, and Youth Services, and the County Houses of Correction. NESSS is a subunit in the ESIS organizational framework.

In 1984, the assistant secretary of education in charge of special education services in Massachusetts asked Dr. Margaret Reilly if she would create a plan for a prototype curriculum framework and common core of learning for schools in ESIS. This plan attempted to sketch out in a broad and general way the kinds of knowledge and skills students in ESIS schools would need to demonstrate. In the end, the suggestions were never developed into a formal framework. Teachers and administrators in ESIS schools believed that any kind of common standards would standardize the curriculum and reduce the faculty's ability to individualize their programs. As discussed earlier, this kind of thinking is also prevalent at NESSS, which contributes to the policy gap described.

Problem Solutions Proposed in the Course
of Current Policy Debates

In August 1995, Allen Cameron, chief administrator of the ESIS unit of the Massachusetts Department of Education, conducted a summer institute for all principals and teachers who work in schools under the rubric of ESIS. This institute aimed to inform principals and teachers that they needed to update their educational programs to comply with the standards and expectations of the Common Core of Learning and the Curriculum Frameworks. After attending this institute, Carol

Kaplan, principal of NESSS, worked with members of the faculty to create a plan for incorporating these requirements into the school's educational program. This plan has four distinct stages:

The Preimplementation Stage.   This first stage consists of (a) creating a faculty newsletter and bulletin board to explain the purposes and elements of the Common Core of Learning and the Curriculum Frameworks and, (b) developing a professional development resource library with materials that provide practical suggestions for implementing these new standards at NESSS.

The Implementation Stage.   This second stage consists of (a) an open house in which teachers inform parents about the new standards, answer questions, and note their concerns and (b) NESSS teachers working to foster mutual respect and understanding between teachers and members of the medical staff. Staff meetings, interagency committees, bulletin boards, and open house activities are opportunities for NESSS teachers to collaborate with medical staff in implementing the new standards.

The Focus on Curriculum Stage.   This third stage consists of (a) promoting the ideal of faculty and staff as a community of learners, (b) recognizing the relationship between the IEP goals and the goals of the Curriculum Frameworks, (c) developing individual faculty implementation plans for the subjects and programs in which they teach, (d) demonstrating of the use of student-centered learning strategies by faculty, and (e) establishing teacher research groups so that faculty can share their individual plans for the way they will use the Common Core of Learning and the Curriculum Frameworks in their classrooms.

The Evaluation Stage.   This fourth and final stage consists of (a) a staff evaluation based on the extent to which faculty encourage active student participation in learning situations, the extent to which faculty require students be responsible for their learning in the classroom, and the extent to which theories of multiple intelligences are used by faculty in teaching, learning, and assessment situations, (b) a student evaluation based on authentic assessments, and (c) a program evaluation conducted every quarter by the administrative staff to monitor the implementation of the Curriculum Frameworks.

This plan has a number of limitations. First, it is broad, vague, and uses educational jargon to convey information to faculty members. Second, it does not make specific policy recommendations. It appears that these recommendations will evolve during the implementation process, and all recommendations are appropriate for guiding the practices of educators. Third, the plan is largely based on improving teaching methodology. It is difficult to know how serious the faculty and administrators are about creating substantive, intellectually coherent academic programs for all students regardless of their intellectual and physical limitations. Fourth, it does not appear that faculty and administrators have given careful thought to what kinds of professional development activities are appropriate to update professional practices. Finally, the plan does not seriously consider how the school will solve the problem of students missing time in instructional settings because of their medical conditions.

Despite these limitations, in general the plan is useful and has number of strong points. First, it encourages the full participation of the faculty in updating the academic program. Second, it focuses on information dissemination, so that teachers and administrators perceive goals of the Curriculum Frameworks and the Common Core of Learning. Third, it encourages the participation of parents by allowing them to ask questions and provide suggestions to teachers. In the end, the researcher feels that this plan is adequate, but it should be augmented to include the solution recommendations considered next.

New Problem Solutions

The researcher would like to propose to the NESSS stakeholders the following policy recommendations and explain how these recommendations relate to the causes of the problem described in Part III.

Clarify Goals. The gap between the standards of the profession and the practices of NESSS is caused, in varying degrees, by vague, undefined, and general program goals. In this way, situational imperatives, prior experiences, professional norms, and organized interests define the essential tasks of teachers and administrators. The organizational culture allows medical care goals to have priority over the goals of teaching and learning in all situations. This culture also helps to create an academic program that is incoherent based on high degrees of individualization in teaching and learning. Furthermore, the focus on the emotional development of students displaces the goals of the Common Core of Learning and the Curriculum Frameworks.

This is not to suggest that, in principle, the goals of NESSS are inappropriate, but faculty and medical staff should work to clarify them. These new goals should be consistent, specific, well defined, understandable, and relatively easy to measure. They should reflect the relationship between the individual goals of the academic and medical care programs. Also, these goals should reflect the standards for teaching and learning outlined in the Common Core of Learning and the Curriculum Frameworks. In this way, clear goals help to define the essential tasks of teachers and administrators; they provide a benchmark for program evaluation and development; and they are the first step in developing a sense of mission in the school.

Create a Curriculum Framework and a Common Core of Learning.
The gap between the standards of the profession and the practices of the school is caused in varying degrees by prior experiences, professional norms, and organized political interests. These factors cause NESSS teachers and administrators to follow

instructional practices that focus on the individual needs of students without considering how common standards can be used to guide teaching and learning. Simply stated, common standards are seen as antithetical to the practice of individualization.

This is not to suggest that these practices are inappropriate, but that teachers and administrators need to incorporate the standards of the profession in a way that fits the individual needs of the students. NESSS student population has a variety of special needs, but, in varying degrees, the elements from the Common Core Learning and the Curriculum Frameworks can be utilized to guide teaching and learning. NESSS students can learn how to study and work effectively, to gain and apply knowledge, and to solve problems (Table 13.4). Faculty should draw on their prior experiences, their professional training, and elements of the Massachusetts Common Core of Learning to create an NESSS common core. In addition, they should consider the clarified goals of the organization in creating this new document.

After the common core is developed, faculty and administrators should create curriculum frameworks for each of the school's academic programs using the NESSS Common Core as the basis for framework development. These frameworks should outline what the students in each program need to learn. In this way, teachers could accommodate for the individual needs of students while outlining common standards.

It is highly recommended that teachers in the academic program create curriculum frameworks that are intellectually challenging; they should consult the Massachusetts Curriculum Frameworks to guide them in this. NESSS students in the academic program must learn to read, write, and communicate with high levels of precision if they are going to attend college after graduation.

These frameworks also should form the basis for (a) integrating technology into teaching and learning situations, (b) using portfolio assessment to determine student progress in the instructional setting, (c) guiding the TEAM in the development of the IEP, and (d) generating professional development activities. Professional development is especially important because teachers need to learn how to utilized curriculum frameworks in their daily supervision of students with severe special needs. High-quality professional development programs, tied to the goals of the NESSS Common Core of Learning, will be intellectually challenging and practical. Such professional development is essential if NESSS is going to close the policy gap described in Table 13.4.

In addition, a framework should be created that outlines the extent to which essential medical and physical therapies can be integrated into instructional settings. This is needed to control the constant movement of students in and out of instructional situations. NESSS also needs to create a framework that outlines those meetings with physicians that are essential, and those meetings (e.g., routine dentist appointments) that can be scheduled around time in instruction. In the end, clear organizational goals, a well-written common core of learning, well-written curriculum frameworks, high-quality professional development activities, and a framework for integrating medical services into the academic program will bring coherence to the educational program. This coherence is needed to create a strong organizational mission that limits the influence of situational imperatives, prior experiences, and professional norms in determining the essential tasks of teachers and administrators.

Extend the School Day. As described earlier, situational imperatives, organized political interests and organizational culture define the essential tasks of NESSS teachers to the extent that the goals of medical care have priority over the goals of teaching. This makes the implementation of the standards of the profession problematic for the school. Perhaps teachers and administrators should consider extending the school day. Instruction could be offered from 9 a.m. to 5 p.m., Monday through Friday, instead of the present 9 a.m. to 3 p.m. schedule. The faculty and medical staff should work together to outline blocks of time in the school day that are reserved only for instruction in some cases and medical care in others. Exceptions could be made for emergency situations or essential appointments. In addition, block scheduling would allow teachers and students to focus on academic goals without the goals of medical care having priority in all situations. This practice would also afford relatively equal consideration for the goals of medical care and instruction.

Identification of Unsatisfactory Policy Recommendations

Perhaps the gap between the standards of the profession and the practices of the NESSS academic program could be closed if NESSS reorganized its academic program to operate more like that of a traditional public school. NESSS teachers and administrators could develop a standardized curriculum, create traditional grading structures, and deemphasize the use of the IEP in instructional practices. In this way, it would be easy to implement the standards of the Common Core of Learning and the Curriculum Frameworks because these standards are primarily designed for traditional public school curricula.

This approach is unacceptable for three reasons. First, NESSS students have a diverse set of needs, and they cannot be taught in traditional ways. The academic program must be flexible enough to accommodate for individual differences. Standardized curricula do not allow for such accommodations. Second, the students at NESSS operate at developmental levels that are not commensurate with their ages. A traditional grading structure would not allow these students to be grouped appropriately on the basis of their cognitive capabilities. Finally, the IEP is a document that should be carefully followed by teachers. This document protects the individual rights of students by documenting educationally appropriate teaching and learning activities.

Explication of a Broad Strategic Plan
for Implementing Recommended Policies

The solution recommendations proposed by the NESSS faculty and the additional policy recommendations made by the researcher should be combined to create a broad strategic plan for implementation as follows.

Preimplementation Stage

1. Faculty members work to create a faculty newsletter and bulletin board to explain the purposes and the elements of the Common Core of Learning and the Curriculum Frameworks.
2. Faculty work to create a professional development resource library with materials that provide practical suggests for how these standards can be implemented in the academic program.
3. Administrators recruit faculty members, and medical staff members to serve on school-wide committees (i.e., goal-clarification committee, Common Core of Learning committee, Curriculum Frameworks committee, and the committee on extending the school day).

Implementation Stage

1. Faculty and administrators conduct an open house to inform parents about new academic standards, answer their questions, and note their concerns.
2. NESSS teachers actively work to foster mutual respect and understanding between teachers and members of the medical staff. Staff meetings, interagency committees, bulletin boards, and open house activities are opportunities for NESSS teachers to encourage collaboration with medical staff in the implementation of the new standards.
3. Goal-clarification committee works to reformulate NESSS program goals so that they are clear, measurable, consistent, and easy to understand. This committee consists of administrators, teachers, and members of the medical staff.

Focus on Curriculum Stage

1. Faculty and administrators promote the ideal of NESSS as a community of learners.
2. Faculty and administrators create a committee that develops an NESSS common core of learning based on the NESSS program goals and the goals for student learning outlined in the Massachusetts Common Core of Learning.
3. After the NESSS Common Core of Learning is developed, faculty in each academic cluster create curriculum frameworks based on the Massachusetts

Curriculum Frameworks and the NESSS common core of learning. Teaching strategies, appropriate learning activities, assessment techniques and professional development activities are described.

4. Faculty and administrators work to recognize the relationship between the IEP goals and those of the Massachusetts Curriculum Frameworks. IEPs should be developed based on the NESSS curriculum framework.
5. Faculty and administrators develop individual implementation plans for their respective subjects and programs.
6. Faculty and administrators engage in professional development activities.
7. Faculty members demonstrate of the use of student-centered learning strategies in their classroom teaching.
8. Faculty and administrators establish teacher research groups in which faculty members share their individual plans for the use of the common core of learning and the curriculum frameworks in their classrooms.
9. Faculty and administrators establish a schoolwide committee to consider the feasibility of an extended school day. The use of block scheduling is considered to work out current discontinuities in the academic program created by the high degree of time missed by students in instructional settings because of medical care needs.
10. Faculty and administrators establish a schoolwide committee to develop a framework that denotes medical care needs that need prolonged absences from class and those routine needs that can be integrated into instructional settings or attended to during nonclass hours.

Evaluation Stage

1. Faculty are evaluated on the basis of the extent to which they encourage active student participation in learning situations, require students to be responsible for their own learning in the classroom, and use theories of multiple intelligences in teaching and assessment situations.
2. Authentic assessment techniques are used to evaluate students by standards developed in the NESSS curriculum frameworks.
3. A program evaluation is conducted every quarter by the administrative staff to monitor the implementation of the curriculum frameworks.
4. Faculty and administrators elicit feed back from parents.

Potential Facilitating and Hindering Factors

Three factors help to facilitate this plan in the following manner. First, faculty, administrators, and medical care staff are involved in the process of implementing the new standards. They have ownership in solving this problem, and they can bend the new standards to fit the individual needs of the students Also, in general, medical care staff and faculty have a positive, collegial working relationship that should make the clarification of the school's goals, the development of the common core of learning, and the development of the curriculum frameworks proceed smoothly.

Second, Allen Cameron supports the new standards. He regularly provides information to teachers and administrators and the resources needed for professional development activities. His support makes the new standards legitimate. Faculty and administrators are more likely to comply with the new standards if the chief administrator of special education programs confirms it as an appropriate standard.

Third, standards-based educational reforms are supported by influential members of the business community, elected officials, and educators. These groups are working in the state legislature to support the Massachusetts Education Reform Act. This behavior facilitates implementation of the act state-wide because it focuses political energy and resources on this issue. In addition, discussion of educational standards is pervasive in the public policy debates and in the educational literature. NESSS teachers and administrators are well informed about the arguments in favor of standards-based reforms.

A potential hindering factor to the implementation of this plan is that educational standards are subject to change on the basis of trends in the larger political environment. For example, John Silber and Edwin Delattre, members of the Massachusetts Board of Education, have been openly critical of the standards in the present Common Core of Learning and the Curriculum Frameworks. In fact, Delattre (1996) has called the current Common Core "intellectual rubbish." These recent comments and the changes that may be pursued by Silber and Delattre would hinder the implementation of the standards at NESSS. Faculty and staff cannot implement the standards if they are unclear, and subject to change.

Furthermore, the faculty's continual support is needed because the Chapter 766 regulations and Public Law 94–142 affords them a high degree of discretion in planning academic programs. The law allows them to disregard the use of common standards if they do not see its relevance to educational practice. Ultimately, faculty are professionals, and they cannot be forced to comply with the mandates in the new standards.

Recommended Policies Keyed to Individual Stakeholders

Stakeholder 1: Allen Cameron, Chief Administrator of ESIS

- Continue to support the goals of the Massachusetts Education Reform Act of 1993.
- Continue to provide NESSS with adequate resources for professional development activities.

- Provide accurate, timely, and useful information to faculty and administrators about how they can implement the new standards in the educational program.
- Lobby in the state legislature, at the Department of Education, and at the Board of Education meetings to clarify the extent to which the mandates of educational reform will apply to students with special needs.

Stakeholder 2: Carol Kaplan, Principal of NESSS

- Work with Allen Cameron to gain resources for professional development activities.
- Work with Allen Cameron to provide faculty and medical staff with accurate, timely, and up-to-date information on how they can implement the new standards in the educational program.
- Work with Allen Cameron to define how the Education Reform Act will apply to students with severe special needs.
- Facilitate the creation of the goal-clarification committee, the common core of learning committee, the curriculum frameworks committee, and a committee on extending the school day. Recruit faculty and staff to work on these committees.
- Create a realistic time line of implementation events. This time line should outline a sequence of events so that the implementation plan has a sense of coherence.
- Provide advice, support, and guidance to faculty members working on school committees.
- Provide faculty and staff with high-quality in-school professional development activities.
- Gain input from parents as to what they want their children to know and be able to demonstrate.
- Evaluate the academic program against the standards established in the NESSS common core of learning and the NESSS curriculum frameworks.

Stakeholder 3: Dr. Margaret Reilly, Executive Director, Potentials Inc.

- Work with Carol Kaplan to gain resources for professional development activities.
- Seek out grants from state, federal agencies, and foundations to support individual and in-school professional development activities.
- Work with Carol Kaplan to provide faculty and medical staff with accurate, timely, and up-to-date information on how they can implement the new standards in the educational program.
- Work with Carol Kaplan to facilitate the creation of the goal clarification committee, the common core of learning committee, the curriculum frame

works committee, and the committee on extending the school day. Recruit faculty and staff to work on these committees.

- Work with Carol Kaplan to create a realistic time line of events for implementing the new standards.
- Provide advice, support, and guidance to faculty members working on the school committees.
- Gain input from parents as to what they want their children to know and be able to demonstrate.
- Work with Carol Kaplan to evaluate the academic program against the standards established in its common core of learning and NESSS curriculum frameworks.

Stakeholder 4: Claretta di Stefano, NESSS Faculty Member

- Work with Carol Kaplan to facilitate the creation of the goal-clarification committee, the common core of learning committee, the curriculum frameworks committee, and the committee on extending the school day.
- Work on the goal-clarification committee and recruit faculty and staff to work with her on this committee.
- Work with Carol Kaplan to create a realistic time line of events for the implementation of the new standards.
- Provide advice, support, and guidance to faculty members working on the school committees.
- Work to gain input from parents as to what they want their children to know and be able to demonstrate.
- Work with Carol Kaplan to evaluate the academic program against the standards established in the NESSS common core of learning and its curriculum frameworks.

14

Analysis of an Organizational Decision: The Placement Process for the Honors Track at Brandywine Regional High School*

Alan Bernstein

DESCRIPTION OF THE DECISION

The Decision and Its Context

At Brandywine Regional High School (BRHS) there are three academic tracks: honors, college preparatory, and junior college/technical. The following analysis will look at the decisional process undertaken by students who seek to enter the honors track. For the purposes of brevity, only the honors track is examined in this chapter.

Within the honors track, there are advanced placement courses and those labeled "honors." The differences between the two are profound, even though both are considered honors track courses. Advanced placement courses (AP) are highly structured and geared toward preparation for the national AP subject tests, which (if successfully completed) may earn the student college credits. The curriculum for the AP courses is highly prescribed and content rich as it must be to prepare students for the AP exams. The honors courses are more proprietary in nature, meaning that each instructor has more latitude in determining the complexity level of the course being offered. The honors courses are not geared for any national exam, and successful completion does not gain a student equivalent college credit.

*This chapter was originally submitted as a term paper for a class in Organizational Analysis, Department of Administration, Training and Policy Studies, School of Education, Boston University, Spring 1990. Names have been altered to protect the identities of the school and key participants.

The honors track (i.e., AP and honors courses) is touted as being significantly more rigorous than the college preparatory track.

The honors track is varied depending on the academic discipline under which the course falls. However, some would argue that no honors track exists at BRHS because students may enroll in as many or as few honors courses as they choose. Although there is truth in this, most of the students who register for an honors course in one subject also register for its equivalent in another academic discipline. Few students genuinely cross-register among the three academic tracks even though it is permissible to do so, and for this reason it can be maintained that an honors track exists. The following list shows all the honors track courses offered along with the prerequisites needed to register for each. As is evident, the prerequisites vary widely across the academic disciplines and even within the disciplines. As discussed later, the listed prerequisites are not in themselves automatic disqualifiers for entry into the courses.

ENGLISH
English 9 (A average in English 8 or B with submission of a writing sample)
English 10 (B average in honors English 9 or A average in college prep English with teacher approval)
English 11 (B average in honors English 10 or A average in college prep English with teacher approval)
English 12 (B average in honors English 11 or A average in college prep English with teacher approval)
World Studies (Teacher recommendation)
English 11 AP (A average in honors English 10, teacher approval, and successful completion of entrance exam)
English 12 AP (A average in honors English 11 or B average in AP English 11, teacher approval, and successful completion of entrance exam)

MATH
Advanced Algebra 2 (B or better in Algebra 1 and department head approval)
Advanced Geometry (C or better in Advanced Algebra 2 honors or department head approval)
Pre-Calculus (C- or better in Advanced Geometry honors or B in Algebra 2)
AP Calculus (B- or better in Pre-Calculus honors or department head approval)

SCIENCE
Honors Earth Science (B or better in grade 8 science and teacher approval)
Honors Biology (B or better in Earth Science or Honors Earth Science and teacher approval)
Honors Chemistry (pass Algebra 2 or Honors Algebra 2, pass honors or Lab Biology)
Honors Physics (C or better in Pre-Calculus or Trigonometry)

AP Biology (B or better in honors or Lab Biology with department head approval)

AP Chemistry (B in honors Chemistry or Lab Chemistry with department head approval)

SOCIAL STUDIES
Government (teacher approval)
World History (teacher approval)
World Studies (teacher approval)
U.S. History (teacher approval)
AP U.S. History (B+ or better in honors U.S. History or honors World History or honors World Studies)
AP European History (B or better in honors World History or honors U.S. History or AP U.S. History)

WORLD LANGUAGES
French 3 (C or better in French 2)
French 4 (C or better in French 3)
AP French (B- in French 4 and/or department head approval)
German 3 (C or better in German 2)
German 4 (C or better in German 3)
Spanish 3 (C or better in Spanish 2)
Spanish 4 (C or better in Spanish 3)
AP Spanish (B- or better in Spanish 4 and/or department head approval)

Sources and Types of Information Used

Types of Information

Six broad types of information are used in deciding whether a student is eligible for the honors track. Each of the five disciplines is prioritized and weighted differently depending on the academic department, and this is partially evident in the preceding list.

1. *Grades in the previous courses.* Because many honors courses either have prerequisites or courses that logically precede them, the grades in these courses are used as determinants. The minimal grades necessary vary, from "A" in certain English courses, to "C" in most language courses.
2. *Mandatory prerequisites.* In some honors courses, a student must successfully complete prerequisites to qualify. In the case of science, some of the prerequisites fall outside of the discipline itself.
3. *Teacher approval.* In the case of social studies, most honors courses require only teacher approval.

4. *Department head approval.* This approval varies depending on the department. In some departments, the department head has no prescribed role. In others the decision rests largely on his or her approval.

5. *Entrance examination.* Used only for the AP English courses, the examination is an essay type that asks students to respond to a set question.

6. *Writing sample.* Used only for entrance into English honors 9, it is not clear whether the students provide a writing sample from a previous class or if they must write an essay similar to the one in the entrance examination and submit it for qualification.

Sources of Information

Parents.   The parents meet with prerequisite teachers of relevant courses, department heads, and guidance counselors to discuss the expectations of the honors courses, the strengths and weaknesses of their student registering for honors, and the likelihood of success for that student. Parents meet during parent-orientation night, in informal settings, or by appointment with the respective guidance counselor and department head. There are many opportunities for parents to receive information, especially by word of mouth, from neighbors, friends, relatives, and so forth who know more intimately the demands of the honors courses and the teachers teaching them. Parents are privy to an informal network of subjective and impressionistic information regarding the demands of honors courses. In terms of what the parents may offer to the knowledge base behind the decision, they possess the medical and psychological information about their child that others may not know. In a sense, they have a more holistic view than anyone else involved in the decision-making process, except perhaps the student him or herself.

Students.   The students are privy to an informal network of subjective and impressionistic information from other students (and parents) regarding the rigors and demands of honors studies. They may also receive feedback and advice from a variety of sources on their suitability for the honors track. That source of that information may be former teachers, current teachers, advisors, guidance counselors, deans of students, parents, friends, students previously or currently enrolled in honors courses, teachers of the honors courses, former teachers of honors courses, department heads, and the principal. From the individual standpoint, each student knows his or her own motivations, strengths, and weaknesses, and thus provides an important knowledge base in the decision whether to enroll in the honors track. After receiving information from a variety of sources and validating that against a personal sense of his or her capabilities, the individual student is probably the most important source of information in the decision process.

Teachers Teaching Prerequisite Courses. One most influential source of information regarding the decision whether to enroll in honors courses is the teachers of the prerequisite courses (or other related preceding courses). They are asked to approve of the decision and to advise and guide the student in his or her decision. Their source of information about the student is both objective (grades, percentage of attendance, GPA, etc.) and subjective (commitment, participation, motivation, drive, desire, etc.). The teachers provide a wealth of information to students, parents, and guidance counselors regarding any student's decision to enroll in the honors track.

Teachers Teaching Honors Courses. Teachers who teach the honors track courses have a good sense of who is likely to succeed or do poorly on the basis of a track record of previous students. This information may be impressionistic, or it may be more objective. There is both a statistical and an impressionistic profile of who is likely to succeed in honors, and the teachers of the honors courses know this. The honors teachers also know the demands of the courses they teach and perhaps which prerequisite teachers are easy or rigorous graders (e.g., students coming from Teacher X with B's or better are more likely to succeed than B students coming from Teacher Y whose grading is inconsistent).

Department Heads. Department heads have a good overall sense of how well students are prepared for honors studies on the basis of which courses and teachers the students had before deciding to enroll in the honors track. They also know the honors curriculum, the demands, as well as the statistical and impressionistic profiles of who is likely to succeed. Many department heads teach honors courses or have taught them in the past. Thus there is an intimate knowledge of what is required in these courses. The department heads also have created the qualifications and prerequisite lists for the honors courses in their respective departments, and in the case of the English department, they grade the entrance examinations for the AP courses.

Guidance Counselors. If the teachers know the content and demands of the honors courses in their departments, the counselors know the students' overall academic and personal track records in ways that teachers may not. Because counselors follow the students through the four years of their high school experience and have the records going back to kindergarten, they have a fuller knowledge base from which they may draw. Teachers may have only a unidisciplinary, cross-sectional view of the student, whereas the counselors may have a longitudinal view that cuts across the disciplines. They also are privy to attendance and discipline files to which teachers have no access.

The Decisional Process

The placement process has roughly eight steps. However, no two decisions are made in precisely the same manner, so there are hybrids and variations for each applicant. The following description is an instructive (not authoritative) look at how the process unfolds.

1. *Orientation night.* Parents and students attend an orientation night before registering for next year's courses. At the event, all the teachers are present, and each department has illustrative examples of what is expected in all the courses offered. This evening provides parents with an opportunity to discuss honors studies (or anything else) with department heads and teachers.
2. *Classroom registration.* Guidance counselors circulate among the classrooms to distribute the program of studies/registration forms and answer any questions about registration. They also encourage students to make an appointment with their counselor regarding course selection. Forms are completed and returned in a 15-min homeroom period several weeks later.
3. *Teacher approval.* Subject area teachers are asked to sign off on any course selections chosen by the students. They may meet privately with students to discuss why they are unwilling to approve courses, including honors courses, for which a student wishes to register.
4. *Department head approval (where applicable).* For certain honors courses, the respective department head must approve of the course selection. In cases of course registration conflict between student and teacher, the department head would automatically be involved in the decision process.
5. *Entrance examination (where applicable).* The English department gives an entrance examination for those seeking to register for AP courses.
6. *Parental approval.* All registration materials must be signed by a parent. In cases of conflict with honors registration, there are meetings as outlined later.
7. *Guidance overview.* The guidance office receives the course selection materials, makes certain that each has parental authorization, and cross-checks to see that students have met prerequisites and approval signatures for honors courses. Students are then registered for courses and funneled into the school's master schedule.
8. *Parental conference (where applicable).* In cases of conflict involving honors registration, the guidance counselor, relevant teacher(s), department head(s), and parent(s) meet to discuss the registration request. Only in rare instances are parents ever turned down or asked to discuss the matter with the principal. As the guidance counselors are apt to repeat, "Students have a right to fail." At most, the team will strongly encourage the parent(s) not to proceed with registering the student for honors. As a caveat, they may inform the parent that decisions made against the wishes of the team could result in the student being denied the opportunity to switch out of honors should failure occur.

ANALYSIS OF THE DECISION USING FOUR
SOCIOLOGICAL PARADIGMS

Burrell and Morgan's Functionalist Paradigm

This paradigm weds the attributes of conservatism with objectivism so that the type of analysis here would be rational, quantitative, legalistic, and bureaucratic. A premium is placed on decisions that are standardized and classified with objective, reliable data. The following discussion analyzes the BRHS honors placement process using the functionalist paradigm.

Critique of the Sources and Types of Information Used. From a functionalist perspective, the BRHS placement process is lacking objectivity and standardization.

First, no objective test scores are used in determining placement. By the time the students are ready to register for honors courses, many have already taken the California Achievement Test (CAT), Scholastic Aptitude Test (SAT), Iowa Test of Basic Skills (ITBS), and Massachusetts Educational Assessment Program (MEAP), yet none of the scores from these standardized tests are even factored into the decision.

Second, and closely related, there is too much reliance on individual grades from previous teachers. Some teachers are easy graders and others are more demanding. This may result in some students getting into the program who are not qualified and others being denied because of their grades. Without a more standardized measure, either from a score on a national standardized test or a grade on a school-created objective test, there is too much uncertainty in relying on individual grades.

Third, the requirements of each department are too variegated. For example, social studies requires only teacher approval for registration in honors courses, whereas other departments require minimum grades, prerequisite courses, teacher approval, and department head approval. The requirements need to be more streamlined.

Fourth, no objective data base exists from which students and parents can draw from to determine more objectively whether the student is suitable for the honors level. There is too much impressionistic data, hearsay evidence, and word-of-mouth advice for the consumer to make an objective decision even if he or she is a qualified applicant. The knowledge base on which the decision rests is not sufficiently complete. At the minimum, a syllabus of the course should be made available for the consumer in this process.

Fifth, there exists no quantitative statistical profile of who is most likely to succeed in an honors course.

Critique of the Decisional Process. The process is rational to a point, but functional flaws are still evident, the most significant being the parent's right to override decisions made by teachers, guidance counselors, and department heads. It makes no sense to allow wholly unqualified applicants to proceed into the honors track simply because parents want them there.

Recommendations Using the Functionalist Paradigm. The following recommendations exist for using the paradigm:

1. Make greater use of standardized test scores in the decision-making process.
2. Streamline the requirements for honors courses among the different depts.
3. Create an objective database from which the consumer can make a more informed decision.
4. Create a quantitative statistical profile of the successful honors candidate.
5. Eliminate the parental veto of the teachers, department heads, and counselors.

Critique of the Decision Itself Using the Functionalist Paradigm.
Functionalists have no problem with the concept of an honors program, nor with a natural weeding out process, so long as the process is rational. The decision to eliminate some applicants and dissuade others from registering for honors courses is entirely just. All are not of equal intelligence, so it is within the purview of educational institutions to create enrichment opportunities for those who are more gifted. If an honors track is to be a going concern, then those of only average intelligence should not be allowed to participate for fear of compromising the integrity and standards of the honors courses.

Burrell and Morgan's Interpretive Paradigm

The interpretive paradigm is a combination of ideological conservatism and epistemological subjectivism. It is an attempt to understand decisions as would an anthropologist, using "thick description" and qualitative investigations and interviews. This paradigm does not seek radically to alter the status quo so much as to understand it from the position of "other." A critique of the BRHS honors placement decision using the interpretive paradigm follows.

Critique of the Sources and Types of Information Used. The sources and types of information used in the decision-making process for honors courses are by and large interpretive. A broad array of personal information used in the process is qualitative in nature. Teacher recommendations, for example, are not entirely based on grades or other quantitative measures, but rather on the impressions that teachers acquire after spending so much time with the student who is seeking the honors track. Teachers often recommend students on the basis of their desire, motivation, motive, and willingness to work hard, not because of their raw intelligence and GPA. Also, parents play an integral role in the knowledge base. By meeting with counselors, teachers, and department heads, parents can fill in the missing personal dimensions (along with the mitigating factors that do not appear on transcripts) that are crucial to properly placing an individual.

The process is interpretive to a point, but the attempts to "get inside" the student are never adequate. Counselors do not spend sufficient time with each student individually to fully explore his or her suitability for honors courses, and parents, who know the student better than anyone else, are only involved in the process when they proactively choose to be involved. Parents have too few opportunities to "educate" the teachers, counselors, and department heads about the student and vice versa. A one-night orientation program is wholly insufficient, yet too few parents choose to pursue more intense contact with the relevant team members. More opportunities need to be created for a fuller, deeper, and richer knowledge base about the student for the purposes of better informed placement decisions.

Critique of the Decisional Process.   With the parental veto, along with the opportunity for the team of teachers, counselors, and department heads to meet, the process is reasonably interpretive. However, more opportunities should exist at the outset for the team to come together before conflicts arise. Conferences built into the process would facilitate more interpretive interaction. This may be difficult given the constraints of time and the inordinately large number of students who would need to be processed in this manner. The fault may lie with the prerequisites listed after each honors course that may lead some to believe the process is more functional than interpretive. There may be no need to include any prerequisites for the honors courses. Instead, those students seeking entry to the honors track should be interviewed in a team conference in order to discuss the issues and present all relevant artifacts, such as a portfolio of prior work.

Recommendations Using the Interpretive Paradigm.   The following recommendations exist for using the interpretive paradigm.

1. Eliminate the prerequisites from the honors courses and replace them with a mandatory team conference that includes parents, student, relevant teachers, counselor, and department head.
2. Create more opportunities for parents to present information about their child so that conflicts over honors enrollment is minimized.
3. Allow counselors more contact time with students, especially those seeking entry to the honors track.

Critique of the Decision Itself Using the Interpretive Paradigm.

Because the interpretive paradigm is along conservative ideological lines, the existence of an honors program would not be questioned per se. The interpretivists would want to ensure that the decision and information used to deny or grant individuals entrance into the honors track was as holistic as possible. It may be impossible for outsiders ever really to "get inside" the student to assess his or her capabilities, but if the selection process is replete with conferences, interviews, portfolios of prior work, and strong parental involvement, then the interpretivists may be sufficiently satisfied that the decision reached is adequate.

Burrell and Morgan's Radical Structuralist Paradigm

This paradigm weds ideological radicalism with epistemological objectivism so that, on the one hand, the status quo is unacceptable because it oppresses individuals, yet on the other, individuals are not the locus through which change occurs. Collective societal structures, such as political, economic, and social state apparatuses, are the cause of power imbalances and oppression of individuals. Such oppression is a product of large forces, with social reality not open to individual interpretation and the making of personal meaning.

Critique of the Sources and Types of Information and the Decisional Process Used.

The sources and types of information used in determining eligibility for the honors track are wholly insufficient. No statistical data exist to determine the ratios between males and females, nonminorities and minorities, rich and poor, and so forth who are seeking entry to the honors track. In fact, societal imbalances are in no way addressed in the types of information used, with the result that the process only perpetuates asymmetrical power relationships. A quota system would help to alleviate some of the imbalances so that minorities, women, and low-income students would have more opportunities to enter the honors track.

The school itself is reactive rather than proactive in cultivating honors candidates because there are no recruitment efforts to bring more nontraditional students into the honors track. Thus, the school creates or perpetuates inequality among the student population, yet has no mechanism in place to redress the imbalance through active cultivation and recruitment. The honors track at BRHS is seen as meritocratic: Those who have the abilities are invited, those who do not are strongly discouraged from participating. The school is culpable in maintaining the status quo, and worse still, does not acknowledge any role in bringing in more nontraditional candidates.

Recommendations Using the Radical Structuralist Paradigm.

The recommendations that exist for using the radical structuralist paradigm follow:

1. Create a statistical database from which the ratios between males and females, nonminorities and minorities, rich and poor can be determined in the honors track.
2. Develop a quota system so that nontraditional students are not denied entry or bumped by disproportionate traditional participation in the program.
3. Develop an active recruitment drive, beginning in the earliest grades, so that more nontraditional students have the aptitude to enter the honors track once they are in high school.
4. Move away from a meritocratic system. The school needs to assume responsibility for the asymmetrical power imbalances and take steps to redress oppression: first by acknowledging its role in perpetuating the status quo, then in creating a means to rectify imbalances.

Critique of the Decision Itself Using the Radical Structuralist Paradigm. Because the present honors system takes no account of power imbalances, it is wholly unjust and should be discontinued until a more equitable system is put in its place. No good results from maintaining an honors program that buttresses inequality and oppression in the name of merit while a new one is being created. The first should be scrapped until something better is put into operation.

Burrell and Morgan's Radical Humanist Paradigm

The radical humanist paradigm is a blending of radical ideology and subjective epistemology. Similar to the radical structuralists approach, this paradigm sees the status quo as unacceptable because of the asymmetrical power relationships at work that oppress individuals, but unlike the structuralist approach, reality and the making of meaning in the radical humanist paradigm are individual enterprises. Individual consciousness raising and empowerment—eliminating false consciousness—lies at the heart of the radical humanist's prescription for change. Large societal apparatuses that keep individuals disempowered need to be delegitimized in favor of individual education leading to mass mobilization.

Critique of Sources and Types of Information and the Decisional Process Used. The sources and types of information used in the decision whether to admit a student into the honors program are inadequate because they disempower individual students. The teachers, counselors, and department heads who have a say in the decision are largely seeking to maintain the status quo, to keep the honors program meritocratic. A better informational source would start from a position of empowering the individual student. The act of judging and evaluating another individual is a form of oppression if it is meant to exclude rather than educate, and so long as the honors program is exclusive and limited, those denied entry are being oppressed, not educated and empowered in any meaningful way. Perhaps the best method would be to open the honors program up to all who wish to take the classes. The sources and types of information would come from the individual—who in a sense is the best judge of self. Each student would evaluate his or her own motives for seeking entry to the honors program and then map out a strategy for successfully completing the program.

The present process for entering the honors track is much too external to the individual, with far too many outside actors judging and evaluating what is best for the student. Because individuals can probably never really know the "other," it is best that the individual decides for him- or herself. The present process itself is disempowering and dehumanizing. The teachers, department heads, and counselors in the team are often more interested in maintaining the meritocratic integrity of the honors program than they are in empowering individual students. The process creates a fundamental disconnection between individual student goals and larger programmatic goals, and because it is probably impossible to separate the two, it is best that they not become entangled.

Recommendations Using the Radical Humanist Paradigm. The recommendations that exist for using the radical humanist paradigm follow:

1. The honors program should be open to all who wish to enroll in the courses.
2. Teachers, counselors, and department heads should focus on providing content-rich, empowering, and meaningful honors courses rather than on whom to include and exclude from the program.
3. The decision to enroll in the honors courses should be managed in a way that is empowering and affirming to the individual student.

Critique of the Decision Itself Using the Radical Humanist Paradigm. The honors program as presently constituted is an unjust, disempowering mechanism that not only alienates individuals, but maintains asymmetrical power relationships. The program can be humanized by opening up the enrollment to all who seek to register in the courses and by reforming the content so that a radical critique of society is taught. The courses and process itself can be humanized, can raise the consciousness level of the participants, but only if a radical restructuring takes place.

CONCLUSIONS AND RECOMMENDATIONS BASED ON THE FOUR CRITIQUES

The honors program at BRHS is largely interpretive because parents can veto almost any decision made by teachers, department heads, and counselors. There are no standardized test scores or rigid criteria that automatically disqualify anyone from participating in the program, and the prerequisites listed for each honors course are more suggestions or guidelines than they are disqualifiers. Parents and students have ample opportunity to discuss course expectations and individual academic promise with the team. The process is accessible (to a point) and flexible enough to accommodate almost all parent or student objections. A mutual learning experience can grow out of the decision, and all parties can come away from the process more knowledgeable about the needs of the individual student.

The process as it presently exists appears to be a good one. Some fine tuning should be done so that more opportunities exist for team meetings and counselor–student interaction before conflicts arise, but no radical restructuring is needed. As mentioned in the interpretive recommendation section, a mandatory conference, interview, and demonstration of portfolio for all those seeking to enroll in the honors track would be a novel idea, but it may work against the student's interests. Creating further barriers may only dissuade good candidates. The process should remain largely as is, in part because the sources and types of information used in the decision are open and flexible enough to ensure that proper placement decisions are made.

The functionalists would standardized the process to a point where some good candidates may be disqualified. There are as many flaws in relying on objective, normative criteria as there are in the present interpretive arrangement. For example, relying too heavily on standardized tests may unduly penalize those who suffer from test anxiety, those who felt lousy on the day of the test, or those who did not try hard on the test because they believed there were no "high stakes" involved. Also, relying too heavily on standardized results works to the disadvantage of those with particular learning disabilities such as dyslexia. In the researcher's view, no further functional criteria should be imposed on the decisional process.

The radical critiques are interesting and do merit discussion. The school could do more to ensure a better balance between males and females, rich and poor, and minorities and nonminorities, but no quota system should be imposed. Schooling is about creating opportunities, not attempting to socially reengineer society into some ideal type. Quotas would only create hostilities, and in light of recent court cases, may not be legal anyway. However, the school could do more to affirmatively recruit more nontraditional students, beginning in the earliest grades, so that the balance is better maintained by the time the students reach high school.

Doing away with the program (as some radical structuralists may recommend) in the name of some abstract concept of justice would only hurt the students who want to participate and who currently benefit by enrolling in the courses. Yet, creating an open-enrollment honors program, although interesting and thoroughly democratic, creates its own set of problems. Despite the desires of some individuals who may want to enroll in the program, the integrity of the honors track must also be maintained. Viewing the world only through the lens of individual desire is as extreme as viewing the world only through the lens of programmatic integrity. A healthier arrangement lies in balancing individual desires with programmatic goals and intents, and only when there is a rough accommodation between the two will both benefit in the long run.

15

Analysis of an Organizational Decision: The Placement Process of the Latin American Scholarship Program of American Universities*

Josephine Jane Pavese

EXECUTIVE SUMMARY

This chapter introduces, discusses, and analyzes an organizational decision situation with regard to the information base on which the decision is made and the larger decision context. Both the information base and the context will be analyzed using four sociological paradigms.

The first two sections introduce the decision to be analyzed and place it in the larger context of the organization. The third section discusses the information base for the decision, presenting six main sources of information as well as five types of information necessary and available to decision makers. The six sources of information are then analyzed individually to determine the types of information each provides to decision makers and the ways in which it is made available to them.

The fourth section examines the sequential steps typically followed in the decision situation. In light of the previous section's information base analysis, it attempts to explore in detail how the types of information, gathered from various sources, are used in the stepwise decision process.

With this outline of the decision process and the information base on which it rests in mind, the article proceeds to analyze the sociological and epistemological

---

*This chapter was originally submitted as a term paper for a class in Organizational Analysis, Department of Administration, Training and Policy Studies, School of Education, Boston University, Spring 1990.

underpinnings of the decision situation. The fifth section focuses on the decision information base from the perspectives of four sociological paradigms. The purpose is to determine the types of information that are meaningful to the decision as it is located in each paradigm, thereby providing new and potentially useful perspectives on the decision situation. The sixth section then discusses the decision process as it is currently followed, with specific comparison between its theoretical bases and those of the paradigms presented.

Analyzing the sociological aspects of the decision information base, however, raises larger questions about the theoretical orientation of the decision itself. The seventh section, then, analyzes the decision context according to a radical-conservative and objective-subjective framework. The purpose is to reveal compatibilities and conflicts between the decision situation and the larger theoretical decision context.

The recommendations offered in the eighth section are meant to draw attention to the possibilities for change or alternative ways of thinking and decision making, with specific reference to the information base and decision context. The final section briefly summarizes the objectives of the chapter.

INTRODUCTION

Organizational Context

The Latin American Scholarship Program of American Universities (LASPAU) is a sponsoring agency for Latin American and Caribbean scholars who have won awards through programs such as the United States Information Agency and the United States Agency for International Development. All scholars are faculty members at Latin American and Caribbean institutions of higher education and are sponsored by them to pursue graduate study that will strengthen the development needs of the institution and the nation.

Program officers at LASPAU have the responsibility to place these Latin American and Caribbean scholarship winners in appropriate graduate programs in the United States. A graduate program is considered appropriate if its curriculum and resources will satisfy the scholar's academic and professional needs as well as the development objectives of his own or his sponsoring institution (these are often the same as the scholar's goals). The objective of program officers is to match as accurately as possible scholars' proposed programs of study with the interests, curricula, and resources at an accredited U.S. institution of higher education.

Placement Process

Placement is defined as gaining admission for a scholar in an appropriate graduate program. The placement process performed by program officers has six general steps:

1. Gather information about the scholar's proposed program of study.
2. Research U.S. graduate programs in the scholar's field of study.
3. Contact U.S. university departments and administrative offices directly to discuss the individual scholar.
4. Synthesize all information to determine the most suitable U.S. university.
5. Present dossier to the admissions office of the university selected by the program officer.
6. Follow up on the dossier until a letter of admission is received from the university.

Should the scholar not be admitted, the program officer must repeat the process to determine an alternative program. Depending on the amount of information gathered during the first time through the placement process, the program officer may not start at Step 1, but actually at a later point.

As an organization, LASPAU has had 26 years of placement experience. In the organization's yearly cycle of activities, the placement process usually occurs between December and June.

TYPE OF DECISION

Within the organizational context just described, this chapter analyzes the decision-making process surrounding the placement activity. Put simply, it addresses the question: How is the decision to place a scholar in a particular university program reached?

Because the scholar's success relies on the appropriateness of the placement, that is the specialized fit of the scholar's proposal and the U.S. university's program, it is important to state that making arbitrary placement decisions is not a strategy option for program officers: They must follow the placement process outlined earlier, and base their decisions on the information gathered during its steps. Therefore, this analysis of the decision-making process will focus on the available information that is taken advantage of by program officers, the sources of that information, and in what phase of the process it is used.

SOURCES AND TYPES OF INFORMATION

Sources of Information

Six sources of information affect the placement process and final placement decision: (a) the scholar, (b) the sponsoring Latin American or Caribbean institution, (c) funding agency representatives, (d) the U.S. university, (e) the program officer her or himself, and (f) LASPAU colleagues/organizational history.

Types of Information

Five broad categories or types of information that program officers use during the placement process have been identified. Placement is essentially a match between a scholar and a U.S. university program (including its faculty and administrators). Therefore, program officers need to know all five types of information for both the scholar and the U.S. university. The information types are categorized as follows:

1. *Personal* characteristics. Of the scholar: personal traits, religious or political beliefs, family and economic situation, and previous experiences abroad. Of the U.S. university faculty and administration: experiences abroad, teaching style, individual attitudes toward international, Latin American, or Caribbean students.
2. *Professional* expertise. Of the scholar and U.S. university faculty and administration: professional experiences, technical skills, publications, research accomplishments.
3. *Academic* information. From the scholar: the content of his or her undergraduate education, conferences, research. From the U.S. universities: content of the curriculum, academic prerequisites for admission.
4. *Programmatic* information. About the scholar: his or her role in the development plan of the Latin American or Caribbean sponsoring institution, how the scholarship will affect the scholar's duties upon return home, and any financial terms of the award, restrictions, and dictates such as degree level or priority fields of study. About the U.S. university: any formal or informal *convenios* (linkages) that may exist between their institutions and those abroad.
5. *Cultural* information. About the scholar and his or her sponsoring institution: the environment and set of beliefs and norms. About the U.S. university: the environment and set of beliefs and norms.

Types of Information Examined by Source

It is possible to examine the information available to program officers during the placement process by creating a framework that focuses either on sources of information or types of information. This analysis will focus on the six sources mentioned earlier. Under each of these categories, the types of information available from the sources and the way in which it is made accessible to program officers will then be discussed.

A framework based on the sources of information was chosen for two reasons: (a) it roughly corresponds to the chronological order in which information is made available to program officers in the annual placement cycle, and (b) in formulating recommendations to improve the information base (next to the last section of this chapter), a framework based on information sources may facilitate implementation by readily identifying the individuals who can assist in these efforts.

Source 1: The Scholar

The scholar is the individual who has been selected to receive a scholarship. This person has undergone extensive and competitive review at three levels: in the sponsoring institution, in a preselection of the entire candidate pool, and in the final selection of all preselected finalists.

Information.   Information is gathered from the scholar in three ways: the in-country interview, the written application, and postselection correspondence.

1. *Interview.* Each scholar is interviewed in his or her home country before being selected for the program. The interview is seen as a valuable source of information for two reasons: (a) It allows a program officer to meet the individual and gain another, more personal, perspective on the candidate's potential as a scholar and (b) it permits the scholar to explain more fully his or her proposal for study in the United States and to expand on the academic and professional needs this study will fulfill.
Types of information: personal, professional, academic, cultural

2. *Written application.* Each candidate completes an extensive LASPAU application, which requests information regarding academic and professional training and experience, proposal for study, and sponsoring institution support.
Types of information: personal, professional, academic

3. *Postselection correspondence.* After selection, scholars and program officers often correspond concerning the placement process as it is taking place. Scholars sometimes provide additional information about their programs, backgrounds, and academic needs at this time.
Types of information: personal, professional, academic

Source 2: Sponsoring Latin American
or Caribbean Institution

Each scholar is sponsored by the Latin American or Caribbean institution of higher education where he or she is on the faculty. The institutions choose candidates from among their staff to assist in concrete ways in the university's development plan. Usually the goals of this plan address both institutional and national needs.

Information.   Information that may affect the placement process is available through: the institution's written documents and visits by staff members.

1. *Written documents.* Latin American and Caribbean universities provide several written sources about their offerings, faculty, educational philosophy, and facilities. These can be in the form of university catalogues, essays, LASPAU contracts, and newspapers and journals.

Types of information: professional, academic

2. *Staff visits.* LASPAU staff members travel to Latin America and the Caribbean twice a year; the first time to do promotional work and the second time to conduct interviews of preselected candidates. During those trips they visit the sponsoring institutions' offices or campuses and meet with university administrators and teachers. These visits are considered extremely valuable because they provide first-hand information about the universities, the program administrators, and their preferences and priorities. Program officers also learn how the universities feel the scholarship program is meeting their needs and objectives.

Types of information: personal, professional, academic, programmatic, cultural

Source 3: Funding Agency and Its Representatives

U.S. government agencies that fund international scholarships have representatives of the programs in participating countries. For example, the United States Information Agency, which funds Fulbright scholarships, has a representative—usually the cultural affairs officer (CAO)—in the United States Information Service office in each embassy. Usually funding agency representatives are responsible to the Washington office for the success of the programs but, within the broad guidelines, have a certain amount of autonomy in their administration. LASPAU usually works directly with the in-country funder.

Information.   Information is received from the funder/funder representatives in three ways: the LASPAU in-country visit, communications to and from the in-country funder representative, and communications to and from the Washington-based funder.

1. *LASPAU in-country visit.* During the visits made by the LASPAU staff member, the in-country funder representative plays a major role in organizing the interviews and any institutional visits, describing the funder's view of the scholarship program in terms of meeting funder, as well as national, needs and objectives.

Types of information: personal, professional, programmatic, cultural

2. *Communications: in-country representatives.* Program officers communicate by telephone, cable, mail, and FAX.

Types of information: personal, programmatic, cultural

3. *Communications: Washington-based funder.* Program officers communicate by telephone, mail, FAX, and personal visit.

Types of information: personal, programmatic

Source 4: U.S. University

Admission of a scholar into an appropriate U.S. university academic program is the objective of placement. Therefore, the program officer must know as much as possible about programs around the country so as to direct the application of scholars who could benefit most from the match between their skills and needs and the resources and interests of the university. A university is described as an accredited institution of higher education located in any of the 50 states and Puerto Rico.

Information.   Program officers obtain information from U.S. institutions in three ways: personal visits, written materials, and telephone conversations with faculty and administrators.

1. *Personal Visits.* Every year, each program officer is required to take one 2-week trip to visit a group of 8 or 10 U.S. universities. During these visits program officers find out and record information about admissions requirements, department requirements, faculty interests, and financial aid. In addition, as LASPAU representatives, they try to promote interest in the organization and its scholars.
Types of information: professional, academic, cultural

2. *Written Materials.* U.S. universities produce general catalogues and brochures about their institutions. Their departments often create their own documents with information that is area and degree specific. The LASPAU office has many of these documents on file for reference.
Types of information: professional, academic

3. *Telephone contact with faculty and administrators.* It is common practice for program officers to call academic departments and administrative offices at U.S. universities to discuss both the programs offered and the proposal of a specific scholar. It is during these detailed conversations that a feel for the appropriateness of the match begins to take shape. Questions of a very specific nature are asked by both the faculty member or administrator and the program officer, and it is often during this activity that the program officer will make the final placement choice on behalf of a scholar.
Type of information: academic, cultural

Source 5: The Program Officer

Every program officer is a source of information for him or herself. Personal experiences of every sort—on the job, in academic programs, as a member of a family, in international settings (a person's life) all provide a filter through which to make meaning out of information and a backdrop against which information can be used to make decisions.

Types of information: personal, professional, academic, programmatic, cultural

Source 6: LASPAU History and Colleagues

LASPAU has 26 six years of placement experience. The process has been more or less well-documented for the last 10 to 15 years. During that time, the personal contacts made and nurtured by placement staff among Latin American and Caribbean university administrators, funding agency representatives, and U.S. university faculty and administrators have become a resource base for future organizational operations. New contacts are made every day, and program officers share and use this information to make the best possible choices on behalf of scholars.

Information.   Information is available to program officers in the following forms: scholar files and electronic database, LASPAU colleagues, and alumni questionnaires.

1. *Files and electronic database.* It is possible to trace the progress of past placements through information and documentation in individual scholar files and the computer database.
Types of information: professional, academic, programmatic

2. *LASPAU colleagues.* Communication among staff members is a valued and required activity at LASPAU. Much information is shared from person to person and, although program officers have their own case loads, they are constantly requesting information and insight from each other. This is especially true of new program officers who call on colleagues with more experience and a broader sense of LASPAU's placement history.
Types of information: professional, academic, programmatic, cultural

3. *Alumni questionnaires.* At the end of their programs, scholars are asked to fill out a questionnaire that requests information about their academic departments as well as reactions to the services provided by LASPAU. These questionnaires are on file and often are used by program officers who are thinking about making placements at schools or departments in which a scholar has studied in the past.

It has been the organization's experience that the scholars offer honest and candid responses to these questions and try to use them as a vehicle to bring important points, both good and bad, to the attention of the administration. Precisely because of their frankness, these responses are extremely valuable to the staff and are taken seriously by the organization.

Types of information: personal, professional, academic, programmatic, cultural

HOW INFORMATION IS USED: A SECOND LOOK
AT THE PLACEMENT PROCESS

Having identified the sources and types of information used in the placement process, we can now take a second and more detailed look at the process to see how and when program officers use the information they have.

Step 1: Gather Information About the Scholar's Proposal for Study

In this phase of the placement process, the program officer uses information primarily from the scholar, funder representatives, and the sponsoring Latin American or Caribbean institution. The types of information most relevant to this step are academic, cultural, personal, and programmatic. The goals of this step are to: (a) assess academic strengths and weaknesses, (b) try to understand the purpose and content of the proposed program of study, and (c) evaluate the scholar as an individual to determine as much as possible the kind of U.S. university environment in which he or she would succeed. Program officers spend a good deal of time reading the scholar's own proposal for study, reflecting on notes and impressions from the interview, and reading the statements of support from the scholar's sponsoring institution.

Academic strengths and weaknesses are assessed with the help of transcripts, description and reputation of the scholar's undergraduate program, and test scores, if available, as well as what scholars say during their interviews. In addition, programmatic information can provide a context for the scholar's performance. Funder representatives often have extensive knowledge of a nation's educational system and can give their interpretations of university and even individual scholar excellence.

Similarly, understanding the proposal for study requires program officers to rely heavily on statements from the sponsoring institution about its faculty and curriculum and notes from the interview, during which the scholar has been asked to provide as much detail as possible about the subject to be studied in the United States. When program officers are unfamiliar with an academic subject (information from his or her own academic experience), the task becomes one of "learning" a new field.

Perhaps the most difficult information to ascertain in this initial step is of a cultural and personal nature. The organization has found that for scholars to be successful, they must be personally suited to or comfortable with the kind of environment into which they are sent to study. Somehow the program officer must get a "feel" for the scholar, and determine from written statements and the personal meeting the "kind" of person he or she really is, so that the match between scholar and school will be a good one.

This certainty would be difficult to achieve within the program officer's own culture, but with individuals from a different culture, it is even more so. Yet the success of the placement very often hangs in the balance. Program officers try to understand and evaluate another person's professional and academic experience; political, social, and economic background; and personal goals and ambitions, then act upon their assessments on the scholar's behalf.

Step 2: Research U.S. Graduate Programs in the Scholar's Field of Study

There are thousands of academic programs in the United States. The job of the program officer is to choose one program that will satisfy the academic and professional needs of a scholar. The diversity of department interests, facilities, size, approaches, and faculty is enormous, and the task of selecting one department seems monumental. However, program officers have a number of important sources of information about universities and specific programs that help them to put the task into perspective.

Information from LASPAU colleagues and written records about past experience is of primary importance. Successful past placements often point a program officer toward a number of schools that have proven to be good sites for scholars with particular interests and academic needs. Program officers' knowledge of past history, their personal visits to specific universities, and written records of suggestions and departmental information are used to advantage. Repeat placements (sending a new scholar every few years to a specific department that has proved successful) are common although there is a slight tendency to view excessive repetition as an overuse and reflects badly on the creativity of the program officer.

This information, together with the written materials from universities—catalogues, brochures, public relations information—helps program officers to narrow down their many choices to a few possibilities for final placements. Even a thorough review of this information cannot provide more than an overview of an institution's offerings. Therefore, program officers proceed to Step 3 of the process in which they begin to contact, individually and personally, personnel at the institutions they have chosen for further investigation.

Step 3: Contact U.S. University

This placement step is equal in importance to the first step described previously, because it is meant to elicit information on an institutional level, from U.S. universities and academic departments, similar to that obtained about individual scholars. Contact is made directly with faculty and administrators to ascertain information about specific faculty interests, research and laboratory facilities, interest in international students, and specific admissions requirements. From these personal conversations, program officers hope to get a "feel" for the school and the department and to gather information and impressions that might help to inform the final placement decision. The aim of an ideal match between scholar and university is what drives this step of the process.

Step 4: Synthesize All Information and Choose Final Placement

The information from Step 1 guides the program officers' conversations with university administrators and teachers. The personal, academic, and professional information from the universities is matched with the profile of the scholar formulated in that first step. A careful review all of the alternatives in light of this profile results in the choice of a final placement.

Step 5: Present Dossier to the University

This step is sometimes considered to be strictly technical in nature: The materials requested by the U.S. university (transcripts, letters of recommendations, essays) are assembled in a folder that identifies the scholar with the LASPAU program and sent to the official LASPAU contact on campus. However, even this fairly mechanical step makes liberal use of programmatic, academic, institutional, personal, and cultural information. In presenting the scholar officially to the U.S. university through the admission process, program officers have the opportunity to "package" scholars' documents in such away as to make the most of their personal attributes, academic skills, and professional experiences and accentuate the match between scholars' credentials and the universities' stated requirements.

Step 6: Follow Up on the Application Until a Letter of Admission is Received

This final step in the process primarily involves providing information to evaluators at the university as the application makes its way through the admissions process. Program officers often help faculty and administrators interpret documents contained in the dossier. They do so because they have information about the specific academic and professional environments from which scholars come that university personnel do not have. At the same time that this information is helpful for the university, the program officer also has an additional opportunity to make use of programmatic, cultural, academic, and professional information. If the program officer's assessments have been accurate, this last step can serve to reinforce the appropriateness of the match and result in a letter of admission.

ANALYSIS OF THE DECISION INFORMATION
BASE USING FOUR SOCIOLOGICAL PARADIGMS

Burrell and Morgan (1979) state that "all theories of organisation are based upon a philosophy of science and a theory of society" (p. 1). Using an objective-subjective ontological-epistemological axis and a radical-conservative ideological axis, they have constructed a framework in which four paradigms for the analysis of social theory are identified. They are the radical humanist, radical structuralist, interpretive, and functionalist paradigms.

There are fundamental differences between and among these paradigms with regard to the social theories and knowledge bases on which they rest. Because of this, each has a different requirement for the type (or combination of types) of information that would be appropriate or meaningful in decision making from that perspective.

This section will look at the LASPAU placement process from the point of view of each of the four paradigms. The purpose of such a study is twofold. First, it will identify the types of information that would meaningfully inform decision making from that perspective. In doing so, it will show how the information requirements change for each paradigm from those used currently at LASPAU. Second, studying the process from the perspectives of four paradigms may provide glimpses at alternative reasoning that may inform the current process. A third benefit, discussed more fully later, relates to how the analysis may reveal sources of conflict, confirm fundamental programmatic beliefs on which the present process is based, or point out alternative sources or types of information that were not recognized as necessary or appropriate.

Functionalist Paradigm

Within the functionalist paradigm, the decision maker has a problem-oriented approach based on the model of scientific inquiry. Reasoning and observation are combined to know and understand notions of the universe that are absolute (Burrell & Morgan, 1979, p. 41). From a functionalist perspective, placement would require a scientific analysis of each scholar's dossier, through the use of quantitative methods, to rate or classify such measures as skill, intelligence, and experience. Academic GPA, years of teaching experience, rank in class, and test scores on standardized tests, for example, would play a significant role in the decision-making process. Because the universe is constructed of discernible absolutes, the functionalist placement officer would view these quantitative measures as a satisfactory, if not mandatory, method of comparing one scholar to another, and a particular scholar to the stated requirements of a U.S. university.

Information most appropriate to the functionalist paradigm, then, would probably take a quantitative form. Functionalist program officers would agree that there are known standards for acceptable levels of academic and professional preparation and performance against which they can compare their scholars. These standards support a status quo with regard to academic and professional variables and do not provide for consideration of individual characteristics that cannot be measured on an absolute scale. Therefore, information referred to earlier as personal and cultural, such as economic or social background, learning style, and level of commitment to national development, would be, if not irrelevant, of secondary importance.

The information base at LASPAU, from a functionalist perspective, would require standardized measures of achievement, performance, and intelligence. In effect, program officers would not have to ask scholars for personal and cultural information of the type currently sought because it would not affect placement decisions, and the "figures" would speak for themselves.

Interpretive Paradigm

An interpretive approach to social theory includes the important notion that the social world is an emergent social process created by the individuals involved. The approach to decision making and information gathering in this paradigm would emphasize the view that "one can only understand the social world by obtaining firsthand knowledge of the subject under investigation" (Burrell & Morgan, 1979, p. 6). The interpretivist program officer would try to "get inside" the scholar's situation (Burrell & Morgan, 1979, p. 6). On the ontological axis, however, this paradigm is conservative and supports a sociological status quo.

Interpretivist program officers would therefore try to gather information that would enlighten them concerning scholars' individual lives (e.g., their national realities, economic and social backgrounds, and personal and professional experiences). In addition, because program officers recognize that the institutional structures of society (higher education and universities) set standards for preparation and performance, they must gather quantifiable data as well for each scholar in order to work on behalf of scholars in the institutional contexts.

Since interpretivist program officers know that reality is individual, they may have to accept the reality that their attempts to "get inside" scholars will never be adequate. Neither can they be sure that they are asking scholars the right questions to elicit information they desire. Similarly, program officers must also recognize that what they think they understand scholars to say, in fact, may not be what scholars believe they are meaning to say. Therefore, individual information sought in the interpretive paradigm is of a particularly sensitive and peculiarly uncertain nature.

Radical Humanist Paradigm

The radical humanist paradigm is "a sociology of radical change from a subjective standpoint" (Burrell & Morgan, 1979, p. 32). Like the interpretive paradigm, this approach believes in an individualistic view of reality, but in addition it seeks to transcend the conservative sociological status quo by identifying and changing the social patterns that limit individual expression and demonstration of full potential.

A radical humanist program officer might reject the placement process as unsatisfactory and irrelevant to the needs of individuals because: (a) in the placement process program officers make decisions on behalf of an individual whose needs and nature cannot be determined external to the individual, and (b) it supports a status quo for resource distribution (e.g., education, economic opportunity) that relies on "standards" that consciously favor certain forms of behavior, background, and achievement, while functionally excluding all others.

In this paradigm, information may be inadequate, or it may be impossible to gather. As in the interpretive paradigm, the radical humanist program officers cannot know the souls of the scholars. They can only make more or less effective attempts at understanding personal meaning from their external positions. Therefore, as in the preceding paradigm, the questions asked of scholars and their responses can be only partially understood.

However, because the paradigm rejects the conservative status quo, which LASPAU tends to accept, program officers must look at the nature of the questions they ask and the system in which they are working on behalf of scholars. LASPAU's current models for nomination and selection are conventional in nature; that is, by seeking scholars from specific positions (university teachers) in the social structure, they effectively exclude individuals from other stations in the social system. In addition, the decision-making models base their assessments of scholars on a (modified) ranking system. This reinforces the resource distribution dictated by the existing social structure by focusing on the candidates who appear to be the "top."

The paradigm's radical emphasis gives the radical humanist program officer a clear mandate to secure other types of information that reveal existing power relationships, resource distribution, gender and race issues, and economic and social hierarchy in order to bring about change through individual empowerment. The program officer, then, would strive to obtain this kind of information, which is not sought formally through the present process. Sources for this might include economists, political scientists, and the man or woman on the street.

Radical Structuralist

From the radical structuralist perspective, "society is characterised by fundamental conflicts which generate radical change through political and economic crises. It is through such conflict and change that the emancipation of men from the social structure in which they live is seen as coming about" (Burrell & Morgan, 1979, p. 34). Radical structuralism acknowledges a structured social world, and it is through structural interrelationships that individual fulfillment and potential is achieved.

For the radical structuralist program officer, supporting the status quo is as unacceptable as it was for the radical humanist. However, in this paradigm social reality is not interpreted by each individual member. Rather, personal potential and meaning is derived through a recognizable and universal reality when it responds to economic and political pressures. With respect to the placement process, the LASPAU program officer would once again be focused toward change and away from the status quo, but this would be achieved through the interrelationships of societal structures, and not through empowerment or understanding of each individual member of society.

The types of information needed for a radical structuralist approach to the placement process, then, would include political, social, and economic data, which, as mentioned earlier, is not now collected formally. However, quantitative information would be appropriate because the epistemological basis for this paradigm is objective.

THE CURRENT PLACEMENT PROCESS

I believe that the interpretive paradigm comes closest to describing the sociological underpinnings of the present LASPAU placement process. Although program officers recognize that there are norms for performance and preparation, they attempt to expand the boundaries imposed by these standards through the conscious inclusion of information that is individually pertinent. LASPAU seeks cultural information in recognition of the belief that reality (or at least some important part of it) is known only by scholars themselves. In compliance with norms set by a system beyond their control (U.S. higher education), and in which they also tend to believe, at least in part, program officers also gather quantifiable data about each scholar.

As it is done at LASPAU, placement follows the methodical stepwise process described earlier, informed by the program officer's interpretation of personal, individual information gained about each scholar. It is believed by the organization that if program officers try to "get inside" the scholar and understand national and personal context, the best placement will result. It seems more accurate to say that perhaps a better placement will result, better than if program officers ignored completely all individual information and considered only quantitative measures in assessing placement possibilities (a functionalist approach). The distinction between these two ways of thinking about placement is very important, because in my view, it explains the source of some of the conflict that results between the program officers' and the scholars' conceptions of the ideal placement.

At the end of their programs in the United States, scholars are asked to fill out a questionnaire about their academic, programmatic, and personal experiences. The question requesting information about the placement choice overwhelmingly receives responses such as the following (please note that these are quoted from individuals whose native language is not English):

> "I am not discontented with ___, but I think that my academic needs could have been better met in a university with a stronger ___ orientation."
> "It did not meet my previous expectations."
> "It was not bad but it could be better choices."
> "What seems to be adequate for LASPAU is far from adequate for the scholar."

It is possible, then, that the real and documented discrepancy between the program officer's placement and the scholar's ideal placement at LASPAU, demonstrates the validity of subjective sociological paradigms' claim that, to a certain extent, individual reality cannot be known by others. It may also indicate that the placement process, as it is designed and practiced, does not, or perhaps cannot, capture individual or subjective information that is the essence of scholars' expectations and hopes. Compound the difficulty of "getting inside" one's own culture with the forces and frameworks of another culture, and the task becomes daunting.

It could be argued that the discrepancy between the program officer's placement and the scholar's expectations lies in the officer's ability to carry out the placement process more or less better than his or her colleagues. However, in an informal reading of approximately 60 alumni questionnaires over the last 3 or 4 years, about 75% had comments similar to those quoted earlier. That is the reason why I feel it is important to highlight the distinction between making an ideal placement and making an honest best effort.

If the placement process remains as it is, comments like those quoted earlier may not be eliminated. The organization will have to accept the fact that the best that can be done is being done, and that the end result will not change dramatically by harder effort or by hiring better program officers. Fundamental changes would have to be made in the process, for dramatically different results (and not necessarily better, given the complexity of the task) to take place.

ANALYSIS OF PROBLEM AND DECISION CONTEXT ACCORDING TO RADICAL-CONSERVATIVE AND OBJECTIVE-SUBJECTIVE FRAMEWORKS

It seems that improving the placement decision process, to a large extent, may depend on improving the information base on which it rests. However, before exploring what fundamental changes might be made regarding the process of obtaining and using information, this section analyzes the decision itself in the larger context of organizational ideology and epistemology.

The LASPAU Program: A Radical Approach
to Development

The LASPAU program founders and its current administration and staff believe that education is one of the most important keys to the development of economically developing nations. There is no single definition of development, and projects carried out in its name range from industrial support to nutrition programs. However, research literature increasingly suggests that, from all perspectives, education is an important way to raise the ability of individuals and nations to begin to address for themselves the problems and needs that have hampered economic growth, political and administrative capability, and social justice.

According to Burrell and Morgan's framework, then, the LASPAU program could be seen as a radical activity. That is, its objective is to effect positive change in the social condition through education. This objective is reached in two ways: (a) The education of individuals in priority fields means, presumably, that these experts will have the knowledge to effect change at a national or macro level (in fact, LASPAU scholars do just that), and (b) that these experts will teach other individuals in formal and informal educational settings (also an activity of LASPAU alumni/ae). At either level, the aim is to foster change through the educational empowerment of individuals.

Why is that important to LASPAU scholars from Latin America and the Caribbean? It is because the participants in the programs and their sponsoring institutions feel that, in certain formal and informal ways, the distribution of resources, and perhaps power, has not been equitable. Scholars are professors teaching and advising students in provincial universities who are often overlooked for advanced training opportunities, biologists working in rural health with the poorest citizens who often do not have the up-to-date information with which to combat problems of nutrition, social workers and anthropologists working with indigenous populations forgotten by their governments. The issues involved in the work of each scholar are those of power and distribution, not only for themselves but for the people with whom they work and have influence.

Implementation of the LASPAU program, then, is accomplished, not at the level of the nation or even the university, but by the case-by-case placement of 250 individuals each year in programs that will equip them with the knowledge they need to effect change at home. The goals and priorities of the program take on a related but entirely new meaning for every scholar, each with a background and a future filled with personal knowledge, failures, joys, and dreams. The success of the program depends on the success of the individual who participates in its process.

The Placement Process: A Conservative Response
to a Radical Question?

The placement process is a method of extracting information from many sources, synthesizing it in light of the complementary and competing goals and objectives of LASPAU, the sponsoring Latin American and Caribbean universities, and the individual scholar, then matching it with a U.S. university program that will maximize the possibility of attaining these goals. A conscientious assessment of the information gives the program officer a good idea of the limitations, strengths, and capabilities of the scholar. Coupled with similar information, at an institutional level about U.S. university programs, the program officer makes a best guess at the fit of the placement match.

Although program officers visit the countries to which they are assigned and are able to see firsthand the conditions and situations of scholars and their sponsoring universities, they cannot be certain of their interpretations of the information they receive; they cannot "know" what they see in the same way as the scholars can. With a limited understanding of both cultural and personal information, then, it can be asked if the LASPAU program can know at all what is appropriate for scholars, and if it can or should be making important choices on their behalf.

It may be important to emphasize that cultural information is not limited to the influence of culture on individual behavior (e.g., rules of decorum, gender roles, or ethics). In the context of the placement process, such information is also implicit in educational norms such as patterns of academic curriculum, concepts of satisfactory performance, the structure of student–teacher relationships, and the societal role of education. In this light, it could be questioned whether the cultural assumptions and priorities on which the U.S. university system is based have any meaning for and can respond appropriately to the needs of students from other nations.

Possible Ideological Conflict

Placement as a scientific or interpretive process (i.e., it attempts to be informed by individually cultural and personal meaning), then, might be ill-suited to the implementation of a radical subjective activity if empowerment of individuals should (and must) take precise account of them as Brazilians, nuns, Mayans, parents, mapmakers, and ballet dancers.

On the programmatic scale, possible conflicts of ideology could arise for program officers if there was tension between the radical aim (education for empowerment) and a more conservative program structure (a funder's vision of economic development, for example). The problem of competing ideologies that surround the placement decision might also occur if the quest for subjective meaning for each individual scholar must be joined to the objective scientific framework of U.S. higher education systems of admissions and degree requirements.

It is possible, therefore, that LASPAU asks program officers to combine a positivist belief in predictive knowledge of the external world with a conventionalist approach to a subjective reality (Hatch, 1985, p. 161). At the same time, it also may be asking economically developing nations to match their ideas for radical reform with a conservative status quo vision of social order.

Responses to the alumni questionnaire touch indirectly on this topic under the question, "How do you think the placement process could be improved?" Here are sample responses to this question:

> "The scholar should have a say as to the type of educational institution he/she is placed."
> "LASPAU should also ask the [scholars] to support the selection they have made."
> "A new [scholar] maybe needs more orientation to really choose a program."

These statements, and many similar to them, indicate that scholars believe in the power to determine their own placements and that the role of LASPAU should change from decision maker to facilitator. In their discussion of Fourth Generation Evaluation, Guba and Lincoln described the evaluator in this alternative evaluation model as moving from "the role of judge to orchestrator of the judgmental process" (Guba & Lincoln, 1985, p. 141; see also, Guba & Lincoln, 1989). The program officer has taken on the role of the evaluator/orchestrator as he or she tries to "enter" the placement "scene as a learner." However, unlike the fourth generation model evaluator, who does not make a final decision, program officers, at least at present, must. Therefore, program officers have no choice but to emerge finally as "experts," even though the radical and interpretive social paradigms in which they dabble rule that this is impossible.

Even the cherished belief that knowledge is universally transferable is uncertain in this analysis. Are educational systems compatible? On which norms are they based? Scholars have made pointed comments on this topic:

> "Graduate work in the U.S. is very different than what I expected."
> "The problem was the way the studies were approached."
> "Please make sure with your oncoming scholars which is their expectation and what is what they plan to solve when thinking of [the United States] as a source of the possible solution."

What Is to Be Done?

Does this conflict mean that program officers should give up trying to understand their scholars and that international students should not study in the United States? Of course not. *Open Doors*, published annually by the Institute for International Education, indicates that record numbers of international students are coming to enroll in U.S. institutions of higher education. The contributions of LASPAU alumni to their sponsoring institutions and their nations alone bear witness to the knowledge and expertise that can be and is acquired by international students during their U.S. studies.

In addition, LASPAU scholars have stated that they were very pleased to have come to the U.S. through LASPAU rather than other sponsoring agencies, specifically noting the staff's efforts to understand and work with them toward personal and national goals. Perhaps, in spite of the alumni questionnaires, the subjective aims of program officers are desirable, however imperfect.

RECOMMENDATIONS

The section offers recommendations for change in the placement decision process, with specific reference to the issues raised in the analyses of the decision information base and the decision context. Some aspects of the recommendations could possibly be incorporated in the organization's present structure. However, some are offered from the perspective of alternative paradigms and may be less likely, or impossible, to implement. In any case, it is hoped that these latter suggestions do serve to broaden the vision of placement, development, and program structure.

Recommendation 1: Increase Scholar Involvement in the Placement Process

It is recommended that scholars be given a greater role in the placement process. This recommendation stems from the interpretive and radical humanist paradigms, which recognize subjective information as valuable and valid, projecting a radical vision of the social system that sees development as a process of individual empowerment for change. If scholars alone know their own needs and the national and individual contexts of their work, then they should play a prominent role in their own placement.

When considering implementation, however, a question arises from this recommendation concerning the extent of scholar participation in the process and the type of role scholars could or should play. At the organizational level, the range of scholar roles depends on the strength of the subjective component of LASPAU's social vision. At the program level, this issue is closely related to scholars' knowledge of U.S. programs and educational culture.

Organizational Capabilities

Theoretically, greater participation of scholars would probably be supported by LASPAU because the organization is guided, at least in part, by an interpretive philosophy that values subjective types of information in addition to its sociological approach, which corresponds to individual empowerment. This has been discussed in detail in previous sections. Accommodations for greater scholar participation would probably be possible and encouraged by the organization. However, as participation increases toward scholar control of the process, serious organizational problems begin to arise.

As a service organization, LASPAU's working philosophy of personal empowerment through education and its individual approach to problem solving and decision making are a framework on which it bases the work of contract implementation. However, the extent to which the organization can exercise this philosophy to a greater or lesser degree is actually dependent on the funder's own perspective on development. Such organization restrictions could greatly affect the role of the scholar or beneficiary in the project.

Scholar Capabilities

From the perspective of scholar capabilities, development workers note that a paradox sometimes exists between beneficiaries' desire (and right) to manifest control during the development process and their deficiencies (seeming or real) in preparedness to do so. At LASPAU, scholars' desire to choose their own placements is confounded by the documented scarcity of information available to them at home about U.S. universities and the culture of U.S. education. Therefore, scholars' ability to make realistic placement choices becomes an important question in the attempt to determine their role in the placement process. Because much time and resources would be needed to supply scholars with the appropriate information for making informed decisions, changes in project planning to provide such information would likely conflict with the time and financial constraints of projects.

A Word About Cultural Chauvinism

It should be noted that cultural chauvinism plays an important role in a discussion of both the programmatic and scholar constraints that determine the role of scholars in placement. First, social paradigms that promote the status quo do so by supporting a view that some sectors of a population (globally or nationally) receive access to resources and opportunities at the expense of other sectors. According to the previous analyses, processes that support the status quo are part of the environment in which the LASPAU placement process takes place. Programmatically, then, LASPAU may be limiting its ability to incorporate scholar control into its structure because of philosophical constraints about the structure of society.

In addition, the sociological visions of conservative paradigms can dictate patterns of thought and action about the actual distribution of information. Information's potential for creating changes in the balance, or imbalance, of power is a serious consideration to those who defend or perpetuate the status quo. In the case of many LASPAU scholars, the physical scarcity of information requires that decisions be made for them by people who have a great deal of relevant information.

Possible Scholar Roles

Given these constraints and considerations, we look briefly at three specific roles along a continuum of scholar participation.

Role 1: Scholars Provide More Detailed Subjective Information.

Scholars would provide even more information of the cultural and personal type than is currently sought, either in oral (more interview questions or questioning over the entire placement process) or written (more extensive application) form. This would continue to place scholars in dependent positions, but it would assist program officers in working on their behalf. Although it would mean more work for both scholars and program officers in preparation and interpretation, respectively, more cultural and personal information would give further clarification to an admittedly imperfect task and would have the potential to improve the chances of arranging a good placement.

One important organizational concern, however, would be regarding the validity of both oral and written questioning. Because language is so distinctly and beautifully linked to culture, program officers cannot be sure that they are asking the questions they think they are asking, nor can they be certain that they are interpreting correctly the information they receive. (Neither can scholars be sure they are providing the right information.) Thus, for example, the development of a new questionnaire or more essay questions, which at first seems unproblematic, may actually be less helpful than anticipated.

Therefore, more and continued cross-checking between what people are saying and what they are understanding would be advisable, if this recommendation were to be implemented. Such cross-checking could be incorporated into the system as it is practiced today, although time and labor would be a serious constraint. Implementation of this role recommendation would not change the placement process or the structure of the organization, both of which, it should be noted here, and in further discussion later, have tendencies to support a conservative sociological status quo.

Role 2: Scholars Take Responsibility for Actively Researching Programs Along With Program Officers to Find Those That Seem to Satisfy Their Needs.

Scholars and program officers should work together on placements, with both parties researching university programs at the same time and sharing ideas and suggestions. This scheme places scholars and program officers more or less on an equal basis, although the latter group would still retain control over the final arrangements. In addition, it would bolster the personal, cultural, academic, and programmatic types of information available to program officers through more direct scholar contact.

This recommendation would require that LASPAU or some other agency provide scholars with detailed information about U.S. universities either when scholars are home in Latin America and the Caribbean or in the United States studying English. Government agencies such as the United States Information Service maintain libraries at embassies with an assortment of catalogues and counseling services that range from excellent to practically nonexistent. Latin American and Caribbean institutions sometimes have their own campus services for such information but with the same range of delivery. Stepping up the provision of detailed educational information could not be accomplished by LASPAU, and the organization has no control over other means of distribution. Therefore, this part of the recommendation would probably not be implemented in a formal way.

Instead, a compromise might be planned in which program officers research universities and offer scholars detailed information about four or five of them, from which scholars would choose the program they feel is most appropriate. This scheme has been suggested by scholars many times in the alumni questionnaires. However, the time involved in having each program officer personally engage 70 scholars in such a labor-intensive exchange of information in the short period when placements occur is not practical from a programmatic perspective. A solution might be to hire more program officers, but the financial limitations of this action likely would be prohibitive.

This recommendation should not be dismissed out of hand, however, because it seems to hold the most potential for improving the placement process. It is a recommendation that addresses, to some extent, the radical paradigm roots of the development program. An important point that scholars seems anxious to make in their alumni questionnaires and that has become apparent to me in the previous analyses, is that they have a right to power and ownership in the decision-making process.

Role 3: Scholars Take Over the Process Completely and Place Themselves.   This role is an interesting consideration because of its potential effects. This recommended role seems to be derived from a purer interpretation of the radical humanist paradigm. In this role, scholars find out the information they need to the extent they desire and apply to whatever schools they wish. Yet, this role possesses a conservative element as well, because it is a role that infers support of the status quo in the form of existing U.S. graduate admissions requirements.

Some scholars taking on this role might soon find themselves running into this functionalist wall. Working without proper information for self-evaluation and institutional assessment, scholars could make unrealistic or inappropriate choices. If the scholars happened not to support a status quo distribution of power and intellectual opportunity, they might experience some conflict with requirements for prerequisites and experience at particular schools.

Some scholars, however, would do just fine. Universities in Latin America and the Caribbean graduate excellent scholars and professionals who are quickly recognized in the admissions process for their talents. For these scholars, perhaps, there might be no conflict between the status quo for educational opportunity and the reward.

Practically speaking, LASPAU would have to change its philosophical vision to implement this role recommendation. It believes that assistance in the placement process is necessary and helpful to scholars because so many do not have the information and resources they need to reach the goal of higher education. However, some funders consider a program desirable in which no overhead is incurred through the work of a third-party sponsoring agency, and such programs do exist today in the United States, Latin America, and the Caribbean.

Recommendation 2: Increase Program Officer Effectiveness Regarding Cultural Information

The preceding recommendation places the burden of providing increased information of the personal and cultural type on the scholar. This recommendation, however, expands the role of the program officers' source of information and suggests that they become more effective agents in knowing and understanding the cultural and personal contexts that affect scholars. That is, it recommends that LASPAU increase the amount of personal, academic, and cultural information available to it by expanding the opportunities to receive such information through the program officers.

Because social paradigms with a subjective emphasis state that information is known only to individuals themselves, ways of implementing this recommendation must be considered over a spectrum, none of which, from this perspective, can or will be entirely successful. Three examples illustrate this range: (a) program officers could ask more individual questions of scholars and their sponsors, continuously checking their understanding of information with the appropriate individuals; (b) program officers could spend more time in-country when interviewing or during the year to learn about national and individual contexts; or (c) program officers could be selected on the basis of Latin American or Caribbean nationality, matching officers with scholars from their own nations.

The following discussion will review each of these possible roles individually to highlight their theoretical and informational bases as well as any implementation possibilities.

Possible Program Officer Roles

Role 1: Program Officers Elicit More Information of the Cultural and Personal Type.   This role corresponds closely with the scholar's Role 1 in the first recommendation. However, in this case it is the program officer's responsibility to attempt new levels of understanding instead of merely collecting more information. Along this line, it should be noted that neither of these recommendations mean to suggest that an increase of any kind of information is necessarily better or helpful.

Rather, both call for a reasoned approach to finding out from both program officers and scholars what information is essential and appropriate to placement decision making (personal meetings and discussions during the placement process and mutual agreement on what seems to satisfy all needs are recommended), and then devising the means to obtain it (mutual agreement on what methods elicit this information best such as essays, visits, photographs).

As in Role 1 discussed earlier, this recommendation does not alter the decision making structure of the program and would probably be encouraged by the organization.

Role 2: Program Officers Spend More Time Abroad. There is no way to determine categorically if increased exposure to a foreign culture causes a corresponding increase in discernment of or sensitivity to important cultural information. LASPAU sends its program officers abroad to interview candidates because it believes that the power of personal assessment and experience will affect the placement process in positive ways. The office consensus, though without benefit of quantifiable proof, is that, in fact, it does.

Furthermore, the extent to which increasing time abroad would produce correspondingly greater positive effects on decision making is presently unknown, but it is believed to be substantial. I am encouraged in presenting this role recommendation by a move in the office to give program officers greater in-country responsibility and presence this coming year. Over a decade ago, the office had an administrative structure that required representatives to spend a great deal of time in-country. This was abandoned in favor of a different office structure, but the requirement has resurfaced in recent months as a possible method of reactivating closer country ties.

This recommendation does not change the structure of the placement process. It does, however, intend to provide a greater infusion of cultural and personal information into placement and the organization as a whole through the program officer. In addition, this recommendation would increase the amount of institutional, academic, and programmatic type information through longer and closer contact with in-country funder representatives and Latin American and Caribbean university administrators. It also reinforces the organization's subjective social approach.

Role 3: Hire Individuals Only From Latin America and the Caribbean as Program Officers. Previous analyses have pointed out the potential difficulties in trying to understand meaning and experience in other cultures. It is possible that scholars' fellow nationals would be more effective as program officers than people from other cultures. In fact, LASPAU has tried to attract more Latin American and Caribbean employees to the organization because it believes in the importance of a regional perspective in all phases of its operations.

Because ability and job effectiveness are individual issues, Latin American and Caribbean Program Officers could be more or less skilled than U.S. personnel in the technical aspects of placement. However, a greater level of cultural understanding would be an important asset in the placement process, so this recommendation should be considered a serious one. Regarding implementation, it would be impractical and financially unfeasible to have a different program officer for each country. However, to the extent that a compromise could result in program officers with personal regional affiliation, I believe that the organization might tend to support it.

Regarding the decision information base, a side effect of this role recommendation might be the discovery of presently unidentified sources of all types of information. Program officers with cultural knowledge and personal experience may know of individuals and agencies that are more culturally appropriate sources, perhaps, than those identified by outsiders.

Recommendation 3: Economically Developing Nations Should Manage the Project Themselves

Recommendations 1 and 2 suggest that changes in the behavior of scholars and program officers, respectively, might have beneficial effects on the placement process. As has been mentioned, however, these changes leave the basic structure of the funder/beneficiary system intact: The funder and its agents are charged with management and decision making on behalf of project beneficiaries. This recommendation, however, seeks to make an important change in the structure of the system by placing the beneficiary, not the benefactor, in charge.

It could be suggested in this recommendation that Latin American and Caribbean nations be given the dollars that fuel the LASPAU program, and others like it, directly, to spend however they choose. For purposes of this analysis, though, it is assumed that these countries regard a program to provide advanced training to university faculty members as desirable. I therefore suggest that the program funder give over the funds to them for design and implementation.

Development project analysts and implementors such as Samuel Paul (1982) and Elliott Morss (1981, 1982, 1986) have noted that beneficiaries are rarely given the power to design or manage projects that affect them directly and that seek to address problems about which they are most familiar. Cultural chauvinism, as well as the realities of financial and political power, often dictate that beneficiaries play passive or nonmanagerial roles in project planning, implementation, and evaluation.

It cannot be stated with certainty what shape a faculty development program might take under beneficiary administration because so many variables enter into project construction. But it can be imagined that some fundamental changes could take place. For example, countries could decide to develop their own criteria for selection of scholars rather than follow the culturally established requirements of the funder, choose their own priority fields of study instead of those that the funder wishes to promote, send faculty to countries other than the funder's for training, demand funder or sponsoring agency personnel accountability and in-country presence, or place nationals in charge of the management and evaluation.

At LASPAU, a small number of projects receive no U.S. government support at all, but are funded and administered entirely by Latin American national scholarship agencies. For these, expectations on the part of the managers are high both for project participants and LASPAU performance. The demands made on LASPAU by these agencies are extremely compelling for two reasons: (a) because the funder and the beneficiary are one and the same, project results are easily scrutinized and direct accountability is high, and (b) direct contact with project administrators, as opposed to a large government bureaucracy, impresses on personnel the immediacy and reality of funder/beneficiary needs.

In these cases, the information base used by LASPAU would change because an even greater amount of programmatic information is needed. Not only is a greater amount of programmatic information needed, but it must necessarily be very specific to the detailed project agenda of the funder nation. Should the funder decide that LASPAU played a minor role in the project, the variety of information needed by the latter could be reduced from the six types discussed in earlier, to perhaps only one or two that would satisfy its diminished role.

An important element that must be noted, however, which was discussed earlier, is the scarcity of information that exists in many Latin American and Caribbean countries about U.S. universities and graduate education in general. Some nations are richer than others and have more sophisticated means of communication or mobility. For the poorer nations or those with less in information, management of a project may be difficult or unfeasible. However, in an effort to continue the notion of an inverted structure that leaves the beneficiary in control, the determination of capability should be left up to nations themselves, rather than having the assessment be made by other nations.

I speculate that a change in program structure that transfers power and control to the beneficiary might be unacceptable to some project fundraisers. As a compromise, beneficiaries might be to allowed a greater voice in the process and decision making in areas where they are directly involved. In some LASPAU projects, the funder determines the priority fields of study, the selection criteria (including political orientation), and the number of participants. I advocate more beneficiary control over areas such as these.

This recommendation is presented for two reasons, even though its chances for implementation are limited. First, it is hoped that the discussion suggests the sociological principles on which the reluctance to make a change in project management is based. Second, an examination of changes in management structure might be overdue.

Recommendation 4: Universities Should Accept
Any Student Who Applies

Although Recommendation 3 changes the importance and definition of roles in the funder/beneficiary structure, it still maintains the conservative objectives of that system. That is, Recommendation 3 does not address the principles of the system that support a status quo regarding the distribution of the resource—knowledge. The system outlined in Recommendation 3 recognizes that education is available only to those who "qualify" for participation, a vision that rewards those who already have some training (which in economically developing nations can be equivalent to those who have financial and social means) and perpetuates a structure in which the "rich get richer." This then maintains the inequitable distribution of resources—jobs, money, status, control—when highly educated scholars return home.

Recommendation 4 suggests that education be available to all who seek it, previous experiences, status, or preparation notwithstanding. Theoretically, opportunity would then be distributed equitably, and all persons would be able to improve themselves and their chances for increased financial and social well-being. This recommendation comes from a radical humanist perspective including both personal empowerment and a change in the distribution of resources.

There is evidence of open enrollment at some universities in the United States. However, I believe it unlikely that this recommendation would be implemented, given the pressures from such competing priorities as accreditation, budgetary and financial constraints, and standardization of requirements for advanced degrees. Indeed, if an open enrollment policy did exist, LASPAU's function would change dramatically. It would no longer be responsible for any type of academic assessment, but would be primarily concerned with implementing financial procedures. Information needs would be minimal with respect to the personal and cultural types, but would expand in the programmatic area.

Although it can in no way effect change within the national educational system, LASPAU attempts to promote a flexibility on the part of U.S. universities, by presenting candidates for admission (scholars) who might not have the exact desired prerequisites, but who do possess other important personal and professional characteristics. Moreover, it has been found that universities respond positively because they, too, value the kind of individual achievement and experiential equivalents that many international students have. Yet, this recommendation will not be implemented because universities cannot make a break from the standards and accreditation requirements of the system and can only accommodate in limited ways.

Recommendation 5: Use Only Quantitative
Information in the Placement Process

The four preceding recommendations all have some aspect of personal and cultural information as important aspects. This final recommendation suggests that qualitative information should not play a role in the placement process and that decisions should be made on the basis of standardized, comparable quantitative data.

The analyses of information and context indicate that the placement process is not easy, especially because of what seems to be the considerable difficulty in accurately discerning its subjective components. An alternative process, then, could adopt a strict functionalist approach to placement: Eliminate all subjective information from the process and base decisions on the quantitative, objective information available for each scholar (e.g., test scores, GPA, rank in class).

Decisions based on objective information would be compatible with the standardized parts of U.S. university admissions systems. They would be free of potentially harmful interpretive error on the part of the program officer, and they would be efficient in terms of time and labor. Because placements that include subjective information have proven to be imperfect, why include it at all?

This recommendation actually describes (although not in the strictest sense) the decision-making philosophy of some international sponsoring agencies. However, in the case of LASPAU, this recommendation is not likely either to be adopted or even supported. It conflicts with the humanist aspects of LASPAU's sociological and operational vision. This vision is exemplified by such organizational practices and preoccupations as personal interviews, country visits, and the mechanisms to gather the personal and cultural information explained in detail earlier. Why, indeed, should subjective information be included? As hopefully has been shown, it is undeniably of primary importance.

SUMMARY

The goal of this series of analyses has been to examine an organizational decision in terms of its information base and context. Building on each other, the analyses offer insights into the theoretical and sociological meaning behind organizational procedures and the kinds of information that support organizational choices. These analyses help to confirm and clarify the reasoning that motivates and guides decision making by highlighting it against the organizational context.

What is also helpful about such an examination is that it reveals possible causes of conflict that can then be addressed, individually or organizationally. In the case of the placement process at LASPAU, some conflicts may never be resolved because they are inherent in the system as it is practiced, which is dictated, in part, by factors beyond the organization's control. Other conflicts may, in fact, be resolved through the use of information and information sources that have been underutilized or unidentified in the past.

The recommendations offered in the preceding section are but a few examples of the changes that could be suggested for the placement decision process. Those presented here have all been oriented toward the organizational level in terms of feasibility of implementation, but perhaps meaningful change could also take place through individual implementation of change related to the theoretical and practical bases of decision making examined in this discussion. In addition, the valuable role of some information sources, such as the funder representatives, has not been explored fully. Their limitations notwithstanding, these examples are meant to provide some indication of both the range of possibilities for change and the scope of the effects of organizational decision making itself.

References

Aeschliman, M. D. (1983). *The restitution of man: C. S. Lewis and the case against scientism*. Grand Rapids, MI: William B. Eerdmans.

Aring, M. K. (1993, January). What the "V" word is costing America's economy. *Phi Delta Kappan, 74*(5), 396–404.

Allison, G. T. (1971). *Essence of decision: Explaining the Cuban missile crisis*. Boston: Little, Brown.

Antonucci, R. (1995). In Unpublished class notes. Boston University School of Education, Boston, Massachusetts.

Argyris, C. (1976). Single-loop and double-loop models in research on decision-making. *Administrative Science Quarterly, 21*, 363–375.

Argyris, C., & Schön, D. A. (1978). *Organizational learning: A theory of action perspective*. Reading, MA: Addison-Wesley.

Arnold, H. J. (1981). A test of the validity of the multiplicative hypothesis of expectancy-valence theories of work motivation. *Academy of Management Journal, 24*, 128–141.

Astley, W. G., & Van De Ven, A. H. (1983). Central perspectives and debates in organization theory. *Administrative Science Quarterly, 28*, 245–273.

Bacharach, S. B., & Lawler, E. J. (1980). *Power and politics in organizations*. San Francisco: Jossey-Bass.

Bacharach, S. B., Bamberger, P., Conley, S. C., & Bauer, S. (1990). The dimensionality of decision participation in educational organizations: The value of a multi-domain evaluative approach. *Educational Administration Quarterly, 26*, 126–127.

Bacharach, S. B., & Mitchell, S. M. (1981). Toward a dialogue in the middle range. *Educational Administration Quarterly, 17*(3), 1–14.

Bacon, F. (1620/1960) *The New Organon and Related Writings*. Indianapolis and New York: Bobbs-Merrill Company.

Bakke, E. W., & Argyris, C. (1954). *Organizational structure and dynamics*. New Haven, CT: Yale University.

Barnard, C. I. (1947) Foreward to Simon's *Administrative Behavior*. In H. A. Simon (Ed.), *Administrative Behavior: A Study of Decision-Making Processes in Administrative Organization*. (pp. ix-xii). New York: The Macmillan Company.

Barnard, C. J. (1938). *The functions of the executive*. Cambridge, MA: Harvard University Press.

Bass, B. M. (1981). *Stogdill's handbook of leadership*. New York: Free Press.

Bass, B. M. (1990). *Bass & Stogdill's handbook of leadership* (3rd ed.). New York: Free Press.

Bateson, G. (1935) Culture contact and schismogenesis. *Man, 35*, 178–183.

Bendix, R. (1960). *Max Weber: An intellectual portrait*. Garden City, NY: Doubleday.

Bennis, W., & Nanus, B. (1985). *Leaders: The strategies for taking charge*. New York: Harper & Row.

Benson, J. K. (1977). Organizations: A dialectical view. *Administrative Science Quarterly, 22*, 1–21.

Benson, J. K. (1982). A framework for policy analysis. In D. L. Rogers & D. A. Whetten (Eds.), *Interorganizational Coordination: Theory, Research, and Implementation* (pp. 137–176). Ames, IA: Iowa State University Press.

Berman, P. (1981). Toward an implementation paradigm. In R. Lehming & M. Kane (Eds.), *Improving schools: Using what we know.* Beverly Hills, CA: Sage.

Berman, P., & McLaughlin, M. W. (1975a). *Federal programs supporting educational change, Vol. II: Factors affecting change agent projects.* Santa Monica, CA: Rand.

Berman, P., & McLaughlin, M. W. (1975b). *Federal programs supporting educational change, Vol. IV: The findings in review.* Santa Monica, CA: Rand.

Berman, P., & McLaughlin, M. W. (1977). *Federal programs supporting educational change: Factors affecting continuation and implementation.* (Vol. 7). Santa Monica, CA: Rand.

Berman, P., & McLaughlin, M. W. (1978). *Federal programs supporting educational change: Implementing and sustaining innovation.* (Vol. 8). Santa Monica, CA: Rand.

Berman, P., & McLaughlin, M. W. (1979). *An exploratory study of school district adaptation.* Santa Monica, CA: Rand.

Blake, R. R., & Mouton, J. S. (1964). *The managerial grid.* Houston: Gulf.

Bolman, L. G., & Deal, T. E. (1984). *Modern approaches to understanding and managing organizations.* San Francisco: Jossey-Bass.

Burns, J. M. (1978) *Leadership.* New York: Harper & Row.

Burrell, G., & Morgan, G. (1979). *Sociological paradigms and organizational analysis.* London: Heinemann.

Calder, B. J. (1977). An attribution theory of leadership. In B. Stark & G. Salancik (Eds.), *New directions in organizational behavior* Chicago: St. Clair.

Carnegie Forum on Education and the Economy (1986). *A nation prepared: Teachers for the 21ˢᵗ century.* Washington, DC: The Forum.

Cartwright, D., & Zander, A. (1968). *Group dynamics: Research and method* (3rd ed.). New York: Harper and Row.

Child, J. (1977). *Organizations: A guide to problems and practice.* London: Harper and Row.

Chubb, J. E., & Moe, T. M. (1990). *Politics, markets, and America's school.* Washington, DC: Brookings Institute.

Clauset, K. H., Jr. (1982). Effective schooling: A system dynamics policy study. Unpublished Doctoral Dissertation, Boston University, Boston, Massachusetts.

Clauset, K. H., Jr., & Gaynor, A. K. (1982). A systems perspective on effective schools. *Educational Leadership, 40*(3), 54–59.

Clegg, S., & Dunkerley, D. (1980). *Organization, class and control.* London: Routledge & Kegan Paul.

Cohen, M., & March, J. (1974). *Leadership and ambiguity: The American college presidency.* New York: McGraw-Hill.

Cohen, M., March, J., & Olsen, J. (1972). A garbage can model of organizational choice. *Administrative Science Quarterly, 17*(1), 1–25.

Commonwealth of Massachusetts, Department of Education., Division of Occupational Education. (1977). *Chapter 74 Regulations Governing Vocational Education.* Bureau of Educational Information Services.

Cuban, L. (1975). Hobson v. Hansen: A study in organizational response. *Educational Administration Quarterly, 11*(2), 15–37.

Cushner, K., McClelland, A., & Safford, P. (1992). *Human diversity in education.* New York: McGraw-Hill.

Dahrendorf, R. (1959). *Class and class conflict in industrial society.* London: Routledge and Kegan Paul.

Davis, C. S. (1992) *A description and analysis of an organizational problem based on the social systems model.* Term Paper, Department of Administration, Training, and Policy Studies, Boston University School of Education, Boston, Massachusetts.

Deal, T. E., & Kennedy, A. A. (1982). *Corporate cultures: The rites and rituals of corporate life.* Reading, MA: Addison-Wesley.

Delattre, E. (1996). In Unpublished class notes. Boston University School of Education, Boston, Massachusetts.

Deming, W. E. (1986). *Out of the crisis.* Cambridge, MA: Center for Advanced Engineering Study, MIT.

Dewey, J. (1896). The reflex arc concept in psychology. *Psychological Review, 3,* 357–370.

DeYoung, A. J. (1989). *Economics and American education.* New York: Longman.

Donaldson, L. (1985). *In Defence of organization theory.* Cambridge: Cambridge University Press.

Drucker, P. (November, 1994). The age of social transformation. *The Atlantic Monthly, 274*(5), 53–80.

Ducat, C. R., & Chase, H. W. (1988). *Constitutional interpretation*. New York: West.

Earley, J., Magno, J., & Amico-Porcaro, K. (1995). *New England school for special students program evaluation*. Woburn, MA: Educational Performance Systems, Inc.

Easton, D. (1965). *A systems analysis of political life*. New York: Wiley.

Easton, D. (1971). *The political system* (2nd ed.). New York: Knopf.

Easton, D. (1991). Political science in the United States: Past and present. In *Divided knowledge: Across disciplines, across cultures* (pp. 37–58). Newbury Park, CA: Sage.

Eisner, E. W. (1988). The primacy of experience and the politics of method. *Educational Researcher, 17*(5), 15–20.

Etzioni, A. (1975). *A comparative analysis of complex organizations* (Revised and Enlarged ed.). New York: Free Press.

Eulau, H. (1969). *Micro-macro political analysis: Accents of inquiry*. Chicago: Aldine.

Ferguson, K. E. (1984). *The feminist case against bureaucracy*. Philadelphia: Temple University Press.

Fiedler, F. E., & Chemers, M. M. (1974). *Leadership and effective management*. Glencoe, IL: Scott, Foresman.

Fiedler, F. E., Chemers, M. M., & Maher, L. (1976). *Improving leadership effectiveness: The leader match concept*. New York: Wiley.

Filley, A. C., House, R. J., & Kerr, S. (1976). *Managerial process and organizational behavior*. Glenview, IL: Scott, Foresman.

Firth, R. (1951). *Elements of social organization*. London: Watts.

Forrester, J. W. (1968). *Principles of systems*. Cambridge, MA: MIT Press.

Foster, W. (1986). *Paradigms and promises: New approaches to educational administration*. Buffalo, NY: Prometheus.

Foster, W. (1988). Educational administration: A critical appraisal. In D. E. Griffiths, R. T. Stout, & P. B. Forsyth (Eds.), *Leaders for America's schools: The report and papers of the national commission on excellence in educational administration* (pp. 68–81). Berkeley, CA: McCutchan.

Freeman, R. B. (1971). *The market for college-trained manpower: A study in the economics of career choice*. Cambridge, MA: Harvard University Press.

Furhman, S. (1993). The politics of coherence. In S. F. Furhman (Ed.), *Designing coherent educational policy* (pp. 1–29). San Francisco: Jossey-Bass.

Gadamer, H. G. (1975). *Truth and Method* (J. C. B. Mohr, Trans., G. Barden & J. Cumming, Eds.) New York: The Continuum Publishing Corporation.

Gagnon, P. (December, 1995). What should children learn? *The Atlantic Monthly, 276*(6), 65–78.

Gaynor, A. K., & Evanson, J. L. (1992). *Project planning: A guide for practitioners*. Needham Heights, MA: Allyn & Bacon.

Getzels, J. W., & Guba, E. G. (1957). Social behavior and the administrative process. *School Review, 65*, 423–441.

Getzels, J. W., Lipham, J. M., & Campbell, R. F. (1968). *Educational administration as a social process: Theory, research, practice*. New York: Harper & Row.

Ghemawat, P. (1991). *Commitment: The dynamic of strategy*. New York: The Free Press.

Glenn, C. L. (1987). *The myth of the common school*. Amherst: University of Massachusetts.

Goodlad, J. I. (1984) *A place called school: Prospects for the Future*. New York: McGraw-Hill.

Goodman, N. (1978). *Ways of worldmaking*. Indianapolis, IN: Hackett Publishing Company.

Graen, G. (1969). Instrumentality theory of work motivation: Some experimental results and suggested modifications. *Journal of Applied Psychology Monograph, 53*, 1–25.

Greenfield, T. B. (1984). Leaders and schools: Willfulness and nonnatural order in organizations. In T. J. Sergiovanni & J. E. Corbally (Eds.), *Leadership and organizational culture: New perspectives on administrative theory and practice* (pp. 142–169). Urbana, IL: University of Illinois Press.

Greenstein, F. I., & Polsby, N. W. (Ed.). (1975). *Handbook of political science: Macropolitical theory*. Reading, MA: Addison-Wesley.

Gregory, K. L. (1983). Native-view paradigms: Multiple cultures and culture conflicts in organizations. *Administrative Science Quarterly, 28*, 359–376.

Grubb, W. N., Davis, G., Lum, J., Plihal, J., & Morgaine, C. (1991, July). *The cunning hand, the cultural mind: Models for integrating vocational and academic education*. Berkeley, CA: University of California, National Center for research in Vocational Education.

Guba, E. G., & Lincoln, Y. S. (1985). Fourth generation evaluation as an alternative. *Educational Horizons, 63*(4), 139–141.

Guba, E. G., & Lincoln, Y. S. (1989). *Fourth generation evaluation.* Newbury Park, CA: Sage.

Habermas, J. (1973). *Legitimation crisis* (T. McCarthy, Trans.). Boston: Beacon Press.

Hage, J. (1980). *Theories of organization: Form, process and transformation.* New York: Wiley.

Hage, J., & Azumi, K. (1972). *Organizational systems: A text reader in the sociology of organizations.* Lexington, MA: D.C. Heath.

Hall, R. H. (1977). *Organizations: Structure and process* (2nd ed.). Englewood Cliffs, NJ: Prentice-Hall.

Hanson, N. R. (1958). *Patterns of discovery: An inquiry into the conceptual foundations of science.* Cambridge, England: Cambridge University Press.

Harrington, J. B. (1996). *Changing the paradigm: Expanding the role of schools of education.* Term Paper, Boston University School of Education, Boston, Massachusetts.

Hatch, J. A. (1985). The quantoids versus the smooshes: Struggling with methodological rapprochement. *Issues in Education, 3*(2), 158–167.

Hegel, G. W. F. (1983). *Hegel and the human spirit: A translation of the Jena lectures on the philosophy of spirit* (Felix Meiner, Trans.). Detroit: Wayne State University Press. (Original work published 1805–1806)

Hills, F. S., & Mahoney, T. A. (1978). University budgets and organizational decision making. *Administrative Science Quarterly, 23*, 454–465.

Hodgkinson, C. (1991). *Educational leadership: The moral art.* Albany, NY: State University of New York Press.

Hollway, W. (1991). *Work psychology and organizational behavior.* London, Newbury Park, CA, and New Delhi: Sage.

House, R. J., & Baetz, M. L. (1979). Leadership: Some empirical generalizations and new research directions. In B. M. Staw (Eds.), *Research in organizational behavior* (pp. 341–423). Greenwich, CT: JAI Press.

House, R. J., & Mitchell, T. R. (1974). Path-goal theory of leadership. *Journal of Contemporary Business, 5*, 81–97.

Huberman, A. M., & Miles, M. B. (1984). *Innovation up close: How school improvement works.* New York: Plenum.

Hume, D. (1987). On the balance of trade. In E. F. Miller (Ed.), *Essays, moral, political, and literary,* (Rev. ed., pp. 308–326). Indianapolis: Liberty Classics. (Original work published 1752)

Immegart, G. L. (1988). Leadership and leader behavior. In N. J. Boyan (Eds.), *Handbook of research on educational administration* (pp. 259–278). New York/London: Longman.

Jago, A. G. (1982). Leadership: Perspectives in theory and research. *Management Science, 28*(3), 315–336.

Jentz, B. C., & Wofford, J. W. (1979). *Leadership and learning: Personal change in a professional setting.* New York: McGraw-Hill.

Kahn, R. L., Wolfe, D. M., Quinn, R. P., & Snoek, J. D. (1964). *Organizational stress: Studies in role conflict and ambiguity.* New York: Wiley.

Kessel, J. H., Cole, G. F., & Seddig, R. G. (Ed.). (1970). *Micropolitics: Individual and group level concepts.* New York: Holt, Rinehart & Winston.

Khandwalla, P. N. (1977). *The design of organizations.* New York: Harcourt Brace.

Kluckholn, C., & Murray, H. A. (Eds.). (1953). *Personality in nature, society, and culture.* New York: Knopf.

Kormondy, E. J. (1969). *Concepts of ecology.* Englewood Cliffs, NJ: Prentice-Hall.

Kotter, J. P. (1982). *The general managers.* New York: Free Press.

Kotter, J. P., Schlesinger, L. A., & Sathe, V. (1979). *Organizations: Texts, cases, and readings on the management of organizational design and change.* Homewood, IL: Irwin.

Kozuch, J. A. (1979). Implementing an educational innovation: The constraints of the school setting. *High School Journal, 62*(5), 223–231.

Landau, M. (1988). Foreword. In E. B. Portis & M. B. Levy (Eds.), *Handbook of political theory and policy science* (pp. vii–xii). New York: Greenwood Press.

Lawrence, P. R. & Lorsch, J. W. (June, 1967). Differentiation and integration in complex organizations. *Administrative Science Quarterly, 4*(2), 1–47.

Lawrence, P. R., & Lorsch, J. W. (1967). *Organization and environment.* Cambridge, MA: Harvard University Press.

Lazerson, M., & Grubb, W. N. (Eds.). (1974). *American education and vocationalism: A documentary history 1870–1970.* New York: Teachers College Press.

Lindblom, C. E. (1959). The science of "muddling through." *Public Administration Review, 19,* 79–88.

Lindblom, C. E. (1965). *The intelligence of democracy.* New York: The Free Press.

Lindblom, C. E. (1968). *The policy making process.* Englewood Cliffs, NJ: Prentice-Hall.

Lindblom, C. E., & Cohen, D. K. (1979). *Usable knowledge: Social science and social problem solving.* New Haven, CT: Yale University Press.

Lipham, J. M. (1988). Getzels's models in educational administration. In N. J. Boyan (Ed.), *Handbook of research on educational administration,* (pp. 171–184). New York/London: Longman.

Lippman, W. (1962). *A preface to politics.* Ann Arbor: The University of Michigan Press. (Original work published 1914)

Locke, J. ([1632–1704] 1990) *Drafts for the essay concerning human understanding, and other philosophical writings.* New York and Oxford, England: Oxford University Press and Clarendon Press.

Lortie, D. (1969). The balance of control and autonomy in elementary school teaching. In A. Etzioni (Ed.), *The semi-professions and their organization* (pp. 1–53). New York: Free Press.

Lotka, A. J. (1925/1956). *Elements of physical biology. Reprinted as Elements of mathematical biology.* New York: Dover.

Lytle, W. O. (1993). *Starting an organization design effort: A planning and preparation guide.* Plainfield, NJ: Block, Petrella, Weisbord.

Machiavelli, N. (1942) *The Prince* (Luigi Ricci, rev. by E. R. P. Vincent, Trans.). New York: New American Library of World Literature. (Original work published 1513)

MacIntyre, A. (1984). *After virtue: A study in moral theory* (2nd ed.). Notre Dame, IN: University of Notre Dame Press.

Malthus, T. R. (1798). *First essay on population:* Reprinted. London: Macmillan, 1926, 1966.

March, J. G., & Olsen, J. P. (1976). *Ambiguity and choice in organizations.* Bergen, Norway: Universitetsforlaget.

Martin, R. (1979). The balance of control and autonomy in elementary school teaching. *Educating handicapped children: The legal mandate.* Champaign, IL: Research Press.

Marx, K. ([1818–1883] 1975). *Karl Marx: Economy, class and social revolution* (Z. A. Jordan, Trans.). New York: Scribner.

Massachusetts Board of Education (1995). *Five year master plan.* Malden, MA: Massachusetts Department of Education.

Massachusetts Board of Education, Massachusetts Department of Education (1994). *Massachusetts common core of learning* (Newsletter Publication #176011-4-580,000-9/94-DOE). Malden, MA: Massachusetts Department of Education.

Massachusetts Department of Education (1994a). *First annual implementation report.* (Publication No. 17615-40). Malden, MA: Massachusetts Department of Education.

Massachusetts Department of Education (1994b). *Chapter 766 regulations.* (Publication No. 16914). Malden, MA: Massachusetts Department of Education.

Massachusetts Department of Education (1995). The common chapters. (Publication No. 17684-48-1500) Malden, MA: Massachusetts Department of Education.

Massachusetts Department of Education, Division of Occupational Education (1990, August 18th). *Regulations for vocational technical education.* Quincy, MA: Massachusetts Department of Education.

Massachusetts Department of Public Health (1993). *New England School for Special Students program guide.* Canton, MA: Massachusetts Department of Public Health.

Mayr, O. (1970). *The origins of feedback control.* Cambridge, MA: MIT Press.

McCall, W., Jr. (1976). Leadership research: Choosing gods and devils on the run. *Journal of Occupational Psychology, 49,* 139–53.

McGregor, D. (1960). *The human side of enterprise.* New York: McGraw-Hill.

Merton, R. K. (1948). The self-fulfilling prophecy. *Antioch Review, 6,* 193–210.

Mills, A. J., & Tancred, P. (1992). *Gendering organizational analysis.* Newbury Park, CA: Sage.

Mintzberg, H. (1979). *The structuring of organizations.* Englewood Cliffs, NJ: Prentice-Hall.

Miskel, C., & Ogawa, R. (1988). Work motivation, job satisfaction, and climate. In N. J. Boyan (Ed.), *Handbook of research on educational administration,* (pp. 279–304). New York/London: Longman.

Morecroft, J. D. W., & Sterman, J. D. (Eds.). (1994). *Modeling for learning organizations.* Portland, OR: Productivity Press.

Morgan, G. (1986). *Images of organization.* Beverly Hills, CA: Sage.

Morss, E. R. (1981). *Integrated rural development: Nine critical implementation problems.* Washington, D.C.: DAI, Development Alternatives, Inc.

Morss, E. R. (1982). *U.S. foreign aid: An assessment of new and traditional development strategies.* Boulder, CO: Westview Press.

Morss, E. R. (1986). *The future of Western development assistance.* Boulder, CO: Westview Press.

Murnane, R. J., & Levy, F. (1996). *Teaching the new basic skills: Principles for educating children to thrive in a changing economy.* New York: Free Press.

Mussen, P. H., Conger, J. J., Kagan, J., & Huston, A. C. (1979). *Child development and personality.* New York: Harper & Row.

Myrdal, G. (1939). *Monetary equilibrium.* London: W. Hodge & Company, Ltd.

National Commission on Excellence in Education (1995). A nation at risk: The imperative for educational reform. In K. Ryan & J. Cooper (Eds.), *Kaleidoscope Readings in education* (7th ed., pp. 396–405). Boston: Houghton Mifflin. (Original work published 1983).

Newton, I. (1972). *Philosophiae naturalis principia mathematica* (3rd ed.). Cambridge, MA: Harvard University Press. (Original work published 1726).

Osterman, P. (1989). The job market for adolescents. In D. S. & D. Eichorn (Ed.), *Adolescence and work: Influences of social structure, labor markets, and culture.* Hillsdale, NJ: Lawrence Erlbaum Associates.

Ouchi, W. G. (1981). *Theory Z: How American business can meet the Japanese challenge.* Reading, MA: Addison-Wesley.

Padgett, J. F. (1980). Managing garbage can hierarchies. *Administrative Science Quarterly, 25,* 583–604.

Parsons, T. (1961). An outline of the social system. In T. Parsons, E. Shils, K. D. Naegele, & J. R. Pitts (Eds.), *Theories of society: Foundations of modern sociological theory* (pp. 30–79). New York: The Free Press.

Parsons, T., & Shils, E. A. (1951). *Toward a general theory of action.* Cambridge, MA: Harvard University Press.

Paul, S. (1982). *Managing developing programs: The lessons of success.* Boulder, CO: Westview Press.

Pautler, A. J., Jr. (1990). The job market for adolescents. In A. J. Pautler, Jr. (Ed.), *Vocational education in the 1990s: Major issues.* Ann Arbor, MI: Prakken Publications.

Peters, T., & Austin, N. (1985). *A passion for excellence: The leadership difference.* New York: Random House.

Pfeffer, J. (1977). The ambiguity of leadership. *Academy of Management Review, 2*(1), 104–112.

Pfeffer, J. (1981). *Power in organizations.* Marshfield, MA: Pitman.

Pfeffer, J., & Lawler, J. (1980). Effects of job alternatives, extrinsic rewards, and behavioral commitment on attitude toward the organization. *Administrative Science Quarterly, 25,* 38–56.

Pfeffer, J., & Salancik, G. R. (1983). Organization design: The case for a coalitional model of organizations. In J. R. Hackman, E. E. Lawler, & L. W. Porter (Eds.), *Perspectives on behavior in organizations* (pp. 102–111). New York: McGraw-Hill.

Portis, E. B., & Levy, M. B. (Ed.). (1988). *Handbook of political theory and policy science.* New York: Greenwood.

Powell, A. G. (1995). Being unspecial in the shopping mall high school. In K. Ryan & J. Cooper (Eds.), *Kaleidoscope* (pp. 174–182). Boston, MA: Houghton Mifflin.

Powell, A. G., Ferrar, E., & Cohen, D. K. (1985). *The shopping mall high school.* Boston: Houghton Mifflin.

Ramos, A. G. (1981). *The new science of organizations: A reconceptualization of the wealth of nations.* Toronto: University of Toronto Press.

Reich, R. B. (1991). *The work of nations: Preparing ourselves for 21st century capitalism.* New York: A. A. Knopf.

Reich, R. B. (1992). *The work of nations.* New York: Vintage.

Richardson, G. P. (1991). *Feedback thought in social science and systems theory.* Philadelphia: University of Pennsylvania Press.

Richardson, L. F. (1938). The arms race of 1909–13. *Nature, 142,* 792.

Rist, R. C. (1973). *The urban school: A factory for failure.* Cambridge, MA: MIT Press.

Roethlisberger, F. J. (1956). *Management and morale.* Cambridge, MA: Harvard University Press.

Rokeach, M. (1968). *Beliefs, attitudes, and values.* San Francisco: Jossey-Bass.

Rosenblum, S., & Louis, K. S. (1981). *Stability and change.* New York: Plenum.

Rosenstock, L. (February, 1991). The walls come down: The overdue reunification of vocational and academic education. *Phi Delta Kappan, 72*(6), 434–436.

Rosenthal, R. (1991). Teacher expectancy effects: A brief update 25 years after the Pygmalion experiment. *Journal of Research in Education, 1*(Spring), 3–12.

Rosenthal, R., & Jacobson, L. (1968). *Pygmalion in the classroom: Teacher expectations and pupils' intellectual development.* New York: Holt, Rinehart & Winston.

Rowan, B. (1982). Organizational structure and the institutional environment: The case of public schools. *Administrative Science Quarterly, 27*(2), 259–279.

Rummler, G. A., & Brache, A. P. (1991). *Improving performance: How to manage the white space on the organization chart.* San Francisco/Oxford: Jossey-Bass.

Salancik, G. R., & Pfeffer, J. (1977). An examination of need-satisfaction models of job attitudes. *Administrative Science Quarterly, 22*, 427–456.

Sarason, S. B. (1971). *The culture of the school and the problem of change.* Boston: Allyn & Bacon.

Scheidler, K. (1992). *Stress in a new program structure: A bureaucratic analysis.* Unpublished Term Paper, Boston University, Boston, Massachusetts.

Schein, E. H. (1985). *Organizational culture and leadership.* San Francisco, CA: Jossey-Bass.

Schoonhoven, C. B. (1981). Problems with contingency theory: Testing assumptions hidden within the language of contingency "theory." *Administrative Science Quarterly, 26*, 349–377.

Schriesheim, C. S., House, R. J., & Kerr, S. (1976). Leader initiating structure: A reconciliation of discrepant research results and some empirical tests. *Organizational Behavior and Human Performance, 15*, 197–321.

Scribner, J. D., & Englert, R. M. (1977). The politics of education: An introduction. In J. D. Scribner (Eds.), *The politics of education: The seventy-sixth yearbook of the national society for the study of education, Part II* (pp. 1–29). Chicago: The University of Chicago Press.

Seidman, R. B. (1992). Justifying Legislation: A Pragmatic, Institutionalist Approach to the Memorandum of Law, Legislative Theory, and Practical Reason. *Harvard Journal on Legislation, 29*(1), 1–77.

Senge, P. M. (1990). *The fifth discipline: The art & practice of the learning organization.* New York: Doubleday Currency.

Sergiovanni, T. J., & Corbally, J. (1984). *Leadership and organizational cultures.* Champaign, IL: University of Illinois Press.

Simon, H. A. (1957). *Administrative behavior: A study of the decision-making processes in administrative organization* (2nd ed.). New York: Macmillan.

Simon, H. A. (1957a). *Administrative behavior.* New York: Macmillan.

Simon, H. A. (1957b). *Models of man: Social and rational.* New York: Wiley.

Sizer, T. (1986). *Horace's compromise.* Boston: Houghton Mifflin.

Smircich, L. (1983). Concepts of culture and organizational analysis. *Administrative Science Quarterly, 28*, 339–358.

Smith, A. (1776). *An inquiry into the nature and causes of the wealth of nations.* Edited by Edwin Cannan. New York: The Modern Library.

Spiegelberg, E. J. (1989). *Dropout problem at Laramie Senior High School: A problem analysis using the social systems model* Term Paper Unnumbered, Boston University School of Education, Department of Administration, Training, and Policy Studies, Boston, Massachusetts.

Spring, J. (1996). *American education.* (7th ed.). New York: McGraw-Hill.

Squires, G. D. (1979). *Education and jobs.* New Brunswick, NJ: Transaction Books.

Stern, D., & Eichorn, D. (Eds.). (1989). *Adolescence and work: Influences of social structure, labor markets, and culture.* Hillside, NJ: Lawrence Erlbaum Associates.

Stogdill, R. M. (1974). *Handbook of leadership: A survey of theory and research.* New York: Free Press.

Tarver, S. B. (1989) *Identifying the gifted/talented: An analysis of a problem in Jacksport using Easton's Political Systems Model.* Term Paper, Boston University School of Education, Boston, Massachusetts.

Taylor, F. W. (1911a). *The principles of scientific management.* New York: W. W. Norton.

Taylor, F. W. (1911b). *Shop management.* New York: Harper & Brothers.

Tesch, R. (1989). Introductory guide to HyperQual. Desert Hot Springs, CA: Qualitative Research Management.

Thurow, L. C. (1975). *Generating inequality.* New York: Basic Books.

Thurow, L. C. (1996). *The future of capitalism: How today's economic forces shape tomorrow's world.* New York: William Morrow.

Toch, T. (1991). *In the name of excellence.* New York: Oxford University Press.

Trice, H. M., & Beyer, J. M. (1991). Cultural leadership in organizations. *Organization Science,* 2(2), 149–169.

Tucker, R. C. (1981). *Politics as leadership.* Columbia, MO: University of Missouri Press.

Turner, B. A. (1972). *Exploring the industrial subculture.* New York: Herder and Herder.

Vroom, V. H. (1964). *Work and motivation.* New York: Wiley.

Vroom, V. H. (1976). Leadership. In M. Dunnette (Eds.), *Handbook of industrial and organizational psychology* (pp. 1527–1551). Chicago: Rand-McNally.

Vroom, V. H., & Yetton, P. W. (1973). *Leadership and decision making.* Pittsburgh, PA: University of Pittsburgh Press.

Waldo, D. (1975). Political Science: Tradition, discipline, profession, science, enterprise. In F. I. Greenstein & N. W. Polsby (Eds.), *Handbook of political science: Political science: Scope and theory* (Vol. 1, pp. 1–130). Reading, MA: Addison-Wesley .

Wallace, W. (1968). *Prolegomena to the study of Hegel's philosophy and especially of his logic* (2nd ed.). New York: Russell & Russell. (Original work published 1894).

Waring, S. P. (1991). *Taylorism transformed: Scientific management theory since 1945.* Chapel Hill: The University of North Carolina Press.

Warsh, D. (1996, September 10). Why life is high school. *The Boston Globe.*

Weber, M. (1946). *From Max Weber: Essays in sociology* (H. H. Gerth and C. Wright Mills, Trans.). New York: Oxford University Press.

Weber, M. (1947). *Max Weber: The theory of social and economic organization* (A. M. Henderson & T. Parsons, Trans.). New York: The Free Press.

Weick, K. E. (1982). Administering education in loosely coupled schools. *Phi Delta Kappan,* 63(10), 673–676.

Wilensky, H. (1967) *Organizational intelligence.* New York: Basic Books.

Wilson, J. Q. (1989). *Bureaucracy: What government agencies do and why they do it.* New York: Basic Books.

Wirt, J. G. (1991, February). A new federal law on vocational education: Will reform follow? *Phi Delta Kappan,* 72(6), 425–433.

Wirth, A. G. (1992). *Education and work for the year 2000: Choices we face.* San Fransisco: Jossey-Bass.

Wirth, A. G. (January, 1993). Education and work: The choices we face. *Phi Delta Kappan,* 72(6), 361–366.

Yang, G. (1992). *A description and analysis of an organizational problem based on the bureaucratic model.* Unpublished Term Paper, Boston University, Boston, Massachusetts.

Zald, M. (1970). Political economy: A framework for comparative analysis. In M. Zald (Eds.), *Power in organizations* (pp. 221–261). Nashville, TN: Vanderbilt University Press.

Zuboff, S. (1988). *In the age of the smart machine.* New York: Basic Books.

Suggested Readings

BUREAUCRATIC THEORY

Abbott, M. G., & Caracheo, F. (1988). Power, authority, and bureaucracy. In N. J. Boyan (Ed.), *Handbook of research on educational administration* (pp. 239–258). New York/London: Longman.

Anderson, J. G. (1969). *Bureaucracy in education*. Baltimore, MD: Johns Hopkins University Press.

Argyris, C. (1960). *Understanding organizational behavior.* Homewood, IL: The Dorsey Press, Inc.

Bacharach, S. B., & Lawler, E. J. (1980). *Power and politics in organizations*. San Francisco: Jossey-Bass.

Bacharach, S. B., & Mitchell, S. M. (1981). Toward a dialogue in the middle range. *Educational Administration Quarterly, 17*(3), 1–14.

Beetham, D. (1987). *Bureaucracy* Minneapolis: University of Minnesota Press.

Bendix, R. (1960). *Max Weber: An intellectual portrait*. Garden City, New York: Doubleday.

Beyer, J. M., & Trice, H. M. (1979). A Reexamination of the relation between size and various components of organizational complexity. *Administrative Science Quarterly, 24*(1), 48–63.

Blau, P. M. (1955). *The dynamics of bureaucracy: A study of interpersonal relations in two government agencies* (Rev. ed.). Chicago: The University of Chicago Press.

Blau, P. M. (1956). *Bureaucracy in modern society.* New York: Random House.

Blau, P. M., & Schoenherr, R. A. (1971). *The structure of organizations*. New York: Basic Books, Inc.

Blau, P. M., & Scott, W. R. (1962). *Formal organizations*. San Francisco, CA: Chandler.

Blau, P. M., & Scott, W. R. (1963). *Formal organizations: A comparative approach*. London: Routledge & Kegan Paul.

Brown, D. L. (1983). *Management conflict at organizational interfaces*. Reading, MA: Addison-Wesley.

Brown, R. H. (1978). Bureaucracy as praxis: Toward a political phenomenology of formal organizations. *Administrative Science Quarterly, 23*, 365–382.

Burack, E. H. (1975). *Organization analysis: Theory and Applications*. Hinsdale, IL: The Dryden Press.

Charters, W. W., Jr. (1981). The control of micro-educational policy in elementary schools. In S. E. Bacharach (Eds.), *Organizational behavior in schools and school districts*. New York: Praeger.

Child, J., & Kieser, A. (1979). Organizational and managerial roles in British and West German companies: An examination of the culture-free thesis. In C. J. Lammers & D. J. Hickson (Eds.), *Organizations alike and unlike* (pp. 251–272). London: Routledge & Kegan Paul.

Corwin, R. G. (1961). The professional employee: A study of conflict in nursing roles. *American Journal of Sociology, 66*, 605–615.

Corwin, R. G. (1965). Militant professionalixm, initiative, and compliance in education. *Sociology of Education, 38*, 310–331.

Corwin, R. G., & Borman, K. M. (1988). School as workplace: Structural constraints on administration. In N. J. Boyan (Ed.), *Handbook of research on educational administration* (pp. 209–238). New York/London: Longman.

Coser, L. A., & Rosenberg, B. (Ed.). (1965). *Sociological theory: A book of readings.* New York: Macmillan.

Drucker, P. F. (1974). *Management: Tasks, responsibilities, practices.* New York: Harper & Row.

Duncan, W. J. (1975). *Essentials of management.* Hinsdale, IL: The Dryden Press.

Engel, B. V. (1970). Professional autonomy and bureaucratic organization. *Administrative Science Quarterly, 15,* 12–21.

Fayol, H. (1949). *General and industrial management* (C. Starrs, Trans.). London: Pitman.

Firestone, W. A., & Wilson, B. L. (1985). Using bureaucratic and cultural linkages to improve instruction: The principal's contribution. *Educational Administration Quarterly, 21,* 7–30.

Follett, M. P. (1924). *Creative experience.* New York: Longmans, Green & Co.

French, J. R. P., Jr. (1960). The bases of social power. In D. Cartwright & A. Zander (Eds.), *Group dynamics: Research and theory.* New York: Harper & Row.

Gerth, H., & Mulls, C. W. (Eds.). (1946). *From Max Weber.* New York: Oxford University Press.

Goodsell, C. T. (1977). Bureaucratic manipulation of physical symbols: An empirical study. *American Journal of Political Science, 21,* 79–91.

Gouldner, A. (1948). "Discussion" of industrial sociology. *American Sociological Review, 13,* 396–400.

Gouldner, A. (1954). *Patterns of industrial bureaucracy.* New York: Free Press.

Gouldner, A. (1957). Cosmopolitans and locals: Toward an analysis of latent social roles. *Administrative Science Quarterly, 2,* 281–306.

Haire, M. (Ed.). (1959). *Modern organization theory.* New York: John Wiley & Sons.

Hall, R. H. (1962). Intraorganizational structural variations: Application of the bureaucratic model. *Administrative Science Quarterly, 7,* 296–308.

Hall, R. H. (1963). The concept of bureaucracy: An empirical assessment. *American Journal of Sociology, 69,* 32–40.

Hall, R. H. (1968). Professionalization and bureaucratization. *American Sociological Review, 33,* 92–104.

Hanson, E. M. (1975). The modern educational bureaucracy and the process of change. *Educational Administration Quarterly, 11*(3), 1–20.

Henderson, A. M., & Parsons, T. (1947). *Max Weber: The theory of social and economic organization.* New York: The Free Press.

Hickson, D. J. (1987). Decision-making at the top of organizations. *Annual Review of Sociology, 13,* 165–192.

Hickson, D. J., Butler, R. J., Cray, D., Mallory, G. R., & Wilson, D. C. (1986). *Top decisions: Strategic decision making in organizations.* San Francisco: Jossey-Bass.

Hickson, D. J., Hinings, C. R., McMillan, C. J., & Schwitter, J. P. (1981). The Culture-free context of organizational structure. In D. J. Hickson & C. J. McMillan (Eds.), *Organization and nation* (pp. 3–17). Westinead, England: Gower Publishing.

Hills, F. S., & Mahoney, T. A. (1978). University budgets and organizational decision making. *Administrative Science Quarterly, 23,* 454–465.

Isherwood, G. B., & Hoy, W. K. (1973). Bureaucracy, powerlessness, and teacher work values. *Journal of Educational Administration, 11,* 124–137.

Jermier, J. M., Slocum, J. W., Fry, L. W., & Gaines, J. (1991). Organizational subcultures in a soft bureaucracy: Resistance behind the myth and facade of an official culture. *Organization Science, 2*(2), 170–195.

Kimberly, J. R. (1976). Organizational size and the structuralist perspective. *Administrative Science Quarterly, 21,* 571–597.

Leiberson, S., & O'Connor, J. F. (1972). Leadership and organizational performance: A study of large corporations. *American Sociological Review, 37*(2), 117–130.

Lincoln, J. R. (1990). Japanese organization and organization theory. *Research in organizational behavior, 12,* 255–294.

Lincoln, J. R., & McBride, K. (1987). Japanese industrial organization in comparative perspective. *Annual Review of Sociology, 13,* 289–312.

Litterer, J. A. (1973). *The analysis of organizations.* New York: John Wiley & Sons.

Litwak, E. (1961). Models of bureaucracy which permit conflict. *American Journal of Sociology, 67,* 177–184.

Mansfield, R. (1973). Bureaucracy and centralization: An examination of organizational structure. *Administrative Science Quarterly, 18,* 477–488.

Mayo, E. (1945). *The social problems of an industrial civilization.* Boston: Graduate School of Business Administration, Harvard University.

Merton, R. K. (1940). Bureaucratic structure and personality. *Social Forces, 23,* 405–415.

Merton, R. K. (1957). *Social theory and social structure.* New York: Free Press.

Meyer, J. W., & Associates (Eds.). (1978). *Environments and organizations.* San Francisco: Jossey–Bass.

Meyer, J. W., & Scott, W. R. (1983). *Organizational environments: Ritual and rationality.* Beverly Hills, CA: Sage Publications.

Meyer, M. W. (1968a). Two authority structures of bureaucratic organization. *Administrative Science Quarterly, 13*(2), 216–221.

Meyer, M. W. (1968b). The two authority structures of bureaucratic organizations. *Administrative Science Quarterly, 13,* 211–228.

Miller, D., Friesen, P. H., & Mintzberg, H. (1984). *Organizations: A quantum view.* Englewood Cliffs, NJ: Prentice-Hall.

Miner, J. B. (1982). *Theories of organizational structure and process.* Chicago: The Dryden Press.

Mintzberg, H. (1979). *The Structuring of Organizations.* Englewood Cliffs, NJ: Prentice-Hall.

Moeller, G. H., & Charters, W. W., Jr. (1966). Relation of bureaucratization to sense of power among teachers. *Administrative Science Quarterly, 10,* 444–465.

Newman, K. (1980). Incipient bureaucracy: Anthropological perspectives on bureaucracy. In G. M. Britan & R. Cohen (Eds.), *Hierarchy and society: Anthropological perspectives on bureaucracy* (pp. 143–163). Philadelphia: Institute for Study of Social Issues.

Pfeffer, J., & Salancik, G. R. (1983). Organization design: The case for a coalitional model of organizations. In J. R. Hackman, E. E. Lawler, & L. W. Porter (Eds.), *Perspectives on behavior in organizations* (pp. 102–111). New York: McGraw-Hill.

Porter, L. W., III, Lawler, E. E., & Hackman, J. R. (1975). *Behavior in Organizations* New York: McGraw-Hill.

Pugh, D. S., & Hickson, D. J. (1976). *Organizational structure in its context: The Aston Programme I.* Westmead, Farnborough, Hants, England & Lexington, Massachusetts: Saxon House, D. C. Heath, Ltd. & Lexington Books, D. C. Heath & Co.

Pugh, D. S., Hickson, D. J., & Hinnings, C. R. (1968). Dimensions of organizational structure. *Administrative Science Quarterly, 13,* 65–105.

Roethlisberger, F. J. (1968). *Man-in-organization: Essays of F. J. Roethlisberger* Cambridge, MA: The Belknap Press of Harvard University Press.

Roth, G., & Wittich, C. (Ed.). (1968). *Max Weber, economy and society: An outline of interpretative sociology.* New York: Bedminster.

Rubenstein, A. H., & Haberstroh, C. J. (Eds.). (1960). *Some theories of organization.* Homewood, IL: The Dorsey Press, Inc. & Richard D. Irwin, Inc.

Selznick, P. (1949). *TVA and the grass roots.* Berkeley, CA: University of California Press.

Simmel, G. (1961). On subordination and superordination. In T. Parsons, E. Shils, K. D. Naegle, & J. R. Pitts (Eds.), *Theories of society: Foundations of modern sociological theory* (pp. 540–551). New York: Free Press.

Smith, B. C. (1988). *Bureaucracy and political power.* Sussex, England, & New York: Wheatsheaf Books & St. Martin's Press.

Smith, E. B. (1975). Chester Barnard's concept of leadership. *Educational Administration Quarterly, 11*(3), 37–48.

Taylor, F. W. (1911). *The principles of scientific management.* New York: W. W. Norton.

Thompson, V. A. (1961). *Modern organization.* New York: Knopf.

Thompson, V. A. (1977). *Modern organization* (2nd ed.). New York: Alfred A. Knopf.

Udy, S. H., Jr. (1959). "Bureaucracy" and "rationality" in Weber's Organization Theory: An empirical study. *American Sociological Review, 24,* 791–795.

Waring, S. P. (1991). *Taylorism transformed: Scientific management theory since 1945.* Chapel Hill: The University of North Carolina Press.

Weber, M. (1968). *Economy and society: An outline of interpretive sociology.* (E. Fischoff & T. M. Trans.; G. Roth & C. Wittich, Eds.). New York: Bedminster Press.

Weber, M. (1947). *The theory of social and economic organization* (A. M. Henderson & T. Parsons, Trans.). New York: Oxford University Press.

Weber, M. (1961). Legitimate order and types of authority. In T. Parsons, E. Shils, K. D. Naegle, & J. R. Pitts (Eds.), *Theories of society: Foundations of modern sociological theory.* New York: Free Press.

Weber, M. (1965). Subjective meaning in the social situation. In L. A. Coser & B. Rosenberg (Eds.), *Sociological theory: A book of readings* New York: Macmillan.

Weick, K. E. (1976). Educational organizations as loosely coupled systems. *Administrative Science Quarterly, 21,* 1–19.

Weick, K. E. (1982). Management of organizational change among loosely coupled elements. In P. Goodman & Associates (Eds.), *Changes in organizations: New perspectives on theory, research and practice* (pp. 375–408). San Francisco: Jossey-Bass.

Weick, K. E. (1985). Sources of order in underorganized systems: Themes in recent organization theory. In Y. S. Lincoln (Ed.), *Organizational theory and inquiry* (pp. 106–136). Beverly Hills, CA: Sage Publications.

Wilson, B. L., & Corbett, H. D. (1983). Organization and change: The effects of school linkages on the quality of implementation. *Educational Administration Quarterly, 19,* 84–104.

Woodward, J. (1965). *Industrial organization: Theory and practice* London: Oxford University Press.

Zald, M. (1970). Political economy: A framework for comparative analysis. In M. Zald (Ed.), *Power in organizations* (pp. 221–261). Nashville, TN: Vanderbilt University Press.

CONTINGENCY THEORY

Aldrich, H. E. (1979). *Organizations and environment.* Englewood Cliffs, NJ: Prentice-Hall.

Bacharach, S. B., Bamberger, P., Conley, S. C., & Bauer, S. (1990). The dimensionality of decision participation in educational organizations: The value of a multi-domain evaluative approach. *Educational Administration Quarterly, 26,* 126–127.

Blake, R. R., & Mouton, J. S. (1964). *The managerial grid.* Houston: Gulf.

Burns, T., & Stalker, G. M. (1961). *The management of innovation.* London: Tavistock.

Corwin, R. G. (1987). *The organization-society nexus* New York: Greenwood Press.

Emery, F. E., & Trist, E. L. (1965). The causal texture of organizational environments. *Human Relations, 18,* 21–32.

Fiedler, F., Chemers, M. M., & Maher, L. (1976). *Improving leadership effectiveness: The leader match concept.* New York: John Wiley.

Gaynor, A. K., & Clauset, K. H., Jr. (1983). *Organizations and their environments: A system dynamics perspective* (Report No. ERIC #ED 231 049). American Educational Research Association.

Hanson, E. M. (1979). School management and contingency theory: An emerging perspective. *Educational Administration Quarterly, 15*(2), 98–116.

Hunt, G. (1984). Organizational leadership: The contingency paradigm and its challenges. In B. Kellerman (Eds.), *Leadership: Multidisciplinary Perspectives* (pp. 113–138). Englewood Cliffs, NJ: Prentice-Hall.

Imber, M., & Duke, D. L. (1984). Teacher participation in school decision making: A framework for research. *Journal of Educational Administration, 12,* 24–34.

Kast, F. E., & Rosenzweig, J. E. (Eds.). (1973). *Contingency views of organization and management.* Chicago: Science Research Associates.

Katz, D., & Kahn, R. (1978). *Social psychology of organizations* (2nd ed.). New York: Wiley.

Kiggundu, M. N., Jorgensen, J. J., & Hafsi, T. (1983). Administrative theory and practice in developing countries: A synthesis. *Administrative Science Quarterly, 28*(1), 66–84.

Lawrence, P. R., & Lorsch, J. W. (1967). *Organization and environment.* Cambridge, MA: Harvard University Press.

Lorsch, J. W. (1979). Making behavioral science more useful. *Harvard Business Review, 57*(2), 171–180.

Meyer, A. D. (1982). How ideologies supplant formal structures and shape responses to environments. *Journal of Management Studies, 19*(1), 45–61.

Meyer, J. W., & Associates (Eds.). (1978). *Environments and organizations.* San Francisco: Jossey-Bass.

Meyer, J. W., & Scott, W. R. (1983). *Organizational environments: Ritual and rationality.* Beverly Hills, CA: Sage Publications.

Rice, A. K. (1963). *The Enterprise and Its Environment.* London: Tavistock.

Schoonhoven, C. B. (1981). Problems with contingency theory: Testing assumptions hidden within the language of contingency "Theory". *Administrative Science Quarterly, 26,* 349–377.

Thompson, J. (1967). *Organizations in action.* New York: McGraw-Hill.

Vroom, V. H., & Yetton, P. W. (1973). *Leadership and decision making.* Pittsburgh, PA: University of Pittsburgh Press.

DECISION-MAKING THEORY

Allison, G. T. (1971). *Essence of decision: Explaining the cuban Missile Crisis.* Boston: Little, Brown.

Bacharach, S. B., Bamberger, P., Conley, S. C., & Bauer, S. (1990). The dimensionality of decision participation in educational organizations: The value of a multi-domain evaluative approach. *Educational Administration Quarterly, 26,* 126–127.

Beyer, J. M. (1981). Ideologies, values and decision-making in organizations. In P. Nystrom & W. H. Starbuck (Eds.), *Handbook of organizational design* (pp. 166–197). London: Oxford University Press.

Beyer, J. M., & Lodahl, T. M. (1976). A comparative study of patterns of influence in United States and English universities. *Administrative Science Quarterly, 21,* 104–127.

Beyer, J. M., & Lutze, S. (1992). The ethical nexus: Organizations, values, and decision-making. In C. Conrad (Ed.), *The Ethical nexus: Communication, values, and organizational decisions* (pp. 23–45). Norwood, NJ: Ablex Publishers.

Blau, P. M., & Scott, W. R. (1962). *Formal organizations.* San Francisco, CA: Chandler.

Braybrooke, D., & Lindblom, C. E. (1963). *A strategy of decision: policy evaluation as a social process.* New York: Free Press.

Charters, W. W., Jr. (1981). The control of micro-educational policy in elementary schools. In S. E. Bacharach (Ed.), *Organizational behavior in schools and school districts.* New York: Praeger.

Cohen, M., & March, J. (1974). *Leadership and ambiguity: The American college presidency.* New York: McGraw-Hill.

Cohen, M., March, J., & Olsen, J. (1972, March). A garbage can model of organizational choice. *Administrative Science Quarterly, 17,* 1–25.

Conway, J. (1984). The myth, mystery, and mastery of participative decision-making in education. *Educational Administration Quarterly, 20*(3), 11–40.

Estler, S. (1988). Decision making. In N. J. Boyan (Ed.), *Handbook of research on educational administration* (pp. 305–320). New York/London: Longman.

Farrell, D. C., & Peterson, J. C. (1982). Patterns of political behavior in organizations. *Academy of Management Review, 7,* 403–421.

Field, R. H. G. (1979). A critique of the Vroom-Yetton Contingency Model of Leadership Behavior. *Academy of Management Review, 4,* 249–257.

Frank, R. H. (1987). Shrewdly irrational. *Sociological Forum, 2*(1), 21–39.

Hickson, D. J. (1987). Decision-making at the top of organizations. *Annual Review of Sociology, 13,* 165–192.

Hickson, D. J., Butler, R. J., Cray, D., Mallory, G. R., & Wilson, D. C. (1986). *Top decisions: Strategic decision making in organizations.* San Francisco: Jossey-Bass.

Imber, M., & Duke, D. L. (1984). Teacher participation in school decision making: A framework for research. *Journal of Educational Administration, 12,* 24–34.

Jackofsky, E. F., & Slocum, J. W., Jr. (1988). C.E.O. roles across cultures. In D. C. Hambrick (Ed.), *The executive effect: Concepts and methods for studying top managers.* Greenwich, CT: JAI Press.

Kennedy, M. M. (1984). How evidence alters understanding and decisions. *Educational Evaluation and Policy Analysis, 6*(3), 207–226.

Kunz, D. W., & Hoy, W. K. (1976). Leadership style of principals and the professional zone of acceptance of teachers. *Educational Administration Quarterly, 12*(3), 49–64.

Lindblom, C. E. (1959). The science of "muddling through". *Public Administration Review, 19,* 79–88.

Lindblom, C. E., & Cohen, D. K. (1979). *Usable knowledge: Social science and social problem solving.* New Haven, CT: Yale University Press.

Locke, E. A., & Schweiger, D. M. (1990). Participation in decision-making: One more look. In L. L. Cummings & B. M. Staw (Eds.), *Leadership, participation, and group behavior* (pp. 137–211). Greenwich, CT: JAI Press.

March, J. G. (1982). Emerging developments in the study of organizations. *The Review of Higher Education, 6*(1), 1–18.

March, J. G., & Olsen, J. P. (1976). *Ambiguity and choice in organizations.* Bergen, Norway: Universitetsforlaget.

Meyer, A. D. (1982). How ideologies supplant formal structures and shape responses to environments. *Journal of Management Studies, 19*(1), 45–61.

Meyer, A. D. (1984). Mingling decision making metaphors. *Academy of Management Review, 9*(1), 6–17.

Padgett, J. F. (1980). Managing garbage can hierarchies. *Administrative Science Quarterly, 25*, 583–604.

Perrow, C. (1982). Disintegrating social sciences. *Phi Delta Kappan, 63*(10), 684–688.

Pettigrew, A. W. (1973). *The politics of organizational decision-making.* London: Tavistock Publications.

Pfeffer, J., & Salancik, G. R. (1974). Organizational decision making as a political process: The case of a university budget. *Administrative Science Quarterly, 19*(2), 135–151.

Salancik, G. R., & Pfeffer, J. (1974). The bases and use of power in organizational decision-making: The case of a university. *Administrative Science Quarterly, 19*(4), 453–473.

Simon, H. A. (1957). *Administrative behavior.* New York: Macmillan.

Vroom, V. H., & Yetton, P. W. (1973). *Leadership and decision making.* Pittsburgh, PA: University of Pittsburgh Press.

Walsh, J. P., & Fahey, L. (1986). The role of negotiated belief structures in strategy making. *Journal of Management, 12*, 325–338.

Weick, K. E. (1976). Educational organizations as loosely coupled systems. *Administrative Science Quarterly, 21*, 1–19.

Weick, K. E. (1982). Administering education in loosely coupled schools. *Phi Delta Kappan, 63*(10), 673–676.

Weick, K. E. (1987). Substitutes for strategy. In D. J. Teece (Eds.), *The competitive challenge: Strategies for innovation and renewal* (pp. 221–233). Cambridge, MA: Ballinger.

Weick, K. E. (1988). Enacted sensemaking in crisis situations. *Journal of Management Studies, 25*(4), 305–317.

Weiss, C. H., & Bucuvalas, M. J. (1980). *Social science research and decision-making.* New York: Columbia University Press.

Willower, D. J. (1982). School organizations: Perspectives in juxtaposition. *Educational Administration Quarterly, 18*(3), 89–110.

Wise, A. (1983). Why educational policies often fail: The hyperrationalization hypothesis. In J. V. Baldridge & T. Deal (Eds.), *The dynamics of organizational change in education* (pp. 93–113). Berkeley, CA: McCutchan.

EPISTEMOLOGY

Burrell, G., & Morgan, G. (1979). *Sociological paradigms and organizational analysis.* London: Heinemann.

GENERAL SYSTEMS THEORY

Bakke, E. W., & Argyris, C. (1954). *Organizational structure and dynamics.* New Haven, CT: Yale University.

Bertalanffy, L. V. (1950). The theory of open systems in physics and biology. *Science, 3.*

Boulding, K. E. (1956a). General systems theory—The skeleton of science. *Management Science, 2*(3), 197–208.

Boulding, K. E. (1956b). Management science 2. The institute of management sciences. In J. M. Shafritz & J. M. Ott (Eds.), *Classics of organization theory* (pp. 239–250). Dorsey Press.

Casti, J. (1981). Systemism, system theory, and social modeling. *Regional Science and Urban Economics, 11*, 405–424.

Goldratt, E. M., & Cox, J. (1992). *The Goal* (2nd Rev.). Croton-on-Hudson, NY: North River Press.

Katz, D., & Kahn, R. (1978). *Social psychology of organizations* (2nd ed.). New York: Wiley.

Parsons, T. (1964). *The social system*. Glencoe, IL: The Free Press of Glencoe.

Quade, E. S., & Miser, H. J. (1985). *Handbook of systems analysis*. New York: North-Holland.

Scott, W. R. (1987). *Organizations: Rational, natural, and open systems* (2nd ed.). Englewood Cliffs, NJ: Prentice-Hall.

von Bertalanffy, L. (1952). *Problems of life*. London: Watts.

JOB SATISFACTION AND MOTIVATION THEORY

Anderson, C. S. (1982). The search for school climate: A review of the literature. *Review of Educational Research, 52*, 368–420.

Halpin, A. W., & Croft, D. B. (1963). *The organizational climate of schools*. Chicago: University of Chicago Press.

Hoy, W. K., & Clover, S. I. R. (1986). The elementary school climate: A revision of the OCDQ. *Educational Administration Quarterly, 22*, 93–110.

James, L. R., & Jones, A. P. (1974). Organizational climate: A review of theory and research. *Psychology Bulletin, 81*, 1096–1112.

Kottkamp, R. B., Mulhern, J. A., & Hoy, W. K. (1987). Secondary school climate: A revision of the OCDQ. *Educational Administration Quarterly, 23*, 31–48.

Lewin, K. (1935). *A dynamic theory of personality*. New York: McGraw-Hill.

Likert, J. G., & Likert, R. (1978). *Profile of a school*. Ann Arbor, MI: Likert Associates, Inc.

Likert, R. (1961). *New patterns of management*. New York: McGraw-Hill.

Miskel, C., & Ogawa, R. (1988). Work motivation, job satisfaction, and climate. In N. J. Boyan (Eds.), *Handbook of research on educational administration* (pp. 279–304). New York/London: Longman.

Murray, H. (1938). *Explorations in personality*. New York: Oxford University Press.

Rice, A. K. (1958). *Productivity and social organization: The Ahmedabad experiment*. London: Tavistock.

Schneider, B. (Ed.). (1990). *Organizational climate and culture*. San Francisco: Jossey-Bass.

Steinhoff, C. R. (1965). *Organizational climate in a public school system* (Cooperative Program Contract No. OE-4-225, Project No. S-083, Syracuse University) Washington, DC: U.S. Office of Education.

Stern, G. G. (1970). *People in context: Measuring person-environment in education and industry*. New York: John Wiley.

Tagiuri, R. (1968). The concept of organizational climate. In R. Tagiuri & G. H. Litwin (Eds.), *Organizational climate: Explorations of concept*. Boston, MA: Division of Research, Graduate School of Business Administration, Harvard University.

Trist, E. L., & Bamforth, K. L. (1951). Some social and psychological consequences of the long-wall method of coal-getting. *Human Relations, 4*, 3–38.

Whyte, W. F. (1969). *Organizational behavior*. Homewood, IL: Irwin/Dorsey.

Willower, D. J., & Hoy, W. K. (1967). *The school and pupil control ideology*. University Park, PA: Pennsylvania State University.

Woodward, J. (Ed.). (1970). *Industrial organizations: Behavior and control*. Oxford: Oxford University Press.

LEADERSHIP THEORY

Barnard, C. J. (1938). *The functions of the executive*. Cambridge, MA: Harvard University Press.

Bass, B. M. (1981). *Stogdill's handbook of leadership*. New York: Free Press.

Bass, B. M. (1985). *Leadership and performance beyond expectations*. New York: Free Press.

Bates, R. (1984). Toward a critical practice of educational administration. In T. J. Sergiovanni & J. E. Corbally (Eds.), *Leadership and organizational culture*. Urbana, IL: University of Illinois Press.

Bennis, W. (1984). Transformative power and leadership. In T. J. Sergiovanni & J. E. Corbally (Eds.), *Leadership and organizational culture.* Urbana, IL: University of Illinois Press.

Bennis, W., & Nanus, B. (1985). *Leaders: The strategies for taking charge.* New York: Harper & Row.

Berlew, D. E., & Hall, D. T. (1966). The socialization of managers: Effect of expectations on performance. *Administrative Science Quarterly, 11,* 207–233.

Blake, R. R., & Mouton, J. S. (1964). *The managerial grid.* Houston: Gulf.

Bolman, L., & Deal, T. (1991). *Reframing organizations: Artistry, choice, and leadership.* San Francisco: Jossey-Bass.

Burns, J. M. (1978). *Leadership.* New York: Harper & Row.

Calder, B. J. (1977). An attribution theory of leadership. In B. Stark & G. Salancik (Eds.), *New directions in organizational Behavior* (pp. 179–204). Chicago: St. Clair.

Child, J. (1972). Organizational structure, environment, and performance: The role of strategic choice. *Sociology, 6,* 1–22.

Clark, D. L., & Astuto, T. A. (1988). Paradoxical choice options in organizations. In D. E. Griffiths, R. T. Stout, & P. B. Forsyth (Eds.), *Leaders for America's schools: The report and papers of the National Commission on Excellence in Educational Administration* (pp. 112–130). Berkeley, CA: McCutchan.

Dill, D. D. (1984). The nature of administrative behavior in higher education. *Educational Quarterly, 20*(3), 69–100.

Ehrlich, S. B., Meindl, J. R., & Viellieu, B. (1990). The charismatic appeal of a transformational leader: An empicical case study of a small high-technology contractor. *Leadership Quarterly, 1*(4), 229–247.

Evans, M. G. (1970). The effects of supervisory behavior on the path-goal relationship. *Organizational Behavior and Human Performance, 5,* 277–298.

Feldman, S. P. (1987). The crossroads of interpretation: administration in professional organizations. *Human Organization, 46*(2), 95–102.

Fiedler, F., Chemers, M. M., & Maher, L. (1976). *Improving leadership effectiveness: The leader match concept.* New York: John Wiley.

Fiedler, F. E. (1967). *A theory of leadership effectiveness.* New York: McGraw-Hill.

Field, R. H. G. (1979). A critique of the Vroom-Yetton Contingency Model of Leadership Behavior. *Academy of Management Review, 4,* 249–257.

Filley, A. C., House, R. J., & Kerr, S. (1976). *Managerial process and organizational behavior.* Glenview, IL: Scott, Foresman.

Foster, W. (1988). Educational administration: A critical appraisal. In D. E. Griffiths, R. T. Stout, & P. B. Forsyth (Eds.), *Leaders for America's schools: The report and papers of the National Commission on Excellence in Educational Administration* (pp. 68–81). Berkeley, CA: McCutchan.

Frank, R. H. (1987). Shrewdly irrational. *Sociological Forum, 2*(1), 21–39.

Gibb, C. A. (1954). Leadership. In G. Lindzey (Ed.), *Handbook of social psychology.* Cambridge, MA: Addison-Wesley.

Goodsell, C. T. (1977). Bureaucratic manipulation of physical symbols: An empirical study. *American Journal of Political Science, 21,* 79–91.

Gouldner, A. (1957). Cosmopolitans and locals: Toward an analysis of latent social roles. *Administrative Science Quarterly, 2,* 281–306.

Gowler, D., & Legge, K. (1983). The meaning of management and the management of meaning: A view from social anthropology. In M. J. Earl (Ed.), *Perspectives on management: An interdisciplinary approach.* London: Oxford University Press.

Greenfield, T. B. (1968). Research on the behavior of educational leaders: Critique of a tradition. *Alberta Journal of Educational Research, 14,* 55–76.

Greenfield, T. B. (1984). Leaders and schools: Willfulness and nonnatural order in organizations. In T. J. Sergiovanni & J. E. Corbally (Eds.), *Leadership and organizational culture: New perspectives on administrative theory and practice* (pp. 142–169). Urbana, IL: University of Illinois Press.

Greenfield, T. B. (1988). The decline and fall of science in educational administration. In D. E. Griffiths, R. T. Stout, & P. B. Forsyth (Eds.), *Leaders for America's schools: The report and papers of the National Commission on Excellence in Educational Administration* (pp. 131–159). Berkeley, CA: McCutchan.

Greenfield, W. D. (1985). The moral socialization of school administrators: Informal role learning outcomes. *Educational Administration Quarterly, 21,* 99–119.

Greiner, L. E. (1972, July/August). Evolution and revolution as organizations grow. *Harvard Business Review, 50,* 37–46.

Griffiths, D. E., Stout, R. T., & Forsyth, P. B. (Eds.). (1988). *Leaders for America's schools: The report and papers of the National Commission on Excellence in Educational Administration.* Berkeley, CA: McCutchan.

Grob, L. (1984). Leadership: The Socratic model. In B. Kellerman (Ed.), *Leadership: Multidisciplinary perspectives.* Englewood Cliffs, NJ: Prentice-Hall.

Guba, E. G. (1973). Reaction. In L. L. Cunningham & W. J. Gephart (Eds.), *Leadership: The science and the art today.* Itasca, IL: Peacock.

H. P. Sims, J. (1977). The leader as a manager of reinforcement contingencies. In J. G. Hunt & L. L. Larson (Eds.), *Leadership: The cutting edge.* Carbondale, IL: Southern Illinois University Press.

Hanson, E. M. (1979). School management and contingency theory: An emerging perspective. *Educational Administration Quarterly, 15*(2), 98–116.

Hersey, P., & Blanchard, K. H. (1988). *Management of organizational behavior: Utilizing human resources* (5th ed.). Englewood Cliffs, N.J.: Prentice-Hall.

Hickson, D. J. (1987). Decision-making at the top of organizations. *Annual Review of Sociology, 13,* 165–192.

Hickson, D. J., Butler, R. J., Cray, D., Mallory, G. R., & Wilson, D. C. (1986). *Top decisions: Strategic decision making in organizations.* San Francisco: Jossey-Bass.

Hodgkinson, C. (1983). *The philosophy of leadership.* Oxford: Basil Blackwell.

Hodgkinson, C. (1991). *Educational leadership: The moral art.* Albany, NY: State University of New York Press.

Hollander, E. (1978). *Leadership dynamics: A practical guide to effective relationships.* New York: Free Press.

House, R. J. (1971). A path-goal theory of leader effectiveness. *Administrative Science Quarterly, 16,* 321–338.

House, R. J., & Baetz, M. L. (1979). Leadership: Some empirical generalizations and new research directions. In B. M. Staw (Ed.), *Research in Organizational Behavior* (pp. 341–423).

House, R. J., & Mitchell, T. R. (1974). Path-goal theory of leadership. *Journal of Contemporary Business, 5,* 81–97.

House, R. J., Woycke, J., & Fodor, E. M. (1988). Charismatic and noncharismatic leaders: Differences in behavior and effectiveness. In J. A. Conger & R. Kanungo (Eds.), *Charismatic leadership: The elusive factor in organizational effectiveness* (pp. 98–121). San Francisco: Jossey-Bass.

Hunt, G. (1984). Organizational leadership: The contingency paradigm and its challenges. In B. Kellerman (Ed.), *Leadership: Multidisciplinary perspectives* (pp. 113–138). Englewood Cliffs, NJ: Prentice-Hall.

Hunt, J. G. (1991). *Leadership: A new synthesis.* Newbury Park, CA: Sage Publications.

Hunt, J. G., & Larson, L. L. (Eds.). (1979). *Crosscurrents in leadership.* Carbondale, IL: Southern Illinois University Press.

Immegart, G. L. (1988). Leadership and leader behavior. In N. J. Boyan (Ed.), *Handbook of research on educational administration* (pp. 259–278). New York/London: Longman.

Isabella, L. A. (1990). Evolving interpretations as a change unfolds: How managers construe key organizational events. *Academy of Management Journal, 33*(1), 7–41.

Jackall, R. (1988). *Moral mazes: The world of corporate managers.* New York: Oxford University Press.

Jackofsky, E. F., & Slocum, J. W., Jr. (1988). C.E.O. roles across cultures. In D. C. Hambrick (Ed.), *The executive effect: Concepts and methods for studying top managers.* Greenwich, CT: JAI Press.

Jago, A. G. (1982). Leadership: Perspectives in theory and research. *Management Science, 28*(3), 315–336.

Kanter, R. (1977). *Men and women of the corporation.* New York: Basic Books.

Kegan, R., & Lahey, L. L. (1984). Adult leadership and adult development: A constructionist view. In B. Kellerman (Ed.), *Leadership: Multidisciplinary perspectives* (pp. 199–230). Englewood Cliffs, NJ: Prentice-Hall.

Kerr, S., & Jermier, J. M. (1983). Substitutes for leadership: Their meaning and measurement. In W. R. Lassey & M. Sashkin (Eds.), *Leadership and social change* (pp. 59–73). San Diego: University Associates.

Kiggundu, M. N., Jorgensen, J. J., & Hafsi, T. (1983). Administrative theory and practice in developing countries: A synthesis. *Administrative Science Quarterly, 28*(1), 66–84.

Kilmann, R. H., Saxton, M. J., & Serpa, R., & Associates (1985). *Gaining control of the corporate culture*. San Francisco: Jossey-Bass.

Kmetz, J. T., & Willower, D. J. (1982). Elementary school principals' work behavior. *Educational Administration Quarterly, 18*, 62–78.

Kunz, D. W., & Hoy, W. K. (1976). Leadership style of principals and the professional zone of acceptance of teachers. *Educational Administration Quarterly, 12*(3), 49–64.

Leiberson, S., & O'Connor, J. F. (1972). Leadership and organizational performance: A study of large corporations. *American Sociological Review, 37*(2), 117–130.

Lieberman, A., & Miller, L. (Eds.). (1979). *Staff development: New demands, New realities, New perspectives*. New York: Teachers College Press.

Likert, R. (1967). *The human organization: Its management and value*. New York: McGraw-Hill.

Locke, E. A., & Schweiger, D. M. (1990). Participation in decision-making: One more look. In L. L. Cummings & B. M. Staw (Eds.), *Leadership, participation, and group behavior* (pp. 137–211). Greenwich, CT: JAI Press.

M. W. McCall, J., & Lombardo, M. M. (1978). *Leadership: Where else can we Go?* Durham, NC: Duke University Press.

Machiavelli, N. (1952). *The Prince* (Luigi Ricci, rev. by E. R. P. Vincent, Trans.). New York: New American Library of World Literature. (Original work, 1513).

Martin, W. J., & Willower, D. J. (1981). The Managerial behavior of high school principals. *Educational Administration Quarterly, 17*, 69–90.

Mawhinney, T. C., & Ford, J. D. (1977). The path-goal theory of leader effectiveness: An operant interpretation. *Academy of Management Review, 2*, 398–411.

Maxcy, S. J. (1991). *Educational leadership: A critical pragmatic perspective*. New York: Bergin and Harvey.

McCall, W., Jr. (1976). Leadership research: Choosing gods and devils on the run. *Journal of Occupational Psychology, 49*, 139–153.

Meindl, J. R. (1990). On leadership: An alternative to the conventional wisdom. *Research in Organizational Behavior, 12*, 159–203.

Miklos, E. (1977–78). Ethical aspects of administrative action: Implications for research and preparation. *Administrator's Notebook, 26*(5), 1–5.

Mintzberg, H. (1973). *The nature of managerial work*. New York: Harper & Row.

Mintzberg, H. (1979, December). An emerging strategy of "direct" research. *Administrative Science Quarterly, 24*, 582–588.

Nystrom, P. C., & Starbuck, W. H. (1984). Managing beliefs in organizations. *Journal of Applied Behavioral Science, 20*(3), 277–287.

Perrow, C. (1972). *Complex organizations: A critical essay* (2nd ed.). Glenview, IL: Scott-Foresman.

Peters, T., & Austin, N. (1985). *A passion for excellence: The leadership difference*. New York: Random House.

Peters, T., & Waterman, R. (1982). *In search of excellence*. New York: Harper & Row.

Pfeffer, J. (1977). The ambiguity of leadership. *Academy of Management Journal, 2*, 104–112.

Pondy, L. R. (1978). Leadership is a language game. In M. W. McCall & M. M. Lombardi (Eds.), *Leadership: Where else can we go?* Durham, NC: Duke University Press.

Porter, L. W., & E. E. Lawler, I. (1968). *Managerial attitudes and performance*. Homewood, IL: Dorsey.

Puffer, S. M. (1990). Attributions of charismatic leadership: The impact of decision style, outcome, and observer characteristics. *Leadership Quarterly, 1*(3), 177–199.

Roberts, N., & Bradley, R. T. (1988). Limits of charisma. In J. A. Conger & R. N. Kanungo & Associates (Eds.), *Charismatic leadership: The elusive factor in organizational effectiveness* (pp. 253–276). San Francisco: Jossey-Bass.

Sashkin, M., & Garland, H. (1979). Laboratory and field research on leadership: Integrating divergent streams. In J. G. Hunt & L. Larson (Eds.), *Crosscurrents in Leadership* (pp. 64–87). Carbondale, IL: Southern Illinois University Press.

Schein, E. H. (1983). The role of founder in creating organizational culture. *Organizational Dynamics* (Summer), 13–28.

Schein, E. H. (1985). *Organizational culture and leadership*. San Francisco, CA: Jossey-Bass.

Schoonhoven, C. B. (1981). Problems with contingency theory: Testing assumptions hidden within the language of contingency "theory". *Administrative Science Quarterly, 26*, 349–377.

Schriesheim, C. S., House, R. J., & Kerr, S. (1976). Leader initiating structure: A reconciliation of discrepant research results and some empirical tests. *Organizational Behavior and Human Performance, 15,* 197–321.

Selznick, P. (1957). *Leadership in administration.* New York: Harper & Row.

Sergiovanni, T. J., & Corbally, J. (1984). *Leadership and organizational cultures.* Champaign, IL: University of Illinois Press.

Smith, E. B. (1975). Chester Barnard's concept of leadership. *Educational Administration Quarterly, 11*(3), 37–48.

Smyth, J. (Ed.). (1989). *Critical perspectives on educational leadership.* London: Falmer Press.

Stogdill, R. M. (1974). *Handbook of leadership: A survey of theory and research.* New York: Free Press.

Stogdill, R. M. (1977). *Leadership: Abstracts and bibliography 1904 to 1974.* Columbus, OH: College of Administrative Science, The Ohio State University.

Swidler, A. (1986). Culture in action: Symbols and strategies. *American Sociological Review, 51,* 273–286.

Trice, H. M., & Beyer, J. M. (1985). Using six organizational rites to change cultures. In R. H. Kilmann, M. J. Saxton, & R. Serpa (Eds.), *Gaining control of the corporate culture* (pp. 370–399). San Francisco: Jossey-Bass.

Trice, H. M., & Beyer, J. M. (1991). Cultural leadership in organizations. *Organization Science, 2*(2), 149–169.

Trice, H. M., & Beyer, J. M. (1993). *The cultures of work organizations.* Englewood Cliffs, NJ: Prentice-Hall.

Tucker, R. C. (1981). *Politics as leadership.* Columbia, MO: University of Missouri Press.

Van Maanen, J., & Schein, E. H. (1979). Toward a theory of organizational socialization. *Research in Organizational Behavior, 1,* 209–259.

Vroom, V. H. (1976). Leadership. In M. Dunnette (Ed.), *Handbook of industrial and organizational psychology.* Chicago: Rand-McNally.

Vroom, V. H., & Yetton, P. W. (1973). *Leadership and decision making.* Pittsburgh, PA: University of Pittsburgh Press.

Watkins, P. (1989). Leadership, power, and symbols in educational administration. In J. Smyth (Ed.), *Critical perspectives on educational leadership.* London: Falmer Press.

Weick, K. E. (1982a). Administering education in loosely coupled schools. *Phi Delta Kappan, 63*(10), 673–676.

Weick, K. E. (1982b). Management of organizational change among loosely coupled elements. In P. S. Goodman & Associates (Eds.), *Changes in organizations: New perspectives on theory, research and practice* (pp. 375–408). San Francisco: Jossey-Bass.

Weick, K. E. (1987). Substitutes for strategy. In D. J. Teece (Ed.), *The competitive challenge: Strategies for innovation and renewal* (pp. 221–233). Cambridge, MA: Ballinger.

Weiss, C. H., & Bucuvalas, M. J. (1980). *Social science research and decision-making.* New York: Columbia University Press.

Zaleznik, A. (1977). Managers and leaders: Are they different? *Harvard Business Review, 55*(3), 67–68.

MATHEMATICAL AND ECONOMIC MODELS

Deming, W. E. (1986). *Out of the crisis.* Cambridge, MA: Center for Advanced Engineering Study, MIT.

Halberstam, D. (1991). *The next century.* New York: William Morrow and Company.

Quade, E. S., & Miser, H. J. (1985). *Handbook of systems analysis.* New York: North-Holland.

ORGANIZATIONAL CHANGE THEORY

Aldrich, H. E. (1979). *Organizations and environment.* Englewood Cliffs, NJ: Prentice-Hall.

Argyris, C. (1982). How learning and reasoning processes affect organizational change. In P. S. Goodman & Associates (Eds.), *Change in Organizations* (pp. 47–86). San Francisco: Jossey-Bass.

Argyris, C., & Schön, D. A. (1978). *Organizational learning: A theory of action perspective.* Reading, MA: Addison-Wesley.

Baldridge, J. V. & Deal, T. E. (1975). *Managing change in educational organizations.* Berkeley, CA: McCutchan.

Baldridge, J. V., & Deal, T. (Eds.). (1983). *The dynamics of organizational change in education.* Berkeley, CA: McCutchan.

Baldridge, J. V., & Deal, T. E. (1975). Overview of change processes in educational organizations (pp. 1–23). In J. V. Baldridge & T. E. Deal (Eds.), *Managing change in educational organizations.* Berkeley, CA: McCutchan.

Bass, B. M. (1985). *Leadership and performance beyond expectations.* New York: Free Press.

Berman, P. (1981). Toward an implementation paradigm. In R. Lehming & M. Kane (Eds.), *Improving schools: Using what we know* Beverly Hills, CA: Sage Publications.

Berman, P., & McLaughlin, M. W. (1975). *Federal programs supporting educational change.* Santa Monica, CA: Rand.

Berman, P., & McLaughlin, M. W. (1975). *Federal programs supporting educational change: The findings in review.* Santa Monica, CA: Rand.

Berman, P., & McLaughlin, M. W. (1977). *Federal programs supporting educational change: Factors affecting continuation and implementation.* Santa Monica, CA: Rand.

Berman, P., & McLaughlin, M. W. (1978). *Federal programs supporting educational change: Implementing and sustaining innovation.* Santa Monica, CA: Rand Corporation.

Berman, P., & McLaughlin, M. W. (1979). *An exploratory study of school district adaptation.* Santa Monica, CA: Rand.

Biggart, N. W. (1977). The creative-destructive process of organizational change: The case of the post office. *Administrative Science Quarterly, 22,* 410–426.

Bolman, L., & Deal, T. (1991). *Reframing organizations: Artistry, choice, and leadership.* San Francisco: Jossey-Bass.

Burns, J. M. (1978). *Leadership.* New York: Harper & Row.

Cameron, K. S., & Quinn, R. E. (1988). Organizational paradox and transformation. In K. S. Cameron & R. E. Quinn (Eds.), *Paradox and transformation* (pp. 1–18). Cambridge, MA: Ballinger Publishing.

Child, J. (1972). Organizational structure, environment, and performance: The role of strategic choice. *Sociology, 6,* 1–22.

Child, J., Ganter, H. D., & Kieser, A. (1987). Technological innovation and organizational conservatism. In J. M. Pennings & A. Buitendam (Eds.), *New technology as organizational innovation* (pp. 87–116). Cambridge, MA: Ballinger Publishing.

Child, J., & Smith, C. (1987, November). The context and process of organizational transformation—Cadbury limited in its sector. *Journal of Management Studies, 24,* 565–593.

Clark, D., Lotto, L., & Astuto, T. (1984). Effective schools and school improvement: A comparative analysis of two lines of inquiry. *Educational Administration Quarterly, 20*(3), 41–68.

Corbett, H. D. (1981). School impacts on technical assistance roles: An in-depth analysis. *Knowledge: Creation, Diffusion, Utilization, 3*(2), 249–267.

Corbett, H. D., Dawson, J. A., & Firestone, W. A. (1984). *School context and school change: Implications for effective planning.* New York: Teachers College Press.

Corwin, R. G., & Borman, K. M. (1988). School as workplace: Structural constraints on administration. In N. J. Boyan (Ed.), *Handbook of research on educational administration* (pp. 209–238). New York/London: Longman.

Crandall, D. P., & Loucks, S. F. (1983). *People, policies, and practices: Examining the chain of school improvement.* Andover, MA: The Network.

Deal, T. E., & Kennedy, A. A. (1982). *Corporate cultures: The rites and rituals of corporate life.* Reading, MA: Addison-Wesley.

Deal, T. E., & Wiske, M. S. (1983). Planning, plotting and playing in education's era of decline. In J. V. Baldridge & T. E. Deal (Eds.), *The dynamics of organizational change in education* (pp. 451–472). Berkeley, CA: McCutchan.

Emrick, J. W., Peterson, W. S. M., & Agarwala-Rogers, R. (1977). *Evaluation of the national diffusion network.* Menlo Park, CA: Stanford Research Institute.

Firestone, W. A., & Corbett, H. D. (1988). Planned organizational change. In N. J. Boyan (Eds.), *Handbook of research on educational administration* (pp. 321–340). New York/London: Longman.

Fullan, M. (1982). *The meaning of educational change.* New York: Teachers College Press, Columbia University.

Fullan, M. (1985). Change processes and strategies at the local level. *Elementary School Journal, 85*, 391–421.

Fullan, M., & Pomfret, A. (1977). Research on curriculum and instruction implementation. *Review of Educational Research, 47*(1), 335–397.

Gagliardi, P. (1986). The creation and change of organizational cultures: A conceptual framework. *Organizational Studies, 7*(2), 117–134.

Gersick, C. J. G. (1991). Revolutionary change theories: A multilevel exploration of the punctuated equilibrium paradigm. *Academy of Management Review, 16*, 10–36.

Giacquinta, J. (1973). The process of organizational change in schools. In F. N. Kerlinger (Ed.), *Review of Research in Education* (pp. 178–208). Itasca, IL: Peacock.

Goodman, P. S., & Associates (1982). *Change in Organizations*. San Francisco: Jossey-Bass.

Gross, N., Giacquinta, J. B., & Bernstein, M. (1971). *Implementing organizational innovations*. New York: Basic Books.

Hall, G., & Hord, S. (1984). Analyzing what change facilitators do. *Knowledge: Creation, Diffusion, Utilization, 5*(3), 275–307.

Hannan, M. T., & Freeman, J. (1984). Structural inertia and organizational change. *American Journal of Sociology, 82*, 929–964.

Havelock, R. G. (1973). *The change agent's guide to innovation in education*. Englewood Cliffs, NJ: Educational Technology Publications.

House, E. R. (1981). Three perspectives on educational innovation: Technological, political and cultural. In R. Lehming & M. Kane (Eds.), *Improving schools: Using what we know* (pp.17–41). Beverly Hills, CA: Sage Publications.

Huberman, A. M. (1983, November). School improvement strategies that work: Some scenarios. *Educational Leadership, 41*(3), 23–27.

Huberman, A. M., & Miles, M. B. (1982). *Innovation up close: A field study in twelve school settings*. Andover, MA: The Network.

Huberman, A. M., & Miles, M. B. (1984). *Innovation up close: How school improvement works*. New York: Plenum.

Isabella, L. A. (1990). Evolving interpretations as a change unfolds: How managers construe key organizational events. *Academy of Management Journal, 33*(1), 7–41.

James, T., & Tyack, D. (1983). Learning from past efforts to reform the high school. *Phi Delta Kappan, 64*(6), 400–406.

Kanter, R. M. (1985). Change masters and the intricate architecture of corporate culture change. In E. A. Gibson (Ed.), *Organizations close up* (pp. 351–368). Plano, TX: Business Publications.

Kirst, M., & Jung, R. (1980). The utility of a longitudinal approach in assessing implementation: A thirteen year view of Title I, ESEA. *Educational Evaluation and Policy Analysis, 2*(5), 17–34.

Kozuch, J. A. (1979). Implementing an educational innovation: The constraints of the school setting. *High School Journal, 62*(5), 223–231.

Lewin, K. (1951). *Field theory in social science*. New York: Harper.

Lippitt, G. L. (1982). *Organizational renewal: A holistic approach to organization development* (2nd ed.). Englewood Cliffs, NJ: Prentice-Hall.

Louis, K. S. (1981). External agents and knowledge utilization: Dimensions for analysis and action. In R. Lehming & M. Kane (Eds.), *Improving schools: Using what we know* (pp. 168–211). Beverly Hills, CA: Sage Publications.

Louis, K. S., & Sieber, S. D. (1979). *Bureaucracy and the dispersed organization: The educational extension agent experiment*. Norwood, NJ: Ablex.

Meyer, J. W., & Associates (Eds.). (1978). *Environments and organizations*. San Francisco: Jossey-Bass.

Meyer, J. W., & Scott, W. R. (1983). *Organizational environments: Ritual and rationality*. Beverly Hills, CA: Sage Publications.

Meyerson, D., & Martin, J. (1987). Cultural change: An integration of three different views. *Journal of Management Studies, 24*, 623–648.

Miles, M. B. (1983, November). Unraveling the mystery of institutionalization. *Educational Leadership, 41*(3), 14–19.

Oakes, J., & Sirotnik, K. (1983, April). *An immodest proposal: From critical theory to critical practice for school renewal*. Paper presented at the annual meeting of the American Educational Research Association, Montreal, Canada.

Pondy, L. (1983). The role of metaphors and myths in organization and in the facilitation of change. In L. Pondy, P. J. Frost, G. Morgan, & T. C. Dandridge (Eds.), *Organizational symbolism* (pp. 157–166). Greenwich, CT: JAI Press.

Pondy, L., Frost, P. J., Morgan, G., & Dandridge, T. C. (Ed.). (1983). *Organizational symbolism.* Greenwich, CT: JAI Press.

Popkewitz, T. (1982, April). *Motion as education change: The misuse and irrelevancy of two research paradigms.* Paper presented at the annual meeting of the American Educational Research Association, New York, NY.

Popkewitz, T., & Tabachnik, B. (Ed.). (1981). *The study of schooling: Field based methodologies in educational research and evaluation.* New York: Praeger.

Rogers, E. M., & Shoemaker, F. F. (1971). *Communication of innovations: A cross-cultural approach* (2nd ed.). New York: Free Press.

Rosenblum, S., & Louis, K. S. (1981). *Stability and change.* New York: Plenum.

Rowan, B. (1982). Organizational structure and the institutional environment: The case of public schools. *Administrative Science Quarterly, 27*(2), 259–279.

Sarason, S. B. (1971). *The culture of the school and the problem of change.* Boston: Allyn and Bacon.

Schein, E. H. (1969). The mechanisms of change. In W. Bennis, K. Benne, & R. Chin (Eds.), *The planning of change* New York: Holt, Rinehart & Winston.

Schein, E. H. (1985). *Organizational culture and leadership.* San Francisco, CA: Jossey-Bass.

Schmuck, R. A., Runkel, P. J., Arends, J. H., & Arends, R. I. (1977). *The second handbook of organization development in schools.* Eugene, OR: Center for Educational Policy and Management, University of Oregon.

Sieber, S. (1981). Knowledge utilization in public education: Incentives and disincentives. In R. Lehming & M. Kane (Eds.), *Improving schools: Using what we know* (pp. 115–167). Beverly Hills, CA: Sage Publications.

Smith, L. M., & Keith, P. M. (1971). *Anatomy of an Educational innovation: An organizational analysis of an elementary school.* New York: John Wiley.

Trice, H. M., & Beyer, J. M. (1985). Using six organizational rites to change cultures. In R. H. Kilmann, M. J. Saxton, & R. Serpa (Eds.), *Gaining control of the corporate culture* (pp. 370–399). San Francisco: Jossey-Bass.

Tushman, M. L., & Romanelli, E. (1985). Organizational evolution: A metamorphosis model of convergence and reorientation. *Research in Organizational Behavior, 7,* 171–222.

Weick, K. E. (1982). Management of Organizational change among loosely coupled elements. In P. Goodman & Associates (Eds.), *Changes in organizations: New perspectives on theory, research and practice* (pp. 375–408). San Francisco: Jossey-Bass.

Wilson, B. L., & Corbett, H. D. (1983). Organization and change: The effects of school linkages on the quality of implementation. *Educational Administration Quarterly, 19,* 84–104.

Wise, A. (1983). Why educational policies often fail: The hyperrationalization hypothesis. In J. V. Baldridge & T. Deal (Eds.), *The dynamics of organizational change in education* (pp. 93–113). Berkeley, CA: McCutchan.

Wolcott, H. F. (1977). *Teachers vs. Technocrats.* Eugene, OR: Center for Educational Policy and Management, University of Oregon.

Zald, M. (1970). Political economy: A framework for comparative analysis. In M. Zald (Ed.), *Power in organizations* (pp. 221–261). Nashville, TN: Vanderbilt University Press.

Zaltman, G., & Duncan, R. (1977). *Strategies for planned change.* New York: John Wiley.

POLITICAL SYSTEMS THEORY

Easton, D. (1965). *A systems analysis of political life.* New York: Wiley.

Easton, D. (1966). *Varieties of political theory.* Englewood Cliffs, NJ: Prentice-Hall.

Mawhinney, H. B. (1994, Winter). Bringing the state back into theorizing on educational policy making: A neo-institutional perspective. *Organizational Theory Dialogue, 1,* 6–13.

Tarver, S. B. (1989) Identifying the gifted/talented: An analysis of a problem in Jacksport using Easton's political systems model. Term paper, Boston University School of Education.

POSTSTRUCTURAL PERSPECTIVES

Astley, W. G., & Van de Ven, A. H. (1983). Central perspectives and debates in organization theory. *Administrative Science Quarterly, 28*, 245–273.

Bates, R. (1984). Toward a critical practice of educational administration. In T. J. Sergiovanni & J. E. Corbally (Eds.), *Leadership and organizational culture* Urbana, IL: University of Illinois Press.

Benson, J. K. (1977a). Innovation and crisis in organizational analysis. In J. K. Benson (Eds.), *Organizational analysis: critique and innovation.* Beverly Hills, CA: Sage Publications.

Benson, J. K. (1977b). Organizations: A dialectical view. *Administrative Science Quarterly, 22*, 1–21.

Benson, J. K. (1983). Paradigms and praxis in organizational analysis. In L. L. Cummings & B. M. Staw (Eds.), *Research in organizational behavior.* Greenwich, CT: JAI Press.

Brown, R. H. (1978). Bureaucracy as praxis: Toward a political phenomenology of formal organizations. *Administrative Science Quarterly, 23*, 365–382.

Burrell, G., & Morgan, G. (1979). *Sociological paradigms and organizational analysis.* London: Heinemann.

Clegg, S., & Dunkerley, D. (1980). *Organization, class and control.* London: Routledge & Kegan Paul.

Czarniawska-Joerges, B. (1992). *Exploring complex organizations.* Newbury Park, CA: Sage Publications.

Foster, W. (1986). *Paradigms and promises: New approaches to educational administration.* Buffalo, NY: Prometheus.

Foster, W. (1988). Educational administration: A critical appraisal. In D. E. Griffiths, R. T. Stout, & P. B. Forsyth (Eds.), *Leaders for America's schools: The report and papers of the National Commission on Excellence in Educational Administration* (pp. 68–81). Berkeley, CA: McCutchan.

Giddens, A. (1979). *Central problems in social theory: Action, structure, and contradictions in social analysis.* Berkeley and Los Angeles: University of California Press.

Greenfield, T. B. (1988). The decline and fall of science in educational administration. In D. E. Griffiths, R. T. Stout, & P. B. Forsyth (Eds.), *Leaders for America's schools: The report and papers of the National Commission on Excellence in Educational Administration* (pp. 131–159). Berkeley, CA: McCutchan.

Greenfield, W. D. (1985). The moral socialization of school administrators: Informal role learning outcomes. *Educational Administration Quarterly, 21*, 99–119.

Grob, L. (1984). Leadership: The Socratic model. In B. Kellerman (Ed.), *Leadership: Multidisciplinary perspectives.* Englewood Cliffs, NJ: Prentice-Hall.

Hodgkinson, C. (1983). *The philosophy of leadership.* Oxford: Basil Blackwell.

Kegan, R., & Lahey, L. L. (1984). Adult leadership and adult development: A constructionist view. In B. Kellerman (Ed.), *Leadership: Multidisciplinary perspectives* (pp. 199–230). Englewood Cliffs, NJ: Prentice-Hall.

Morgan, G. (1980). Paradigms, metaphors, and puzzle solving in organization theory. *Administrative Science Quarterly, 25*, 605–622.

Oakes, J., & Sirotnik, K. (1983, April). *An immodest proposal: From critical theory to critical practice for school renewal.* Paper presented at the annual meeting of the American Educational Research Association, Montreal, Canada.

Papagianiss, G. J., Bickel, R. N., & Fuller, R. H. (1983). The social creation of school dropouts: Accomplishing the reproduction of an underclass. *Youth & Society, 14*(3), 363–392.

Popkewitz, T. (1982, April). *Motion as education change: The misuse and irrelevancy of two research paradigms.* Paper presented at the Annual meeting of the American Educational Research Association, New York, NY.

Popkewitz, T., & Tabachnik, B. (Eds.). (1981). *The study of schooling: Field based methodologies in educational research and evaluation.* New York: Praeger.

Ranson, S., Hinings, B., & Greenwood, R. (1980). The structuring of organizational structures. *Administrative Science Quarterly, 25*, 1–17.

Robinson, V. M. J. (1994). The practical promise of critical research in educational administration. *Educational Administration Quarterly, 30*(1), 56–76.

Salancik, G. R., & Pfeffer, J. (1978). A social information processing approach to job attitudes and task design. *Administrative Science Quarterly, 23*, 224–253.

Sharp, R. (1980). *Knowledge, ideology and the politics of schooling: Towards a Marxist analysis of education.* London: Routledge & Kegan Paul.

Smyth, J. (Ed.). (1989). *Critical perspectives on educational leadership.* London: Falmer Press.

Tesch, R. (1989). *Introductory guide to HyperQual.* Desert Hot Springs, CA: Qualitative Research Management.

UCEA (1992). Organizational studies overview: UCEA Knowledge Domains Project (Draft for Reviewers).

Watkins, P. (1989). Leadership, power, and symbols in educational administration. In J. Smyth (Eds.), *Critical perspectives on educational leadership.* London: Falmer Press.

Willis, P. E. (1977). *Learning to labour: How working class kids get working class jobs.* Hampshire, England: Gower Press.

PROCESS MANAGEMENT

Capper, C. A., & Jamison, M. T. (1992a, October). The saga of outcomes-based education: Paradigm pioneer or reproduction of the status quo? Paper presented at the Annual Conference of the University Council for Educational Administration, Minneapolis, MN.

Capper, C. A., & Jamison, M. T. (1992b, October). Total quality management. Paper presented at the Annual Conference of the University Council for Educational Administration, Minneapolis, MN.

Deming, W. E. (1986). *Out of the crisis.* Cambridge, MA: Center for Advanced Engineering Study, MIT.

Lewis, R. G., & Smith, D. H. (1993). *Total quality in higher education.* Delray Beach, FL: St. Lucie Press.

Rummler, G. A., & Brache, A. P. (1991). Improving performance: How to manage the white space on the organization chart. San Francisco/Oxford: Jossey-Bass.

SOCIAL SYSTEMS THEORY

Argyris, C. (1957). *Personality and organization: The conflict between the system and the individual.* New York: Harper & Row.

Argyris, C. (1960). *Understanding organizational behavior* Homewood, IL: The Dorsey Press, Inc.

Argyris, C. (1962). *Interpersonal competence and organizational effectiveness.* Homewood, IL: Dorsey Press.

Argyris, C. (1964). *Integrating the individual and the organization.* New York: Wiley.

Argyris, C. (1982). *Reasoning, learning, and action.* San Francisco: Jossey-Bass.

Getzels, J. W., & Guba, E. G. (1957). Social behavior and the administrative process. *School Review, 65,* 423–441.

Getzels, J. W., Lipham, J. M., & Campbell, R. F. (1968). *Educational administration as a social process: Theory, research, practice.* New York: Harper & Row.

Lipham, J. M. (1988). Getzels's models in educational administration. In N. J. Boyan (Ed.), *Handbook of research on educational administration* (pp. 171–184). New York/London: Longman.

O'Reilly, C. A., Chatman, J., & Caldwell, D. F. (1991). People and organizational culture: A profile comparison approach to assessing person-organization fit. *Academy of Management Journal, 34,* 487–516.

Parsons, T. (1964). *The social system.* Glencoe, IL: The Free Press of Glencoe.

Spiegelberg, E. J. (1989). *Dropout problem at Laramie senior high school: A problem analysis using the Social Systems Model* Term Paper, Boston University School of Education, Department of Administration, Training, and Policy Studies.

SYSTEM DYNAMICS

Forrester, J. W. (1987). Lessons from system dynamics modeling. *System dynamics review, 3*(2), 136–149.

Forrester, J. W. (1961). *Industrial dynamics.* Cambridge, MA: MIT Press.

Forrester, J. W. (1968). *Principles of Systems*. Cambridge, MA: MIT Press.

Forrester, J. W., Low, G. W., & Mass, N. J. (1974, June). The debate on world dynamics: A Response to Nordhaus. *Policy Sciences, 5*(2), 169–190.

Forrester, J. W. (1987). Nonlinearity in high-order models of social systems. *European Journal of Operations Research, 30*, 104–109.

Forrester, J. W. (1993). System dynamics as an organizing framework for pre-college education. *System Dynamics Review, 9*(2), 183–194.

Forrester, J. W., & Senge, P. M. (1980). Tests for building confidence in system dynamics models. In J. A. A. Legasto, J. W. Forrester, & J. M. Lyneis (Eds.), *System Dynamics* (pp. 209–228).

Gaynor, A. K., & Clauset, K. H., Jr. (1983). *Organizations and their environments: A system dynamics perspective* (Report No. ERIC #ED 231 049). American Educational Research Association.

Lane, D. C. (1994). Modeling as learning: A consultancy methodology for enhancing learning in management teams. In J. D. W. Morecroft & J. D. Sterman (Eds.), *Modeling for learning organizations* (pp. 85–117). Portland, OR: Productivity Press.

Machuca, J. A. D. (1992). Are we losing one of the best features of system dynamics? *System Dynamics Review, 8*(2), 175–177.

Morecroft, J. D. W., & Sterman, J. D. (Ed.). (1994). *Modeling for learning organizations*. Portland, OR: Productivity Press.

Goodman, M. R. (1974). *Study notes in system dynamics*. Cambridge, MA: Wright-Allen Press.

Richardson, G. P. (1986). Problems with causal-loop diagrams. *System Dynamics Review, 2*(2), 158–170.

Richardson, G. P. (1991). *Feedback thought in social science and systems theory*. Philadelphia: University of Pennsylvania Press.

Richardson, G. P., & A. L. Pugh, I. (1981). *Introduction to system dynamics modeling with DYNAMO*. Cambridge, MA: Productivity Press.

Richmond, B., Peterson, S., & Vescuso, P. (1987). *An academic user's guide to STELLA*. Lyme, NH: High Performance Systems.

Roberts, N., Andersen, D., Deal, R., Garet, M., & Shaffer, W. (1983). *Introduction to computer simulation: A system dynamics modeling approach*. Reading, MA: Addison-Wesley.

Saeed, K. (1992). Slicing a complex problem for system dynamics modeling. *System Dynamics Review, 8*(3), 251–261.

Senge, P. M. (1990). *The fifth discipline: The art & practice of the learning organization*. New York: Doubleday Currency.

Vennix, J. A. M., & Gubbels, J. W. (1994). Knowledge elicitation in conceptual model building: A case study in modeling a regional Dutch health care system. In J. D. W. Morecroft & J. D. Sterman (Eds.), *Modeling for learning organizations* (pp. 121–145). Portland, OR: Productivity Press.

Vennix, J. A. M., Gubbels, J. W., Post, D., & Poppen, H. J. (1990). A structured approach to knowledge elicitation in conceptual model building. *System Dynamics Review, 6*(2), 194–208.

Wolstenholme, E. F. (1994). A systematic approach to model creation. In J. D. W. Morecroft & J. D. Sterman (Eds.), *Modeling for learning organizations* (pp. 175–194). Portland, OR: Productivity Press.

Author Index

A

Aeschliman, M. D., 97
Allison, G., 25n
Amico-Porcaro, K., 211–212
Antonucci, R., 178
Argyris, C., 20, 62, 101
Aring, M. K., 152
Arnold, H.J., 25n
Astley, W. G., 32
Austin, N., 32
Azumi, K., 8

B

Bacharach, S. B., 25n, 72
Bacon, F., 96
Baetz, M. L., 87
Bakke, E. W., 62
Bamberger, P., 25n
Barnard, C. I., 3, 27, 32
Bass, B. M., 32, 87–89
Bateson, G., 110
Bauer, S., 25n
Becker, G., 154
Bendix, R., 39–42, 54
Bennis, W., 27, 32, 89–94
Benson, J. K., 32, 71
Berman, P., 126
Beyer, J. M., 32
Blake, R. R., 25n
Bolman, L. G., 8, 69, 72
Brache, A. P., 32, 44
Burns, J. M., 30
Burrell, G., x, 28, 32, 35, 95–96, 247–249

C

Calder, B. J., 25n

Campbell, R. F., 55
Carnegie Forum on Education and the Economy, 157
Cartwright, D., 87
Chase, H. W., 174
Chemers, M. M., 25n, 32
Child, J., 8
Chubb, J. E., 206–207
Clauset, K. H., Jr., 113, 127
Cohen, D. K., 4
Cohen, M., 25
Cole, G. F., 70
Commonwealth of Massachusetts, 144
Conley, S. C., 25n
Corbally, J., 32, 57
Cuban, L., 25
Cushner, K., 174–175

D

Dahrendorf, R., 25
Davis, C. S., 13–14, 17–18
Deal, T. E., 8, 57, 69, 72
Delattre, E., 192, 220
Deming, W. E., 32
Dewey, J., ix, 110
DeYoung, A. J., 157
Donaldson, L., 8
Drucker, P., 175
Ducat, C. R., 174
Dunkerley, D., 32

E

Earley, J., 211–212
Easton, D., 25, 69–70, 72–83
Eisner, E. W., 97–98
Englert, R. M., 69

Etzioni, A., 8
Eulau, H., 70
Evanson, J. L., 33

F

Farrar, E., 151
Ferguson, K. E., 32
Fiedler, F. E., 25n, 32, 87
Filley, A. C., 87
Forrester, J. W., 71
Foster, W., 32
Freeman, R. B., 154
Fuhrman, S., 175

G

Gadamer, H. G., 131
Gagnon, P., 175–176
Gaynor, A. K., 33
Getzels, J. W., 25n, 55–56, 58–64
Ghemawat, P., 32
Glenn, C. L., 185
Goodlad, J. I., 138
Graen, G., 25n
Greenfield, T. B., 32
Greenstein, F. I., 70
Gregory, K. L., 57
Grubb, W. N., 138, 160
Guba, E. G., 25n, 55, 254

H

Habermas, J., 71
Hage, J., 8
Hall, R. H., 8
Hanson, N. R., 25
Harrington, J. B., 15–16
Hatch, J. A., 254
Hegel, G. W. F., 110
Hills, F. S., 72
Hodgkinson, C., 32
Hollway, W., 54–55
House, R. J., 25n, 87
Huberman, A. M., 126
Hume, D., 110
Huston, A. C., 151

I

Immegart, G. L., 32, 87

J

Jacobson, L., 121
Jago, A. G., 32, 87–89
Jentz, B. C., 92

K

Kagan, J., 151
Kahn, R. L., 53, 59
Kennedy, A. A., 57
Kerr, S., 87
Kessel, J. H., 70
Khandwalla, P. N., 8
Kluckholn, C., 63
Kotter, J. P., 8, 40, 91
Kozuch, J. A., 57

L

Landau, M., 70
Lawler, J., 32, 72
Lawrence, P. R., 25n, 46, 190–191, 193
Lazerson, M., 138
Levy, F., 157
Levy, M. B., 71
Lincoln, Y. S., 254
Lindblom, C. E., 4, 25, 72
Lipham, J. M., 55
Lippmann, W., 12
Locke, J., 96
Lorsch, J. W., 25n, 46, 190–191, 193
Lortie, D., 203–205
Lotka, A. J., 110
Louis, K. S., 126
Lytle, W. O., 33

M

Machiavelli, N., 87
MacIntyre, A., 7
Magno, J., 211–212
Maher, L., 25n, 32
Mahoney, T. A., 72
Malthus, T. R., 110
March, J. G., 25
Martin, R., 173–174
Marx, K., 110
Massachusetts Board of Education, 184
Massachusetts Department of Education, 144,
        172, 181–182
Massachusetts Department of Public Health,
        197–198, 207
Mayr, O., 109
McCall, W., Jr., 87
McClelland, A., 174–175
McGregor, D., 53
McLaughlin, M. W., 126
Miles, M. B., 126
Mills, A. J., 32
Mintzberg, H., 8
Miskel, C., 32, 54
Mitchell, S. M., 72

Mitchell, T. R., 25n
Moe, T. M., 206–207
Morecroft, J. D. W., 111
Morgan, G., x, 28, 32, 35, 95–96, 247–249
Morss, E. R., 261
Mouton, J. S., 25n
Murnane, R. J., 157
Murray, H. A., 63
Mussen, P. H., 151
Myrdal, G., 110

N

Nanus, B., 27, 32, 89–94
National Commission on Excellence in Education, 176
National Public Television, 131
Newton, I., 96

O

O'Neill, T. P., 34
Ogawa, R., 32, 54
Olsen, J. P., 25
Osterman, P., 153–154
Ouchi, W. G., 25n, 32

P

Padgett, J. F., 25
Parsons, T., 58, 90
Paul, S., 261
Pautler, A. J., Jr., 139, 144
Peters, T., 32
Pfeffer, J., 25n, 32, 72
Polsby, N. W., 70
Portis, E. B., 71
Powell, A. G., 151, 177

Q

Quinn, R. P., 53

R

Ramos, A. G., 95–96
Reich, R. B., 156, 175, 185
Richardson, G. P., 109–111
Richardson, L. F., 110
Rist, R. C., 121
Roethlisberger, F. J., 54

Rokeach, M., 25
Rosenblum, S., 126
Rosenstock, L., 165
Rosenthal, R., 121
Rowan, B., 72
Rummler, G. A., 32, 44

S

Safford, P., 174–175
Salancik, G. R., 25n, 32, 72
Sarason, S. B., 67
Sathe, V., 8
Scheidler, K., 43, 45, 47–49
Schein, E. H., 32, 57
Schlesinger, L. A., 8
Schön, D. A., 101
Schoonhoven, C. B., 25n
Schriesheim, C. S., 87
Scribner, J. D., 69
Seddig, R. G., 70
Seidman, R. B., 24
Senge, P., 46, 108
Sergiovanni, T. J., 32, 57
Shils, E. A., 58
Simon, H. A., 4, 25
Sizer, T., 177–178
Smircich, L., 57
Smith, A., 110
Snoek, J. D., 53
Spiegelberg, E. J., 55, 57–65
Spring, J., 184–186
Squires, G. D., 154
Sterman, J. D., 111
Stern, D., 151
Stogdill, R. M., 87

T

Tancred, P., 32
Tarver, S. B., 75–82
Taylor, F. W., 54
Tesch, R., 35
Thurow, L. C., 90, 155
Toch, T., 175
Trice, H. M., 52
Tucker, R. C., 72
Turner, B. A., 57

V

Van de Ven, A. H., 32
Verhulst, P. F., 110
Vroom, V. H., 25n, 32

W

Waldo, D., 69
Wallace, W., 96

Warsh, D., 157
Weber, M., 39–42, 53–54
Weick, K. E., 25
Wilensky, H., 191, 193
Wilson, J. Q., 172, 192–194, 196–203
Wirt, J. G., 159–160
Wirth, A. G., 139, 156
Wofford, J. W., 92
Wolfe, D. M., 53

Y

Yang, G., 44–49
Yetton, P. W., 25n

Z

Zald, M., 72
Zander, A., 87
Zuboff, S., 155

Subject Index

A

Analysis, *see* Problem analysis
Authority, charismatic, 40

B

Bureaucracy
   and legal domination, 40
   characteristics of, 41
   dangers of, 40, 42, 54
   dominance of, 42
   dehumanizing potential of, 54
   principles of, 40–41
   tension between nomothetic and idiographic
      dimensions of, 54
   the nine elements of, 43–49
Bureaucratic official, attributes and position of,
      41
Bureaucratic theory, 39–52, *see also* Bureaucracy
   as a framework for analysis, 42–49
   place in the literature, 39
Burrell and Morgan's meta-framework, 95–107
   application of for analysis, 100–102
   decision analysis using, 101–102
   dimensions of, 98–99
   four paradigms of, 99–100
   intellectual background of, 96–98

C

Case examples, *see* Examples, case
Causal analysis, 24–29, *see also* Theoretical
      analysis
   essentially qualitative in nature, 35
   and "characterizing," 24–25
   and diverse actors and groups, 25
   and selective patterning, 25
   and personal experience, 24

Causal-loop diagramming, and modeling prob-
      lem systems, 9n
Causes of problems, *see* Problems, causes of
Change, organizational, *see* Systems thinking
Communication, in leadership theory, 90–91
Communication channels, in political systems
      theory, 78–79
Conceptual frameworks, 26–29, *see also*
      Frames; Theoretical analysis
   and fit with the problem, 27–28
   definition of, 26–27
   driving the causal analysis, 28
Conclusions, drawing of, 30–32
   across theoretical analyses, 32
   from information collected, 31–32
Constituencies, political, *see* Political constituen-
      cies
Continuous organization, in bureaucratic theory,
      43
Contractual relationships, in bureaucratic theory,
      49
Culture, organizational, in social systems theory,
      56–58; *see also* Subculture

D

Decision analysis, using Burrell and Morgan's
      meta-framework, examples of,
      223–265
   based on the functionalist paradigm, 229–230
   based on the interpretive paradigm, 230–232
   based on the radical-humanist paradigm,
      233–234
   based on the radical-structuralist paradigm,
      232–233
   description of the decision and decisional
      process, 223–228, 237–246
   recommendations, 234–235, 255–264

Decisions, political, *see* Political decisions
Decision makers, in problem analysis, 22–23
Decision makers, political, *see* Political decision
    makers
Demands, political, *see* Political demands
Division of labor, in bureaucratic theory, 43–44

E

Everyday language, importance of translating
    theoretical analyses into, 35
Examples, case, 136–265

F

Facilitating factors, *see* Problem analysis, poten-
    tial facilitating and hindering factors in
Feedback, history of thought, 109–111, *see also*
    Systems thinking
    in political systems theory, 74–75
    positive and negative, 119–126
Frames, organizational; *see* Theoretical frame-
    works
Functional authority, in bureaucratic theory, 44–45
Functional specificity of authority, in bureaucratic
    theory, 45

H

Hierarchy of authority, in bureaucratic theory,
    46–47
Hindering factors, *see* Problem analysis, potential
    facilitating and hindering factors in
Human relations movement, historical develop-
    ment of, 54

I

Information, collecting of, 31
Indicators, *see* Problem indicators

L

Leadership, definition of, 88–89
    theories of, 88
    typology of, 88
Leadership theory, 87–94
    an overview of, 87–89
    as a framework for analysis, 89–92
    major elements of, 89–92

M

Misperceptions, *see* Perceptions and mispercep-
    tions
Models, system dynamics, *see also* Systems think-
    ing
    advantage of, 109
    avoiding external variables in, 126
    building of, 111–129
    defining problems for analysis in, 112–115

developing confidence in, 129
    hypotheses in; mathematical equations in,
        127–128
    multiplier effects in, 121
    relationships among variables in, 115–118
    setting the boundaries of, 112, 118–119
    state variables in, 111
    steps in building, 112
    testing the logical coherence of, 128
    time delays in, 111, 125

N

Needs and dispositions, in social systems theory,
    56
Need-dispositions, of individuals in organizations,
    63–64
    patterning of, 63
    variability of, 63
Nomothetic dimension, of social systems theory,
    56–61

O

Outline, illustrative
    for a bureaucratic problem analysis, 52
    for a leadership problem analysis, 94
    for a political problem analysis, 85–86
    for a social systems problem analysis, 67–68
    for a system dynamics problem analysis, 130
    for a Burrell and Morgan decision analysis,
        102–107

P

Perceptions and misperceptions, 65
Policy gap, 15–18
    qualitative, 15–16
    quantitative, 15, 17–18
Policy recommendations, *see* Problem analysis,
    policy recommendations in
Political constituencies, active and latent, 75
    definition of, 75
    feedback to, 81–82
Political decision makers, 76–78
    definition of, 76
    importance of their identification in analysis,
        77
Political decisions
    categories of, 73n
    types of, 80
Political demands, 78
    categories of, 73n
    flow of, 78
Political science, 69–71
    and neo-Marxism, 71

definition of, 69
separation of from policy studies, 70–71
Political stress, *see* Stress, political
Political support, 79–80
and passive resistance, 80
categories of, 73n
Political systems theory, 69–86
and public relations, 82
and systems thinking, 73–75
an overview of, 69–71
as a framework for analysis, 72–84
as applied to organizations, 69
data collection in, 73
elements of, 72–73, 75–84
rationale for, 72
Potentialities, in social systems theory, 56
of an individual in an organization, 62
Problem, *see also* Policy gap; Problem analysis
as a discrepancy between indicators and
standards of comparison, 15
an example of, 147
background statement for a, an example of,
172–178
causes of a, an example of, 172, 150–153,
190–193
description and documentation of a, 5–6
an example of, 181–187
history and importance of a, 13
identifying a, 12
importance of a, an example of, 140–141,
178–180
indicators of a, 13–15
an example of, 142, 187–188
meaning of a, 14–15
qualitative examples of a, 13
quantitative examples of a, 13–14
statement of a, an example of, 139, 171
Problem analysis, as a hermeneutic process,
131–133, *see also* Problem; Stakeholders; Standard of comparison;
Theoretical analysis
questions for doing a, using system dynamics, 129
using Burrell and Morgan's meta-framework,
102
using bureaucratic theory, 50–52
using leadership theory, 92–94
using political systems theory, 84–85
using social systems theory, 66–67
policy evaluation in, an example of, 164–167
policy recommendations in, an example of,
158, 164, 169–170, 172, 212–219
potential facilitating and hindering factors in,
an example of, 219–220
stakeholder recommendations in, an example
of, 167–169, 220–222

using human capital theory in, an example
of, 155–158
using Wilson's bureaucratic theory in, an example of, 196–212
Problems, causes of: systematic thinking about, 8

Q

Questions, guiding, *see* Problem analysis, questions for

R

Recommendations, *see* Problem analysis, policy
recommendations in, stakeholder rec-
ommendations in
Role conflict, multiple: definition of, 60–61
Role pressure and role set, 58–59
Roles and role expectations, definition of, 58
in social systems theory, 56, 58–60
Role senders, definition of, 59
Role set and role expectations, 58–59, *see also*
Role pressure
Role stress, *see* Stress, role
Role theory and the human side of organizations,
53
a corollary to bureaucratic theory, 53

S

Separation of administration from ownership, in
bureaucratic theory, 47–48
Social systems theory, 53–68
as a framework for analysis, 55–66
elements and dynamics of, 55–56
focusing on a representative individual in using, 55
rationale for, 55
Solution strategies and multiple causal analyses,
29, *see also* Problem analysis, policy
recommendations in
deciding on satisfactory, 34
evaluating, 33–34
formulating, 32–34
hindering and facilitating factors associated
with, 33
importance of describing in concrete terms,
32–33
using theory to generate ideas about, 9–10
Stakeholders, 20–22, *see also* Problem; Problem
analysis
and solution strategies, 10
distinction between decision makers and, 6

example of, 147–150, 188–190
negative, 22
positive, 21–22
positive and negative, 7
recommendations to, 29, 34
table of characteristics of, 22
Standards of comparison, 15–20, *see also* Problem; Problem analysis
and values, 20, 35
an example of, 144–147, 181–185
alternative, example of, 185–187
definition of, 15–17
rationale for, an example of, 146
types and sources of, 18–20
Stress, political: from demands, 78
from erosion of support, 79–80
from political demands, 82
responses to, 83
sources of, 82–83
Stress, role: from changes over time, 66
sources of, 64–65
Subculture, and values, 61–62
of individuals in organizations, 61–62
Support, political: *see* Political support
System dynamics, *see* Systems thinking; Models, system dynamics
Systems thinking, 108–130, *see also* Feedback thought; Models, system dynamics
and neo-Marxism, 71
and organizational change, 126
the nature of, 108–109

T

Technical competence, in bureaucratic theory, 47
Theoretical analysis, 9–11, *see also* Causal analysis

flow chart of, 11
steps in doing, 9–11, 30–32
the generic process of, 26
usefulness of, 9
the value of, 7–8
Theoretical frameworks, and data collection, 27, *see also* Conceptual frameworks
bureaucratic theory as an example of, 39–52
Burrell and Morgan's meta-framework as an example of, 95–107, 223–235, 236–265
human capital theory as an example of, 153–158
leadership theory as an example of, 87–94
political systems theory as an example of, 69–86
social systems theory as an example of, 53–68
systems theory as an example of, 108–130
Wilson's bureaucratic theory as an example of, 193–212
Trust, in leadership theory, 91–92
through deployment of self, 91–92
through positioning, 91

V

Vision, in leadership theory, 90
Values, in social systems theory, 57; *see also* Standards of comparison

W

Weber, Max: as a thoughtful observer, 42
Written rules and policies, in bureaucratic theory, 48–49